MW00658848

Mastering Scientific Computing with R

Employ professional quantitative methods to answer scientific questions with a powerful open source data analysis environment

Paul Gerrard

Radia M. Johnson

open source*

community experience distilled

BIRMINGHAM - MUMBAI

Mastering Scientific Computing with R

Copyright © 2015 Packt Publishing

All rights reserved. No part of this book may be reproduced, stored in a retrieval system, or transmitted in any form or by any means, without the prior written permission of the publisher, except in the case of brief quotations embedded in critical articles or reviews.

Every effort has been made in the preparation of this book to ensure the accuracy of the information presented. However, the information contained in this book is sold without warranty, either express or implied. Neither the authors, nor Packt Publishing, and its dealers and distributors will be held liable for any damages caused or alleged to be caused directly or indirectly by this book.

Packt Publishing has endeavored to provide trademark information about all of the companies and products mentioned in this book by the appropriate use of capitals. However, Packt Publishing cannot guarantee the accuracy of this information.

First published: January 2015

Production reference: 1270115

Published by Packt Publishing Ltd.
Livery Place
35 Livery Street
Birmingham B3 2PB, UK.

ISBN 978-1-78355-525-3

www.packtpub.com

Cover image by Jason Dupuis Mayer (jdmphoto011@gmail.com)

Credits

Authors
Paul Gerrard

Radia M. Johnson

Reviewers
Laurent Drouet

Ratanlal Mahanta

Mzabalazo Z. Ngwenya

Donato Teutonico

Commissioning Editor
Kartikey Pandey

Acquisition Editor
Greg Wild

Content Development Editor
Akshay Nair

Technical Editors
Rosmy George

Ankita Thakur

Copy Editors
Shivangi Chaturvedi

Pranjali Chury

Puja Lalwani

Adithi Shetty

Project Coordinator
Mary Alex

Proofreaders
Simran Bhogal

Martin Diver

Ameesha Green

Paul Hindle

Bernadette Watkins

Indexer
Priya Subramani

Graphics
Sheetal Aute

Disha Haria

Abhinash Sahu

Production Coordinator
Conidon Miranda

Cover Work
Conidon Miranda

About the Authors

Paul Gerrard is a physician and healthcare researcher who is based out of Portland, Maine, where he currently serves as the medical director of the cardiopulmonary rehabilitation program at New England Rehabilitation Hospital of Portland. He studied business economics in college. After completing medical school, he did a residency in physical medicine and rehabilitation at Harvard Medical School and Spaulding Rehabilitation Hospital, where he served as chief resident and stayed on as faculty at Harvard before moving to Portland. He continues to collaborate on research projects with researchers at other academic institutions within the Boston area and around the country. He has published and presented research on a range of topics, including traumatic brain injury, burn rehabilitation, health outcomes, and the epidemiology of disabling medical conditions.

I would like to thank my beautiful wife, Deirdre, and my son, Patrick. My work on this book is dedicated to the loving memory of Fiona.

Radia M. Johnson has a doctorate degree in immunology and currently works as a research scientist at the Institute for Research in Immunology and Cancer at the Université de Montréal, where she uses genomics and bioinformatics to identify and characterize the molecular changes that contribute to cancer development. She routinely uses R and other computer programming languages to analyze large data sets from ongoing collaborative projects. Since obtaining her PhD at the University of Toronto, she has also worked as a research associate at the University of Cambridge in Hematology, where she gained experience using system biology to study blood cancer.

I would like to thank Dr. Charlie Massie for teaching me to love programming in R and Dr. Phil Kousis for all his support through the years. You are both excellent mentors and wonderful friends!

About the Reviewers

Laurent Drouet holds a PhD in economics and social sciences from the University of Geneva, Switzerland, and a master's degree in applied mathematics from the Institute of Applied Mathematics of Angers, France. He was also a postdoctoral research fellow at the Research Lab of Economics and Environmental Management at the Ecole Polytechnique Federale de Lausanne (EPFL), Switzerland. He was also a researcher at the Public Research Center Tudor, Luxembourg. He is currently a senior researcher at Fondazione Eni Enrico Mattei (FEEM) and a research affiliate at Centro Euro-Mediterraneo sui Cambiamenti Climatici (CMCC), Italy.

His main research is related to integrated assessment modeling and energy modeling. For more than a decade, he designed scientific tools to perform data analysis for this type of modeling. He also built optimization frameworks to couple models of many kinds (such as climate models, air quality models, and economy models). He created and developed the bottom-up techno-economic energy model ETEM to study optimal energy policies at urban or national levels.

I want to thank my wife for her support every day both in my private life and professional life.

Ratanlal Mahanta holds an MSc in computational finance. He is currently working at GPSK Investment Group as a senior quantitative analyst. He has 4 years of experience in quantitative trading and strategies developments for sell side and risk consulting firms. He is an expert in high frequency and algorithmic trading. He has expertise in these areas: quantitative trading (FX, equities, futures and options, and engineering on derivatives); algorithms — partial differential equations, stochastic differential equations, the finite difference method, Monte Carlo, and Machine Learning; code — R programming, C++, MATLAB, HPC, and scientific computing; data analysis — Big Data analytic [EOD to TBT], Bloomberg, Quandl, and Quantopian; and strategies — vol-arbitrage, vanilla and exotic options modeling, trend following, mean reversion, co-integration, Monte Carlo simulations, ValueatRisk, stress testing, buy side trading strategies with high Sharpe ratio, credit risk modeling, and credit rating.

He has reviewed *Mastering R for Quantitative Finance, Packt Publishing*. He is currently reviewing two other books for Packt Publishing: *Mastering Python for Data Science and Machine Learning with R Cookbook*.

Mzabalazo Z. Ngwenya holds a postgraduate degree in mathematical statistics from the University of Cape Town. He has worked extensively in the field of statistical consulting, wherein he utilized varied statistical software including R. His area of interest are primarily centered around statistical computing. Previously, he was involved in reviewing *Learning RStudio for R Statistical Computing, Mark P.J. van der Loo* and *Edwin de Jonge; R Statistical Application Development Example Beginner's Guide, Prabhanjan Narayanachar Tattar; Machine Learning with R, Brett Lantz; R Graph Essentials, David Alexandra Lillis,* and *R Object-oriented Programming, Kelly Black,* all by Packt Publishing. He currently works as a biometrician.

Donato Teutonico has several years of experience in modeling and the simulation of drug effects and clinical trials in industrial and academic settings. He received his PharmD degree from the University of Turin, Italy, specializing in chemical and pharmaceutical technology, and his PhD in pharmaceutical sciences from Paris-Sud University, France.

He is the author of two R packages for pharmacometrics, *CTStemplate* and *panels-for-pharmacometrics*, which are both available on Google Code. He is also the author of *Instant R Starter, Packt Publishing*.

www.PacktPub.com

Support files, eBooks, discount offers, and more

For support files and downloads related to your book, please visit www.PacktPub.com.

Did you know that Packt offers eBook versions of every book published, with PDF and ePub files available? You can upgrade to the eBook version at www.PacktPub.com and as a print book customer, you are entitled to a discount on the eBook copy. Get in touch with us at service@packtpub.com for more details.

At www.PacktPub.com, you can also read a collection of free technical articles, sign up for a range of free newsletters and receive exclusive discounts and offers on Packt books and eBooks.

https://www2.packtpub.com/books/subscription/packtlib

Do you need instant solutions to your IT questions? PacktLib is Packt's online digital book library. Here, you can search, access, and read Packt's entire library of books.

Why subscribe?

- Fully searchable across every book published by Packt
- Copy and paste, print, and bookmark content
- On demand and accessible via a web browser

Free access for Packt account holders

If you have an account with Packt at www.PacktPub.com, you can use this to access PacktLib today and view 9 entirely free books. Simply use your login credentials for immediate access.

Table of Contents

Preface

As an open source computing environment, R is rapidly becoming the lingua franca of the statistical computing community. R's powerful base functions, powerful statistical tools, open source nature, and avid user community have led to R having an expansive library of powerful, cutting-edge quantitative methods not yet available to users of other high-cost statistical programs.

With this book, you will learn not just about R, but how to use R to answer conceptual, scientific, and experimental questions.

Beginning with an overview of fundamental R concepts, including data types, R program flow, and basic coding techniques, you'll learn how R can be used to achieve the most commonly needed scientific data analysis tasks, including testing for statistically significant differences between groups and model relationships in data. You will also learn parametric and nonparametric techniques for both difference testing and relationship modeling.

You will delve into linear algebra and matrix operations with an emphasis not on the R syntax, but on how these operations can be used to address common computational or analytical needs. This book also covers the application of matrix operations for the purpose of finding a structure in high-dimensional data using the principal component, exploratory factor, and confirmatory factor analysis in addition to structural equation modeling. You will also master methods for simulation, learn about an advanced analytical method, and finish by going to the next level with advanced data management focused on dealing with messy and problematic datasets that serious analysts deal with daily.

By the end of this book, you will be able to undertake publication-quality data analysis in R.

What this book covers

Chapter 1, Programming with R, presents an overview of how data is stored and accessed in R. Then, we will go over how to load data into R using built-in functions and useful packages for easy import from Excel worksheets. We will also cover how to use flow control statements and functions to reduce complexity and help you program more efficiently.

Chapter 2, Statistical Methods with R, presents an overview of how to summarize your data and get useful statistical information for downstream analysis. We will show you how to plot and get statistical information from probability distributions and how to test the fit of your sample distribution to well-defined probability distributions.

Chapter 3, Linear Models, covers linear models, which are probably the most commonly used statistical methods to study the relationships between variables. The *Generalized linear model* section will delve into a bit more detail than typical R books, discussing the nature of link functions and canonical link functions.

Chapter 4, Nonlinear Methods, reviews applications of nonlinear methods in R using both parametric and nonparametric methods for both theory-driven and exploratory analysis.

Chapter 5, Linear Algebra, covers algebra techniques in R. We will also learn linear algebra operations including transposition, inversion, matrix multiplication, and a number of matrix transformations.

Chapter 6, Principal Component Analysis and the Common Factor Model, helps you understand the application of linear algebra to covariance and correlation matrices. We will cover how to use PCA to account for total variance in a set of variables and how to use EFA to model common variance among these variables in R.

Chapter 7, Structural Equation Modeling and Confirmatory Factor Analysis, covers the fundamental ideas underlying structural equation modeling, which are often overlooked in other books discussing SEM in R, and then delve into how SEM is done in R.

Chapter 8, Simulations, explains how to perform basic sample simulations and how to use simulations to answer statistical problems. We will also learn how to use R to generate random numbers, and how to simulate random variables from several common probability distributions.

Chapter 9, Optimization, explores a variety of methods and techniques to optimize a variety of functions. We will also cover how to use a wide range of R packages and functions to set up, solve, and visualize different optimization problems.

Chapter 10, Advanced Data Management, walks you through the basic techniques for data handling and some basic memory management considerations.

What you need for this book

The software that we require for this book is R Version 3.0.1 or higher, OpenMx Version 1.4, and RStudio.

Who this book is for

If you want to learn how to quantitatively answer scientific questions for practical purposes using the powerful R language and the open source R tool ecosystem, this book is ideal for you. It is ideally suited for scientists who understand scientific concepts, know a little R, and want to start applying R to be able to answer empirical scientific questions. Some R exposure is helpful, but not compulsory.

Conventions

In this book, you will find a number of text styles that distinguish between different kinds of information. Here are some examples of these styles and an explanation of their meaning.

Code words in text, database table names, folder names, filenames, file extensions, pathnames, dummy URLs, user input, and Twitter handles are shown as follows: "You can also retrieve additional information on the objects stored in your environment using the str() function."

A block of code is set as follows:

```
> integer_vector <- c(1L, 2L, 12L, 29L)
> integer_vector
[1]  1  2 12 29
```

New terms and important words are shown in bold. Words that you see on the screen, for example, in menus or dialog boxes, appear in the text like this: "To install R on Windows, click on **Download R for Windows**, and then click on **base** for the download link and installation instructions."

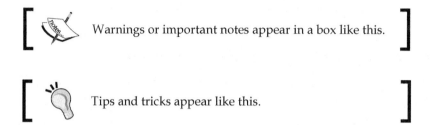

> Warnings or important notes appear in a box like this.

> Tips and tricks appear like this.

Reader feedback

Feedback from our readers is always welcome. Let us know what you think about this book—what you liked or disliked. Reader feedback is important for us as it helps us develop titles that you will really get the most out of.

To send us general feedback, simply e-mail feedback@packtpub.com, and mention the book's title in the subject of your message.

If there is a topic that you have expertise in and you are interested in either writing or contributing to a book, see our author guide at www.packtpub.com/authors.

Customer support

Now that you are the proud owner of a Packt book, we have a number of things to help you to get the most from your purchase.

Downloading the example code

You can download the example code files from your account at http://www.packtpub.com for all the Packt Publishing books you have purchased. If you purchased this book elsewhere, you can visit http://www.packtpub.com/support and register to have the files e-mailed directly to you.

Downloading the color images of this book

We also provide you with a PDF file that has color images of the screenshots/ diagrams used in this book. The color images will help you better understand the changes in the output.

You can download this file from: `https://www.packtpub.com/sites/default/ files/downloads/5253OS_ColoredImages.pdf`.

Errata

Although we have taken every care to ensure the accuracy of our content, mistakes do happen. If you find a mistake in one of our books — maybe a mistake in the text or the code — we would be grateful if you could report this to us. By doing so, you can save other readers from frustration and help us improve subsequent versions of this book. If you find any errata, please report them by visiting `http://www.packtpub. com/submit-errata`, selecting your book, clicking on the **Errata Submission Form** link, and entering the details of your errata. Once your errata are verified, your submission will be accepted and the errata will be uploaded to our website or added to any list of existing errata under the Errata section of that title.

To view the previously submitted errata, go to `https://www.packtpub.com/books/ content/support` and enter the name of the book in the search field. The required information will appear under the **Errata** section.

Piracy

Piracy of copyrighted material on the Internet is an ongoing problem across all media. At Packt, we take the protection of our copyright and licenses very seriously. If you come across any illegal copies of our works in any form on the Internet, please provide us with the location address or website name immediately so that we can pursue a remedy.

Please contact us at `copyright@packtpub.com` with a link to the suspected pirated material.

We appreciate your help in protecting our authors and our ability to bring you valuable content.

Questions

If you have a problem with any aspect of this book, you can contact us at `questions@packtpub.com`, and we will do our best to address the problem.

1

Programming with R

Scientific computing is an informatics approach to problem solving using mathematical models and/or applying quantitative analysis techniques to interpret, visualize, and solve scientific problems. Generally speaking, scientists and data analysts are concerned with understanding certain phenomena or processes using observations from an experiment or through simulation. For example, a biologist may want to understand what changes in gene expression are required for a normal cell to become a cancerous cell, or a physicist may want to study the life cycle of galaxies through numerical simulations. In both cases, they will need to collect the data, and then manipulate and process it before it can be visualized and interpreted to answer their research question. Scientific computing is involved in all these steps.

R is an excellent open source language for scientific computing. R is broadly used in companies and academics as it has great performance value and provides a cutting-edge software environment. It was initially designed as a software tool for statistical modeling but has since then evolved into a powerful tool for data mining and analytics. In addition to its rich collection of classical numerical methods or basic actions, there are also hundreds of R packages for a wide variety of scientific computing needs such as state-of-the-art visualization methods, specialized data analysis tools, machine learning, and even packages such as **Shiny** to build interactive web applications. In this book, we will teach you how to use R and some of its packages to define and manipulate your data using a variety of methods for data exploration and visualization. This book will present to you state-of-the-art mathematical and statistical methods needed for scientific computing. We will also teach you how to use R to evaluate complex arithmetic expressions and statistical modeling. We will also cover how to deal with missing data and the steps needed to write your own functions tailored to your analysis requirements. By the end of this book, you will not only be comfortable using R and its many packages, but you will also be able to write your own code to solve your own scientific problems.

This first chapter will present an overview of how data is stored and accessed in R. Then, we will look at how to load your data into R using built-in functions and useful packages, in order to easily import data from Excel worksheets. We will also show you how to transform your data using the `reshape2` package to make your data ready to graph by plotting functions such as those provided by the `ggplot2` package. Next, you will learn how to use flow-control statements and functions to reduce complexity, and help you program more efficiently. Lastly, we will go over some of the debugging tools available in R to help you successfully run your programs in R.

The following is a list of the topics that we will cover in this chapter:

- Atomic vectors
- Lists
- Object attributes
- Factors
- Matrices and arrays
- Data frames
- Plots
- Flow control
- Functions
- General programming and debugging tools

Before we begin our overview of R data structures, if you haven't already installed R, you can download the most recent version from `http://cran.r-project.org`. R compiles and runs on Linux, Mac, and Windows so that you can download the precompiled binaries to install it on your computer. For example, go to `http://cran.r-project.org`, click on **Download R for Linux**, and then click on **ubuntu** to get the most up-to-date instructions to install R on Ubuntu. To install R on Windows, click on **Download R for Windows**, and then click on **base** for the download link and installation instructions. For Mac OS users, click on **Download R for (Mac) OS X** for the download links and installation instructions.

In addition to the most recent version of R, you may also want to download RStudio, which is an integrated development environment that provides a powerful user interface that makes learning R easier and fun. The main limitation of RStudio is that it has difficulty loading very large datasets. So if you are working with very large tables, you may want to run your analysis in R directly. That being said, RStudio is great to visualize the objects you stored in your workplace at the click of a button. You can easily search help pages and packages by clicking on the appropriate tabs. Essentially, RStudio provides all that you need to help analyze your data at your fingertips. The following screenshot is an example of the RStudio user interface running the code from this chapter:

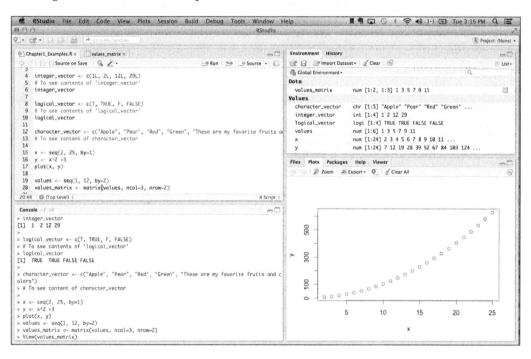

You can download RStudio for all platforms at http://www.rstudio.com/products/rstudio/download/.

Finally, the font conventions used in this book are as follows. The code you should directly type into R is preceded by > and any lines preceded by # will be treated as comment in R.

```
> The user will type this into R
This is the response from R
> # If the user types this, R will treat it as a comment
```

[Note that all the code written in this book was run with R Version 3.0.2.]

Data structures in R

R objects can be grouped into two categories:

- **Homogeneous**: This is when the content is of the same type of data
- **Heterogeneous**: This is when the content contains different types of data

Atomic vectors, **Matrices**, or **Arrays** are data structures that are used to store homogenous data, while **Lists** and **Data frames** are typically used to store heterogeneous data. R objects can also be organized based on the number of dimensions they contain. For example, atomic vectors and lists are one-dimensional objects, whereas matrices and data frames are two-dimensional objects. Arrays, however, are objects that can have any number of dimensions. Unlike other programming languages such as Perl, R does not have scalar or zero-dimensional objects. All single numbers and strings are stored in vectors of length one.

Atomic vectors

Vectors are the basic data structure in R and include atomic vectors and lists. Atomic vectors are flat and can be logical, numeric (double), integer, character, complex, or raw. To create a vector, we use the `c()` function, which means combine elements into a vector:

```
> x <- c(1, 2, 3)
```

To create an integer vector, add the number followed by L, as follows:

```
> integer_vector <- c(1L, 2L, 12L, 29L)
> integer_vector
[1]  1  2 12 29
```

To create a logical vector, add TRUE (T) and FALSE (F), as follows:.

```
> logical_vector <- c(T, TRUE, F, FALSE)
> logical_vector
[1]  TRUE  TRUE FALSE FALSE
```

Downloading the example code

You can download the example code files from your account at
`http://www.packtpub.com` for all the Packt Publishing books
you have purchased. If you purchased this book elsewhere, you
can visit `http://www.packtpub.com/support` and register
to have the files e-mailed directly to you.

To create a vector containing strings, simply add the words/phrases in
double quotes:

```
> character_vector <- c("Apple", "Pear", "Red", "Green", "These are my
favorite fruits and colors")
> character_vector
[1] "Apple"
[2] "Pear"
[3] "Red"
[4] "Green"
[5] "These are my favorite fruits and colors"
> numeric_vector <- c(1, 3.4, 5, 10)
> numeric_vector
[1]  1.0  3.4  5.0 10.0
```

R also includes functions that allow you to create vectors containing repetitive
elements with `rep()` or a sequence of numbers with `seq()`:

```
> seq(1, 12, by=3)
[1]  1  4  7 10
> seq(1, 12) #note the default parameter for by is 1
 [1]  1  2  3  4  5  6  7  8  9 10 11 12
```

Instead of using the `seq()` function, you can also use a colon, `:`, to indicate that
you would like numbers 1 to 12 to be stored as a vector, as shown in the
following example:

```
> y <- 1:12
> y
 [1]  1  2  3  4  5  6  7  8  9 10 11 12
> z <- c(1:3, y)
> z
 [1]  1  2  3  1  2  3  4  5  6  7  8  9 10 11 12
```

To replicate elements of a vector, you can simply use the `rep()` function, as follows:

```
> x <- rep(3, 14)
> x
 [1]  3  3  3  3  3  3  3  3  3  3  3  3  3  3
```

You can also replicate complex patterns as follows:

```
> rep(seq(1, 4), 3)
 [1] 1 2 3 4 1 2 3 4 1 2 3 4
```

Atomic vectors can only be of one type so if you mix numbers and strings, your vector will be coerced into the most flexible type. The most to the least flexible vector types are **Character**, **numeric**, **integer**, and **logical**, as shown in the following diagram:

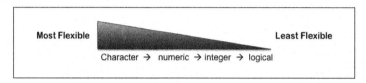

This means that if you mix numbers with strings, your vector will be coerced into a character vector, which is the most flexible type of the two. In the following paragraph, there are two different examples showing this coercion in practice. The first example shows that when a character and numeric vector are combined, the class of this new object becomes a character vector because a character vector is more flexible than a numeric vector. Similarly, in the second example, we see that the class of the new object x is numeric because a numeric vector is more flexible than an integer vector. The two examples are as follows:

Example 1:

```
> mixed_vector <- c(character_vector, numeric_vector)
> mixed_vector
[1] "Apple"
[2] "Pear"
[3] "Red"
[4] "Green"
[5] "These are my favorite fruits and colors"
[6] "1"
[7] "3.4"
[8] "5"
[9] "10"
> class(mixed_vector)
[1] "character"
```

Example 2:

```
> x <- c(integer_vector, numeric_vector)
> x
[1]  1.0  2.0 12.0 29.0  1.0  3.4  5.0 10.0
> class(x)
[1] "numeric"
```

At times, you may create a group of objects and forget its name or content. R allows you to quickly retrieve this information using the `ls()` function, which returns a vector of the names of the objects specified in the current workspace or environment.

```
> ls()
[1] "a"    "A"    "b"    "B"    "C"    "character_vector"  "influence.1"
[8] "influence.1.2"  "influence.2"  "integer_vector"  "logical_vector"
"M"    "mixed_vector"    "N"
[15] "numeric_vector"    "P"    "Q"    "second.degree.mat"    "small.network"
"social.network.mat" "x"
[22] "y"
```

At first glance, the workspace or environment is the space where you store all the objects you create. More formally, it consists of a frame or collection of named objects, and a pointer to an enclosing environment. When we created the variable x, we added it to the global environment, but we could have also created a novel environment and stored it there. For example, let's create a numeric vector y and store it in a new environment called `environB`. To create a new environment in R, we use the `new.env()` function as follows:

```
> environB <- new.env()
> ls(environB)
character(0)
```

As you can see, there are no objects stored in this environment yet because we haven't created any. Now let's create a numeric vector y and assign it to `environB` using the `assign()` function:

```
> assign("y", c(1, 5, 9), envir=environB)
> ls(environB)
[1] "y"
```

Alternatively, we could use the $ sign to assign a new variable to `environB` as follows:

```
> environB$z <- "purple"
> ls(environB)
[1] "y" "z"
```

To see what we stored in y and z, we can use the `get()` function or the $ sign as follows:

```
> get('y', envir=environB)
[1] 1 5 9
> get('z', envir=environB)
[1] "purple"
> environB$y
[1] 1 5 9
```

You can also retrieve additional information on the objects stored in your environment using the `str()` function. This function allows you to inspect the internal structure of the object and print a preview of its contents as follows:

```
> str(character_vector)
 chr [1:5] "Apple" "Pear" "Red" "Green" ...
> str(integer_vector)
 int [1:4] 1 2 12 29
> str(logical_vector)
 logi [1:4] TRUE TRUE FALSE FALSE
```

To know how many elements are present in our vector, you can use the `length()` function as follows:

```
> length(integer_vector)
[1] 4
```

Finally, to extract elements from a vector, you can use the position (or index) of the element in square brackets as follows:

```
> character_vector[5]
[1] "These are my favorite fruits and colors"
> numeric_vector[2]
[1] 3.4
> x <- c(1, 4, 6)
> x[2]
[1] 4
```

Operations on vectors

Basic mathematical operations can be performed on numeric and integer vectors similar to those you perform on a calculator. The arithmetic operations used are given in the following table:

Arithmetic operators
+ x
- x
x + y
x - y
x * y
x / y
x ^ y
x %% y
x %/% y

For example, if we multiply a vector by 2, all the elements of the vector will be multiplied by 2. Let's take a look at the following example:

```
> x <- c(1, 3, 5, 10)
> x * 2
[1]   2   6 10 20
```

You can also add vectors to each other, in which case the computation will be performed element-wise as follows:

```
> x <- c(1, 3, 5, 10)
> y <- c(13, 15, 17, 22)
> x + y
[1] 14 18 22 32
```

If the vectors are of different lengths, the shorter vector will be extended to match the length of the longer vector by recycling its elements starting from the first element. However, you will also get a warning message from R in case you did not intend to add vectors of differing length, as follows:

```
> x
[1]   1   3   5 10
> z <- c(1,3, 4, 6, 10)
> x + z #1 was recycled to complete the operation.
[1]   2   6   9 16 11
Warning message:
In x + z : longer object length is not a multiple of shorter object
length
```

In addition to this, the standard operators also have %%, which indicates x mod y, and %/%, which indicates integer division as follows:

```
> x %% 2
[1] 1 1 1 0
> x %/% 5
[1] 0 0 1 2
```

Lists

Unlike atomic vectors, lists can contain different types of elements including lists. To create a list, you use the list() function as follows:

```
> simple_list <- list(1:4, rep(3, 5), "cat")
> str(simple_list)
List of 3
 $ : int [1:4] 1 2 3 4
 $ : num [1:5] 3 3 3 3 3
```

```
  $ : chr "cat"
> other_list <- list(1:4, "I prefer pears", logical_vector, x, simple_
list)
> str(other_list)
List of 5
 $ : int [1:4] 1 2 3 4
 $ : chr "I prefer pears"
 $ : logi [1:4] TRUE TRUE FALSE FALSE
 $ : num [1:3] 1 4 6
 $ :List of 3
  ..$ : int [1:4] 1 2 3 4
  ..$ : num [1:5] 3 3 3 3 3
  ..$ : chr "cat"
```

If you use the c() function to combine lists and atomic vectors, c() will coerce the vectors to lists of length one before proceeding. Let's go through a detailed example in R:

```
> new_list <- c(list(1, 2, simple_list), c(3, 4), seq(5, 6))
```

Now, let's take a look at the output of the list we just created by entering new_list in R:

```
> new_list
[[1]]
[1] 1

[[2]]
[1] 2

[[3]]
[[3]][[1]]
[1] 1 2 3 4

[[3]][[2]]
[1] 3 3 3 3 3

[[3]][[3]]
[1] "cat"


[[4]]
[1] 3

[[5]]
```

```
[1]  4

[[6]]
[1]  5

[[7]]
[1]  6
# Output truncated here
```

We can further inspect the new_list object that we just created using the str() function as follows:

```
> str(new_list)
List of 7
 $ : num 1
 $ : num 2
 $ :List of 3
  ..$ : int [1:4] 1 2 3 4
  ..$ : num [1:5] 3 3 3 3 3
  ..$ : chr "cat"
 $ : num 3
 $ : num 4
 $ : int 5
 $ : int 6
```

You can also coerce an atomic vector into a list using the as.list() function as follows:

```
> x_as_list <- as.list(x)
> str(x_as_list)
List of 4
 $ : num 1
 $ : num 3
 $ : num 5
 $ : num 10
```

To access different elements in your list, you can use the index position in square brackets [], as you would for a vector, or double square brackets [[]]. Let's take a look at the following example:

```
> simple_list
[[1]]
[1] 1 2 3 4
[[2]]
[1] 3 3 3 3 3
```

```
[[3]]
[1] "cat"
> simple_list[3]
[[1]]
[1] "cat"
```

As you will no doubt notice, by entering `simple_list[3]`, R returns a list of the single element `"cat"` as follows:

```
> str(simple_list[3])
List of 1
 $ : chr "cat"
```

If we use the double square brackets, R will return the object type as we initially entered it. So, in this case, it would return a character vector for `simple_list[[3]]` and an integer vector for `simple_list[[1]]` as follows:

```
> str(simple_list[[3]])
 chr "cat"
> str(simple_list[[1]])
 int [1:4] 1 2 3 4
```

We can assign these elements to new objects as follows:

```
> animal <- simple_list[[3]]
> animal
[1] "cat"
> num_vector <- simple_list[[1]]
> num_vector
[1] 1 2 3 4
```

If you would like to access an element of an object in your list, you can use double square brackets `[[ ]]` followed by single square brackets `[ ]` as follows:

```
> simple_list[[1]][4]
[1] 4
> simple_list[1][4] #Note this format does not return the element
[[1]]
NULL
#Instead you would have to enter
> simple_list[1][[1]][4]
[1] 4
```

Attributes

Objects in R can have additional attributes ascribed to objects that you can store with the `attr()` function, as shown in the following code:

```
> attr(x_as_list, "new_attribute") <- "This list contains the number
of apples eaten for 3 different days"
> attr(x_as_list, "new_attribute")
[1] "This list contains the number of apples eaten for 3 different
days"
> str(x_as_list)
List of 3
 $ : num 1
 $ : num 4
 $ : num 6
 - attr(*, "new_attribute")= chr "This list contains the number of
apples eaten for 3 different days"
```

You can use the `structure()` function, as shown in the following code, to attach an attribute to an object you wish to return:

```
> structure(as.integer(1:7), added_attribute = "This vector contains
integers.")
[1] 1 2 3 4 5 6 7
attr(,"added_attribute")
[1] "This vector contains integers."
```

In addition to attributes that you create with `attr()`, R also has built-in attributes ascribed to some of its functions, such as `class()`, `dim()`, and `names()`. The `class()` function tells us the class (type) of the object as follows:

```
> class(simple_list)
[1] "list"
```

The `dim()` function returns the dimension of higher-order objects such as matrices, data frames, and multidimensional arrays. The `names()` function allows you to give names to each element of your vector as follows:

```
> y <- c(first =1, second =2, third=4, fourth=4)
> y
 first second  third fourth
     1      2      4      4
```

You can use the `names()` attribute to add the names of each element to your vector as follows:

```
> element_names <- c("first", "second", "third", "fourth")
> y <- c(1, 2, 4, 4)
> names(y) <- element_names
> y
 first second  third fourth
     1      2      4      4
```

You can also modify the names of vector elements using the `setNames()` function as follows:

```
> setNames(y, c("alpha", "beta", "omega", "psi"))
alpha beta, omega    psi
    1     2      4      4
```

If you do not provide names for some of your vector elements, the `names()` function will return empty strings, `<NA>`, for the missing ones as follows:

```
> y <- setNames(y, c("alpha", "beta", "psi"))
> names(y)
[1] "alpha" "beta"  "psi"    NA
```

However, this does not mean that all vectors require names. In the event that you haven't provided any, `names()` will return `NULL` as follows:

```
> x <- 1:12
> x <- 1:12
> names(x)
NULL
```

You can remove names using the `unname()` function or by replacing the names with `NULL`:

```
> unname(y)
[1] 1 2 4 4
> names(y) <- NULL
> names(y)
NULL
```

Factors

When dealing with categorical data, R provides an alternative framework to store character data termed **Factors**. These are specialized vectors that contain predefined values referred to as **Levels**. For example, say you have data for `"placebo"` and `"treatment"` for four patients, you could store this information as factors instead of a character vector by using the following code:

```
> drug_response <- c("placebo", "treatment", "placebo", "treatment")
> drug_response <-  factor(drug_response)
> drug_response
[1] placebo    treatment placebo    treatment
Levels: placebo treatment
```

To check the integers used for each level, you can use the `as.integer()` function as follows:

```
> as.integer(drug_response)
[1] 1 2 1 2
```

Note that you can only adjust elements in a factor with data stored as levels. Say you wanted to change the `drug_response` attribute for the fourth patient from `"treatment"` to `"refused treatment"`, you will get the following warning message:

```
> drug_response[4] <- "refused treatment"
Warning message:
In `[<-.factor`(`*tmp*`, 4, value = "refused treatment") :
  invalid factor level, NA generated
```

In order to correct this error, you need to first add a new level to the factor using the `factor()` function with the `levels` argument as follows:

```
> drug_response <- factor(drug_response, levels = c(levels(drug_
response), "refused treatment"))
> drug_response[4] <- "refused treatment"
> drug_response
[1] placebo            treatment           placebo           refused
treatment
Levels: placebo treatment refused treatment
> as.integer(drug_response)
[1] 1 2 1 3
```

Multidimensional arrays

Multidimensional arrays are created by adding dimensions to the atomic vector created. In computer science, an array is defined as a data structure consisting of elements identified by at least one array index. So, atomic vectors can be seen as one-dimensional arrays. However, as mentioned earlier, arrays can have more than one dimension. These arrays are termed multidimensional arrays. In R, you can create multidimensional arrays using the `array()` function. For example, you can create a three-dimensional array using the `array()` function and specify the dimensions with the `dim` argument using a vector. Let's create a three-dimensional array of coordinates where the maximal indices in each dimension is 2, 8, and 2 for the first, second, and third dimension, respectively:

```
> coordinates <- array(1:16, dim=c(2, 8, 2))
> coordinates
, , 1
     [,1] [,2] [,3] [,4] [,5] [,6] [,7] [,8]
[1,]    1    3    5    7    9   11   13   15
[2,]    2    4    6    8   10   12   14   16
, , 2
     [,1] [,2] [,3] [,4] [,5] [,6] [,7] [,8]
[1,]    1    3    5    7    9   11   13   15
[2,]    2    4    6    8   10   12   14   16
```

You can also change an object into a multidimensional array using the `dim()` function as follows:

```
> values <- seq(1, 12, by=2)
> values
[1]  1  3  5  7  9 11
> dim(values) <- c(2,3)
> values
     [,1] [,2] [,3]
[1,]    1    5    9
[2,]    3    7   11
> dim(values) <- c(3,2)
> values
     [,1] [,2]
[1,]    1    7
[2,]    3    9
[3,]    5   11
```

To access elements of a multidimensional array, you will need to list the coordinates in square brackets [ ] as follows:

```
> coordinates[1, , ]
      [,1] [,2]
[1,]     1    1
[2,]     3    3
[3,]     5    5
[4,]     7    7
[5,]     9    9
[6,]    11   11
[7,]    13   13
[8,]    15   15
> coordinates[1, 2, ]
[1] 3 3
> coordinates[1, 2, 2]
[1] 3
```

Matrices

Matrices are a special case of two-dimensional arrays and are often created with the matrix() function. Instead of the dim argument, the matrix() function takes the number of rows and columns using the ncol and nrow arguments, respectively. Alternatively, you can create a matrix by combining vectors as columns and rows using cbind() and rbind(), respectively:

```
> values_matrix <- matrix(values, ncol=3, nrow=2)
> values_matrix
      [,1] [,2] [,3]
[1,]     1    5    9
[2,]     3    7   11
```

We will create a matrix using rbind() and cbind() as follows:

```
> x <- c(1,5,9)
> y <- c(3,7,11)
> m1  <- rbind(x, y)
> m1
   [,1] [,2] [,3]
x     1    5    9
y     3    7   11
> m2 <- cbind(x,y)
> m2
       x  y
[1,]   1  3
[2,]   5  7
[3,]   9 11
```

You can access elements of a matrix using its row and column number as follows:

```
> values_matrix[2,2]
[1] 7
```

Alternatively, matrices and arrays are also indexed as a vector, so you could also get the value at (2, y) using its index as follows:

```
> values_matrix[4]
[1] 7
> coordinates[3]
[1] 3
```

Since matrices and arrays are indexed as a vector, you can use the `length()` function to determine how many elements are present in your matrix or array. This property comes in very handy when writing `for` loops as we will see later in this chapter in the *Flow control* section. Let's take a look at the length function:

```
> length(coordinates)
[1] 32
```

The `length()` and `names()` functions have attributes with higher-dimensional generalizations. The `length()` function generalizes to `nrow()` and `ncol()` for matrices, and `dim()` for arrays. Similarly, `names()` can be generalized to `rownames()`, `colnames()` for matrices, and `dimnames()` for multidimensional arrays.

 Note that `dimnames()` takes a list of character vectors corresponding to the names of each dimension of the array.

Let's take a look at the following functions:

```
> ncol(values_matrix)
[1] 3
> colnames(values_matrix) <- c("Column_A", "Column_B", "Column_C")
> values_matrix
     Column_A Column_B Column_C
[1,]        1        5        9
[2,]        3        7       11
> dim(coordinates)
[1] 2 8 2
> dimnames(coordinates) <- list(c("alpha", "beta"), c("a", "b", "c",
"d", "e", "f", "g", "h"), c("X", "Y"))
> coordinates
, , X

      a b c d  e  f  g  h
alpha 1 3 5 7  9 11 13 15
beta  2 4 6 8 10 12 14 16
```

```
, , Y

      a b c d  e  f  g  h
alpha 1 3 5 7  9 11 13 15
beta  2 4 6 8 10 12 14 16
```

In addition to these properties, you can transpose a matrix using the `t()` function and an array using the `aperm()` function that is part of the `abind` package. Another interesting tool of the `abind` package is the `abind()` function that allows you to combine arrays the same way you would combine vectors into a matrix using the `cbind()` or `rbind()` functions.

You can test whether your object is an array or matrix using the `is.matrix()` and `is.array()` functions, which will return TRUE or FALSE; otherwise, you can determine the number of dimensions of your object with `dim()`. Lastly, you can convert an object into a matrix or array using the `as.matrix()` or `as.array()` function. This may come in handy when working with packages or functions that require that an object be of a particular class, that is, a matrix or an array. Be aware that even a simple vector can be stored in multiple ways, and depending on the class of the object and function they will behave differently. Quite frequently, this is a source of programming errors when people use built-in or package functions and don't check the class of the object the function requires to execute the code.

The following is an example that shows that the `c(1, 6, 12)` vector can be stored as a matrix with a single row or column, or a one-dimensional array:

```
> x <- c(1, 6, 12)
> str(x)
 num [1:3] 1 6 12 #numeric vector
> str(matrix(x, ncol=1))
 num [1:3, 1] 1 6 12 #matrix of a single column
> str(matrix(x, nrow=1))
 num [1, 1:3] 1 6 12 #matrix of a single row
> str(array(x, 3))
 num [1:3(1d)] 1 6 12 #a 1-dimensional array
```

Data frames

The most common way to store data in R is through data frames and, if used correctly, it makes data analysis much easier, especially when dealing with categorical data. Data frames are similar to matrices, except that each column can store different types of data. You can construct data frames using the `data.frame()` function or convert an R object into a data frame using the `as.data.frame()` function as follows:

```
> students <- c("John", "Mary", "Ethan", "Dora")
> test.results <- c(76, 82, 84, 67)
```

```
> test.grade <- c("B", "A", "A", "C")
> thirdgrade.class.df <- data.frame(students, test.results, test.
grade)
> thirdgrade.class.df
  students test.results test.grade
1    John           76          B
2    Mary           82          A
3   Ethan           84          A
4    Dora           67          C
> # see page 18 for how values_matrix was generated
> values_matrix.df  <- as.data.frame(values_matrix)
> values_matrix.df
  Column_A Column_B Column_C
1        1        5        9
2        3        7       11
```

Data frames share properties with matrices and lists, which means that you can use colnames() and rownames() to add the attributes to your data frame. You can also use ncol() and nrow() to find out the number of columns and rows in your data frame as you would in a matrix. Let's take a look at an example:

```
> rownames(values_matrix.df) <- c("Row_1", "Row_2")
> values_matrix.df
      Column_A Column_B Column_C
Row_1        1        5        9
Row_2        3        7       11
```

You can append a column or row to data.frame using rbind() and cbind(), the same way you would in a matrix as follows:

```
> student_ID <- c("012571", "056280", "096493", "032567")
> thirdgrade.class.df <- cbind(thirdgrade.class.df, student_ID)
> thirdgrade.class.df
  students test.results test.grade student_ID
1    John           76          B     012571
2    Mary           82          A     056280
3   Ethan           84          A     096493
4    Dora           67          C     032567
```

However, you cannot create data.frame from cbind() unless one of the objects you are trying to combine is already a data frame because cbind() creates matrices by default. Let's take a look at the following function:

```
> thirdgrade.class <- cbind(students, test.results, test.grade,
student_ID)
> thirdgrade.class
     students test.results test.grade student_ID
```

```
[1,] "John"    "76"         "B"         "012571"
[2,] "Mary"    "82"         "A"         "056280"
[3,] "Ethan"   "84"         "A"         "096493"
[4,] "Dora"    "67"         "C"         "032567"
> class(thirdgrade.class)
[1] "matrix"
```

Another thing to be aware of is that R automatically converts character vectors to factors when it creates a data frame. Therefore, you need to specify that you do not want strings to be converted to factors using the `stringsAsFactors` argument in the `data.frame()` function, as follows:

```
> str(thirdgrade.class.df)
'data.frame':   4 obs. of  4 variables:
 $ students    : Factor w/ 4 levels "Dora","Ethan",..: 3 4 2 1
 $ test.results: num  76 82 84 67
 $ test.grade  : Factor w/ 3 levels "A","B","C": 2 1 1 3
 $ student_ID  : Factor w/ 4 levels "012571","032567",..: 1 3 4 2
> thirdgrade.class.df <- data.frame(students, test.results, test.
grade, student_ID, stringsAsFactors=FALSE)
> str(thirdgrade.class.df)
'data.frame':   4 obs. of  4 variables:
 $ students    : chr  "John" "Mary" "Ethan" "Dora"
 $ test.results: num  76 82 84 67
 $ test.grade  : chr  "B" "A" "A" "C"
 $ student_ID  : chr  "012571" "056280" "096493" "032567"
```

You can also use the `transform()` function to specify which columns you would like to set as character using the `as.character()` or `as.factor()` functions. This is because each row and column can be seen as an atomic vector. Let's take a look at the following functions:

```
> modified.df <- transform(thirdgrade.class.df, test.grade  =
as.factor(test.grade))
> str(modified.df)
'data.frame':   4 obs. of  4 variables:
 $ students    : chr  "John" "Mary" "Ethan" "Dora"
 $ test.results: num  76 82 84 67
 $ test.grade  : Factor w/ 3 levels "A","B","C": 2 1 1 3
 $ student_ID  : chr  "012571" "056280" "096493" "032567"
```

You can access elements of a data frame as you would in a matrix using the row and column position as follows:

```
> modified.df[3, 4]
[1] "096493"
```

You can access a full column or row by leaving the row or column index empty, as follows:

```
> modified.df[, 1]
[1] "John"  "Mary"  "Ethan" "Dora"
#Notice the command returns a vector
> str(modified.df[,1])
 chr [1:4] "John" "Mary" "Ethan" "Dora"
> modified.df[1:2,]
  students test.results test.grade student_ID
1     John           76          B     012571
2     Mary           82          A     056280
#Notice the command now returns a data frame
> str(modified.df[1:2,])
'data.frame':  2 obs. of  4 variables:
 $ students    : chr  "John" "Mary"
 $ test.results: num  76 82
 $ test.grade  : Factor w/ 3 levels "A","B","C": 2 1
 $ student_ID  : chr  "012571" "056280"
```

Unlike matrices, you can also access a column by using its object_name$column_name attribute, as follows:

```
> modified.df$test.results
[1] 76 82 84 67
```

Loading data into R

There are several ways to load data into R. The most common way is to enter data using the read.table() function or one of its derivatives, read.csv() for the .csv files, or read.delim() for .txt files. You can also directly upload Excel data in the .xls or .xlsx format using the gdata or XLConnect package. Other file formats such as Minitab Portable Worksheet (.mtp) and SPSS (.spss) files can also be opened using the foreign package.

To download a package from within R, you can use the install.packages() function as follows:

```
> install.packages(pkgname.tar.gz, repos = NULL, type = "source" )
```

Next, load the package (otherwise known as a **library**) using the library() or require() function. The require() function is designed to use in functions because it returns FALSE and a warning message, instead of the error message that the library() returns when the package is missing. You only need to load a package once per R session.

The first thing to do before loading a file is to make sure that R is in the right working directory. You can see where R will read and save files, by default, using the getwd() function. Then, you can change it using the setwd() function. You should use the full path when setting the working directory because it is easier to avoid unwanted error messages such as Error in setwd("new_directory") : cannot change working directory.

For example, execute the following function on a Mac operating system:

```
> getwd()
[1] "/Users/johnsonR/"
> setwd("/Users/johnsonR/myDirectory")
```

To work with data in the C: drive in the myDirectory folder on a Windows version of R, you will need to set the working directory as follows:

```
> setwd("C:/myDirectory")
```

Then, you can use the read.table() function to load your data as follows:

```
#To specify that the file is a tab delimited text file we use the sep
argument with "\t"
> myData.df <- read.table("myData.txt", header=TRUE, sep="\t")
> myData.df
    A  B C
1 12   6 8
2  4   9 2
3  5 13 3
```

Alternatively, you could use the read.delim() function instead as follows:

```
> read.delim("myData.txt", header=TRUE)
    A  B C
1 12   6 8
2  4   9 2
3  5 13 3
> myData2.df <-read.csv("myData.csv", header=FALSE)
> myData2.df
   V1 V2 V3
1  A  B  C
2 12  6  8
3  4  9  2
4  5 13  3
```

By default, these functions return data frames with all string-containing columns converted to factors unless you set `stringsAsFactors=FALSE` in `read.table()`, `read.delim()`, and `read.csv()`. Let's take a look at an example:

```
> str(myData2.df)
'data.frame':  4 obs. of  3 variables:
 $ V1: Factor w/ 4 levels "12","4","5","A": 4 1 2 3
 $ V2: Factor w/ 4 levels "13","6","9","B": 4 2 3 1
 $ V3: Factor w/ 4 levels "2","3","8","C": 4 3 1 2
> myData2.df <-read.csv("myData.csv", header=FALSE,
stringsAsFactors=FALSE)
> str(myData2.df)
'data.frame':  4 obs. of  3 variables:
 $ V1: chr  "A" "12" "4" "5"
 $ V2: chr  "B" "6" "9" "13"
 $ V3: chr  "C" "8" "2" "3"
```

To upload Excel sheets using the `gdata` package, you load the package into R and then use the `read.xls()` function as follows:

```
> library("gdata")
> myData.df <- read.xls("myData.xlsx", sheet=1) #also uploads .xls
files and returns a data frame
```

Alternatively, you could upload a complete workbook and read the worksheets separately using the `XLConnect` package as follows:

```
> library("XLConnect")
> myData.workbook <- loadWorkbook("myData.xlsx")
> myData3.df <- readWorksheet(myData.workbook, sheet="Sheet1")
```

To read the `.mtp` and `.spss` files, you will first load the `foreign` package, and then use the `read.mtp()` and `read.spss()` functions. By default, these functions return a list of components so you will have to convert the data into a data frame afterwards. Alternatively, for `.spss` files, the `read.spss()` function has a `to.data.frame` argument that allows it to return a data frame instead.

```
> myData4.df <- read.spss("myfile.spss", to.data.frame=TRUE)
```

Saving data frames

To save an object, preferably a matrix or data frame, you can write a `.txt` file or a file using another delimiter using the `write.table()` function. You can choose to include `row.names` and `col.names` by setting these arguments to TRUE. The output file will be saved to your current directory. Note that the `write.table()` function often saves character vectors with quotation marks in the output file. So, I also suggest that you set the quote argument to FALSE to avoid seeing quotation marks should you open the file with a text editor. Let's take a look at a few examples:

```
> write.table(myData.df, file="savedata_file.txt", quote = FALSE, sep
= "\t", row.names=TRUE, col.names=TRUE, append=FALSE)
```

By default, there is no column name for a column of row names. So your output would look like this:

```
V1    V2    V3
1      A     B    C
2     12     6    8
3      4     9    2
4      5    13    3
```

To correct this problem to view in a spreadsheet viewer such as Excel, you can write the table setting as `col.names=NA` and `row.names=TRUE`, as follows:

```
> write.table(myData.df, file="savedata_file.txt", quote = FALSE, sep
= "\t",col.names = NA, row.names = TRUE, append=FALSE)
      V1    V2    V3
1      A     B    C
2     12     6    8
3      4     9    2
4      5    13    3
```

Alternatively, you could use the `write.csv()` function, which has `col.names=NA` and `row.names=TRUE` set as defaults:

```
> write.csv(myData.df, file = "savedata_file.csv") #same output as
above
```

If you would like to save a series of data frames in an Excel workbook, we recommend that you use the `WriteXLS` package, which greatly simplifies the task. Here is an example of the code you could use to save two data frames (`df1` and `df2`) as two separate worksheets with the sheet names set as `"df1_results"` and `"df2_results"` in a file called `combined_dfs_workbook.xls`:

```
> library("WriteXLS")
> dfs.tosave <- c("df1", "df2")
```

```
> sheets.tosave <- c("df1_results", "df2_results")
> WriteXLS(dfs.tosave, ExcelFileName = "combined_dfs_workbook.xls",
SheetNames = sheets.tosave)
```

You can also save and reload R objects for future sessions using the `dump()` and `source()` functions. For example, say you created several `list` objects containing important data for routine analysis. Saving a `list` object to a spreadsheet or `.txt` file can be difficult to reload afterwards, since most read functions return a data frame. A simpler way to proceed will be to save (or dump) the object to a file that R can reopen (source) in another session.

The following data shows how you can save that object:

```
> dump("myData.df", "myData.R")
> #Or if you would like to save all objects in your session:
> dump(list=objects(), "all_objects.R")
```

The `myData.R` file created will contain all the commands necessary to recreate that object in a future session. At a later date, you can retrieve the data as follows:

```
> source("mydata.R")
```

You can also use the `save()` and `load()` functions to save and retrieve your objects at a later time, as follows:

```
> save(myData.df, file="myData.R")
> load("myData.R")
```

A good alternative to the `save()` and `load()` functions are the `saveRDS()` and `readRDS()` functions, respectively. The `saveRDS()` function doesn't save the object and its name; instead, it just saves a representation of the object. Therefore, when you retrieve the data with the `readRDS()` function, you will need to store it in an object. However, unlike the `save()` function, you can only save one object at a time with the `saveRDS()` function. For example, to save the `myData.df` object and retrieve it later, you can execute the following lines of code:

```
# To save the object
> saveRDS(myData.df, "myData.rds")
# To load and save the object to a new object
> myData2 <- readRDS("myData.rds")
```

You can also redirect the R output to a file using the `sink(file="filename")` function as follows:

```
> sink("data_session1.txt")
> x<-c(1,2,3)
> y <-c(4,5,6)
> #This is a comment
> x+y #Note the sum of x+y is redirected to data_session1.txt
```

To stop redirecting the output to the file and print a new output to the screen, just run the `sink()` function again without any arguments as follows:

```
> sink()
> 3+4
[1] 7
```

When you open the `data_session1.txt` file, you will notice that only the result of the sum of x+y is saved to the file and not the commands or comments you entered.

The following is the output in the `data_session1.txt` file:

```
[1] 5 7 9
```

As you can see, comments and standard input aren't included in the output. Only the output is printed to the file specified in the `sink()` function.

Basic plots and the ggplot2 package

This section will review how to make basic plots using the built-in R functions and the `ggplot2` package to plot graphics.

Basic plots in R include histograms and scatterplots. To plot a histogram, we use the `hist()` function:

```
> x <- c(5, 7, 12, 15, 35, 9, 5, 17, 24, 27, 16, 32)
> hist(x)
```

The output is shown in the following plot:

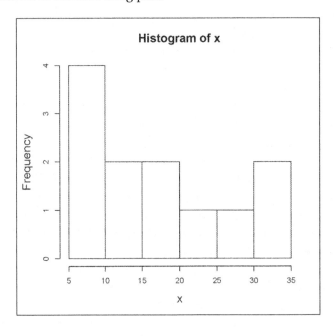

You can plot mathematical formulas with the plot() function as follows:

```
> x <- seq(2, 25, by=1)
> y <- x^2 +3
> plot(x, y)
```

The output is shown in the following plot:

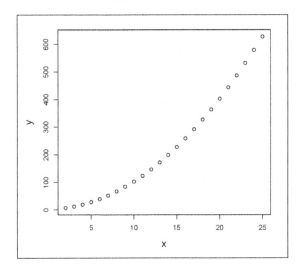

You can graph a univariate mathematical function on an interval using the `curve()` function with the `from` and `to` arguments to set the left and right endpoints, respectively. The `expr` argument allows you to set a numeric vector or function that returns a numeric vector as an output, as follows:

```
# For two figures per plot.
> par(mfrow=c(1,2))
> curve(expr=cos(x), from=0, to=8*pi)
> curve(expr=x^2, from=0, to=32)
```

In the following figure, the plot to your left shows the curve for `cox(x)` and the plot to the right shows the curve for x^2. As you can see, using the `from` and `to` arguments, we can specify the x values to show in our figure.

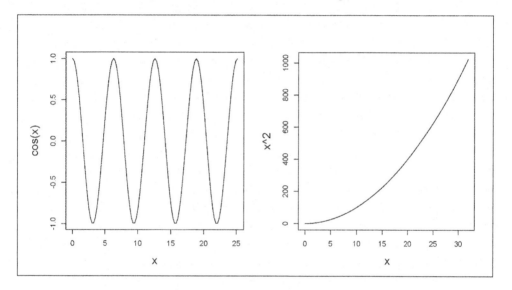

You can also graph scatterplots using the `plot()` function. For example, we can use the `iris` dataset as part of R to plot `Sepal.Length` versus `Sepal.Width` as follows:

```
> plot(iris$Sepal.Length, iris$Sepal.Width, main="Iris sepal length vs
width measurements", xlab="Length", ylab="Width")
```

The output is shown in the following plot:

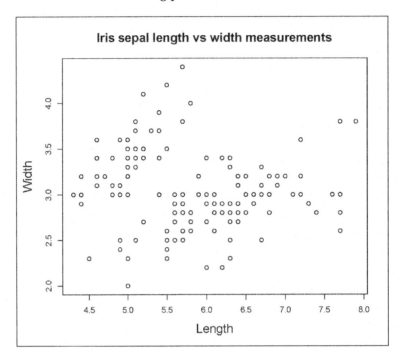

R has built-in functions that allow you to plot other types of graphics such as the `barplots()`, `dotchart()`, `pie()`, and `boxplot()` functions. The following are some examples using the `VADeaths` dataset:

```
> VADeaths
       Rural Male Rural Female Urban Male Urban Female
50-54       11.7          8.7       15.4          8.4
55-59       18.1         11.7       24.3         13.6
60-64       26.9         20.3       37.0         19.3
65-69       41.0         30.9       54.6         35.1
70-74       66.0         54.3       71.1         50.0
> barplot(VADeaths, beside=TRUE, legend=TRUE, ylim=c(0, 100),
ylab="Deaths per 1000 population", main="Death rate in VA") #Requires
that the data to plot be a vector or a matrix.
```

The output is shown in the following plot:

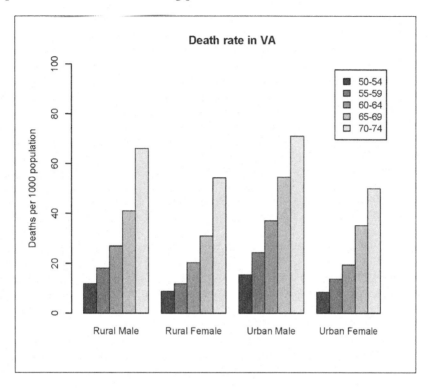

However, when working with data frames, it is often much simpler to use the ggplot2 package to make a bar plot, since your data will not have to be converted to a vector or matrix first. However, you need to be aware that ggplot2 often requires that your data be stored in a data frame in long format and not wide format.

The following is an example of data stored in wide format. In this example, we look at the expression level of the MYC and BRCA2 genes in two different cell lines, after these cells were treated with a vehicle-control, drug1 or drug2 for 48 hours:

```
> geneExpdata.wide <- read.table(header=TRUE, text='
cell_line gene control drug1 drug2
      CL1    MYC     20.4  15.9  1.5
      CL2    MYC     26.9  18.1  6.7
      CL1    BRCA2    109.5  18.1  89.8
      CL2    BRCA2    121.3  24.4  120.2
  ')
```

The following is the data rewritten in long format:

```
> geneExpdata.long <- read.table(header=TRUE, text='
  cell_line  gene variable value
1        CL1   MYC  control  20.4
2        CL2   MYC  control  26.9
3        CL1 BRCA2  control 109.5
4        CL2 BRCA2  control 121.3
5        CL1   MYC    drug1  15.9
6        CL2   MYC    drug1  18.1
7        CL1 BRCA2    drug1  18.1
8        CL2 BRCA2    drug1  24.4
9        CL1   MYC    drug2   1.5
10       CL2   MYC    drug2   6.7
11       CL1 BRCA2    drug2  89.8
12       CL2 BRCA2    drug2 120.2
')
```

Instead of rewriting the data frame by hand, this process can be automated using the melt() function, which is a part of the reshape2 package:

```
> library("reshape2")
> geneExpdata.long<- melt(geneExpdata.wide, id.vars=c("cell_
line","gene"), measure.vars=c("control", "drug1", "drug2" ), variable.
name="condition", value.name="gene_expr_value")
```

Now, we can plot the data using ggplot2 as follows:

```
> library("ggplot2")
> ggplot(geneExpdata.long, aes(x=gene, y= gene_expr_value)) + geom_
bar(aes(fill=condition), colour="black", position=position_dodge(),
stat="identity")
```

The output is shown in the following plot:

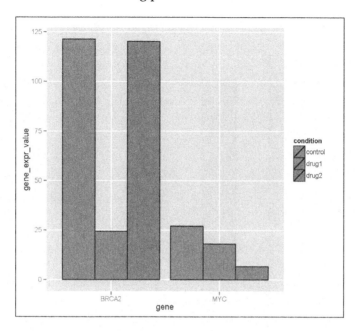

Another useful trick to know is how to add error bars to bar plots. Here, we have a summary data frame of standard deviation (`sd`), standard error (`se`), and confidence interval (`ci`) for the `geneExpdata.long` dataset as follows:

```
> geneExpdata.summary <- read.table(header=TRUE, text='
  gene condition N gene_expr_value       sd      se        ci
1 BRCA2   control 2         115.40  8.343860   5.90   74.96661
2 BRCA2     drug1 2          21.25  4.454773   3.15   40.02454
3 BRCA2     drug2 2         105.00 21.496046  15.20  193.13431
4   MYC   control 2          23.65  4.596194   3.25   41.29517
5   MYC     drug1 2          17.00  1.555635   1.10   13.97683
6   MYC     drug2 2           4.10  3.676955   2.60   33.03613
')
> #Note the plot is stored in the p object
> p<- ggplot(geneExpdata.summary, aes(x=gene, y= gene_expr_value,
fill=condition)) + geom_bar(aes(fill=condition), colour="black",
position=position_dodge(), stat="identity")
> #Define the upper and lower limits for the error bars
> limits <- aes(ymax = gene_expr_value + se, ymin= gene_expr_value -
se)
> #Add error bars to plot
> p + geom_errorbar(limits, position=position_dodge(0.9), size=.3,
width=.2)
```

The result is shown in the following plot:

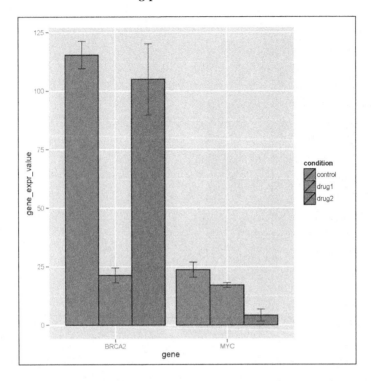

Going back to the VADeaths example, we could also plot a Cleveland dot plot (dot chart) as follows:

```
> dotchart(VADeaths,xlim=c(0, 75), xlab=Deaths per 1000, main="Death
rates in VA")
```

 Note that the built-in dotchart() function requires that the data be stored as a vector or matrix.

The result is shown in the following plot:

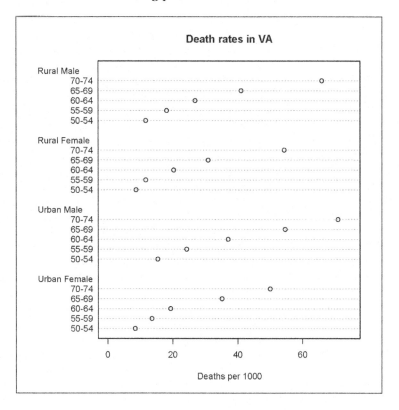

The following are some other graphics you can generate with built-in R functions:

You can generate pie charts with the `pie()` function as follows:

```
> labels <- c("grp_A", "grp_B", "grp_C")
> pie_groups <- c(12, 26, 62)
> pie(pie_groups, labels, col=c("white", "black", "grey")) #Fig. 3B
```

You can generate box-and-whisker plots with the `boxplot()` function as follows:

```
> boxplot(value ~ variable, data= geneExpdata.long, subset=gene ==
"MYC", ylab="expression value", main="MYC Expression by Condition",
cex.lab=1.5, cex.main=1.5)
```

 Note that unlike other built-in R graphing functions, the `boxplot()` function takes data frames as the input.

Using our cell line drug treatment experiment, we can graph MYC expression for all cell lines by condition. The result is shown in the following plot:

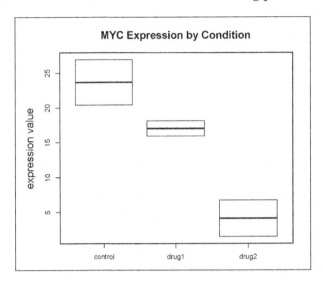

The following is another example using the iris dataset to plot `Petal.Width` by `Species`:

```
> boxplot(Petal.Width ~ Species, data=iris, ylab="petal width", cex.
lab=1.5, cex.main=1.5)
```

The result is shown in the following plot:

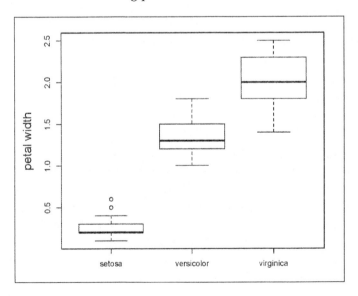

Flow control

In this section, we will review flow-control statements that you can use when programming with R to simplify repetitive tasks and make your code more legible. Programming with R involves putting together instructions that the computer will execute to fulfill a certain task. As you have noticed this far, R commands consist mainly of expressions or functions to be evaluated. Most programs are repetitive and depend on user input prior to executing a task. Flow-control statements are particularly important in this process because it allows you to tell the computer how many times an expression is to be repeated or when a statement is to be executed. In the rest of this chapter, we will go through flow-control statements and tips that you can use to write and debug your own programs.

The for() loop

The `for(i in vector){commands}` statement allows you to repeat the code written in brackets {} for each element (i) in your vector in parenthesis.

You can use `for()` loops to evaluate mathematical expressions. For example, the `Fibonacci` sequence is defined as a series of numbers in which each number is the sum of the two preceding numbers. We can get the first 15 numbers that make up the `Fibonacci` sequence starting from `(1, 1)`, using the following code:

```
> # First we create a numeric vector with 15 elements to store the
data generated.
> Fibonacci <- numeric(15)
> Fibonacci
 [1] 0 0 0 0 0 0 0 0 0 0 0 0 0 0 0
```

Next, we need to write down the code that will allow us to generate the `Fibonacci` sequence. If the first two elements of the sequence are `(1, 1)` and every subsequent number is the sum of the two preceding numbers, then the third element is *1 + 1 = 2* and the fourth element is *1 + 2 = 3*, and so on.

So, let's add the two first elements of the `Fibonacci` sequence in our `Fibonacci` vector as shown:

```
> Fibonacci[1:2] <- c(1,1)
```

Next, let's create a `for()` loop, which will add the sum of the two preceding numbers indexed at `i-2` and `i-1` from `i=3` to `i=15` (the length of the `Fibonacci` numeric vector we initially created):

```
> for(i in 3:length(Fibonacci)){Fibonacci[i] <- Fibonacci[i-2] +
Fibonacci[i-1]}
> Fibonacci
 [1]   1   1   2   3   5   8  13  21  34  55  89 144 233 377 610
```

In this example, the vector evaluated by the `for()` loop is `3:length(Fibonacci)`, but we could have also expressed the vector as `c(3, 4, 5, 6, 7, 8, 9, 10, 11, 12, 13, 14, 15)` or `seq(3, 15, by=1)`. To simplify our code, we can create a separate vector to store the sequence and then write our `for()` loop as follows:

```
> Fibonacci_terms <- seq(3, 15, by=1)
> for(i in Fibonacci_terms){Fibonacci[i] <- Fibonacci[i-2] +
Fibonacci[i-1]}
```

You don't always have to use a numeric or integer vector when writing `for()` loops. For example, you can use a character vector in a `for()` loop to update strings in another vector as follows:

```
> fruits <- c("apple", "pear", "grapes")
> other_fruits <- c("banana", "lemon")
> for (i in fruits){other_fruits <-c(other_fruits, i)} #appends fruits
to other_fruits vector
> other_fruits
[1] "banana" "lemon"  "apple"  "pear"   "grapes"
```

The apply() function

A good alternative to the `for()` loop is the `apply()` function, which allows you to apply a function to a matrix or array by row, column, or both. For example, let's calculate the mean of a matrix by row using the `apply()` function. First, let's create a matrix as follows:

```
> m1 <-matrix(1:12, nrow=3)
> m1
     [,1] [,2] [,3] [,4]
[1,]    1    4    7   10
[2,]    2    5    8   11
[3,]    3    6    9   12
```

The second argument of the `apply()` function is MARGIN, which allows you to specify whether the function should be applied by row with 1, by column with 2, or both with `c(1,2)`. Since we want to calculate the mean by row, we will use 1 for MARGIN, as follows:

```
> meanByrow <- apply(m1, 1,   mean)
> meanByrow
[1] 5.5 6.5 7.5
```

The last argument of the `apply()` function is FUN, which refers to the function to be applied to the matrix. In our last example, we used the `mean()` function. However, you can use any function including those you wish to write yourself. For example, let's apply the x+3 function to each value in the matrix as follows:

```
# Notice there is no comma between function(x) and x+3 when defining
the function in apply()
> m1plus3 <- apply(m1, c(1,2), function(x) x+3)
> m1plus3
     [,1] [,2] [,3] [,4]
[1,]    4    7   10   13
[2,]    5    8   11   14
[3,]    6    9   12   15
```

In the event that you want to specify arguments of a function, you just need to add them after the function. For example, let's say you want to apply the mean function by column to a second matrix but this time by specifying the `na.rm` argument as TRUE instead of the default (FALSE). Let's take a look at that in that in the following example:

```
> z <- c( 1, 4, 5, NA, 9,8, 3, NA)
> m2 <- matrix(z, nrow=4)
> m2
     [,1] [,2]
[1,]    1    9
[2,]    4    8
[3,]    5    3
[4,]   NA   NA
# Notice you need to separate the argument from its function with a
comma
> meanByColumn <- apply(m2, 2, mean, na.rm=TRUE)
> meanByColumn
[1] 3.333333 6.666667
```

The if() statement

The `if(condition){commands}` statement allows you to evaluate a condition and if it returns TRUE, the code in brackets will be executed. You can add an `else {commands}` statement to your `if()` statement if you would like to execute a block of code if your condition returns FALSE:

```
> x <- 4
> # we indent our code to make it more legible
> if(x < 10) {
  x <-x+4
  print(x)
}
[1] 8
```

If you have several conditions to test before running an `else {}` statement, you can use an `else if(condition){commands}` statement as follows:

```
> x <- 1
> if(x == 2) {
  x <- x+4
  print("X is equal to 2, so I added 4 to it.")
} else if (x > 2) {
  print("X is greater than 2, so I did nothing to it.")
} else {
  x <- x -4
  print("X is not greater than or equal to 2, so I subtracted 4 from it.")
}
[1] "X is not greater than or equal to 2, so I subtracted 4 from it."
```

The while() loop

The `while(condition){commands}` statement allows you to repeat a block of code until the condition in the parenthesis returns FALSE. If we look back at our `Fibonacci` sequence example, we could have written our program using a `while()` loop instead, as follows:

First, we create two objects to store the first and second number of the `Fibonacci` sequence:

```
> num1 <- 1
> num2 <- 1
```

Then, we create a numeric vector to contain the first two numbers of the `Fibonacci` sequence:

```
> Fibonacci <- c(num1, num2)
```

Next, we create a `count` object to store the number of elements added to the `Fibonacci` vector. We start the count at 2 since the first two numbers have already been added to the `Fibonacci` vector as follows:

```
> count <- 2 #set count to start from 2

>  while(count < 15) {

#We update the count number so that we can track the number of times
the loop is repeated.
count <- count +1

#Next we make sure to store the 2nd number in a new object before it
is overwritten.
oldnum2 <- num2

#Then we calculate the next number in the Fibonacci sequence.
num2 <- num1 + num2

#Then we update the Fibonacci vector with the 2nd number each time the
loop is repeated.
Fibonacci <- c(Fibonacci, num2)

#Lastly, we assign the 2nd number as the new first number to use in
the next iteration of the loop.
num1 <- oldnum2

}
> Fibonacci
 [1]   1   1   2   3   5   8  13  21  34  55  89 144 233 377 610
```

The repeat{} and break statement

The `repeat{commands}` statement is similar to the `while()` loop except that you do not need to set a condition to test, and your code is repeated endlessly unless you include a `break` statement. Typically, a `repeat{}` statement includes an `if(condition) break` line, but this is not required. The `break` statement causes the loop to terminate immediately.

If we go back to our Fibonacci example, we could have written the code as follows:

```
> num1 <- 1
> num2 <- 1
Fibonacci <- c(num1, num2)
> count <- 2
> repeat {
count <- count +1
oldnum2 <- num2
num2 <- num1 + num2
Fibonacci <- c(Fibonacci, num2)
num1 <- oldnum2
if (count >= 15) { break }
}
```

Functions

Functions are bits of code that perform a particular task and print or return its output to an object. Writing functions are particularly useful to avoid rewriting code over and over in your program; instead, you can write a function and every time you would like to perform that particular task, you can call that function. In fact, all the code we used so far in our examples call built-in or third-party R package functions.

For example, we ask for the mean of x using the following code:

```
> x <- c(2, 6, 7, 12)
> mean(x)
[1] 6.75
```

In the preceding code, we are actually asking R to call the mean() function. Each function takes arguments. If you would like to know what arguments could be passed to a particular R function, you can consult the help page. There are several ways to access the help documentation in R. First, you can use the help() function as follows:

```
> help(mean)
Description
Generic function for the (trimmed) arithmetic mean.
Usage
mean(x, ...)

## Default S3 method:
mean(x, trim = 0, na.rm = FALSE, ...)
Arguments
```

```
x  An R object. Currently there are methods for numeric/logical
vectors and date, date-time, and time interval objects. Complex
vectors are allowed for trim = 0, only.
trim  the fraction (0 to 0.5) of observations to be trimmed from each
end of x before the mean is computed. Values of trim outside that
range are taken as the nearest endpoint.
na.rm  a logical value indicating whether NA values should be stripped
before the computation proceeds.
... further arguments passed to or from other methods.
[...]
```

Alternatively, you can use the ? symbol to obtain the documentation page for the mean function as follows:

```
> ?mean #Returns the same output as above
```

Alternatively, you may also want to search all the help topics as shown in the following screenshot for the mean word with the ?? symbol as follows:

```
> ??mean
```

Topic	Package	Description
DateTimeClasses	base	Date–Time Classes
Date	base	Date Class
colSums	base	Form Row and Column Sums and Means
difftime	base	Time Intervals
mean	base	Arithmetic Mean
sunspot	boot	Annual Mean Sunspot Numbers
runmean	caTools	Mean of a Moving Window
dates	chron	Generate Dates and Times Components from Input
CKME	clue	Cassini Data Partitions Obtained by K–Means
meanabsdev	cluster	Internal cluster functions
effectiveSize	coda	Effective sample size for estimating the mean
dispersionPlot	cummeRbund	Mean count vs dispersion plot
IDate	data.table	Integer based date class
fitDispersionFunction	DEXSeq	Fit the mean-variance function.
dglmStdResid	edgeR	Visualize the mean-variance relationship in DGE data using standardized residuals
loessByCol	edgeR	Locally Weighted Mean By Column
binMeanVar	edgeR	Explore the mean-variance relationship for DGE data
ghMoments	fBasics	Generalized Hyperbolic Distribution Moments
ghtMoments	fBasics	Generalized Hyperbolic Student-t Moments
hypMoments	fBasics	Hyperbolic Distribution Moments
nigMoments	fBasics	Moments for the Normal Inverse Gaussian
%in%-methods	flowCore	Filter-specific membership methods
kmeansFilter	flowCore	Class "kmeansFilter"

As you can see in the preceding screenshot, R returns a table of all the search results matching the word "mean" for all the packages you have installed on your computer.

The help page is very useful because it tells you what type of object the function takes as input and a list of all the arguments it takes. The help page also informs you of the default settings used for all the arguments the function takes. By consulting the help page for the mean() function, you learn that the default settings are trim=0 and na.rm=FALSE. With trim set to 0, no observations or values are removed prior to calculating the mean, and with na.rm set to FALSE, all NA entries are not removed before calculating the mean. Consider the following example:

```
> x <- c(2, 6, 7, 12, NA, NA)
> mean(x)
[1] NA
```

If we specify na.rm=TRUE, the NA entries are ignored as follows:

```
> mean(x, na.rm=TRUE)
[1] 6.75
```

So far, we have been changing default parameters by explicitly specifying which arguments to change, that is, na.rm=TRUE. However, R also allows you to change default parameters using the argument position only. This means we can rewrite the last command as follows:

```
> #notice "," is used to specify unchanged missing arguments in the
order they appear in the function definition on the help page
> mean(x, ,TRUE)
[1] 6.75
```

This also holds true for the functions you may write as well. Let's write a simple function called vectorContains() to test whether a vector contains the number 3. To define a function in R, we write the word function and our list of arguments contained in parenthesis () followed by curly braces that contains the sequence of commands we want our function to execute. For example, let's write a function to check whether the value 3 is present in a vector. Here are the steps we will take to write a function to check whether a value (in this case, 3) is present in an input vector:

1. We create a function called vectorContains and use an argument (variable) value.to.check to store the value we want to check.

2. We check that the input object type is numeric using the is.numeric() function.

3. We ensure that there are no missing (NA) values using the any() and is.na() functions. The any() function will check each entry and the is.na() function will return TRUE if NA is present. Because we want to return TRUE when there is no NA present instead of when an NA is present, we use the ! sign before the any(is.na()) command.

4. We use an `if else {}` statement to return an error message if the vector isn't numeric and/or contains NA values using the `stop()` function.

5. We create an object `value.found` to keep track of whether the value to be checked is found. We initially set `value.found` to FALSE because we assume the value is not present.

6. We check each value of our input vector using a `for()` loop. If an element (`i`) of our vector matches `value.to.check`, we set `value.found` to "yes" and break out of the `for()` loop.

7. Depending on whether `value.found` is set to "yes" or "no", we return TRUE or FALSE as follows:

```
> vectorContains <- function(v1, value.to.check=3){
    if(is.numeric(v1) && !any(is.na(v1))) {
    value.found <- "no"
    for (i in v1){
      if(i == value.to.check) {
        value.found <- "yes"
        break
      }
    }
    if(value.found == "yes") {
      return(TRUE)
    } else {
      return(FALSE)
    }
  } else {
#When it exits the function it will print the following error
message
    stop("This function takes a numeric vector without NAs as
input.")
  }
}
```

Now, let's test our function as follows:

```
> x <- c(2, 6, 7, 12, NA, NA)

> vectorContains(x)
Error in vectorContains(x) :
  This function takes a numeric vector without NAs as input.
> y <- c(1, 4, 6, 8, 3, 12, 15)
> vectorContains(y)
[1] TRUE
```

Suppose we want to test whether a vector contains the value 6 instead of 3, we can easily change the default `value.to.check` from `3` to `6`, as follows:

```
> vectorContains(y, 6)
[1] TRUE
> vectorContains(y, value.to.check=17)
[1] FALSE
```

Hopefully, in the preceding example, you can see that the beauty of writing functions instead of individual commands because you can reuse this function to check whether a vector contains any particular value. Moreover, by saving these lines of code to a text document (for example, `vectorfunction.R`), you can reload this function in a later session using the `source()` command instead of rewriting the function, as follows:

```
> source("/PathToFile/vectorfunction.R")
```

General programming and debugging tools

Since this chapter is meant to review R programming, I will not go into too much detail on how to write a program step by step, but I will present some general advice on how to write a successful program.

First, it is essential that you understand the problem because R will only do what you tell it to do. So if you don't have a clear picture of the problem, it's best you sit down and work out what you want your program to do and think about what R tools and/or packages are available to help you fulfill your task. Once you've explored the R functions and packages available to you to help address your question, you should simplify your problem by writing down general steps and functions you can use to solve your problem and then translate your general ideas into a detailed implementation.

A good strategy to adopt when working on a detailed implementation for a program is to use the "top-down" design approach, which consists of writing the whole program in a couple of steps like you would an essay outline. Then, expand each step with additional key steps and keep expanding until you have a full program. To save time and make your code more legible, I would suggest breaking up each of your key steps into functions, and then run and check each function iteratively. As a general rule of thumb, if your function starts to get really long, that is, dozens of line, I would suggest thinking of ways to break down that function into a bunch of smaller functions or "subfunctions", in the same way you would break down really long paragraphs into smaller ones when writing an essay.

The beauty of programming resides in the ability to write and reuse functions in several programs. By writing generic functions that fulfill specific tasks, you can reuse that code in another program by simply executing the following code:

```
> source("someOtherfunctions.R")
```

The trickiest part of programming is finding and solving errors (debugging). The following is a list of some generic steps you can take when trying to solve a bug:

1. Recognize that your program has a bug. This can be easy when you get an error or warning message but harder when you get an output that is not the output expected or the true answer to your problem.

2. Make the bug reproducible. It is easier to fix a bug that you know how to trigger.

3. Identify the cause of the bug. For example, this can be a variable, not updating it the way you wanted it to in a function, or a condition statement that can never return TRUE as written. Other common causes of error for beginners include testing for a match (equality) by writing if(x = 12) instead of if(x==12), or the inability of your code to deal with missing data (NA values).

4. Fix the error in your code and test whether you successfully fixed it.

5. Look for similar errors elsewhere in your code.

 One trick you can use to help you tease out the cause of your error message is the traceback() function. For example, when we tried to the vectorContains(x), we got the error message "This function takes a numeric vector as input." If someone wanted to see where the error message was coming from, they could run traceback() and get the location as follows:

```
> traceback()
2: stop("This function takes a numeric vector as
input.") at #38
1: vectorContains(x)
```

Other useful functions include the browser() and debug() functions. The browser() function allows you to pause the execution of your function, and examine or change local variables, and even execute other R commands. Let's inspect the vectorContains() function we wrote earlier with the browser() function as follows:

```
> x <- c(2, 6, 7, 12, NA, NA)
> browser()
```

```
# We have now entered the Browser mode.
Browse[1]> x <-c(1, 2, 3)
Browse[1]> vectorContains(x)
Error in vectorContains(x) :
  This function takes a numeric vector without NAs as input.
Browse[1]> x <-c(1, 2, 3)
Browse[1]> vectorContains(x)
[1] TRUE
Browse[1]> Q #To quit browser()
```

 Note that the variable x we changed in the browser mode was stored to our workspace. So if we enter x after we quit, the values stored in browser mode will be returned, as follows:

```
> x
[1] 1 2 3
```

When we call the debug() function, we also enter the browser mode. This allows us to execute a single line of code at a time by entering n for next, continue to run the function by entering c, or quit the function by entering Q like in browser mode. Note that each time you call the function, you will enter the browser mode unless you run the undebug() function.

The following is an example using debug to inspect our vectorContains() function:

```
>  debug(vectorContains)
> x <- c(1, 2, 3, 9)
> vectorContains(x)
debugging in: vectorContains(x)
debug at #1: {
    if (is.numeric(v1) && !any(is.na(v1))) {
        value.found <- "no"
        for (i in v1) {
            if (i == value.to.check) {
                value.found <- "yes"
                break
            }
        }
        if (value.found == "yes") {
            return(TRUE)
        }
        else {
            return(FALSE)
```

```
        }
    }
    else {
        stop("This function takes a numeric vector as input.")
    }
}
Browse[2]> c
exiting from: vectorContains(x)
[1] TRUE
> undebug(vectorContains)
> vectorContains(x)
[1] TRUE
```

 Notice that debug only enters the browser mode when you call the vectorContains function.

Summary

In this chapter, we saw how data is stored and accessed in R. We also discussed how to write functions. You should now be able to write and access data in vectors, arrays, and data frames, and load your data into R. We also learned how to make basic plots using built-in R functions and the ggplot2 package. You should also know how to use flow-control statements in your code and write your own functions and use built-in tools to troubleshoot your code.

Now that you have a foundation in R data structures, we will move on to statistical methods in the next chapter, where you will find out how to obtain useful statistical information from your dataset and fit your data to known probability distributions.

2
Statistical Methods with R

This chapter will present an overview of how to summarize your data and get useful statistical information for downstream analysis. We will also show you how to plot and get statistical information from probability distributions and how to test the fit of your sample distribution to well-defined probability distributions. We will also go over some of the functions used to perform hypothesis testing including the Student's t-test, Wilcoxon rank-sum test, z-test, chi-squared test, Fisher's exact test, and F-test.

Before we begin, we will load the gene expression profiling data from the E-GEOD-19577 study entitled "MLL partner genes confer distinct biological and clinical signatures of pediatric AML, an AIEOP study" from the ArrayExpress website to use as a sample dataset for some of our examples. For simplicity, we will not go into the details of how the data was generated, except to mention that the study evaluates the expression level of 54,675 probes in 42 leukemia patients' samples. If you would like to learn more about the study, please consult the experiment web page at `http://www.ebi.ac.uk/arrayexpress/experiments/E-GEOD-19577`. Here are the steps we will follow to load the data into R:

1. Download the R ExpressionSet (`E-GEOD-19577.eSet.r`).
2. Load the dataset with the `load()` function. This command will create the `study` object, which contains the raw experimental data.
3. Rename the `study` object as `MLLpartner.dataset`.
4. Load the `Biobase` and `affy` bioconductor packages.
5. Normalize the data with the `rma()` function.
6. Inspect the data.

These steps can be implemented in R, as follows:

```
> load(url("http://www.ebi.ac.uk/arrayexpress/files/E-GEOD-19577/E-
GEOD-19577.eSet.r"))
> MLLpartner.ds <- study
> library("affy")
> library("Biobase")
> AEsetnorm = rma(MLLpartner.ds)
Background correcting
Normalizing
Calculating Expression
> head(exprs(AEsetnorm)) #output shown truncated
          GSM487973 GSM487972 GSM487971 GSM487970 GSM487969
1007_s_at  4.372242  4.293080  4.210850  4.707231  4.345101
1053_at    8.176033  8.541016  8.338475  7.935021  7.868985
117_at     5.730343  8.723568  5.172717  5.404062  5.731468
121_at     7.744487  6.951332  7.202343  7.158402  6.959318
1255_g_at  2.707115  2.717625  2.699625  2.698669  2.701679
1294_at    9.077232  7.611238  9.649630  7.911132  9.732346
```

Now, let's get the expression values for two probes to be used in our examples, as follows:

```
> probeA <- as.numeric(exprs(AEsetnorm)[1,])
> probeA <- setNames(probeA, colnames(exprs(AEsetnorm)))
> probeB <- as.numeric(exprs(AEsetnorm)[2,])
> probeB <-setNames(probeB, colnames(exprs(AEsetnorm)))
```

Now, let's create a matrix with all the expression values for each probe evaluated in the 42 patient samples, as follows:

```
> MLLpartner.mx <- as.matrix(exprs(AEsetnorm))
> #Lets save the object to our session
> dump("MLLpartner.mx", "MLLpartner.R")
> class(MLLpartner.mx)
[1] "matrix"
> dim(MLLpartner.mx)
[1] 54675    42
```

Descriptive statistics

A useful tool to evaluate your data before you begin your analysis is the `summary()` function, which provides a summary of the non-parametric descriptors of a sample, as follows:

```
> summary(probeA)
   Min. 1st Qu.  Median    Mean 3rd Qu.    Max.
  4.211   4.645   4.774   4.774   4.892   5.231
```

You can also get a summary for each column of the matrix using the `summary()` function, as follows:

```
> summary(MLLpartner.mx) #output truncated
   GSM487973           GSM487972           GSM487971
 Min.   : 2.112   Min.   : 1.805   Min.   : 1.994
 1st Qu.: 3.412   1st Qu.: 3.410   1st Qu.: 3.411
 Median : 4.736   Median : 4.745   Median : 4.731
 Mean   : 5.342   Mean   : 5.346   Mean   : 5.355
 3rd Qu.: 6.870   3rd Qu.: 6.851   3rd Qu.: 6.933
 Max.   :14.449   Max.   :14.453   Max.   :14.406
```

We can also get this information by calling the individual functions used to determine these parameters, namely the `mean`, `median`, `min`, `max`, and `quantile` functions, as follows:

```
> min(probeA)
[1] 4.21085
> max(probeA)
[1] 5.231199
> mean(probeA)
[1] 4.773866
> median(probeA)
[1] 4.774236
> quantile(probeA)
      0%      25%      50%      75%     100%
4.210850 4.644994 4.774236 4.892259 5.231199
```

You can also specify which probabilities to use with the `probs` argument, as follows:

```
> quantile(probeA, probs = c(0.1, 0.2, 0.6, 0.9))
     10%      20%      60%      90%
4.375377 4.576501 4.821101 5.118735
```

To avoid getting a string of numbers in your output, you can specify the number of decimal places to be displayed using the `round()` function, as follows:

```
> round(mean(probeA), 2)
[1] 4.77
```

Suppose we also had information on the response to the `drugA` treatment for those 42 patient samples, we could include it to the `probeA` and `probeB` gene expression levels, as follows:

```
> df <- data.frame(expr_probeA=probeA, expr_probeB=probeB, drugA_
response= factor(rep(c("success", "fail"), 21)))
> head(df)
          expr_probeA expr_probeB drugA_response
GSM487973    4.372242    8.176033        success
GSM487972    4.293080    8.541016           fail
GSM487971    4.210850    8.338475        success
GSM487970    4.707231    7.935021           fail
GSM487969    4.345101    7.868985        success
GSM487968    4.586062    7.909702           fail
```

Now, we can get a summary for each column by response to the `drugA` treatment using the `by()` function, as follows:

```
> by(df, df$drugA_response, summary)
df$drugA_response: fail
   expr_probeA        expr_probeB        drugA_response
 Min.   :4.293    Min.   :6.960    fail   :21
 1st Qu.:4.687    1st Qu.:7.935    success: 0
 Median :4.766    Median :8.245
 Mean   :4.786    Mean   :8.201
 3rd Qu.:4.895    3rd Qu.:8.575
 Max.   :5.218    Max.   :8.926
-------------------------------------------------
df$drugA_response: success
   expr_probeA        expr_probeB        drugA_response
 Min.   :4.211    Min.   :6.652    fail   : 0
 1st Qu.:4.571    1st Qu.:7.597    success:21
 Median :4.776    Median :7.921
 Mean   :4.762    Mean   :7.950
 3rd Qu.:4.885    3rd Qu.:8.338
 Max.   :5.231    Max.   :9.033
```

Data variability

In addition to general information from the `mean`, `median`, and `quantiles` functions, we are often interested in knowing how variable our data points are from each other. The simplest measure of variability is the range, which is the difference between the largest and smallest value. We can obtain the range by subtracting the maximum value from the minimum value, or simply using the `range()` function, as shown in the following code:

```
> max(probeA) - min(probeA)
[1] 1.02035
> range(probeA)
[1] 4.210850 5.231199
```

Other measures of variability include the variance and standard deviation. The variance is defined as the average squared deviation of the data values from the mean. More formally, the population variance is defined as:

$$\sigma^2 = \frac{1}{N}\sum_{i=1}^{N}(x_i - \mu)^2$$

In the preceding formula, N is the size and μ is the mean of the population given by each data point x_i. The sample variance is defined as:

$$s^2 = \frac{n}{n-1}\sigma_y^2 = \frac{1}{n-1}\sum_{i=1}^{n}(y_i - \bar{y})^2$$

In the preceding formula, n is the number of samples from the population, n is less than N and $\bar{y}$ is the sample mean.

In other words, the sum of squares divided by the number of data values (n) for a population and the degrees of freedom (n-1) for a sample. We can find the mean using the `mean()` function, as follows:

```
> mean(probeA)
[1] 4.773866
```

We can calculate the sum of squares in R using the `sum()` function, as follows:

```
> probeA.soq <- sum((probeA-mean(probeA))^2)
[1] 2.734039
```

Now, we can easily calculate the unbiased sample variance by dividing the sum of squares by the number of degrees of freedom defined as *(n-1)*, where *n* is `length()` of the `probeA` vector, as shown in the following command:

```
> d.f <- length(probeA) - 1
> probeA.soq/(d.f)
[1] 0.06668388
```

A quicker way to get the variance would be to use the `var()` function, as shown in the following command:

```
> var(probeA)
[1] 0.06668388
```

Another measure of variability is the **standard deviation** defined as the square root of the sample variance. To get the standard deviation for our `probeA` data, we can write the formula using the `sqrt()` function to get the square root of the variance or, more simply, use the `sd()` function, as shown in the following command:

```
> sqrt(var(probeA))
[1] 0.2582322
> sd(probeA)
[1] 0.2582322
```

Often, it is important to determine how reliable our measures are by calculating the **standard error of the mean**, defined as the square root of the variance divided by the number of samples, as shown in the following command:

```
> sqrt(var(probeA)/length(probeA))
[1] 0.0398461
```

Confidence intervals

Another way we can assess the reliability of our measurements is by determining the confidence intervals for the mean of our data points. **Confidence intervals (CI)** estimate the range the mean would fall in, should the experiment or exercise be repeated. We can calculate the confidence intervals for the mean of our sample distribution by multiplying the standard error by the *t* value associated with a significance level of α equal to 0.025 or 0.975 quantile of the t-distribution with 41 degrees of freedom. The `qt()` function gives us the quantiles of the t-distribution for *n* degrees of freedom, which we can apply in the formula to calculate the confidence interval, as shown in the following code:

```
> std.err.s2A <- sqrt(var(probeA)/length(probeA))
> qt(.975, d.f)* std.err.s2A
[1] 0.08047082
```

Therefore, the mean of the gene expression values for `probeA` is 4.77 ± 0.080 for the 42 samples with a 95 percent confidence interval.

Probability distributions

R makes it very easy to plot and get statistical information on many probability distributions. For those who are not familiar with probability distributions, they are defined as a table or an equation that links each outcome of a statistical experiment with its probability of occurrence. A summary of many common probability distributions available in R is available in the following table:

Probability distribution	R name
Beta	beta
Binomial	binom
Cauchy	cauchy
Chi square	chisq
Exponential	exp
F	f
Gamma	gamma
Geometric	geom
Hypergeometric	hyper
Logistic	logis
Lognormal	lnorm
Negative Binomial	nbinom
Normal	norm
Poisson	pois
Student t	t
Uniform	unif
Tukey	tukey
Weibull	weib
Wilcoxon	wilcox

You can also get this summary in R by entering `help("distributions")`. For additional probability distributions, and the packages needed to load them, you can consult the CRAN distributions page at `http://cran.r-project.org/web/views/Distributions.html`.

For each probability distribution, you can obtain the function that generates the mass or the probability function by adding the d prefix, the cumulative density function by adding the p prefix, and the quantile function by adding the q prefix to the R name, shown in the previous table. You can also generate random numbers from these probability distributions by adding the r prefix to the R name. For example, you can use qnorm() to call the quantile function for a normal distribution and rpois() to generate random numbers from a Poisson distribution.

For the 0.65 quantile of a normal distribution with a mean of 7.5 and standard deviation of 4, we would enter:

```
> qnorm(0.65, mean=7.5, sd=4)
[1] 9.041282
```

To generate seven random numbers from a Poisson distribution with a lambda equal to 4, we would enter:

```
> rpois(7, lambda=4)
[1] 2 3 5 4 6 3 5
```

Now, let's consider a more detailed example using probability distribution functions to solve a particular problem. Say the average number of liters of water consumed per day for children under the age of 12 has a normal distribution with a mean of 7.5 and a standard deviation of 3.5. Since the 68–95–99.7 rule (also known as the three-sigma rule or empirical rule) states that 99.7 percent randomly generated values will fall within three standard deviations of the mean in a normal distribution, we can approximate the interval values to be used for the x values in our plot, as follows:

```
> ld.mean <- 7.5
> ld.sd <- 1.5
> ld.mean+3*ld.sd
[1] 12
> ld.mean-3*ld.sd
[1] 2
```

So, from these calculations, we can use an interval of [0, 16] because most random numbers generated will fall between 2 and 12:

```
> x <- seq(0, 16, length=100)
```

Next, we will use the dnorm() function, along with our mean and standard deviation, to return the density curve for average liters of water consumed per day for children under the age of 12:

```
> nd.height <- dnorm(x, mean = 7.5, sd = 1.5)
```

Now, we can plot the normal curve for probability distribution in R using the `plot()` function. We will set `type = "l"` in the `plot()` function to graph a line instead of points, as shown in the following command:

```
> plot(x, nd.height, type = "l", xlab = "Liters per day",  ylab =
"Density", main = "Liters of water drank by school children < 12 years
old")
```

The graph for this normal curve is shown in the following plot:

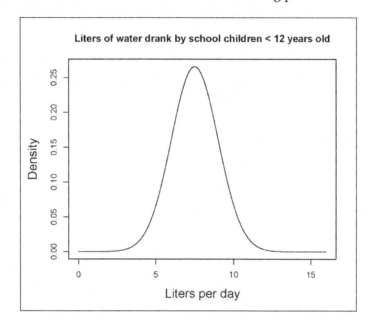

Suppose we want to evaluate the probability of a child drinking less than 4 liters of water per day. We can get this information by measuring the area under the curve to the left of 4 using `pnorm()`, as shown in the following code to return the cumulative density function. Since we want to measure the area to the left of the curve, we set `lower.tail=TRUE` (default command) to the `pnorm()` function; otherwise, we will enter `lower.tail=FALSE` to measure the area to the right of the curve:

```
> pnorm(4, mean = 7.5, sd = 1.5, lower.tail = TRUE)
[1] 0.009815329
```

We can plot the cumulative density function for x, as follows:

```
> ld.cdf <- pnorm(x, mean = 7.5, sd = 1.5, lower.tail = TRUE)
> plot(x, ld.cdf, type = "l", xlab = "Liters per day", ylab =
"Cumulative Probability")
```

The result is shown in the following graph:

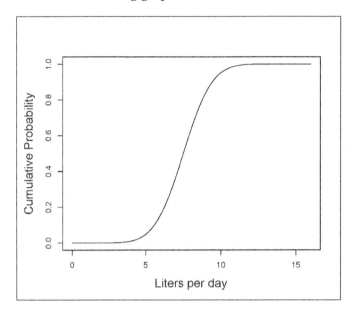

We can also plot the cumulative probability of a child drinking more than 8 liters of water per day on our normal curve by setting upper and lower boundaries and then coloring in that area using the `polygon()` function. By looking at our cumulative density function plot (shown in the previous diagram), we can see that the probability of a child drinking more than 15 liters per day approaches zero so we can set our upper limit to 15.

Plot the normal curve using the `plot()` function, as follows:

```
>   plot(x, nd.height, type = "l", xlab = "Liters per day",  ylab =
"Density")
```

Set the lower and upper limits, as follows:

```
>   ld.lower <- 8
>   ld.upper <- 15
```

Get all values of *x* that fall between 8 and 15:

```
>   i <- x >= ld.lower & x <= ld.upper #returns a logical vector
```

Now, we can highlight the area under the curve corresponding to the probability of a child drinking more than 8 liters of water in red with the `polygon()` function:

```
> polygon(c(ld.lower,x[i], ld.upper), c(0, nd.height [i],0),
col="red")
> abline(h = 0, col = "gray")
```

Calculate the cumulative probability of a child drinking more than 8 liters of water per day:

```
> pb <- round(pnorm(8, mean = 7.5, sd = 1.5, lower.tail = FALSE)
> pb
[1] 0.37
```

Use the `paste()` function to create a character vector that will concatenate the `pb` value to our text:

```
> pb.results <- paste("Cumulative probabily of a child drinking > 8L/
day", pb, sep=": ")
```

Add the `pb.results` text as the title of our plot:

```
> title(pb.results)
```

The result is shown in the following graph:

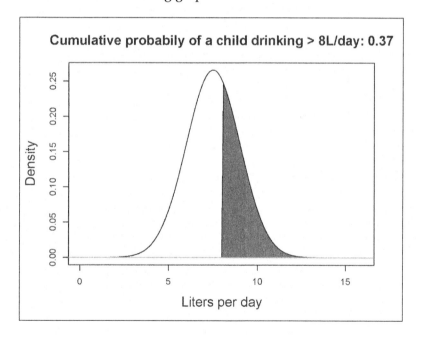

Fitting distributions

Now that we have seen how to plot and gain statistical information from probability distributions, we will show you how to use R to fit your data to theoretical distributions. There are several methods you can use to test whether your sample distribution fits a theoretical distribution. For example, you may want to see if your sample distribution fits a normal distribution using a **Quantile-Quantile plot (Q-Q plot)**. In R, you can use the qqnorm() function to create a Q-Q plot to evaluate the data. R also has a more generic version of this function called qqplot() to create Q-Q plots for any theoretical distribution. To illustrate the use of these functions, let's create a Q-Q plot to test whether the gene expression values of probeA follow a normal or gamma distribution.

First, let's set the plot settings to display two figures in the same layout:

```
> par(mfrow=c(1,2))
```

Use qqnorm() to fit the data to a normal distribution:

```
qqnorm(probeA)
```

Add the theoretical line for a normal distribution using the default first and third quantiles:

```
> qqline(probeA, distribution = qnorm, probs = c(0.25, 0.75))
```

To examine the fit of our data to a gamma distribution, let's estimate the shape and rate parameters using the fitdistr() function part of the MASS package:

```
> require("MASS")
> fitdistr(probeA, 'gamma')
      shape        rate
  341.75868     71.58950
 ( 74.52444) ( 15.62234)
```

Let's store the gamma parameters in an object for future use:

```
> gamma.par <- fitdistr(probeA, 'gamma')
```

To know what is stored in our `gamma.par` object, we can use the `str()` function we mentioned earlier in *Chapter 1, Programming with R*. Let's have a look at the following function:

```
> str(gamma.par)
List of 5
 $ estimate: Named num [1:2] 341.8 71.6
  ..- attr(*, "names")= chr [1:2] "shape" "rate"
 $ sd      : Named num [1:2] 74.5 15.6
  ..- attr(*, "names")= chr [1:2] "shape" "rate"
 $ vcov    : num [1:2, 1:2] 5554 1163 1163 244
  ..- attr(*, "dimnames")=List of 2
  .. ..$ : chr [1:2] "shape" "rate"
  .. ..$ : chr [1:2] "shape" "rate"
 $ loglik  : num -2.37
 $ n       : int 42
 - attr(*, "class")= chr "fitdistr"
```

By inspecting the structure of the `gamma.par` object, we now know how to access the shape and rate values. We need to use the appropriate index from the `gamma.par$estimate` parameter named numeric vector or use the name of the index, as follows:

```
> gamma.par$estimate['shape'] #or gamma.par$estimate[1]
   shape
341.7587
> s <- gamma.par$estimate['shape']
> r <- gamma.par$estimate['rate']
```

Now, we can calculate the theoretical quantiles for a gamma distribution with the estimated values for the shape and rate, as shown:

```
> theoretical.probs <- seq(1:length(probeA))/(length(probeA)+1)
> theoretical.quantiles <- qgamma(theoretical.probs,shape=s,rate=r)
> plot(theoretical.quantiles, sort(probeA),xlab="Theoretical
Quantiles",ylab="Sample Quantiles",main="Gamma QQ-plot")
```

Now, let's add a line to the first and third quantiles using the `qqline()` function. Since we are not using the default `qnorm` function for the `distribution` argument in the `qqline()` function, we need to create our own settings using the `qgamma()` function with the appropriate shape and rate settings, as follows:

```
> qF <- function(p) qgamma(p, shape=s, rate=r)
> qqline(y=sort(probeA), distribution=qF)
```

The graph for theoretical quantiles of a Normal Q-Q plot and Gamma Q-Q plot is shown in the following diagram:

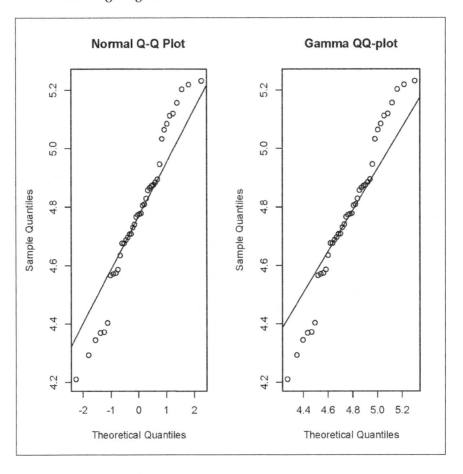

Before going any further, let's return our plot parameter settings to its default settings using the `par()` function:

```
>par(mfrow=c(1,1))
```

Instead of Q-Q plots, you may choose to use a well-defined statistical test for fitting distributions such as the **Kolmogorov-Smirnov, Anderson-Darling**, or **Chi-square test**. For example, let's use the Kolmogorov-Smirnov method to test whether our `probeA` data fits a gamma distribution with a shape of three and rate of two using the `ks.test()` function, as follows:

```
> ks.test(probeA, "pgamma", 3, 2)
One-sample Kolmogorov-Smirnov test
data:  probeA
D = 0.9901, p-value = 2.22e-16
alternative hypothesis: two-sided
```

Alternatively, we can use the Anderson-Darling test to test whether our `probeA` dataset fits a normal distribution using the `ad.test()` function available in the `nortest` package:

```
> require("nortest")
> ad.test(probeA)
Anderson-Darling normality test
data:  probeA
A = 0.378, p-value = 0.3923
```

Higher order moments of a distribution

Higher order moments of a sample distribution are often used to estimate shape parameters, such as skewness and kurtosis, or to measure the deviation of a sample distribution from a normal distribution. For example, we might want to know if the skew we observed in our `probeA` distribution has a long drawn out tail to the left (negative skewing) or right (positive skewing) compared to a normal curve. You quantify the degree of skewing using the `skewness()` function available in the `fBasics` package and test whether the degree of skewing you calculate from your dataset is significantly different from the theoretical value for the skew of a normal distribution, which is zero.

Let's have a look at the following code:

```
> require("fBasics")
> skewness(probeA)
[1] -0.1468461
attr(,"method")
[1] "moment"
```

Now, we can determine whether the absolute value of the -0.147 skew is significantly different from zero by performing a t-test. The approximate standard error of a skew is defined as the square root of 6 divided by the total number of samples:

```
> abs(skewness(probeA))/sqrt(6/length(probeA))
[1] 0.3885183
attr(,"method")
[1] "moment"
```

Now, we just need to calculate the probability of obtaining a t-value of 0.389 by chance when the skew value is truly zero:

```
> 1- pt(0.389, 41)
[1] 0.3496446
```

Since the `p-value` is greater than 0.05, we cannot reject the null hypothesis and conclude that the skew is not significantly different from zero. Thus, the skew is not significantly different from a normal curve.

Instead of calculating the skew, we can also evaluate the kurtosis value to get an idea of the peak or flat-top nature of the distribution. A normal curve has a kurtosis value of zero and the approximate standard error of kurtosis is calculated by taking the square root of 24 divided by the total number of samples. To obtain the kurtosis value in R, we can use the `kurtosis()` function, which is also available in the `fBasics` package:

```
> kurtosis(probeA)
[1] -0.5670091
attr(,"method")
[1] "excess"
> abs(kurtosis(probeA))/sqrt(24/length(probeA))
[1] 0.7500826
attr(,"method")
[1] "excess"
> 1-pt(0.750, 41)
[1] 0.2287686
```

Since the `p-value` is greater than 0.05, we cannot reject the null hypothesis and conclude that the kurtosis of our sample distribution is not significantly different from a normal distribution.

Other statistical tests to fit distributions

R also has many other functions available to help fit your sample distribution to many other types of distributions. For convenience, you can find a list of R functions available to fit distributions in the following table. You can also consult Vito Ricci's document on fitting distributions at `http://cran.r-project.org/doc/contrib/Ricci-distributions-en.pdf` for more information on how to use these functions to fit distributions.

Test	Function	Package
Anderson-Darling test for normality	`ad.test()`	nortest
Chi-squared test	`chisq.test()`	stats
Cramer-von Mises test for normality	`cvm.test()`	nortest
Empirical cumulative distribution function	`ecdf()`	stats
Maximum-likelihood fitting of univariate distributions	`fitdistr()`	MASS
Discrete count data distribution for goodness-of-fit tests	`goodfit()`	vcd
Jarque-Bera test for normality	`jarque.bera.test()`	tseries
Augmented Dickey–Fuller test	`adf.test()`	tseries
Kolmogorov-Sminorv test	`ks.test()`	stats
Returns kurtosis value	`kurtosis()`	fBasics
Lilliefors test for normality	`lillie.test()`	nortest
Estimate parameters by the method of maximum likelihood	`mle()`	stats4
Pearson chi-square test for normality	`pearson.test()`	nortest
Normal Q-Q plot	`qqnorm()`	stats
Q-Q plot of two datasets	`qqline()`, `qqplot()`	stats
Shapiro-Francia test for normality	`shapiro.test()`	stats
Returns skewness value	`skewness()`	fBasics

The propagate package

You may also find the `propagate` package particularly useful because it allows you to fit your data to many distributions at once and tells you which one is the most appropriate. For example, we can use the `fitDistr()` function to fit your data to a variety of distributions. The fits for the data will be sorted by ascending **Akaike information criterion** (**AIC**) value, where the preferred model is the one with the minimum AIC value. The AIC value takes into account the trade-off between the goodness-of-fit of the model and the complexity of the model. Let's have a look at the following example:

```
> install.packages("propagate")
> library("propagate")
```

The `fitDistr()` function allows you to use a vector of observation or an object generated using the `propagate()` function. In our first example, let's consider a simple example using the `rnorm()` function to simulate 10,000 numerical observations. Let's have a look at the following example:

```
> set.seed(275) #so you get the same results
> observations <- rnorm(10000, 5)
> distTested <- fitDistr(observations)
Fitting Normal distribution...Done.
Fitting Skewed-normal distribution...Done.
Fitting Generalized normal distribution...........10.........20.......
Done.
Fitting Log-normal distribution...Done.
Fitting Scaled/shifted t- distribution...Done.
Fitting Logistic distribution...Done.
Fitting Uniform distribution...Done.
Fitting Triangular distribution...Done.
Fitting Trapezoidal distribution...Done.
Fitting Curvilinear Trapezoidal distribution...Done.
Fitting Generalized Trapezoidal distribution...Done.
Fitting Gamma distribution...Done.
Fitting Cauchy distribution...Done.
Fitting Laplace distribution...Done.
Fitting Gumbel distribution...Done.
Fitting Johnson SU
distribution...........10.........20.........30.........40.........50
.........60..........70.........80.Done.
Fitting Johnson SB
distribution...........10.........20..........30.........40.........50
.........60.........70.........80.Done.
```

```
Fitting 3P Weibull distribution...........10.........20.......Done.
Fitting 4P Beta distribution...Done.
Fitting Arcsine distribution...Done.
Fitting von Mises distribution...Done.
```

As you can see, the `fitDistr()` function automatically plots the best distribution based on the AIC value. To disable this feature, you can set `plot=FALSE` value. The plot is shown in the following graph:

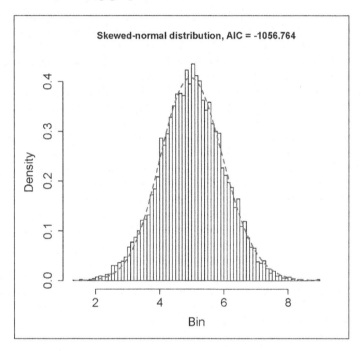

You can see the AIC values for the other distributions by accessing the `aic` data frame of the `distTested` object. Let's have a look at the following example:

```
> distTested$aic
                 Distribution         AIC
2                Skewed-normal  -1056.7637
16                  Johnson SU  -1055.2898
3           Generalized normal  -1055.1193
17                  Johnson SB  -1053.0655
19                     4P Beta  -1051.5507
11 Generalized Trapezoidal  -1049.0981
1                       Normal  -1047.0616
5            Scaled/shifted t-  -1046.9436
18                  3P Weibull  -1005.1263
```

```
12                          Gamma   -998.3562
6                        Logistic   -984.4944
21                      von Mises   -947.3471
8                       Triangular  -941.3394
9                      Trapezoidal  -940.3361
4                      Log-normal   -929.9566
15                         Gumbel   -809.9676
14                         Laplace  -733.8516
13                          Cauchy  -650.7236
10 Curvilinear Trapezoidal          -581.6016
7                          Uniform  -391.3259
20                         Arcsine  -261.7417
```

Alternatively, you can use the `fitDistr()` function to fit results obtained from the `propagate()` function. Consider the following example:

$$x^{3y} - 1$$

$$\mu_x = 6, \sigma_x = 0.1$$

$$\mu_x = 6, \sigma_y = 0.1$$

First, we enter the equation in R using the `expression()` function and the mean and standard deviation for the x and y variables into separate numeric vectors, as follows:

```
> EXPR <- expression(x^(3 * y)-1)
> x <- c(6, 0.1)
> y <- c(2, 0.1)
```

Then, we create a matrix that stores the means in the first row and the standard deviations in the second row for each variable, as follows:

```
> DF <- cbind(x, y)
```

Next, we use the `propagate()` function to generate the kernel density of the Monte Carlo simulation results to be used in the `fitDistr()` function, as follows:

```
> RES <- propagate(expr = EXPR, data = DF, type = "stat", do.sim =
TRUE, verbose = TRUE)
```

Now, we can fit our data to the 21 distributions, as shown in the following code, with the `fitDistr()` function:

```
> testedDistrEXPR <- fitDistr(RES)
Fitting Normal distribution...Done.
Fitting Skewed-normal distribution...Done.
Fitting Generalized normal distribution...........10.........20.......
Done.
Fitting Log-normal distribution...Done.
Fitting Scaled/shifted t- distribution...Done.
Fitting Logistic distribution...Done.
Fitting Uniform distribution...Done.
Fitting Triangular distribution...Done.
Fitting Trapezoidal distribution...Done.
Fitting Curvilinear Trapezoidal distribution...Done.
Fitting Generalized Trapezoidal distribution...Done.
Fitting Gamma distribution...Done.
Fitting Cauchy distribution...Done.
Fitting Laplace distribution...Done.
Fitting Gumbel distribution...Done.
Fitting Johnson SU
distribution..........10.........20.........30.........40.........50
.........60.........70.........80.Done.
Fitting Johnson SB
distribution..........10.........20.........30.........40.........50
.........60.........70.........80.Done.
Fitting 3P Weibull distribution..........10.........20.......Done.
Fitting 4P Beta distribution...Done.
Fitting Arcsine distribution...Done.
Fitting von Mises distribution...Done.
```

The plot generated for the best distribution fitted is shown in the following graph:

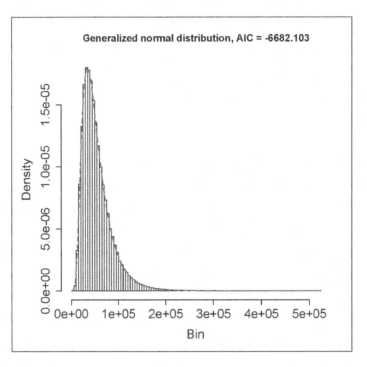

The AIC values for all the distributions tested are as follows:

```
> testedDistrEXPR$aic
                  Distribution       AIC
3            Generalized normal  -6682.103
16                  Johnson SU   -6680.099
4                   Log-normal   -6670.469
2                Skewed-normal   -5847.043
18                  3P Weibull   -5691.254
12                       Gamma   -5667.074
15                      Gumbel   -5611.167
9                  Trapezoidal   -5541.594
5              Scaled/shifted t-  -5284.617
6                    Logistic    -5274.231
1                      Normal    -5256.894
14                     Laplace   -5220.417
13                      Cauchy   -5216.931
11  Generalized Trapezoidal     -5105.354
20                     Arcsine   -4674.931
7                     Uniform    -4661.630
```

```
8            Triangular -4661.388
10 Curvilinear Trapezoidal -4603.581
21              von Mises -4603.451
17             Johnson SB -4602.456
19                4P Beta -4599.451
```

Hypothesis testing

Often when we analyze data, we would like to know whether the mean of our sample distribution is different from some theoretical value or expected average. Suppose we measured the height of 12 females and wanted to know if the average we calculated from our sample population is significantly different from the theoretical average height of females, which is 171 cm. A simple test we could perform to test this hypothesis would be the **Wilcoxon signed-rank test**. To do this in R, we will use the `wilcox.test()` function with the `mu` argument set to `171`:

```
> female.heights <- c(117, 162, 143, 120, 183, 175, 147, 145, 165,
167, 179, 116)
> mean(females.heights)
[1] 151.5833
> wilcox.test(female.heights, mu=171)
Wilcoxon signed rank test with continuity correction
data:  female.heights
V = 11.5, p-value = 0.0341
alternative hypothesis: true location is not equal to 171

Warning message:
In wilcox.test.default(female.heights, mu = 171) :
  cannot compute exact p-value with ties
```

Because the p-value is less than 0.05, we accept the alternative hypothesis that the mean of our sample set is not equal to 171. You will also notice in the output that R produces a warning message stating that the exact p-value cannot be computed with ties in the data. This is because there are repeats of the same measurement in our dataset, which cause ties in the data. When there are ties in the data, the `wilcox.test()` function will return a `p-value` and, if specified, confidence interval estimates based on a normal approximation to the signed-rank statistics. Let's have a look at the following function:

```
> wilcox.test(female.heights, mu=171, conf.int = TRUE, conf.level =
0.99)
   Wilcoxon signed rank test with continuity correction
data:  female.heights
```

```
V = 11.5, p-value = 0.0341
alternative hypothesis: true location is not equal to 171
99 percent confidence interval:
 120 175
sample estimates:
(pseudo)median
      151.9893
Warning messages:
1: In wilcox.test.default(female.heights, mu = 171, conf.int = TRUE,
:
   cannot compute exact p-value with ties
2: In wilcox.test.default(female.heights, mu = 171, conf.int = TRUE,
:
   cannot compute exact confidence interval with ties
```

Instead of using the Wilcoxon signed-rank test with continuity correction, we can test if the mean of our sample distribution is different from the theoretical average of 171 using a **bootstrap approach** that would estimate the mean from taking the mean for a large number of random samples (in this case 10,000), each with a size of 12 and values part of our `female.heights` dataset. To allow R to generate these samples, we will use the `sample()` function and specify `replacement=TRUE` so that repetitions are allowed and we don't always end up with all twelve values from our sample dataset.

Here is the code you would use in R to apply the bootstrap approach to test whether the mean of our sample population is significantly different from the theoretical average.

First, we create a numeric vector to store the 10,000 means generated from sampling the `female.heights` dataset, as follows:

```
> f <- numeric(10000)
> for(i in 1:10000) {
 f[i] <- mean(sample(female.heights, replace=TRUE))
}
> hist(f, xlab="bootstrap means")
```

The result is shown in the following plot:

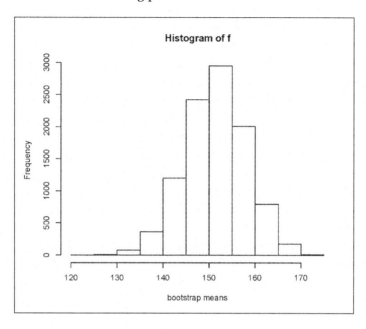

Now, we can perform a t-test to determine whether the mean of our sampling distribution is different for the theoretical value using the t.test() function with the mu argument set to 171, as follows:

```
> t.test(female.heights, mu=171)
   One Sample t-test
data:   female.heights
t = -2.7861, df = 11, p-value = 0.01771
alternative hypothesis: true mean is not equal to 171
95 percent confidence interval:
 136.2446 166.9221
sample estimates:
mean of x
 151.5833
```

Since the p-value is less than 0.05, we can accept the alternative hypothesis and conclude that the female heights in our dataset are significantly different from the theoretical average.

Instead of comparing the mean of two sample distributions, you might want to compare their variance by performing an **F-test**. You can perform this test in R using the var.test() function, as follows:

```
> var.test(probeA, probeB)
  F test to compare two variances
data:  probeA and probeB
F = 0.2301, num df = 41, denom df = 41, p-value =
7.182e-06
alternative hypothesis: true ratio of variances is not equal to 1
95 percent confidence interval:
 0.1236921 0.4281015
sample estimates:
ratio of variances
          0.2301147
```

Another useful statistical test is the **Kruskal-Wallis test** used to determine whether two sample populations are identical without assuming that they follow a normal distribution. For example, if we go back to our data frame containing the gene expression values for probeA and probeB and their response to the drugA treatment (df), we can determine if the mean expression value for probeA is dependent on the response to the drugA treatment using the kruskal.test() function. Let's have a look at this function:

```
> head(df)
          expr_probeA expr_probeB drugA_response
GSM487973    4.372242    8.176033        success
GSM487972    4.293080    8.541016           fail
GSM487971    4.210850    8.338475        success
GSM487970    4.707231    7.935021           fail
GSM487969    4.345101    7.868985        success
GSM487968    4.586062    7.909702           fail
> kruskal.test(expr_probeA ~ drugA_response, data = df)
  Kruskal-Wallis rank sum test
data:  expr_probeA by drugA_response
Kruskal-Wallis chi-squared = 0.0571, df = 1, p-value =
0.8111
```

Since the p-value is greater than 0.05, we cannot reject the null hypothesis and conclude that the probeA expression values in response to the drugA treatments are indeed from the same population.

Proportion tests

Sometimes we want to evaluate proportions instead of individual measurements. Several statistical tests are used to determine whether the proportion observed in your dataset is significantly different from some theoretical value. Two useful statistical tests used in hypothesis testing for proportions are the traditional **Z-test** and the **binomial exact test**. Say we wanted to test that 50 percent of patients have to wait more than 4 hours to see a doctor. We can record the waiting period for 11 patients and store that information in a numerical vector as follows:

```
> waiting.period <- c(3, 5, 4, 5.5, 3.5, 2.5, 3, 5, 4.5, 3, 3.5)
```

Next, we can count the number of patients who waited for more than 4 hours by creating a table using the following commands:

```
> above4.hrs <- ifelse(waiting.period > 4, "yes", "no")
> above4hs.table <- table(above4.hrs)
> above4hs.table
above4.hrs
 no yes
  7   4
```

Now, if we can assume the waiting period to see a doctor is indeed 50 percent, then we can use a Z-test to this hypothesis using the `prop.test()` function:

```
> prop.test(4, n=11, p=0.5, alternative="two.sided", correct=FALSE)
   1-sample proportions test without continuity correction
data:  4 out of 11, null probability 0.5
X-squared = 0.8182, df = 1, p-value = 0.3657
alternative hypothesis: true p is not equal to 0.5
95 percent confidence interval:
 0.1516647 0.6461988
sample estimates:
        p
0.3636364
```

By explicitly stating `correct=FALSE` in the `prop.test()` function, we are ensuring that no continuity correction is applied when determining the Z value.

Since the sample size of our `female.heights` dataset is small (n=11), it might be a better idea to use "continuity-adjusted" Z value when determining whether to accept or reject the null hypothesis by setting the `correct` argument to TRUE.

```
> prop.test(4, n=11, p=0.5, alternative="two.sided", correct=TRUE)
  1-sample proportions test with continuity correction
data:  4 out of 11, null probability 0.5
X-squared = 0.3636, df = 1, p-value = 0.5465
alternative hypothesis: true p is not equal to 0.5
95 percent confidence interval:
 0.1236508 0.6838637
sample estimates:
        p
0.3636364
```

From the statistical test, we can accept the null hypothesis and conclude that we don't have sufficient evidence to say that 50 percent of patients wait more than four hours to see a doctor. In fact, from the 95 percent confidence interval, we can see that the proportion of patients that will likely wait for more than four hours to see a doctor is potentially between 0.12 and 0.68.

Instead of using the continuity-adjusted Z-statistic to choose whether to accept or reject the null hypothesis, we can also perform a **binomial exact test** with the `binom.test()` function, as follows:

```
> binom.test(4, n=11, p=0.5)
  Exact binomial test
data:  4 and 11
number of successes = 4, number of trials = 11, p-value =
0.5488
alternative hypothesis: true probability of success is not equal to
0.5
95 percent confidence interval:
 0.1092634 0.6920953
sample estimates:
probability of success
             0.3636364
```

Similarly, the binomial exact test indicates that we don't have enough evidence to reject the null hypothesis and that the proportion of patients that wait for more than four hours to see a doctor likely falls between 11 to 69 percent.

Two sample hypothesis tests

So far, we have covered how to use statistical tests for hypothesis testing on a single sample distribution. However, these statistical tests can also be applied to compare two sample distributions. For example, we could test whether the mean of the `probeA` sample distribution was significantly different from the `probeB` sample distribution. If we can assume that the error of both samples are normally distributed, then we can use a t-test to compare the mean of both samples by entering `t.test(probeA, probeB)`, as follows:

```
> t.test(probeA, probeB)
   Welch Two Sample t-test
data:  probeA and probeB
t = -35.8398, df = 58.92, p-value < 2.2e-16
alternative hypothesis: true difference in means is not equal to 0
95 percent confidence interval:
 -3.486162 -3.117460
sample estimates:
mean of x mean of y
 4.773866  8.075677
```

If the errors are not normally distributed for these samples, we can run the Wilcoxon rank-sum test, as follows:

```
> wilcox.test(probeA, probeB)
   Wilcoxon rank sum test
data:  probeA and probeB
W = 0, p-value < 2.2e-16
alternative hypothesis: true location shift is not equal to 0
```

If these samples are paired, you can run a paired t-test or a Wilcoxon signed-rank test by setting the `paired` argument to TRUE:

```
> wilcox.test(probeA, probeB, paired=T)
   Wilcoxon signed rank test
data:  probeA and probeB
V = 0, p-value = 4.547e-13
alternative hypothesis: true location shift is not equal to 0
```

Instead of comparing the mean of two populations, you might be interested in comparing two proportions by performing a binomial test using the `prop.test()` function. Suppose you want to test the hypothesis that women are favored over men for promotions in company A. If there are 16 out of 430 female employees and 63 out of 1,053 male employees promoted this year, you could perform a binomial proportions test using the `prop.test()` function with two vectors. The first vector will contain the number of female employees and male employees promoted this year and the other vector will store the total number of females and males employed by company A. Let's have a look at the following code:

```
> promoted.employees <-c(16, 63)
> total.employees <- c(430, 1053)
> prop.test(promoted.employees, total.employees)
  2-sample test for equality of proportions with continuity correction
data:  promoted.employees out of total.employees
X-squared = 2.6653, df = 1, p-value = 0.1026
alternative hypothesis: two.sided
95 percent confidence interval:
 -0.04717571  0.00193619
sample estimates:
    prop 1     prop 2
0.03720930 0.05982906
```

You can test for independence in contingency tables using the **Chi-squared** or **Fisher's Exact test** in R, which uses the data stored in a matrix with the `chisq.test()` and `fisher.test()` functions. For example, we can create a matrix that stores the counts observed for blue eyes, brown eyes, blond hair, and brown hair in a sample population of 96 Caucasian males. To test whether eye color and hair color are independent, we can perform a Chi-squared test with the `chisq.test()` function, as follows:

```
> trait.counts <- matrix(c(24, 14, 11, 47), nrow=2)
> colnames(trait.counts) <- c("Blue eyes", "Brown eyes")
> rownames(trait.counts) <- c("Blond hair", "Dark brown hair")
> trait.counts
                 Blue eyes     Brown eyes
Blond hair           24            11
Dark brown hair      14            47
> chisq.test(trait.counts)
   Pearson's Chi-squared test with Yates' continuity correction
data:  trait.counts
X-squared = 17.4938, df = 1, p-value = 2.882e-05
```

As you can see, by default, `Yates' continuity correction` is applied. To remove `Yates' continuity correction`, you just have to specify `correct=FALSE` as follows:

```
> chisq.test(trait.counts, correct=FALSE)
    Pearson's Chi-squared test
data:  trait.counts
X-squared = 19.3544, df = 1, p-value = 1.086e-05
```

Since the `p-value` is less than 0.05, we can reject the null hypothesis that eye color and hair color are independent traits for this sample population.

Instead of a Chi-squared test, you may be interested in performing a Fisher's exact test. This statistical test is usually performed for the analysis of contingency tables in which one or more of the expected frequencies are less than five. To illustrate the `fisher.test()` function, let's create a 2 x 2 matrix containing hypothetical data, as follows:

```
> data.counts <- matrix(c(7, 5, 2, 6), nrow=2)
> fisher.test(data.counts)
    Fisher's Exact Test for Count Data
data:  data.counts
p-value = 0.1968
alternative hypothesis: true odds ratio is not equal to 1
95 percent confidence interval:
  0.438792 55.616983
sample estimates:
odds ratio
  3.895711
```

 You can also use the `fisher.test()` function with matrices much larger than 2 x 2 vectors or you can use two vectors containing factor levels instead of a matrix to save you the trouble of counting the number of events in each combination of traits.

Unit root tests

R has a variety of packages that allow you to perform a variety of statistical tests. For example, the `tseries` package allows you to perform unit root tests to determine whether a time series variable is nonstationary using an autoregressive model. For example, the **Augmented Dickey–Fuller (ADF)** is a test for a unit root in a time series sample. The null hypothesis of this test is that the time series is not stationary. The ADF test statistics is a negative number and the more negative that number, the more strongly we can reject the null hypothesis and accept the alternative hypothesis that there is a unit root in the time series.

For example, let's create a time series representing the fertility rate of women between the age of 35 to 39 and 40 to 44 between 1997 and 2012 for residents of New York City using the annual vital statistic tables provided by the Department of Health at http://www.health.ny.gov/statistics/vital_statistics/. The fertility rates provided in these tables are based on the number of live births per 1,000 females between the age of 35 to 39 and 40 to 44. A summary of this data is provided in the fertility Data.xlsx file, which can be downloaded at (https://www.packtpub.com/books/content/support/19729/fertilityData.xlsx). Save this file to your current working directory, as shown:

```
>setwd("/directory_where_file_was_downloaded/")
```

 You can use the getwd() function to obtain your current working directory file path or change it using the setwd() function.

Next, load the data into your workspace using the read.xls() function, which is available as part of the gdata package:

```
> library("gdata")
> fertility_rates.df <- read.xls("fertilityData.xlsx")

# Change the colnames for the two time series accordingly.
> colnames(fertility_rates.df)[2:3] <- c("Age 35-39", "Age 40-44")
```

We can take a look at the data frame using the head() function:

```
> head(fertility_rates.df)
  year Age 35-39 Age 40-44
1 1997      46.4      12.4
2 1998      48.1      12.8
3 1999      49.7      12.3
4 2000      49.8      13.5
5 2001      49.2      13.2
6 2002      49.4      13.5
```

Next, we need to create a time series object for the fertility rate of each age group using the ts() function. Basically, the ts() function allows us to specify the times of the first and last observation together with the frequency of that occurrence with the start, end, and frequency arguments, respectively. The frequency is the number of observations per unit time, where 1 is equal to annual, 4 is equal to quarterly, and 12 is equal to monthly. To create a time series from our data frame, we will remove the year column and specify the frequency as annual with frequency=1, as shown in the following code:

```
> fertilityRates.ts <- ts(fertility_rates.df[, 2:3], start=c(1997, 1),
end=c(2012, 1), frequency=1)
```

To inspect our time series object, we can print it, as follows:

```
> fertilityRates.ts
Time Series:
Start = 1997
End = 2012
Frequency = 1
     Age 35-39 Age 40-44
1997     46.4      12.4
1998     48.1      12.8
1999     49.7      12.3
2000     49.8      13.5
2001     49.2      13.2
2002     49.4      13.5
2003     51.6      14.8
2004     52.5      14.2
2005     52.0      14.3
2006     53.5      14.5
2007     53.6      15.0
2008     54.5      15.0
2009     58.2      17.1
2010     63.6      18.2
2011     65.2      18.0
2012     66.9      19.1
```

We can also plot the time series with the plot() function, which calls the plot.ts() function in R to create a graph of time series objects, as shown in the following graph:

```
> plot(fertilityRates.ts, main="Fertility Rates for Females in NYC
from 1997 to 2012", xlab="Year")
```

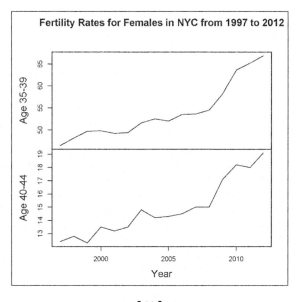

Now, let's use the ADF test to check if our time series is stationary in both female age groups using the adf.test() function as part of the tseries package. Since we can only apply the function on univariate time series, we will evaluate each of them separately. Let's have a look at the following function:

```
> library("tseries")
```

For the time series for women aged 35 to 39, we use the following code:

```
> adf.test(fertilityRates.ts[, 1])
  Augmented Dickey-Fuller Test

data:  fertilityRates.ts[, 1]
Dickey-Fuller = 0.3567, Lag order = 2, p-value = 0.99
alternative hypothesis: stationary


Warning message:
In adf.test(fertilityRates.ts[, 1]) : p-value greater than printed
p-value
```

For the time series for women aged from 40 to 44, we use the following code:

```
> adf.test(fertilityRates.ts[, 2])
  Augmented Dickey-Fuller Test

data:  fertilityRates.ts[, 2]
Dickey-Fuller = -0.3712, Lag order = 2, p-value = 0.9805
alternative hypothesis: stationary
```

In both cases, we cannot reject the null hypothesis. Therefore, we conclude that both time series are not stationary. Indeed, we can see from the graphs that the fertility rate for both age groups increased in the early 2000s. Now, what if we are only interested in the fertility rate of women aged from 40 to 44 between 1997 and 2003? We can test if this time series is stationary, as follows:

```
> testTS <- ts(fertility_rates.df[1:7, 2], start=c(1997, 1),
frequency=1)
>  adf.test(testTS)
  Augmented Dickey-Fuller Test
data:  testTS
Dickey-Fuller = -7.4101, Lag order = 1, p-value = 0.01
alternative hypothesis: stationary
Warning message:
In adf.test(testTS) : p-value smaller than printed p-value
```

In this case, we have a `p-value`, which is much smaller than 0.05, so we can reject the null hypothesis and conclude that the time series for the fertility rate of woman aged from 40 to 44 was stationary between 1997 and 2003.

You may be interested in using the `adf.test()` function to know whether the price at closing of a particular stock is stationary over a given period of time. So, for our next example, we will test whether the Facebook stock price from 2012-06-18 to 2014-11-28 was stationary at closing. We can download the stock price information from Yahoo! using the `getSymbols()` function from the `quantmod` package. Let's have a look at the following function:

```
> install.packages("quantmod")
> library("quantmod")
```

The stock symbol for Facebook is "FB" on the NASDAQ stock exchange:

```
> fbstock <-getSymbols("FB", src="yahoo", from= '2012-06-18',
end='2014-11-28', auto.assign=FALSE)
```

We can inspect the object using the `head()` function to print the first six dates, as follows:

```
> head(fbstock)
           FB.Open FB.High FB.Low FB.Close FB.Volume FB.Adjusted
2012-06-18   29.96   32.08   29.41    31.41  42978900       31.41
2012-06-19   31.54   32.18   30.70    31.91  30849000       31.91
2012-06-20   31.92   31.93   31.15    31.60  15553600       31.60
2012-06-21   31.67   32.50   31.51    31.84  21875300       31.84
2012-06-22   32.41   33.45   32.06    33.05  74834000       33.05
2012-06-25   32.86   33.02   31.55    32.06  24352900       32.06
```

We can plot `fbstock` information using the `chartSeries()` function, which is also part of the `quantmod` package. Since we are just interested in viewing the stock price at closing and the total volume, we will only plot the fourth and fifth columns, as shown in the following code:

```
> chartSeries(fbstock[, 4:5], theme="white", up.col="black")
```

The plot is shown in the following graph:

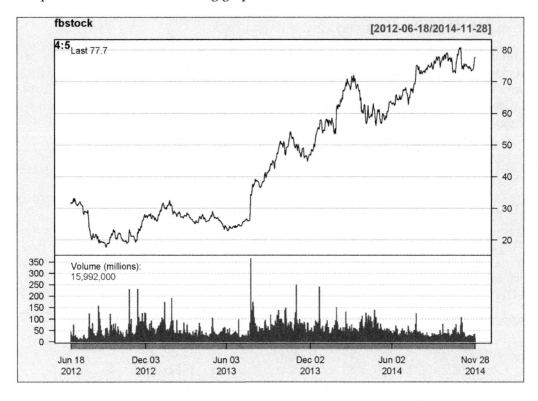

Alternatively, you could plot the `fbstock` data with the `plot.ts` function after converting the `fbstock` data from an extended time series (`xts`) object to a standard time series (`ts`) object with the `as.ts()` function:

```
> plot.ts(as.ts(fbstock[, 4:5]), main="FACEBOOK Stock Information from
2012-06-18 to 2014-11-28")
```

Here is the plot the previous command generated:

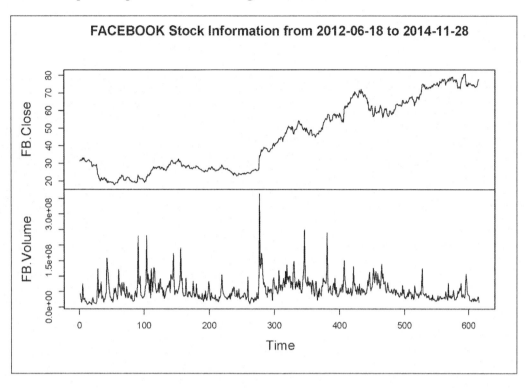

Now, let's perform the ADF test with the `adf.test()` function, which is a part of the `tseries` package, as follows:

```
> require(tseries)
> adf.test(fbstock[, 4])
   Augmented Dickey-Fuller Test
data:  fbstock[, 4]
Dickey-Fuller = -3.123, Lag order = 8, p-value = 0.103
alternative hypothesis: stationary
```

Based on the `p-value`, we cannot reject the null hypothesis and conclude that the time series is not stationary and thus, contains a unit root. We can confirm the ADF test results by performing a **Kwiatkowski–Phillips–Schmidt–Shin (KPSS)** test. The KPSS test is also used to test whether this time series is stationary, except in this case, the null hypothesis is that the observable time series is stationary around a deterministic trend. To perform the KPSS test on our `fbstock` time series, we can use the `kpss.test()` function, which is also part of the `tseries` package.

Again, since we are interested in the Facebook stock price at closing, we will perform the KPSS test on the fourth column:

```
> kpss.test(fbstock[, 4])
KPSS Test for Level Stationarity
data:  fbstock[, 4]
KPSS Level = 9.6561, Truncation lag parameter = 5, p-value = 0.01
Warning message:
In kpss.test(fbstock[, 4]) : p-value smaller than printed p-value
```

As you can see, our `p-value` is below 0.05, so we can reject the null hypothesis and conclude that the time series for the Facebook stock price at closing, between 2012-06-18 and 2014-11-28, is not stationary.

> If you are interested in additional packages for time series analysis in R, we recommend you consult the CRAN R project Time Series Analysis website at http://cran.r-project.org/web/views/TimeSeries.html.

Summary

In this chapter, we saw how to obtain useful statistical information from sample populations and probability distributions. You should now be able to summarize your data and obtain useful statistical information such as the mean, median, variance, and so on. You should also be able to plot and obtain useful statistics from theoretical probability distributions, fit your sample data to theoretical probability distributions, perform hypothesis testing using parametric and non-parametric statistical tests, and plot and test whether time series data is stationary using statistical tests.

Now that you have a foundation of how to apply statistical methods to your sample datasets, we will be moving on to linear models in the next chapter, where you will find out how to study the relationship between variables.

3
Linear Models

This chapter will cover linear models, which are probably the most commonly used statistical methods to study the relationships between variables. The generalized linear model section will delve into a bit more detail than typical R books, discussing the nature of link functions and canonical link functions:

- Linear regression
- Linear model fits
- Analysis of variance models
- Generalized linear models
- Link functions and canonical link functions
- Generalized additive models
- Principal components analysis
- Clustering
- Discriminant analysis

An overview of statistical modeling

In order to explore the relationship between data and a set of experimental conditions, we often rely on statistical modeling. One of the central purposes of R is to estimate the fit of your data to a variety of models that you can easily optimize using several built-in functions and arguments. Although picking the best model to represent your data can be overwhelming, it is important to remember the principle of parsimony when choosing a model. Essentially, you should only include an explanatory variable in a model if it significantly improves the fit of a model. Therefore, our ideal model will try and fulfill most of the criteria in this list:

- Contain *n-1* parameters instead of *n* parameters
- Contain *k-1* explanatory variables instead of *k* variables
- Be linear instead of curved
- Not contain interactions between factors

In other words, we can simplify our model by removing non-significant interaction terms and explanatory variables, and by grouping together factor levels that do not differ from one another or add any new information to the model. In this chapter, we will go over the steps to fit your data to linear models, and in the following chapter, we will go over nonlinear methods to explore your data.

Model formulas

Before we begin, we will go over the model formula and conventions used in R for statistical modeling. This formula will then be the argument of the function defining the model. A detailed overview of statistical modeling in R is available in *Chapter 7* of Michael J.Crawley's book *Statistics An Introduction using R*. Briefly, the basic structure of a model in R is specified as follows:

response_variable ~ explanatory_variable

The tilde (~) symbol signifies that the response variable is modeled as a function of the explanatory variable. The right side of the model formula specifies the following points:

- The number of continuous or categorical explanatory variables and their attributes
- Potential interactions between the explanatory variables
- Nonlinear terms (if required)
- The offset of error terms (in some special cases)

It is important to remember that both the response and explanatory variables can appear as transformations, or as powers, and polynomials. Also, the meaning of mathematical symbols is different from arithmetic expressions in model formulas. Let's take a look at the symbols used for statistical modeling in R in the following table:

Symbol	Explanation
+	Adds this explanatory variable
−	Deletes this explanatory variable
*	Includes this explanatory variables and interactions
/	Nests this explanatory variables

Symbol	Explanation
|	Denotes a condition; for example, $y \sim x \mid z$ reads y as a function of x given z
:	Denotes an interaction; for example, *A:B* indicates the two-way interaction between *A* and *B*
I	Overrides the interpretation of a model symbol to use it as an arithmetic operator

Here are some examples to help understand how these symbols are used in statistical modeling.

For example, $y \sim 1/x$ fits x nested within the intercept, whereas $y \sim I \ (1/x)$ will fit $1/x$ as an explanatory variable.

For categorical variables *A* and *B*, $y \sim A/B$ means fit *A+B* within *A*.

This formula can also be written as follows:

$y \sim A + A{:}B$

$y \sim A + B \ \%in\% \ A$

You can also specify the level of interactions to include using the ^ operator. For example, by writing $(A+B+C)\wedge3$, you are telling R to fit all the main effects and all interactions up to level 3. In other words, $(A+B+C)\wedge3$ can also be written as $A*B*C$ or $A+B+C+A{:}B+A{:}C+B{:}C+A{:}B{:}C$. If you want to exclude the three-way interaction from $A*B*C$, then you could write $(A+B+C)\wedge2$, which means to fit all the main effects and the two-way interactions but not the three-way interaction. Therefore, $(A+B+C)\wedge2$ could also be written as $A*B*C - A{:}B{:}C$. The following table gives the examples of model formulas and their interpretation in R:

To fit A+B within A
y ~ A/B
y ~ A + A:B
y ~ A + B %in % A
To fit all the main effects and interactions
(A+B+C)^3
A*B*C
A+B+C+A:B+A:C+B:C+A:B:C
To fit all main effects and the two-way interactions excluding the three-way interaction
(A+B+C)^2
A*B*C – A:B:C

Explanatory variables interactions

Another thing to bear in mind when writing model formulas is that categorical variables are fitted differently from continuous variables. For example, $y \sim A*B$ means to evaluate the A and B main effect means and the $A:B$ interaction mean (that is, $A + B + A:B$). The number of interaction terms for $A:B$ is $(a - 1)(b - 1)$ for the two categorical variables, where a and b are the number of levels of the factors for A and B, respectively. So, if factor A has two levels and factor B has four levels, R would estimate $(2-1)(4-1) = 3$ parameters for the $A:B$ interaction. In contrast, if x and z are continuous variables, then $y \sim x*z$ tells R to fit $x + z + x:z$, where the $x:z$ interaction behaves like a new variable that was computed from the point-wise product of the two vectors x and z explicitly calculated as $xz.prod < x*z$. Therefore, $x + z + x:z$ can be rewritten as $y \sim x + z + xz.prod$.

In cases that we have interactions between categorical and continuous variables, such as $y \sim A*x$, where x is a continuous variable and A is a categorical variable with n levels, R will fit n regression equations and estimate n parameters from the data. In other words, n slopes and n intercepts.

Error terms

You can also include an error function as part of a model formula when there is nesting or pseudo replication. For example, to include the error to model a three-factorial experiment with categorical variables A, B, and C with three plot sizes and three different error variances, one for each plot, you would write $y \sim A*B*C + Error(A/B/C)$.

The intercept as parameter 1

The null model has just one parameter, a constant, and indicates that y does not depend on any of the explanatory variables provided. The formula to fit your data to the null model is $y \sim 1$, where y is fitted to a mean of y. However, removing parameter 1 from categorical variables has a different effect. For example, if `genotype` is a three-level categorical variable, the model formula $y \sim genotype - 1$ will give the mean for each genotype rather than the overall mean in the summary table.

When fitting a linear model, $y \sim x - 1$ specifies a line through the origin. In other words, by removing parameter 1, we are forcing the regression line through the origin.

Updating a model

You can easily make a modification to a model in R by using the `update()` function. By using the `.` character on the right-hand side of the tilde, you specify that you'll use use the model as it is. So, if your original model is defined as `model <- lm(y ~ A*B*C)`, you can remove the *A:B* interaction term as follows:

```
> model2 <- update(model, ~ . - A:B)
# no need to repeat the response variable y
```

 For more details and information on the formula class in R, you can consult the help page by entering `> ?formula`.

Linear regression

Regression analysis is a statistical method used to estimate the relationship among continuous variables. Linear regression is the simplest and most frequently used type of regression analysis. The aim of linear regression is to describe the response variable *y* through a linear combination of one or more explanatory variables *x1, x2, x3, ..., xp*. In other words, the explanatory variables get weighted with constants and then summarized. For example, the simplest linear model is $y = a + bx$, where the two parameters *a* and *b* are the intercept and slope, respectively. The model formula for this relationship in R is $y \sim x$. Note that all parameters are left out. So, if our linear model was $y = a + bx + cz$, then our model formula will be $y \sim x + z$.

Plotting a slope

Before going into a detailed example of linear regression analysis, I think it's worth going over how to plot a slope (or the change in *y* divided by the change in *x*). Say you wanted to plot a slope given the Cartesian coordinates (3, 7) and (4, 4). The values for *x* that we need to plot are 3 and 4 and the values for *y* are 7 and 4. Let's take a look at the following lines of code:

```
>plot(c(3,4), c(7,4), ylab="y", xlab="x", main="Slope from coordinates
(3, 7) and (4,4)", ylim=c(0,10), xlim=c(0, 10))
```

 The plot arguments do not take Cartesian coordinates but a vector for the *x* coordinates and a vector for the *y* coordinates.

To draw the change in *y* and consequent change in *x*, we use the `lines()` function as follows:

```
>lines(c(3,3), c(7,4))
>lines(c(3,4), c(4,4))
```

We can add "*delta y*" and "*delta x*" to the plot by using the `text()` function and the first two arguments to specify the location where the text should be added, that is, at $x = 2$ and $y = 5.5$ for delta y and $x = 3.5$ and $y = 3.5$ for delta x. Let's take a look at this in the following lines of code:

```
>text(2,5.5, "delta y")
>text(3.5,3.5, "delta x")

#To plot a red line of width=3 between the two coordinates
> lines(c(3,4), c(7,4), col="red", lwd=3)
```

To calculate the slope *b*, we divide the change in *y* by the corresponding change in *x*, which in this case is *(4-7)/(4-3)*, as follows:

```
> (4-7)/(4-3)
[1] -3
```

Then, we can calculate the intercept by solving *a* in the $y = a + bx$ equation. Since we know that $y = 4$ and $x = 4$ from our coordinates (4, 4) and we also know that our slope is -3, we can solve *a* using the $a = y - bx$ equation. Let's take a look at this in the following lines of code:

```
> 4 - (-3)*(4)
[1] 16
```

Now we can add the slope to our plot using the `abline()` function, where the first argument specifies the intercept and the second one specifies the slope as follows:

```
> abline(16, -3)
```

The result is shown in the following plot:

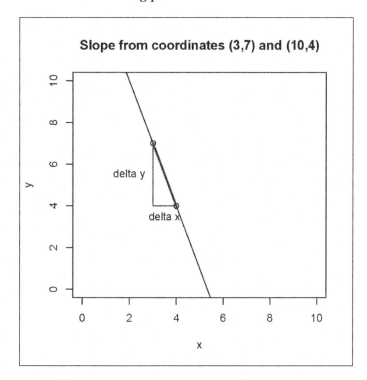

Now, let's look at an example to perform linear regression in R. We will use data generated from a quantitative real-time polymerase chain reaction (PCR) experiment to create a standard curve to quantify GAPDH expression. In this example, we expect the relationship between the quantity of RNA and the threshold cycle values (Ct) to be linear. The Ct values were measured in triplicate and stored in columns A1, A2, and A3. From this data we can get the maximum likelihood estimates for the slope and intercept of our standard curve by performing regression analysis.

First, we load the data into a data frame and check its structure to make sure the data in RNA_ng, A1, A2, A3 columns are stored as numerical vectors so that they will be considered as continuous variables by R in our linear regression analysis. Let's take a look at this in the following lines of code:

```
> gapdh.qPCR <- read.table(header=TRUE, text='
 GAPDH  RNA_ng  A1   A2    A3
std_curve  50   16.5  16.7  16.7
std_curve  10   19.3  19.2  19
std_curve  2    21.7  21.5  21.2
std_curve  0.4  24.5  24.1  23.5
std_curve  0.08 26.7  27    26.5
std_curve  0.016 36.5 36.4  37.2
 ')
> str(gapdh.qPCR)
'data.frame':  6 obs. of  5 variables:
 $ GAPDH : Factor w/ 1 level "std_curve": 1 1 1 1 1 1
 $ RNA_ng: num  50 10 2 0.4 0.08 0.016
 $ A1     : num  16.5 19.3 21.7 24.5 26.7 36.5
 $ A2     : num  16.7 19.2 21.5 24.1 27 36.4
 $ A3     : num  16.7 19 21.2 23.5 26.5 37.2
```

Since A1, A2, and A3 can be considered as levels of one explanatory variable Ct_Value, let's transform our gapdh.qPCR data frame from wide to long format using the melt() function from the reshape2 package. Let's take a look at this in the following lines of code:

```
> library("reshape2")
> gapdh.qPCR <- melt(gapdh.qPCR, id.vars=c("GAPDH", "RNA_ng"), value.name="Ct_Value")
> str(gapdh.qPCR)
'data.frame':  18 obs. of  4 variables:
 $ GAPDH   : Factor w/ 1 level "std_curve": 1 1 1 1 1 1 1 1 1 1 ...
 $ RNA_ng  : num  50 10 2 0.4 0.08 0.016 50 10 2 0.4 ...
 $ variable: Factor w/ 3 levels "A1","A2","A3": 1 1 1 1 1 1 2 2 2 2
...
 $ Ct_Value: num  16.5 19.3 21.7 24.5 26.7 36.5 16.7 19.2 21.5 24.1
...
```

By using the `attach()` function, we can simplify this task by referring to the `gapdh.qPCR` vectors by using the column name only (for example, `RNA_ng`) instead of the long way (`gapdh.qPCR$RNA_ng`) or by including the data argument (`data=gapdh.qPCR`). Let's take a look at the following lines of code:

```
> attach(gapdh.qPCR)
> names(gapdh.qPCR)
[1] "GAPDH"     "RNA_ng"    "variable" "Ct_Value"
```

Now we can easily plot the relationship between our Ct values and the quantity of RNA by plotting `Ct_Values` as a function of `RNA_ng` as follows:

```
> #plots two graphs side by side
> par(mfrow=c(1,2))
> plot(RNA_ng, Ct_Value)
```

As you can see, if we plot the data as is, the data seems to follow a curved model, which we want to avoid in order to follow the principle of parsimony. So let's try and log transform the `RNA_ng` explanatory variable as follows:

```
> plot(log(RNA_ng), Ct_Value)
```

The result is shown in the following plot:

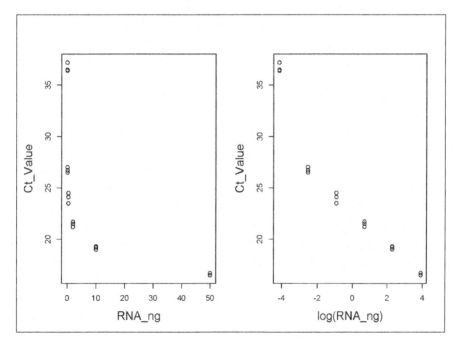

Now, our data is ready to fit a linear model using the `lm()` function as follows:

```
> lm(Ct_Value ~ log(RNA_ng))

Call:
lm(formula = Ct_Value ~ log(RNA_ng))

Coefficients:
(Intercept)   log(RNA_ng)
      23.87         -2.23
```

R reports the intercept *a* and slope *b* as coefficients. In this model, $y = a + bx$, the maximum likelihood estimate for *a* is 23.87 and *b* is -2.23.

If we would like to get more information on our model, such as the residual standard error or the adjusted R-squared value, we can save the model as an object and use the `summary()` function to print these details and more. Let's take a look at this in the following lines of code:

```
> model <- lm(Ct_Value ~ log(RNA_ng))
> summary(model)

Call:
lm(formula = Ct_Value ~ log(RNA_ng))

Residuals:
    Min       1Q   Median       3Q      Max
-3.0051  -1.7165  -0.1837   1.4992   4.1063

Coefficients:
              Estimate Std. Error t value Pr(>|t|)
(Intercept)    23.8735     0.5382   44.36  < 2e-16 ***
log(RNA_ng)    -2.2297     0.1956  -11.40 4.33e-09 ***
---
Signif. codes:  0 '***' 0.001 '**' 0.01 '*' 0.05 '.' 0.1 ' ' 1

Residual standard error: 2.282 on 16 degrees of freedom
Multiple R-squared:  0.8903,   Adjusted R-squared:  0.8835
F-statistic: 129.9 on 1 and 16 DF,  p-value: 4.328e-09
```

You can also see the **Anova** table for the analysis using the `summary.aov()` function as follows:

```
> summary.aov(model)
            Df Sum Sq Mean Sq F value   Pr(>F)
log(RNA_ng)  1  676.1   676.1   129.9 4.33e-09 ***
Residuals   16   83.3     5.2
---
Signif. codes:  0 '***' 0.001 '**' 0.01 '*' 0.05 '.' 0.1 ' ' 1
```

You can check that your data meets the assumptions of a linear model, which are that the variance is constant and the errors are normally distributed by plotting the model object as follows:

```
> par(mfrow=c(2,2))
> plot(model)
```

The result is shown in the following plot:

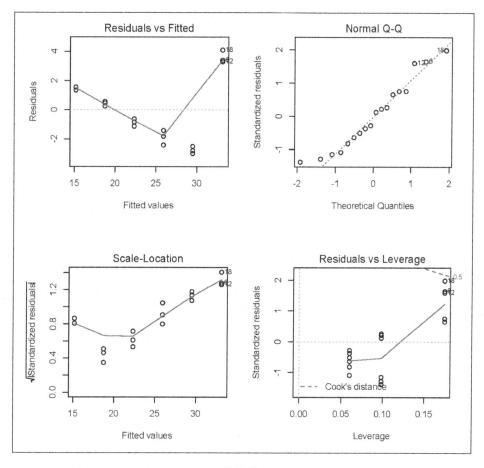

In the preceding plot, the four graphs allow you to inspect your model in more detail. The first plot shows the residuals against the fitted values. For your model to be valid, the residuals (or error terms) must have a mean of zero and constant variance, which means that the residuals should be scattered randomly around zero. In this example, the error seems to be scattered randomly. Of course, with so few points it's not so clear, but ideally you want to avoid situations where the residuals increase or decrease with fitted values since these patterns indicate that the errors may not have constant variance. The second plot is a qqnorm plot, which allows us to ensure that the errors are normally distributed. Ideally, your points should be aligned in a straight line and avoid skewed distributions. The third plot is a repeat of the first plot except that it shows the square root of the residuals against the fitted values. Again, you want to avoid trends in the data. For example, we would have a problem if all the points were distributed in a triangle where the scatter of the residuals increases with the fitted values. Finally, the last plot shows us the Cook's distance in the residuals against leverage plot for each value of the response variable. The Cook's distance plot highlights the points with the greatest influence on the parameter estimates. In this case, the point with the most influence on our model is 18. To see the values for this point, we just need to use its index, which is 18, as follows:

```
> RNA_ng[18]
[1] 0.016
> Ct_Value[18]
[1] 37.2
```

Say we wanted to see the effect of removing this point on the adjusted R-squared value by updating our model and getting the summary as follows:

```
> model2 <- update(model, subset=(Ct_Value !=37.2))
> summary(model2)

Call:
lm(formula = Ct_Value ~ log(RNA_ng), subset = (Ct_Value != 37.2))

Residuals:
   Min      1Q Median     3Q     Max
-2.373 -1.422 -0.470  1.033   4.275

Coefficients:
             Estimate Std. Error t value Pr(>|t|)
(Intercept)   23.6135     0.4970   47.51  < 2e-16 ***
log(RNA_ng)   -2.0825     0.1878  -11.09 1.26e-08 ***
---
Signif. codes:  0 '***' 0.001 '**' 0.01 '*' 0.05 '.' 0.1 ' ' 1
```

```
Residual standard error: 2.047 on 15 degrees of freedom
Multiple R-squared:  0.8913,  Adjusted R-squared:  0.8841
F-statistic:   123 on 1 and 15 DF,  p-value: 1.259e-08
```

As you can see, by removing the (0.016, 37.2) point from the mode, we only slightly increase the adjusted R-squared from 0.8835 to 0.8841. We can also look at the effect of this change on the slope of the curve by using the following lines of code:

```
> model2

Call:
lm(formula = Ct_Value ~ log(RNA_ng), subset = (Ct_Value != 37.2))

Coefficients:
(Intercept)  log(RNA_ng)
     23.613      -2.083
```

As you can see, the slope went from -2.23 to -2.083. Here, we might decide to simply note that the point was influential or gather more data. However, if removing the data point significantly improved the model fit, we would leave the point out and use that model instead.

Analysis of variance

Analysis of variance (Anova) is used to fit data to a linear model when all explanatory variables are categorical. Each of these categorical explanatory variables is known as a factor, and each factor can have two or more levels. When a single factor is present with three or more levels, we use a one-way Anova to analyze the data. If we had a single factor with two levels, we would use a student's t-test to analyze the data. When there are two or more factors, we would use a two-way or three-way Anova. You can easily perform an Anova in R using the aov() function.

In the first example, we will look at the effect of the dose of drugA on the level of fatigue reported by the 20 patients as follows:

```
> patient.fatigue <- read.table(header=TRUE, text='
  patients fatigue drugA_dose
1        1     low        0.2
2        2     low        0.2
3        3     med        0.2
4        4     med        0.2
5        5     med        0.2
6        6     low        0.4
7        7     low        0.4
```

```
8         8        low        0.4
9         9        med        0.4
10        10       med        0.4
11        11       med        0.8
12        12       high       0.8
13        13       med        0.8
14        14       med        0.8
15        15       high       0.8
16        16       high       1.2
17        17       high       1.2
18        18       high       1.2
19        19       high       1.2
20        20       med        1.2 ')
```

```
>attach(patient.fatigue)
> aov(drugA_dose ~ fatigue)
Call:
    aov(formula = drugA_dose ~ fatigue)

Terms:
                    fatigue Residuals
Sum of Squares    1.666444   1.283556
Deg. of Freedom          2         17

Residual standard error: 0.2747786
Estimated effects may be unbalanced
```

A more concise way to view the results of the one-way Anova analysis is to use the `summary()` function as follows:

```
> summary(aov(drugA_dose ~ fatigue))
             Df Sum Sq Mean Sq F value   Pr(>F)
fatigue       2  1.666  0.8332   11.04 0.000847 ***
Residuals    17  1.284  0.0755
---
Signif. codes:  0 '***' 0.001 '**' 0.01 '*' 0.05 '.' 0.1 ' ' 1
```

From the analysis, you can see that the relationship between the levels of fatigue reported is related to the dose of `drug_A` administered. Now, we can plot the model to ensure that the assumptions of the model are met, namely that the variance is constant and the errors are normally distributed. Let's take a look at this in the following lines of code:

```
> modelA <- aov(drugA_dose ~ fatigue)
> par(mfrow=c(2,2))
> plot(modelA)
```

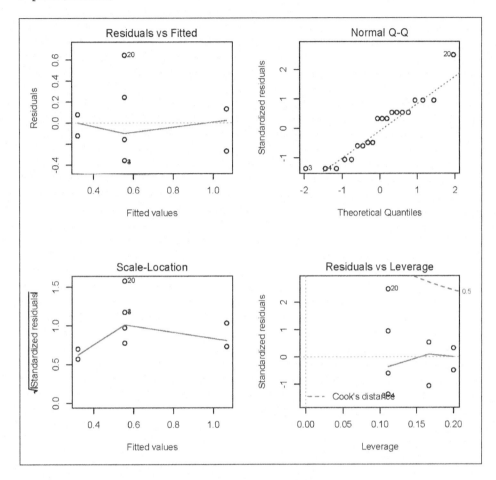

In the residuals versus leverage plot, we can see that the level of fatigue reported by patients[20] greatly influences the data. Let's see what happens when we remove this data point. Let's take a look at the following lines of code:

```
> modelB <- update(modelA, subset=(patients !=20))
> summary(modelB)
             Df Sum Sq Mean Sq F value   Pr(>F)
fatigue       2 1.8152  0.9076   17.79 8.57e-05 ***
Residuals    16 0.8163  0.0510
---
Signif. codes:  0 '***' 0.001 '**' 0.01 '*' 0.05 '.' 0.1 ' ' 1
>
```

As you can see, the *p* value changes but the interpretation remains the same. We can also investigate the effects of the different levels using the `summary.lm()` function as follows:

```
> summary.lm(modelB)

Call:
aov(formula = drugA_dose ~ fatigue, subset = (patients != 20))

Residuals:
    Min      1Q  Median      3Q     Max
-0.2750 -0.1933  0.0800  0.1333  0.3250

Coefficients:
            Estimate Std. Error t value Pr(>|t|)
(Intercept)  1.06667    0.09221  11.567 3.50e-09 ***
fatiguelow  -0.74667    0.13678  -5.459 5.25e-05 ***
fatiguemed  -0.59167    0.12199  -4.850 0.000177 ***
---
Signif. codes:  0 '***' 0.001 '**' 0.01 '*' 0.05 '.' 0.1 ' ' 1

Residual standard error: 0.2259 on 16 degrees of freedom
Multiple R-squared:  0.6898,  Adjusted R-squared:  0.651
F-statistic: 17.79 on 2 and 16 DF,  p-value: 8.575e-05
```

In order to interpret the meaning of these coefficients, we need to remember that `lm(y ~ x)` is interpreted as $y = a + bx$ by R, where a is the intercept and b is the slope. Similarly, the regression model `aov(y ~ x)` is interpreted as $y = a + bx1 + cx2$. Therefore, the intercept in this table refers to a, or based on R convention, the factor level that comes first by alphabetical order. So in our coefficients section of the `summary` table, intercept refers to `fatiguehigh`.

Now, if we wanted to factor in the gender of each patient in addition to fatigue into our model, we can perform a two-way Anova as on the original dataset as follows:

```
> patient.sex <- as.factor(c("F", "F", "F", "M", "M", "F", "M", "M",
"M", "F", "F", "M", "M", "F", "F", "F", "M", "M", "F", "M"))
```

```
> modelC = aov(drugA_dose ~ fatigue*patient.sex)
> summary(modelC)
                    Df Sum Sq Mean Sq F value  Pr(>F)
fatigue              2 1.6664  0.8332   9.243 0.00276 **
patient.sex          1 0.0067  0.0067   0.075 0.78842
fatigue:patient.sex  2 0.0148  0.0074   0.082 0.92158
Residuals           14 1.2620  0.0901
---
Signif. codes:  0 '***' 0.001 '**' 0.01 '*' 0.05 '.' 0.1 ' ' 1
```

From the summary, you can see that the effects of gender and fatigue are not additive. In fact, we also see that there is no significant relationship between drug_A_dose and patient.sex. We can compare the two models using the anova() function as follows:

```
> anova(modelA, modelC)
Analysis of Variance Table

Model 1: drugA_dose ~ fatigue
Model 2: drugA_dose ~ fatigue * patient.sex
  Res.Df    RSS Df Sum of Sq      F Pr(>F)
1     17 1.2836
2     14 1.2620  3  0.021556 0.0797   0.97
```

As you can see, the models are not significantly different from each other based on the p value that is equal to 0.97. So, we can choose the simpler model to explain the data.

Generalized linear models

We just saw how to fit our data to a model using linear regression. However, as we just saw, in order for our model to be valid, it must make the assumption that the variance is constant and the errors are normally distributed. A **generalized linear model (GLM)** is an alternative approach to linear regression, which allows the errors to follow probability distributions other than a normal distribution. GLM is typically used for response variables that represent count data or binary response variables. To fit your data to a GLM in R, you can use the glm() function.

GLM has three important properties:

- An error structure
- A linear predictor
- A link function

The **error structure** informs us of the error distribution to use to model the data and is specified by the `family` argument. For example, you might want to use a Poisson distribution to model the errors for count data and a Gamma distribution to model data showing a constant coefficient of variation as follows:

```
glm(y ~ z, family = poisson)
glm(y ~ z, family = Gamma)
```

The **linear predictor** incorporates the information about the independent variables into the model and is defined as the linear sum of the effects of one or more explanatory variables. The link function specifies the relationship between the linear predictor and the mean of the response variables. By using different link functions, the performance of the models can be compared. Ideally, the best link function to use is the one that produces the minimal residual deviance, where the deviance is defined as a quality of fit statistic for a model that is often used for statistical hypothesis testing. The canonical link functions are default functions used when a particular error structure is specified. Let's take a look at this in the following table:

Error structure	Canonical link function
binomial	`link = "logit"`
gaussian	`link = "identity"`
Gamma	`link = "inverse"`
inverse. gaussian	`link = "1/mu^2"`
poisson	`link = "log"`
quasi	`link = "identity", variance = "constant"`
quasibinomial	`link = "logit"`
quasipoisson	`link = "log"`

To use an alternative link function when fitting our data to a GLM model, we can change the `link` argument as follows:

```
glm(y, family=binomial(link=probit))
```

Now, let's go over a detailed example of how to fit your data to a GLM in R. In the first example, we will look at the effect of the dose of a compound on the death of 20 male and female mice. Let's take a look at this in the following lines of code:

```
> cmp1.ld <- read.table(header=TRUE, text='
  lethaldose sex numdead numalive
1          0   M       1       19
2          1   M       3       17
3          2   M       9       11
4          3   M      14        6
5          4   M      17        3
6          5   M      20        0
7          0   F       0       20
8          1   F       2       18
9          2   F       2       18
10         3   F       3       17
11         4   F       4       16
12         5   F       6       14
')
> attach(cmp1.ld)
```

We can plot the data to take a look at the relationship between the dose of the compound and the proportions of deaths by mouse gender. Let's take a look at this in the following lines of code:

```
> proportion_dead <- numdead/20
> plot(proportion_dead ~ lethaldose, pch=as.character(sex))
```

The result is shown in the following plot:

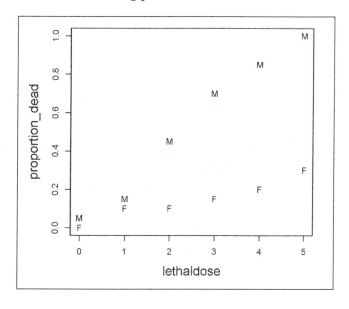

Now we will fit our data to a GLM model. First, we combine the number of dead and alive mice into a `counts` matrix as follows:

```
> counts <- cbind(numdead, numalive)
> cmp1.ld.model <- glm( counts ~ sex * lethaldose, family=binomial)
```

We can summarize the results for the GLM model with the `summary()` function as follows:

```
> summary(cmp1.ld.model)
```

```
Call:
glm(formula = counts ~ sex * lethaldose, family = binomial)

Deviance Residuals:
      Min         1Q     Median         3Q        Max
 -1.23314   -0.14226   -0.03905    0.17624    1.11956

Coefficients:
                  Estimate Std. Error z value Pr(>|z|)
(Intercept)        -3.2507     0.6774  -4.799 1.59e-06 ***
sexM                0.3342     0.8792   0.380  0.70387
lethaldose          0.4856     0.1812   2.681  0.00735 **
sexM:lethaldose     0.7871     0.2804   2.807  0.00500 **
---
Signif. codes:  0 '***' 0.001 '**' 0.01 '*' 0.05 '.' 0.1 ' ' 1

(Dispersion parameter for binomial family taken to be 1)

    Null deviance: 125.811  on 11  degrees of freedom
Residual deviance:   3.939  on  8  degrees of freedom
AIC: 40.515

Number of Fisher Scoring iterations: 4
```

At first glance, there seems to be a significant interaction between the `sex` and the `lethaldose` explanatory variables ($p = 0.0050$). However, before we can make this conclusion, we need to check if there is more variability in the data than expected from the statistical model (**overdispersion**). We can check for overdispersion in our model by dividing the residual deviance by the number of degrees of freedom as follows:

```
> 3.939/8
[1] 0.492375
```

The value is less than 1, which reassures us that the data is not over-dispersed. However, if we get a value greater than 1, we might want to re-fit the model with a quasibinomial error structure to account for the overdispersion. For the sake of argument, let's see if we can improve the model by using a quasibinomial error structure instead of a binomial one. Let's take a look at this in the following lines of code:

```
> summary(glm( counts ~ sex * lethaldose, family=quasibinomial))

Call:
glm(formula = counts ~ sex * lethaldose, family = quasibinomial)

Deviance Residuals:
    Min       1Q    Median       3Q       Max
-1.23314  -0.14226  -0.03905   0.17624   1.11956

Coefficients:
                 Estimate Std. Error t value Pr(>|t|)
(Intercept)       -3.2507     0.3957  -8.214 3.61e-05 ***
sexM               0.3342     0.5137   0.651  0.53355
lethaldose         0.4856     0.1058   4.588  0.00178 **
sexM:lethaldose    0.7871     0.1638   4.805  0.00135 **
---
Signif. codes:  0 '***' 0.001 '**' 0.01 '*' 0.05 '.' 0.1 ' ' 1

(Dispersion parameter for quasibinomial family taken to be 0.3413398)

    Null deviance: 125.811  on 11  degrees of freedom
Residual deviance:   3.939  on  8  degrees of freedom
AIC: NA

Number of Fisher Scoring iterations: 4
```

As you can see, the change in error structure did not change too much except for the p values of the explanatory variables. Now let's see what will happen if we remove the `sex:lethaldose` interaction from our original model. Let's take a look at this in the following lines of code:

```
> cmp1.ld.model3 <- update(cmp1.ld.model, ~ . -sex:lethaldose )
> summary(cmp1.ld.model3)

Call:
glm(formula = counts ~ sex + lethaldose, family = binomial)

Deviance Residuals:
    Min       1Q    Median       3Q       Max
```

```
   -1.2468   -0.6442    0.1702    0.6824    1.8965


Coefficients:
              Estimate Std. Error z value Pr(>|z|)
(Intercept)   -4.8871     0.6169  -7.922 2.34e-15 ***
sexM           2.7820     0.4310   6.455 1.08e-10 ***
lethaldose     0.9256     0.1373   6.740 1.58e-11 ***
---
Signif. codes:  0 '***' 0.001 '**' 0.01 '*' 0.05 '.' 0.1 ' ' 1


(Dispersion parameter for binomial family taken to be 1)

    Null deviance: 125.811  on 11  degrees of freedom
Residual deviance:  11.975  on  9  degrees of freedom
AIC: 46.551


Number of Fisher Scoring iterations: 5
```

The first thing you will notice is that the residual deviance/degrees of freedom ratio is greater than 1, suggesting overdispersion:

```
> 11.975/9
[1] 1.330556
```

Now let's statistically test whether this model was significantly different from our initial model using the `anova()` function with the `test` argument set to Chi-square test since we are dealing with a binomial family. Let's take a look this in the following lines of code:

```
> anova(cmp1.ld.model, cmp1.ld.model3, test="Chi")
Analysis of Deviance Table

Model 1: counts ~ sex * lethaldose
Model 2: counts ~ sex + lethaldose
  Resid. Df Resid. Dev Df Deviance Pr(>Chi)
1         8      3.939
2         9     11.975 -1  -8.0356 0.004587 **
---
Signif. codes:  0 '***' 0.001 '**' 0.01 '*' 0.05 '.' 0.1 ' ' 1
```

From this analysis, we see that the two models are significantly different from each other. Since the second model shows signs of overdispersion, we can stick to the first model as a better fit for this data. The important thing to remember when choosing the best model is to choose the one that has the lowest residual deviance (goodness of fit) while maximizing parsimony.

Generalized additive models

Generalized additive models (GAMs) are a non-parametric extension of GLMs in which the linear predictor depends linearly on unknown smooth functions of some predictor variables. GAMs are typically used to let the data "speak for themselves" since you don't need to specify the functional form of the relationship, the response, and the continuous explanatory variables beforehand. To fit your data to a GAM, you will need to obtain the `gam()` function from the `mgcv` package. It is similar to the `glm()` function except that you add `s()` to each explanatory variable you wish to add smooths. For example, if you wish to describe the relationship between *y* and to smooth three continuous explanatory variables *x*, *z*, and *w*, you would enter `model <- gam(y ~ s(x) + s(z) + s(w))`. Now let's go through a detailed example in R.

In this example, we will explore the relationship between the total number of pregnancies and a variety of measurements taken from 300 mice.

Let's first simulate a dataset for 300 mice with `pregnancies`, `glucose`, `pressure`, `insulin`, and `weight` as explanatory variables. Since the `sample()` and `rnorm()` functions generate pseudorandom numbers, you will get different results when you run the following code in R. Let's simulate our explanatory variables with the following lines of code:

```
> pregnancies <- sample(0:25, 300,replace=T)
> glucose <- sample(65:200, 300,replace=T)
> pressure <-  sample(50:120, 300,replace=T)
> insulinD <- abs(rnorm(150, 450, 100))
> insulinN <- abs(rnorm(150, 65, 75))
> insulin <- c(insulinD, insulinN)
> weight <- sample(20:70, 300,replace=T)
```

Now let's use the `gam()` function part of the `mgcv` package to explore the relationship between diabetes and pregnancies, glucose, pressure, insulin, and weight as follows:

```
> library("mgcv")
> mouse.data.gam <- gam(pregnancies ~ s(glucose) + s(pressure) +
s(insulin) + s(weight))

> summary(mouse.data.gam)

Family: gaussian
Link function: identity

Formula:
pregnancies ~ s(glucose) + s(pressure) + s(insulin) + s(weight)
```

```
Parametric coefficients:
            Estimate Std. Error t value Pr(>|t|)
(Intercept)  13.3467     0.4149   32.17   <2e-16 ***
---
Signif. codes:  0 '***' 0.001 '**' 0.01 '*' 0.05 '.' 0.1 ' ' 1

Approximate significance of smooth terms:
             edf Ref.df     F p-value
s(glucose)  3.225  3.995 1.270   0.282
s(pressure) 1.088  1.171 0.216   0.681
s(insulin)  1.000  1.000 1.080   0.300
s(weight)   1.000  1.000 1.562   0.212

R-sq.(adj) =  0.0118   Deviance explained = 3.26%
GCV = 52.936   Scale est. = 51.646     n = 300
```

As you can see from the summary results of the GAM model, R returns the **effective degrees of freedom (edf)** and other useful information in assessing the fit of our data to the GAM model. Unlike other ordinary **least squares linear regression** models, the number of degrees of freedom is not equivalent to the number of predictors in the model because it also needs to take into account the smoothing process. Therefore, the terms associated with the smoothing process are each penalized to a certain extent, which in turn is reflected in the edf value.

Another important term to consider when evaluating the fit of a GAM is the **generalized cross validation (GCV)** score, which is used as an estimate of the mean square prediction error. We can use the GCV as a comparative measure to choose between different models, where the lower the GCV value, the better the model. To read more about the information returned in the gam object summary, you can consult the documentation page as follows:

```
> ?summary.gam
```

To plot the model to inspect 95 percent Bayesian confidence intervals to determine whether the curvature is real or not, we can use the following function:

```
> par(mfrow=c(2,2))
> plot(mouse.data.gam)
```

The result is shown in the following plot:

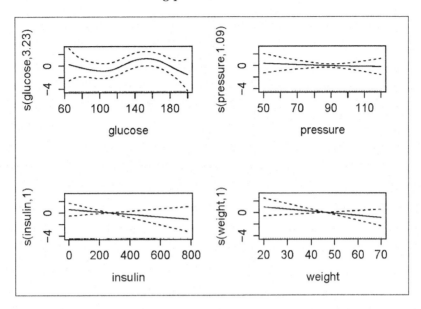

Alternatively, we can use the `vis.gam()` function to visualize the two main effect terms in a perspective plot. In this case, the two main effect terms are `glucose` and `pressure` as follows:

```
> par(mfrow=c(1,1))
> vis.gam(mouse.data.gam,theta=-35,color="topo")
```

The result is shown in the following plot:

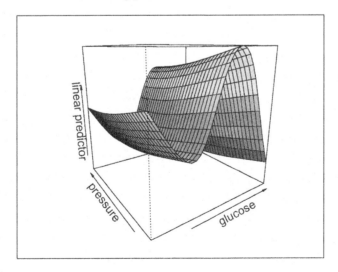

We can also use the `gam.check()` function to inspect our model as follows

```
> gam.check(mouse.data.gam)


Method: GCV   Optimizer: magic
Smoothing parameter selection converged after 13 iterations.
The RMS GCV score gradiant at convergence was 1.813108e-06 .
The Hessian was positive definite.
The estimated model rank was 37 (maximum possible: 37)
Model rank =  37 / 37


Basis dimension (k) checking results. Low p-value (k-index<1) may
indicate that k is too low, especially if edf is close to k'.

              k'   edf k-index p-value
s(glucose)  9.000 3.225  1.030    0.70
s(pressure) 9.000 1.088  0.999    0.44
s(insulin)  9.000 1.000  1.106    0.96
s(weight)   9.000 1.000  1.058    0.82
```

Let's see what happens to the fit of the model when we remove the non-significant explanatory variables as follows:

```
> mouse.data.gam2 <- gam(pregnancies ~ s(insulin))
> summary(mouse.data.gam2)


Family: gaussian
Link function: identity


Formula:
pregnancies ~ s(insulin)


Parametric coefficients:
            Estimate Std. Error t value Pr(>|t|)
(Intercept)  13.3467     0.4174   31.97   <2e-16 ***
---
Signif. codes:  0 '***' 0.001 '**' 0.01 '*' 0.05 '.' 0.1 ' ' 1


Approximate significance of smooth terms:
           edf Ref.df     F p-value
s(insulin)   1      1 0.918   0.339


R-sq.(adj) =  -0.000276   Deviance explained = 0.307%
GCV = 52.626  Scale est. = 52.275    n = 300
```

To better compare the two models, we can use the `AIC()` function, which calculates the **Akaike information criterion (AIC)** to give us an idea of the trade-off between the goodness of fit of the model and the complexity of the model. Generally speaking, a good GAM has a low AIC and and the fewest number of degrees of freedom. Let's take a look at this in the following lines of code:

```
>   AIC(mouse.data.gam, mouse.data.gam2)
                      df       AIC
mouse.data.gam   8.313846 2045.909
mouse.data.gam2  3.000000 2044.313
```

As you can see, the number of degrees of freedom and the AIC value are slightly lower for `mouse.data.gam2`, making the second GAM a better model than the first. That being said, GAMs are best used in the preliminary phase of your analysis to broadly explore the potential relationship between your response and explanatory variables. Some people find it useful to examine the shape of a curve with GAMs and then reconstruct the curve shape parametrically with GLMs for model building. A GLM is preferable to the more complex GAM. As a general rule of thumb, it is usually preferable to rely on a simple well-understood model to predict future cases than on a complex model that is difficult to interpret and summarize.

Linear discriminant analysis

Linear discriminant analysis (LDA) is used to find the linear combinations of explanatory variables that give the best possible separation between the groups in our dataset. More specifically, LDA is used as a linear supervised classifier to form a classification model from the data provided. For example, we can use LDA to classify fish based on their length, weight, and speed underwater. Let's simulate a dataset based on the Ontario warm water fish species Bluegill, Bowfin, Carp, Goldeye, and Largemouth Bass.

```
> set.seed(459)
> Bluegill.length <- sample(seq(15, 22.5, by=0.5), 50, replace=T)
> Bluegill.weight <- sample(seq(0.2, 0.8, by=0.05), 50, replace=T)
> Bowfin.length <- sample(seq(46, 61, by=0.5), 50, replace=T)
> Bowfin.weight <- sample(seq(1.36, 3.2, by=0.5), 50, replace=T)
> Carp.length <- sample(seq(30, 75, by=1), 50, replace=T)
> Carp.weight <- sample(seq(0.2, 3.5, by=0.1), 50, replace=T)
> Goldeye.length <- sample(seq(25, 38, by=0.5), 50, replace=T)
> Goldeye.weight <- sample(seq(0.4, 0.54, by=0.01), 50, replace=T)
> Largemouth_Bass.length <- sample(seq(22, 55, by=0.5), 50, replace=T)
> Largemouth_Bass.weight <- sample(seq(0.68, 1.8, by=0.01), 50,
replace=T)

> weight <-c(Bluegill.weight, Bowfin.weight, Carp.weight, Goldeye.
weight, Largemouth_Bass.weight)

> length <-c(Bluegill.length, Bowfin.length, Carp.length, Goldeye.
length, Largemouth_Bass.length)

> speed <- rnorm(50*5, 7.2, sd=1.8)

> fish <- c(rep("Bluegill", 50), rep("Bowfin", 50), rep("Carp", 50),
rep("Goldeye", 50), rep("Largemouth_Bass", 50))
> fish.data <- data.frame(length, weight, speed, fish)
```

```
> str(fish.data)
'data.frame':   250 obs. of  4 variables:
 $ length: num  17 19 21.5 22.5 19.5 21.5 15 20.5 18.5 15.5 ...
 $ weight: num  0.5 0.5 0.7 0.3 0.75 0.35 0.45 0.5 0.5 0.65 ...
 $ speed : num  6.78 7.74 5.43 4.76 9.03 ...
 $ fish  : Factor w/ 5 levels "Bluegill","Bowfin",..: 1 1 1 1 1 1 1 1
 1 1 ...
```

To help visualize the data, let's make 3D scatterplots using the `scatterplot3d` package. To simplify generating the four 3D scatterplots, we will write a function and call it to plot each figure. Let's take a look at how to do this in the following lines of code:

```
> plot3DfishData <- function(x, y, z, data=fish.data){

    require("scatterplot3d")

    #To store the axis labels
    fish.variable <- colnames(data)

    scatterplot3d(data[, x], data[, y], data[, z], mar = mar0, color =
    c("blue", "black", "red", "green", "turquoise")[data$fish], pch
    = 19,   xlab=fish.variable[x], ylab=fish.variable[y], zlab=fish.
    variable[z])

}

> # Load the scatterplot3d package
> library("scatterplot3d")
```

Now, we can use `plot3DfishData()` to plot the relationship between the length, weight, and speed as follows:

```
> par(mfrow = c(1, 1))
> plot3DfishData(1, 2, 3)
```

To add the figure legend, click on the plot at the position you wish to add the legend after entering the following command:

```
> legend(locator(1),levels(fish.data$fish), col=c("blue", "black",
"red", "green", "turquoise"), lty=c(1, 1, 1, 1, 1), lwd=3, box.lwd =
1,box.col = "black",bg = "white")
```

The result is shown in the following plot:

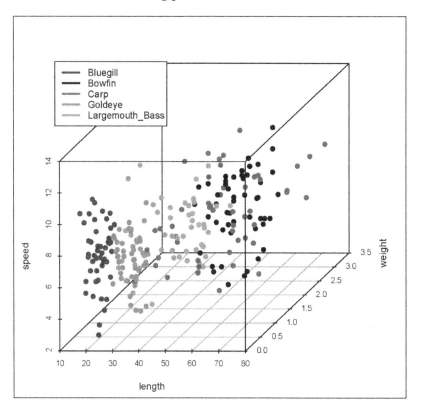

To plot all four figures in the same plot, use the following lines of code:

```
> par(mfrow = c(2, 2))
> plot3DfishData(1, 2, 3)
> plot3DfishData(2, 3, 4)
> plot3DfishData(3, 4, 1)
> plot3DfishData(4, 1, 2)
```

The result is shown in the following plot:

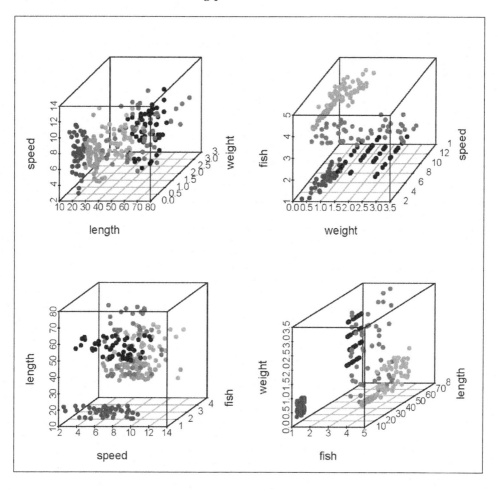

Now let's perform an LDA analysis on fish.data by using the lda() function available as part of the MASS package. To specify the prior probabilities of class membership, we use the prior argument. Say we only had data from these five fishes to classify, then the prior probability would be 1/5 for each fish group.

The probabilities in the prior argument should be specified in the same order of the factor levels.

Let's take a look at this in the following lines of code:

```
> library("MASS")
> fish.lda <- lda(fish ~ ., data=fish.data, prior = c(1,1,1,1,1)/5)

> fish.lda
Call:
lda(fish ~ ., data = fish.data, prior = c(1, 1, 1, 1, 1)/5)

Prior probabilities of groups:
        Bluegill          Bowfin            Carp         Goldeye
             0.2             0.2             0.2             0.2
Largemouth_Bass
             0.2

Group means:
                  length weight     speed
Bluegill           19.25 0.5280 7.222587
Bowfin             53.57 2.1600 7.243531
Carp               52.26 1.7320 7.588852
Goldeye            31.87 0.4748 7.122371
Largemouth_Bass    40.11 1.2428 7.163396

Coefficients of linear discriminants:
                 LD1             LD2              LD3
length    0.10121664  -0.067114012    0.003296811
weight    1.17216477   1.335393654    0.011024527
speed    -0.02745768  -0.009936134   -0.555543270

Proportion of trace:
   LD1    LD2    LD3
0.9730 0.0256 0.0014
```

The lda() function returns the prior probability of each class ($prior), the class-specific means for each covariate ($means), the coefficients for each linear discriminant ($scaling), and the proportion of trace. You can also get the counts for each class in the data with $counts and the singular values (svd) that gives the ratio of the between and within-group standard deviations on the linear discriminant variables with $svd.

```
> fish.lda$counts
        Bluegill          Bowfin            Carp
              50              50              50
```

```
        Goldeye Largemouth_Bass
           50                50
> fish.lda$svd
[1] 16.1282733  2.6175620  0.6155127
```

Using the `predict()` function, we can return the classification and posterior probabilities of a new dataset. As an example, let's use 100 samples from our `fish.data` dataset to train and perform the LDA before predicting the classification 150 samples.

Select 100 samples from the data using the following code:

```
> set.seed(10)
> train100 <- sample(1:nrow(fish.data), 100)
```

The following code will show the sample distribution in a table:

```
> table(fish.data$fish[train100])
```

```
        Bluegill            Bowfin            Carp           Goldeye
            18                25              16                20
Largemouth_Bass
            21
```

Now we can use the `select` argument to provide the indices to use from the `fish.data` dataset for the LDA analysis as follows:

```
> fish100.lda <- lda(fish ~ ., data=fish.data, prior = c(1,1,1,1,1)/5,
subset = train100)
```

 Note that using the `prior` argument, we specify that the probability of belonging to any group is equal; otherwise, R would use the proportions in the sample.

Now let's get information on the model using the `predict()` function to classify the 100 samples we used to create the LDA as follows:

```
> predict.fish100 <- predict(fish100.lda)
> table(fish.data$fish[train100], predict.fish100$class)
```

	Bluegill	Bowfin	Carp	Goldeye	Largemouth_Bass
Bluegill	18	0	0	0	0
Bowfin	0	15	9	0	1
Carp	0	5	7	0	4
Goldeye	1	0	0	19	0
Largemouth_Bass	2	0	2	2	15

As you can see, it classified a couple of the samples in the wrong fish group. To help visualize the implications of these findings, let's plot the results as follows:

```
> par(mfrow = c(1, 1))
> plot(predict.fish100$x,
    type="n",xlab="LD1", ylab="LD2",
    main="TrainingSetLDA Results(n=50)")
> text(predict.fish100$x,
    as.character(predict.fish100$class),
    col=as.numeric(fish.data$fish[train100]),cex=1.5)
> abline(h=0, col="gray")
> abline(v=0, col="gray")
```

The result is shown in the following plot:

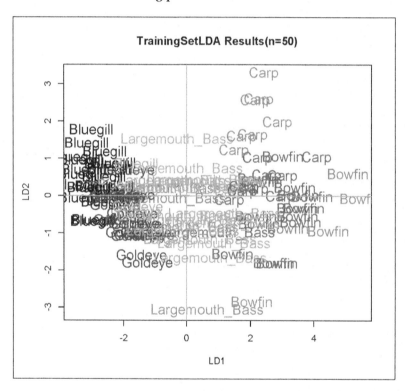

Alternatively, we can plot the figure with the `ggplot()` function from the `ggplot2` package as follows:

```
> library("ggplot2")

> p <- ggplot(as.data.frame(predict.fish100$x),
aes(x=LD1,y=LD2,col=fish.data$fish[train100])) + geom_point() + geom_
text(aes(label = as.character(predict.fish100$class)))
```

```
> # Adjust legend size
> p <- p + theme(legend.title=element_blank(), legend.text = element_
text( size = 20, face = "bold"))

# Adjust axis labels
> p <- p + theme(axis.title = element_text(face="bold", size=20),
          axis.text  = element_text(size=18))

# Display plot
> p
```

The result is shown in the following plot:

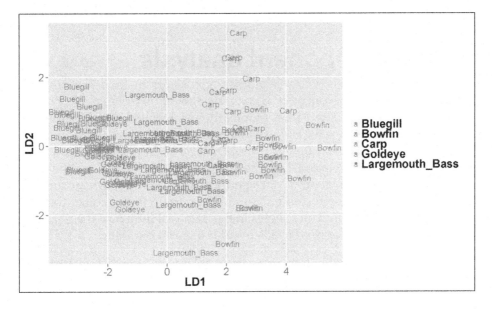

Now let's use `predict()` to classify the remaining data as follows:

```
> predict.new <- predict(fish100.lda, newdata=fish.data[-train100, ])
```

If you want to look at the classification (`$class`) and the posterior probability (`$posterior`) of each sample, you can enter `predict.new$class` and `predict.new$posterior`. Alternatively, you might want to use a table to see how well it classified the data. Let's take a look at this in the following lines of code:

```
> table(fish.data$fish[-train100], predict.new$class)
```

	Bluegill	Bowfin	Carp	Goldeye	Largemouth_Bass
Bluegill	32	0	0	0	0
Bowfin	0	11	13	0	1
Carp	0	16	5	3	10

Goldeye	0	0	0	30	0
Largemouth_Bass	3	0	3	5	18

Now, let's calculate the misclassification rate as follows:

```
> TAB <- table(fish.data$fish[-train100], predict.new$class)
> mcrlda <- 1 - sum(diag(TAB))/sum(TAB)
> mcrlda
[1] 0.36
```

If these results were from a real experiment, we might want to consider taking additional measurements to decrease the misclassification rate to better discriminate between the different groups.

Principal component analysis

Principal component analysis (PCA) is another exploratory method you can use to separate your samples into groups. PCA converts a set of observations of possibly correlated variables into a set of values of linearly uncorrelated variables called principal components. PCA is widely used as a dimension reduction technique to help visualize data. PCA is different from LDA because it doesn't rely on class information to explore the relationship between the variable values and the sample group numbers. For example, let's perform a PCA to explore our simulated fish.data dataset. Before performing PCA, it is important to remember that the magnitude of the variables and any skews in the data will influence the resulting principal components. So, we need to scale and transform our data.

First, we recommend you to log transform the data (if necessary). Then, run PCA using the prcomp() function as follows:

```
> fish.data.mx <- as.matrix(fish.data[, 1:3])
> fish.data.log <- log(fish.data.mx)
> fish.log.pca <- prcomp(fish.data.log, scale=T, center=T)
> summary(fish.log.pca)
Importance of components:
                          PC1    PC2    PC3
Standard deviation     1.2563 0.9953 0.6566
Proportion of Variance 0.5261 0.3302 0.1437
Cumulative Proportion  0.5261 0.8563 1.0000
```

Instead of the summary, you might want to see the standard deviation of each principal component, and their rotation (or loadings), which are the coefficients of the linear combinations of the continuous variables. To get this information, we can use the print() function as follows:

```
> print(fish.log.pca)
Standard deviations:
```

```
[1] 1.2563128 0.9952860 0.6565698

Rotation:
              PC1          PC2          PC3
length 0.7012316  -0.09252202   0.70690444
weight 0.7016076  -0.08648088  -0.70729617
speed  0.1265742   0.99194795   0.00427102
```

We can also plot the variance associated with each principal component as follows:

```
> plot(fish.log.pca, ylim=c(0, 2)) #plot not shown
```

Now let's visualize the loadings on the first principal component with the `qplot()` function from the `ggplot2` package as follows:

```
> library("ggplot2")
> loadings <- as.data.frame(fish.log.pca$rotation)

> # Add a column with the name of each variable to the loadings data
frame.
> loadings$variables <- colnames(fish.data[,1:3])

> # Plot figure with qplot()
> q <- qplot(x = variables, y = PC1, data = loadings, geom = "bar",
stat="identity")

> # Adjust axis label sizes
> q + theme(axis.title = element_text(face="bold", size=20), axis.text
= element_text(size=18))
```

The result is shown in the following plot:

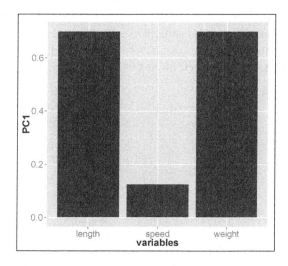

We can also plot the score from our PCA results as follows:

```
> scores <- as.data.frame(fish.log.pca$x)
> q2 <- qplot(x = PC1, y = PC2, data = scores, geom = "point", col =
fish.data$fish)
> q2 <- q2 + theme(legend.title=element_blank(), legend.text =
element_text( size = 20, face = "bold"))
> q2 <- q2 + theme(axis.title = element_text(face="bold", size=20),
axis.text  = element_text(size=18))
> q2
```

The result is shown in the following plot:

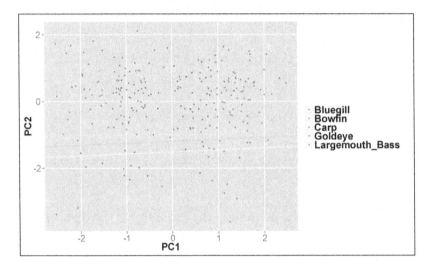

We can also view the PCA results with the `biplot()` function. A biplot allows us to visualize two sets of variables at the same time. It's representation is similar to the last plot we just generated with the `qplot()` function except that it also represents the variables as vectors. Let's take a look at the following `biplot()` function:

```
> biplot(fish.log.pca)
```

The result is shown in the following plot:

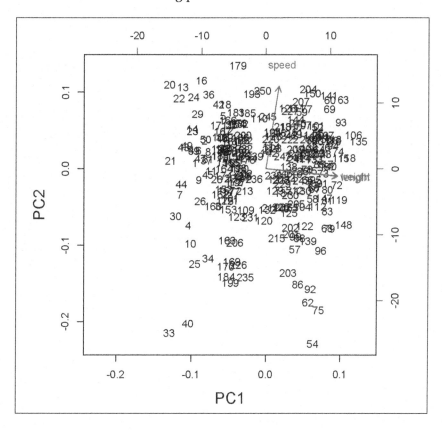

As you can see, in this case, the samples are shown as points and the variables (speed, length, and width) are shown as vectors.

You may also want to take advantage of the `ggbiplot()` function as part of the ggbiplot package (available at `https://github.com/vqv/ggbiplot`) to produce a better figure as follows:

```
> library("devtools")
> install_github("ggbiplot", "vqv")
> library("ggbiplot")

> fish.class   <- fish.data$fish
> g <- ggbiplot(fish.log.pca, obs.scale = 1, var.scale = 1, groups =
fish.class, ellipse = TRUE, circle = TRUE)
> g <- g + scale_color_discrete(name = '')
> g <- g + theme(legend.direction = 'horizontal',
               legend.position = 'top')
> g <- g + theme(legend.title=element_blank(), legend.text = element_
text( size = 20, face = "bold"))
> g <- g + theme(axis.title = element_text(face="bold", size=20),
axis.text  = element_text(size=18))
> g
```

The result is shown in the following plot:

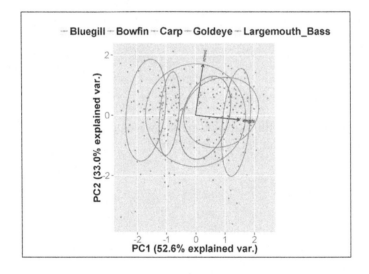

We can also create a three-dimensional view of the principal components with the `plot3d()` function available in the `rgl` package. The `plot3d()` function creates an interactive 3D scatter plot. So you can move around the plot to have a better idea of the separation between the principal components. Let's take a look at the following code:

```
> library(rgl)
> fish.pca.col=c("red", "blue", "green", "magenta", "black")
> plot3d(fish.log.pca$x[,1:3], col=fish.pca.col[sort(rep(1:5, 50))])
```

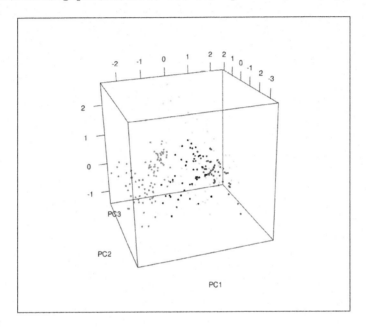

To save an image, we use the `rgl.snapshot()` function as follows:

```
> rgl.snapshot("PCAfigure1.png")
```

Clustering

An alternative approach to PCA is k-means (unsupervised) clustering, which partitions the data into *k* clusters in which each observation belongs to the cluster with the nearest mean, serving as a prototype of the cluster. We can perform k-means clustering with the `kmeans()` function and plot the results with `plot3d()` as follows:

```
> set.seed(44)
> cl <- kmeans(fish.data[,1:3],5)
> fish.data$cluster <- as.factor(cl$cluster)
> plot3d(fish.log.pca$x[,1:3], col=fish.data$cluster, main="k-means
clusters")
```

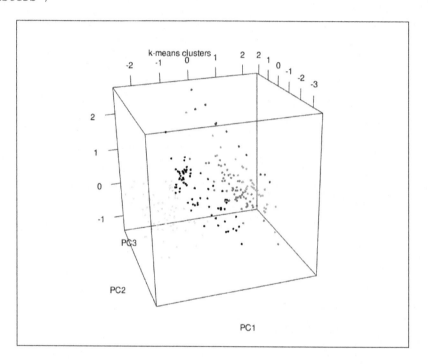

 The color scheme used for the groups is different from the 3D plot of the PCA results. However, the overall distribution of the groups is similar.

Let's now evaluate how well it categorizes the data with a table as follows:

```
> with(fish.data, table(cluster, fish))
        fish
cluster Bluegill Bowfin Carp Goldeye Largemouth_Bass
      1        0      0   14      39              18
      2        0     27   12       0              22
      3        0     23   13       0               2
      4        0      0   11       0               0
      5       50      0    0      11               8
```

As you can see, it nicely groups all the Bluegill fish together but had a much harder time placing the other fish in the right group.

To help improve the classification of the fish into the five groups, we can perform hierarchical clustering as follows:

```
> di <- dist(fish.data[,1:3], method="euclidean")
> tree <- hclust(di, method="ward")

> fish.data$hcluster <- as.factor((cutree(tree, k=5)-2) %% 3 +1)
> plot(tree, xlab="", cex=0.2)
```

Let's add a red box around the five hierarchical clusters as follows:

```
> rect.hclust(tree, k=5, border="red")
```

The result is shown in the following plot:

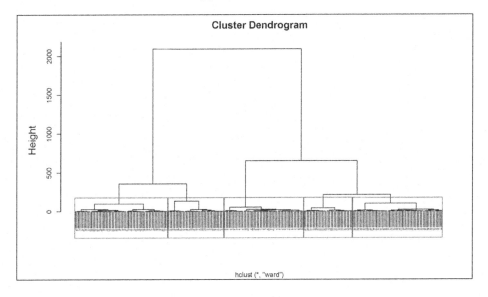

Now, let's create a table to determine how well we can group the fish based on the hierarchical clustering as follows:

```
> with(fish.data, table(hcluster, fish))
         fish
hcluster Bluegill Bowfin Carp Goldeye Largemouth_Bass
      -1       50      0    0       0               4
       0        0     35    8       0              20
       1        0     15   23       0               0
       2        0      0   10       9              14
       3        0      0    9      41              12
```

As you can see, hierarchical clustering didn't drastically improve the classification of the fish. Therefore, you might consider collecting additional measurements to help classify the fish since the information provided by the length, weight, and speed is insufficient.

Summary

In this chapter, we began with an overview of statistical modeling and how to write model formulas in R. Then, we also saw how to fit our data using linear methods. More specifically, we showed you how to use linear regression, generalized linear models, and generalized additive models to model your data and use statistical methods to assess the fit of your model to help choose the best one. Next, we showed you how to use analysis of variance to fit your data to a linear model when all the explanatory variables are categorical. Finally, we also saw how to use exploratory methods such as linear discriminant analysis, principal component analysis, and hierarchical clustering to separate your data into groups. While linear models are the most commonly used statistical models in scientific computing, there are times when nonlinear methods are preferable. Now that you know how to use linear methods to model your data, you will move on to nonlinear methods in the next chapter, where you will find out how to use non-parametric regression for exploratory analysis.

References:

Crawley, Michael J. 2005. *Statistics: An Introduction Using R*. Chinchester: John Wiley & Sons. Ltd.

4

Nonlinear Methods

In the previous chapter, we looked at using R for the estimation of linear models, the groundwork upon which most data analysis is built. However, what is one supposed to do if the relationship between two variables is not linear? For this, we must use nonlinear methods, a topic to which this chapter is devoted.

We will start with extensions to linear regression and then move on to nonparametric regression. In this chapter, we'll cover the following topics:

- Polynomial regression
- Spline regression
- General regression framework
- Point-wise regression
- Kernel density regression
- Local polynomial regression

Nonparametric and parametric models

The exact role of nonlinear methods in statistics is perhaps still a bit contentious. They are largely used for the purposes of exploratory analyses as visual tools, and for this reason data visualization and nonlinear statistical methods are closely tied together. The question is whether or not nonlinear methods can also be used to truly develop statistical models.

Broadly speaking, nonlinear models might be grouped into nonparametric (or semi-parametric) and parametric models. The term "parametric" here has a very different meaning than it does in statistical methods, used in testing for differences between groups. Parametric tests of statistically significant differences are concerned with a parameterization of the sample distribution. For example, the t-test does not actually test for differences in observed data but tests for differences in distributions whose parameters were computed based on observed data. This is to say, that we only need to know the parameters of the t-distribution for a given sample to do a t-test; we don't actually need the original sample values to perform a t-test if we know these parameters.

The term parametric when applied to regression is concerned not with the distribution of the sample being studied but with the statistical model being developed. As such, a parametric regression model is so called because it can be described completely with a few model parameters. For example, in linear regression, once we know that the model is linear, we only need to know two parameters: one is the intercept and the other is the slope of the model to recreate the entire line. Alternatively, if we regress a curve of unknown algebraic form on to a cloud of data points, then we need to know the x and y values of each point on that curve to recreate it, making it a nonparametric model. A nonparametric regression model can in fact make distributional assumptions about the sample.

There are a number of advantages that parametric regression models have over their nonparametric counterparts. They can be easily interpreted and used to advance a general theory from the model, which is not always possible with nonparametric regression models. The proportion of variance explained can give a convenient summary of how well a parametric model explains data, whereas, a similar statistic is not so readily available for nonparametric models. Finally, parametric models are excellent for use in smaller datasets or datasets with a low signal-to-noise ratio, since the strong assumption about the algebraic form of the model will have a tempering effect on model parameter sensitivity to only a few observations. The disadvantage of parametric models is that they require an assumption about the algebraic form of the relationship between two or more variables. It is also worth noting that nonlinear parametric regression models, like polynomial regression, can be thought of as linear regression onto nonlinear transformations of the predictor variables, and as such, it is possible to make all of the same assumptions of linear regression. As such, the term "nonlinear regression" is sometimes used strictly to refer to nonparametric regression models, though in this book, we will use nonlinear regression to refer to both parametric and nonparametric models.

Before getting into either the theory or the practical execution of these methods in R, it is important to first place these methods in context and address the question: What are such statistical methods useful for? There are two potential answers to this question, which have practical implications for how one might use R to execute these methods:

- Nonparametric statistical models are simply exploratory tools and can be used to get an overall sense of how variables relate to one another (that is, they are not really models).

- Nonparametric statistical models are powerful generalizations of linear models that allow us to model the relationships between two or more variables with high fidelity and without being bound to the equation for a line

The adsorption and body measures datasets

In this section, we will use two datasets:

- The adsorption dataset (`adsorption.txt`) is available for download at `http://scholar.harvard.edu/gerrard/mastering-scientific-computation-r`. This data is designed to represent the proportion of a solid surface to which gas is bound at 50 different pressure readings. It contains four variables:
    - P is the pressure at which measurements were taken
    - T1, T2, and T3 are the proportions of the solid covered in gas at temperatures 1, 2, and 3

- Anthropometric data obtained from the Centers for Disease Control's National Health and Nutrition Examination Survey, 2011-2012, provided as a comma-separated values (CSV) file is available for download at `http://scholar.harvard.edu/gerrard/mastering-scientific-computation-r`. This dataset has been cleaned and processed for use and contains 8,602 individuals and four variables:
    - Gender (1 is for male, 2 is for female)
    - Age
    - Height
    - Weight

Theory-driven nonlinear regression

While opinions vary as to how theory-driven data analysis should be in science, nearly all scientists agree that a well thought out theoretical model applied to real data is typically ideal. The clearest use for nonlinear regression is when you know how two or more variables relate to one another theoretically, and your theory tells you that they are not linearly related. An example of this is a classical model of gas adsorption, known as the **Langmuir adsorption model** (other adsorption models also exist).

Adsorption is the phenomenon in which gases tend to concentrate near the surface of a material. Practically speaking, this has applications in engineering for gas separations. We will not delve into the theory of how the Langmuir model was derived but will give its equation, which is as follows:

$$\Theta = \frac{\alpha P}{1 + \alpha P}$$

In the preceding formula, Θ is a proportion of the surface covered by gas. α is a constant for a given gas interacting with a given solid at a given temperature and P is pressure.

As can be seen from this equation, the relationship between pressure and coverage of the solid is nonlinear. A common task in chemical engineering is to estimate the constant α, based on observations of the proportion of the surface covered at given pressures.

> Experimentally, what is done is that a gas cylinder containing a very sensitive scale weighing a solid is maintained at a consistent temperature and the solid sample is weighed at varying pressures. To stay focused on the data analysis and to make this book applicable to non-engineers, we will not delve into the practical details of physical measurement.

Perform the following steps:

1. First, load the dataset using the following code:

```
adsorption <- read.csv('adsorption.txt')
```

2. The simplest way to fit this equation in R is via the `nls` command, which fits a user specified algebraic model to a set of data. The adsorption data frame has three different sets of theta values for three different temperatures: T1, T2, and T3. We can use the estimate, **α**, in the Langmuir equation for each temperature, as follows:

```
langmuir.T1 <- 'T1 ~ (alpha.1 * P) / (1 + alpha.1 * P)'
langmuir.T2 <- 'T2 ~ (alpha.2 * P) / (1 + alpha.2 * P)'
langmuir.T3 <- 'T3 ~ (alpha.3 * P) / (1 + alpha.3 * P)'
fit.T1 <- nls(langmuir.T1, start = list(alpha.1 = 1), data =
adsorption)
fit.T2 <- nls(langmuir.T2, start = list(alpha.2 = 1), data =
adsorption)
fit.T3 <- nls(langmuir.T3, start = list(alpha.3 = 1), data =
adsorption)
```

3. The previous functions define three different nonlinear regressions (one for each temperature) based on the equation for the Langmuir adsorption model. Simply calling the objects fit by the `nls` function will return estimates of **α** for each temperature, while the `summary` command will also give the standard errors of the estimates:

```
fit.T1
fit.T2
fit.T3
```

An important note of caution is that starting values can be important and starting values that are way off might not converge. Therefore, it is often advisable to use multiple starting values and compare the final values.

Visually exploring nonlinear relationships

Let's say that we want to understand the relationship between height, weight, age, and gender. We probably have some preconceived notions about how these variables relate to one another (for example, taller people probably tend to weigh more). Let's perform the following steps:

1. Firstly, load the data and attach the data frame using the following code:
```
body.measures <- read.csv('nhanes_body.txt')
attach(body.measures)
```

2. Now, let's just look at the data visually, as shown in the following diagram, an important first step in most analyses. Let's have a look at the following function:

```
plot(age, height, xlab = 'Age', ylab = 'Height', main = 'Height vs
Age')
```

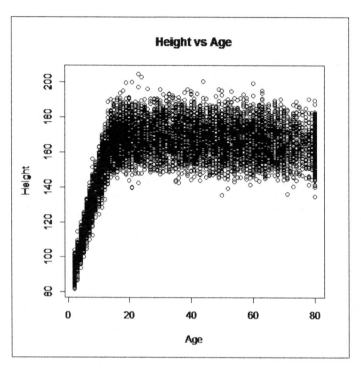

The previous dataset has thousands of data points, so a simple plot with default graphics options looks messy but it is clear that this is not a linear relationship. However, even the previous plot shows us some features about the relationship between age and height. The most obvious feature is that the relationship between height and age is not linear but it does have segments that might be successfully modeled as linear. As expected, those who are relatively young are shorter than those who have reached adulthood. It also looks like there is a slight trend towards decreasing height as adults get older.

Are there data visualization tools in R for examining high density data?

To examine high density data, there are a number of packages available for visualization in R, including `hexbin` and `ggplot2`. These packages are also helpful for creating publication-quality plots.

The following three packages display high density data on two-dimensional plots and shading plot areas to give a visual representation of number of observations.

Using `hexbin`, as shown in the following code:

```
library(hexbin)
bin<-hexbin(age, height)
plot(bin, xlab = 'Age', ylab = 'Height', main = 'Height vs Age')
```

Using `ggplot2`, as shown in the following code:

```
library(ggplot2)
qplot(age, height, data = body.measures, geom="hex", xlim = c(0, 80),
ylim = c(80, 200), binwidth = c(5, 5))
```

Using `graphics`, as shown in the following code:

```
smoothScatter(height ~ age, xlab = 'Age', ylab = 'Height', main =
'Height vs Age')
```

If we wish to try to make sense of an overall pattern using visualization, we can simply use the `scatter.smooth` command. This is not a sophisticated command with many options but it gives a quick view of the relationships between two variables with minimal code. It is generally helpful to set the color of the data points to a light color so that the smoothed line is visible. The plot is probably not publication ready and we might want to try to develop a better statistical model, as the one given by the following code, rather than the one provided by this curve, but this is a quick and dirty method to visualize data:

```
scatter.smooth(age, height, xlab = 'Age', ylab = 'Height', main =
'Height vs Age', col = 'gray', pch = 16)
```

The plot is shown in the following graph:

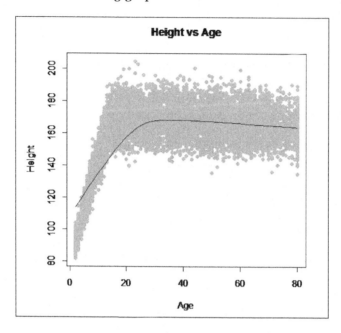

As we cover the next few sections, we will be making many judgments about how sensitive we wish to be to individual data points, which is tantamount to deciding whether we wish to be optimally sensitive to small quirks in the data or whether we wish to minimize our modeling of sample-specific random error in the data. One will come at the cost of the other. If we expect that there will be large changes in one variable with respect to another, and that these changes truly represent a phenomenon worth modeling, then we believe that there is a large signal-to-noise ratio, and we will use methods that are very sensitive to changes in the data. Alternatively, if we believe that there will be only relatively small changes in one variable with respect to another and that large fluctuations are the effect of random errors, then we will be best served by methods that are relatively insensitive to fluctuations.

We will further discuss nonparametric data used to create these plots but first, we will stop and discuss extensions of the linear model to nonlinear relationships.

Extending the linear framework

As discussed in the previous chapter, the basic idea underlying linear regression is that some variables' values can be predicted by the following equation describing a line:

$$Y = \alpha + B_1 X_1 + B_2 X_2 + B_3 X_3 + \ldots$$

Here, the dependent variable Y has a linear relationship with a set of X values (that is, X values that are all raised to the power of 1). Of course, the various X values themselves can be nonlinear functions of other predictor variables; thus, by performing linear regression on nonlinear transformations of predictor variables we will be able to model nonlinear relationships in between variables.

Polynomial regression

The simplest way to extend the linear framework to nonlinear relationships is through polynomial regression. The idea here is that some of the predictor variables are squared or cubed, and the squares or cubes of these predictor variables are themselves treated as distinct predictors. For example, let's say that we want to fit a second degree polynomial, as shown by the equation:

$$Y = \alpha + B_1 X_1 + B_2 X_2 + B_3 X_2^2$$

This is not a linear regression formula but we can make it one by declaring a new variable B_3 and setting it equal to X_2^2, as shown in the following equation:

$$Y = \alpha + B_1 X_1 + B_2 X_2 + B_3 X_3$$

In the preceding equation,

$$X_3 = X_2^2$$

This way, we simply solve α, B_1, B_2, and B_3 as we would in typical least squares linear regression.

Performing a polynomial regression in R

As can be visually seen in the previous plots, the relationship between height and age is clearly nonlinear. For starters, we just fit a line to the data to see what we get:

```
fit.linear <- lm(height ~ age)
summary(fit.linear)
```

Based on the R-squared value of 0.304, it might at first appear that a linear model fits the data well. We know that this is not true because visual inspection of the data, prior to model fitting, showed nonlinear data. The line fit to our dataset clearly misses the key features of the change in height in youth followed by a tapering of height in older age. Thus, it is a poor height versus age model, shown by:

```
plot(age, height, pch = 16, col = 'gray', xlab = 'Age', ylab =
'Height', main = 'Height vs Age')
points(age, fit.linear$fitted, pch = 16, cex = 0.1)
```

The result is shown in the following plot:

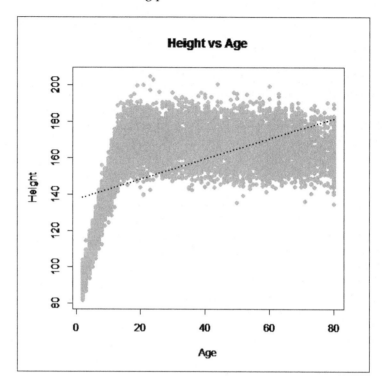

This can also be seen using visual methods for regression diagnostics. Here, we will focus on the residuals versus fitted plots, which we will compare subsequent models against, as shown in the following code:

```
plot(fit.linear, which = 1)
```

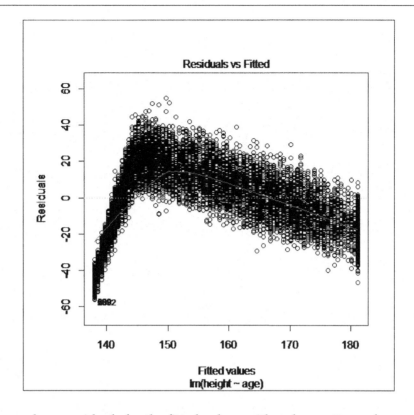

Here, we see large residuals for the fitted values with a clear pattern of very negative, then very positive followed by somewhat negative residuals.

How can we then fit a model in the absence of a theoretical formula relating these two variables? The answer is polynomial regression. This is in fact a kind of linear regression but the regression is performed on a combination of basis functions of x, where each basis function raises X to a higher level power.

Unfortunately, we don't actually know what kind of polynomial is required, so we will start with low order polynomials and advance. We use the function I() to tell R that the contents inside the parentheses are a mathematical function that should be interpreted independently and passed to the regression formula, as follows:

```
fit.quadratic <- lm(height ~ age + I(age^2))
plot(fit.quadratic, which = 1)
fit.cubic <- lm(height ~ age + I(age^2)+ I(age^3))
plot(fit.cubic, which = 1)
```

```
fit.quartic <- lm(height ~ age + I(age^2)+ I(age^3)+ I(age^4))
plot(fit.quartic, which = 1)
fit.quintic <- lm(height ~ age + I(age^2)+ I(age^3)+ I(age^4)+
I(age^5))
plot(fit.quintic, which = 1)
fit.sextic <- lm(height ~ age + I(age^2)+ I(age^3)+ I(age^4)+
I(age^5)+ I(age^6))
plot(fit.sextic, which = 1)
fit.septic <- lm(height ~ age + age + I(age^2)+ I(age^3)+ I(age^4)+
I(age^5) + I(age^6)+ I(age^7))
plot(fit.septic, which = 1)
```

For the sake of saving space, we don't show all of the plots; however, as can be seen in the following diagram, with each higher order polynomial, the residuals versus fitted plot improves:

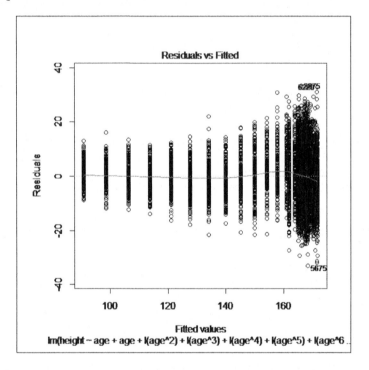

The approach of fitting high order polynomials might seem difficult to many readers to stomach for a variety of reasons. To begin with, it might just intuitively seem ridiculous. Additionally, once you get to a fourth order polynomial, it is not clear whether higher order polynomials are any better. However, we still had to get to a fourth order polynomial in our data modeling exercise. It is generally recommended to use polynomials of no more than cubic order to avoid the problem of nonconvergence.

Nonconvergence is a problem in many estimation algorithms, and a problem of high order polynomials in particular. Practically speaking, this problem can result in a polynomial that produces wildly fluctuating interpolated values. This can generally be avoided if no term in the polynomial is raised to a power higher than three. The problem lies in the distribution of interpolation points. Try the following code illustrating Runge's phenomenon (a prototypical example of the noncovergence problem), as an example:

Using data that has equally spaced interpolation points, as shown in the following code:

```
runge <- function(x) {return(1/(1+x^2))}
x<-seq(-5,5, 0.5)
y <- runge(x)
plot(y~x)
fit.runge <- lm(y~x+I(x^2)+I(x^3)+I(x^4)+I(x^5)+I(x^6))
lines(fit.runge$fitted ~ x)
```

The circles represent the actual points of the function, which one's intuition might suggest is a simple bell-shaped curve but the polynomial curve fit to these points oscillates wildly at the edges.

We can reduce this fluctuation by giving more interpolation points at the extremes of the interpolation interval using data with a high density of points at the extremes and a few points in the middle, as follows:

```
x2<-c(seq(-5,-4.05, 0.05),seq(-4, 4, 1), seq(4.05, 5, 0.05))
y2 <- runge(x2)
fit.runge.2 <- lm(y2~x2+I(x2^2)+I(x2^3)+I(x2^4)+I(x2^5)+I(x2^6))
lines(fit.runge.2$fitted ~ x2, col = 'red')
```

This technique helps to deal with noncovergence in made-up data, in which we get to choose interpolation points. Unfortunately, with real data, we don't get to choose where our interpolation points lie, so this solution can't be used.

The truth is that the relationship that we graphically see does not look like any common polynomial, and as such, it is really a bit unfair to apply polynomial regression to height versus age for all ages. A better approach might be to acknowledge that there are likely to be two distinct regimes; one in which people are growing and maturing and the other in which their growth has leveled off and might be declining. Let's start by breaking the sample into two age groups:

- Those up to the age of 18, whom we expect to be growing
- Those over the age of 18, for whom we expect growth has completed

The following code is used to break the samples:

```
detach(body.measures)
youths <- which(body.measures$age %in% c(2:18))
adults <- which(body.measures$age %in% c(19:80))
body.measures.youths <- body.measures[youths,]
body.measures.adults <- body.measures[adults,]
attach(body.measures.youths)
plot(height ~ age)
```

The result is shown in the following plot:

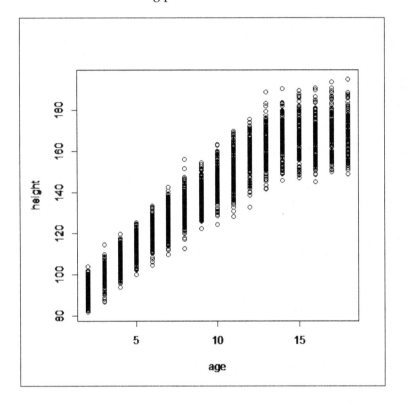

We can understand from the previous plot that there is a curvilinear relationship between age and height. Furthermore, a visual inspection shows that this sort of curve looks like the kind that might be amenable to polynomial modeling. Let's have a look at the following code:

```
fit.cubic.youths <- lm(height ~ age + I(age^2) + I(age^3))
plot(fit.cubic.youths, which = 1)
```

Here, we see a nice plot of residuals versus fitted, with residuals simply showing random errors rather than an organized pattern of misfit. Let's look at how the predicted model looks in comparison to the data:

```
plot(age, height, pch = 16, col = 'gray', xlab = 'Age', ylab =
'Height', main = 'Height vs Age (in youths)')
points(fit.cubic.youths$fitted ~ age, pch = 16, cex = 1)
```

The result is shown in the following code:

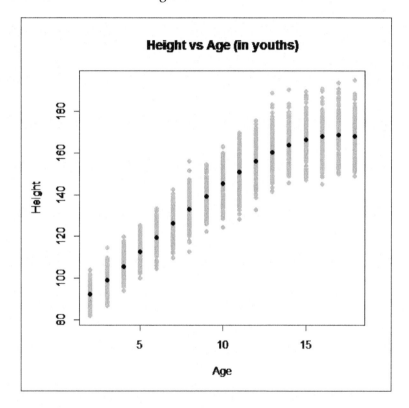

We can also look at the standard model parameters and the proportion of variance explained, which suggests that this cubic spline has an R-squared of 0.93 (excellent value. We can use the same summary command as we did in linear regression (explained in *Chapter 3, Linear Models*):

```
summary(fit.cubic.youths)
```

We could then repeat the same procedure for those aged 19 and above:

```
detach(body.measures.youths)
attach(body.measures.adults)
fit.cubic.adults <- lm(height ~ age + I(age^2)+ I(age^3))
plot(age, height, pch = 16, col = 'gray', xlab = 'Age', ylab =
'Height', main = 'Height vs Age (in adults)')
points(fit.cubic.adults$fitted ~ age, pch = 16, cex = 1)
```

The result is shown in the following plot:

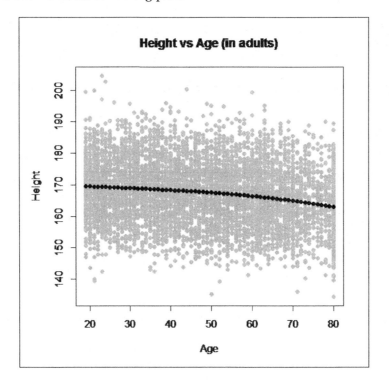

We have, in effect, created two different functions for predicting height: one for those aged 18 and under and one for those aged 19 and older. This regression approach is the basic idea of splines.

Spline regression

To fit curve relationships without high degree polynomials, we can use splines. A spline is essentially a piece-wise function in which the regression formula changes based on the X value. There are a large number of approaches to splines and fortunately R has more sophisticated approaches than our previous approach.

Each point where there is a break in the regression function is called a "knot". Our previous approach had a single knot located at 18 to 19 years. In our piece-wise regression, the value at 18 and the estimated value at 19 could be completely different. True splines stipulate that there can be a continuous function at each knot.

As hinted at the beginning of this chapter, the role of nonlinear methods is debatable and as we progressed, we started to use models in a lesser theory-driven fashion and more in an exploratory manner. In line with this progression, splines make use of a parametric framework but they break the data into pieces to do this, so it takes more than just a few parameters to summarize a function.

One of the most straightforward functions for fitting splines in R is the `smooth.spline` function available in the R base. To demonstrate this, we will go back to the full dataset, as follows:

```
detach(body.measures.adults)
attach(body.measures)
fit.spline.smooth <- smooth.spline(height ~ age, nknots = 4)
plot(age, height, pch = 16, col = 'gray', xlab = 'Age', ylab =
'Height', main = 'Height vs Age')
lines(fit.spline.smooth, pch = 16)
```

The result is shown in the following plot:

This gives us a smooth representation of the plot that appears to fit the quirks in the data. However, it does not tell us anything about the mathematical properties of the data, making it most well suited for exploratory analyses.

Nonparametric nonlinear methods

We will begin by taking a moment to consider linear models in a very general context, since, many nonlinear models can be seen as a generalization of their linear counterparts.

We traditionally see the linear model expressed as an equation giving a variable Y in terms of a linear prediction terms BX, as follows:

$$Y = \alpha + BX$$

The equation is the classic algebraic formula describing a line. However, we can describe regression, linear or otherwise, in a more general framework. What if we don't actually know the formula to relate Y and X to one another? We can still predict Y value for a given X value without any idea about the algebraic relationship between Y and X, so long as we simply rely on the observed X and Y values for predictions of Y given X, by taking the mean of observed Y values for any given X value:

$$\hat{m}(x) = E(Y_x) = \frac{1}{n_x} \sum_{i=1}^{n_x} Y_i$$

The previous formula is a kind of point-wise regression, specifically point-wise mean regression. We define an $\hat{m}(x)$ function, which is equal to the expected value of Y for a given value of X and this expected value is equal to the mean of all observed Y values for that particular value of X. The estimated value of Y for one particular X value is completely independent of the estimated value of Y for all other X values. We can implement a function to do this kind of regression in R relatively easily, as follows:

```
pointwise.regression <- function(x, y) {
..X <- c(min(x):max(x))
..Y <- vector('numeric', length(X))
..for (i in X) {
....Y[i-min(x)+1] <- mean(y[x == i])
..}
..return.frame <- data.frame(X, Y)
..return(return.frame)
}
```

This function takes two vectors of variables as inputs: x and y; extracts the mean value of y for each unique value of x and returns a data frame with each x and its corresponding mean y values. (Note the capitalization of x versus X and y versus Y in the function.)

There are a number of ways to use loops in R to iteratively construct data objects with multiple members (for example, vectors, data frames, or matrices). In general, the slowest way to do this is to lengthen the data object in each iteration, because this method requires reallocating the data object in the system memory with each iteration to accommodate the larger sized object. A much faster method is to simply create a data object of the required length and insert the appropriate values into their positions in the data object.

Using our point-wise regression function, we can create a plot of the mean expected height for each age value. By plotting lines based on these data points, R will connect each of the estimated points with a short straight line segment and we will, in a sense, have a nonparametric curve describing the trend in the data, as follows:

```
expected.height <- pointwise.regression(age, height)
plot(age, height, pch = 16, col = 'gray', xlab = 'Age', ylab =
'Height', main = 'Height vs Age')
lines(expected.height)
```

The result is shown in the following plot:

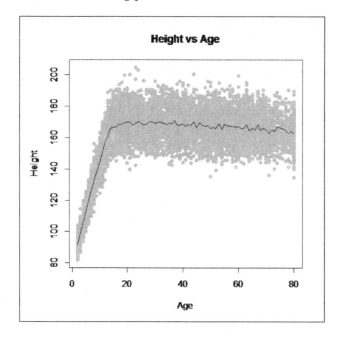

We can, of course, easily extend our point-wise regression function to put out a data frame with 95 percent confidence intervals of the estimated Y values based on the t-distribution or distribution of our choice:

```
pointwise.confint <- function(x, y) {
X <- c(min(x):max(x))
Y.list <- list('numeric', length(X))
for (i in X) {
t.temp <- t.test(y[x == i])
Y.list[[(i-min(x)+1)]] <- c(t.temp$estimate[[1]], t.temp$conf.int[1],
t.temp$conf.int[2])
}
```

```
Y.mat <- do.call('rbind', Y.list)
return.frame <- data.frame(cbind(X, Y.mat))
names(return.frame) <- c('X', 'Y', 'Lower.Y', 'Upper.Y')
return(return.frame)
}
```

We will further discuss that there are other, often more useful, methods to model nonlinear relationships in data but the `pointwise.confint` function is useful because it is easily extensible; the elements of `Y.list` can be filled with any set of functions that the user would like.

Point-wise regression is a term that is not often used within data analysis but it is quite commonly used as a visual tool, going under names such as "box and whisker plots" or "candlestick charts". R contains a base function for doing box and whisker plots:

```
boxplot(height ~ age, xlab = 'Age', ylab = 'Height', main = 'Height vs
Age')
```

The result is shown in the following plot:

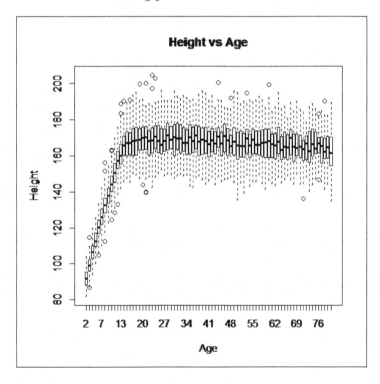

The box and whisker plots have a rectangular box at each X value. The line through the middle of that box is the median, and the bottom and top of the box are the values of the first and third quartiles respectively. The whiskers, by default, extend out 1.5 times the interquartile range (that is, 1.5 times the length of the box), and the individual points represent outliers.

The `boxplot` command in R can take the `add` = `TRUE` argument, which will add the `boxplot` command to an already existing plot. However, the `boxplot` command will not line up with the existing plot unless X values for the pre-existing plot have started at one. If they have started at some other value, then the `at` argument must be passed to `boxplot`, as follows:

```
plot(height ~ age, col = 'gray', pch = 16, xlim = c(2,
80), xlab = '', ylab = '', xaxt = 'n')
boxplot(height ~ age, xlab = 'Age', ylab = 'Height',
main = 'Height vs Age', add = TRUE, at = c(2:80))
```

The most notable feature of this point-wise approach to value estimation or the use of box and whisker plots is that it treats estimated Y values for each X value as completely independent of all Y values for all other X values. Of course, this is likely to ignore important information—a 50 year old male who is 5 feet tall today might have been 5'1" last year but he was likely not 6 feet tall. As such, it makes sense to model the Y value at any given X as having some relationship with adjacent X values as well. We do this by assuming a function, w, to describe the relationship between the observed data points. This adds an additional assumption to the model by requiring that the estimated Y value for each X value be tied somehow to the estimated Y value for other X values.

$$\hat{m}(x) = \sum_{i=1}^{n} w \cdot Y_i$$

If we define w as follows (note the variance term in the denominator), we get a line:

$$w = \frac{(x_i - \bar{x})x}{n \cdot \sum_{i=1}^{n}(x_i - \bar{x})^2}$$

In the next sections, we will discuss the use of weighting functions that relate Y at a given X to neighboring X values as well.

Point-wise regression will capture every kink in the direction of the relationship between two variables. This is good if we think every kink is important but more often than not, these kinks reflect sample-specific errors, which is why weighting functions are useful.

Kernel regression

Kernel smoothing regression is a flexible method to fit a smooth curve to nonlinear data. Instead of estimating the expected Y value at each X value as a function of that particular X alone, it uses a weighted distribution of surrounding points. How these surrounding points are weighted is determined by the particular kernel chosen.

As discussed in the earlier section on theory, regression can be thought of as a function of the sum of observed Y values multiplied by a w function. In the case of kernel density regression, the formula for the Nadaraya-Watson kernel regression formula can be expressed, as follows:

$$\hat{m}(x) = \frac{\sum_{i=1}^{n} K\left(\frac{x_i - \overline{x}}{h}\right) y_i}{\sum_{i=1}^{n} K\left(\frac{x_i - \overline{x}}{h}\right)}$$

In the preceding formula, K is a kernel function, and h is the bandwidth (that is, the smoothing parameter). For example, to apply Gaussian kernel smoothing, we use the probability density function for the normal distribution to describe K. The bandwidth can be either fixed or based on the nearest neighbors. A fixed bandwidth uses all points within the defined range while a nearest neighbor's bandwidth uses a proportion of the sample closest to the point of interest to create estimates. For example, if we used a kernel that weighted all values equally on the height versus age data, then a fixed bandwidth of 10 would be tantamount to estimating the height at a given age as the mean height for all ages within 10 years of the age of interest. Alternatively, if we applied the same kernel to a nearest neighbor's bandwidth of 0.25, then we would be estimating the height of someone at a given age as the mean height of the 25 percent of the sample closest the age of interest.

To apply kernel regression based on the Nadaraya-Watson formula in R, the simplest method is to use the built-in R function `ksmooth`, which uses fixed window bandwidths. This might be thought of as a variant of point-wise regression in an earlier section, in which the estimated Y value is not estimated based on a single point but on a group of adjacent points:

```
smooth.height <- ksmooth(age, height, bandwidth = 10, kernel =
'normal')
```

There are two notable arguments that we explicitly define here in addition to the arguments referencing the data, the bandwidth (h in the previous equation) and the kernel function (K in the previous equation). The bandwidth argument tells R how wide the "local" area is over which we want to regress data points. The `ksmooth` function requires manually declaring this bandwidth; larger bandwidths mean smoother curves and less chance of modeling noise, while smaller bandwidths can result in rougher curves. The choice of appropriate bandwidth is obviously an important concern. Here, a bandwidth of 10 has been arbitrarily chosen but methods for creating "optimal" bandwidths have been described and have implementations in R, which we will discuss shortly.

The kernel argument here is declared as "normal". The other kernel option is "box" (often called a "rectangular" kernel elsewhere). A normal kernel means that R samples the data with weights in a Gaussian distribution, while a box kernel means that R samples all points in the bandwidth with the same weight and all points outside of the bandwidth with a weight of zero.

Let's take a look at how a curve generated with kernel density regression fits the data. We will also ensure that the second plot looks a little cleaner, so that we can actually see the curve:

```
plot(age, height, xlab = 'Age', ylab = 'Height', main = 'Height vs Age
in Males', col = 'gray', pch = 16)
lines(smooth.height, col = 'red')
```

The result is as shown in the following plot:

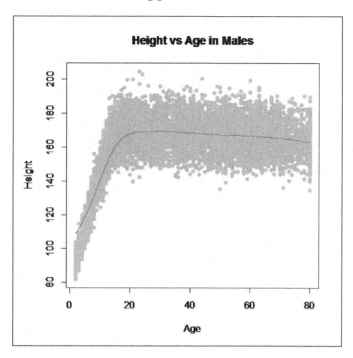

The curve in the previous diagram appears to fit the data relatively well but it might not completely meet our needs. As indicated earlier, one of the reasons to use nonlinear methods is because a better fit to the data is required than what a linear model can provide, and while this curve fits the data relatively well, it appears to over-estimate height for those close to the minimum age. This is caused by excess smoothing, which we can ameliorate by decreasing the bandwidth:

```
plot(age, height, xlab = 'Age', ylab = 'Height', main = 'Height vs
Age', col = 'gray', pch = 16)
smooth.height <- ksmooth(age, height, bandwidth = 2, kernel =
'normal')
lines(smooth.height, col = 'red')
```

The result is as shown in the following plot:

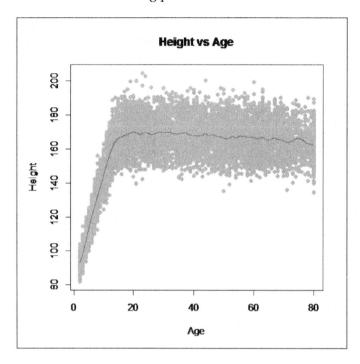

After a few tries, it looks like a bandwidth of about two seems to match the data better, but now it appears to model noise in the data as well. The small decline in height that we previously saw in those of an advanced age is not so evident even now. Before discussing what can be done about this, it is worth taking a moment to think about what we are doing.

We know that children start out at a low height, grow until the end of puberty, and then remain the same height for most of their adult lives with perhaps a small loss of height as they reach advanced ages. We are trying to match a curve to our a-priori expectations about height and age. Notably, we have some expectations about the relationship between these two variables in general, but we also have some expectations about how the relationship between these two variables behaves within very narrow windows. The ksmooth function, unfortunately, only allows us to adjust the overall behavior of the kernel density estimator, which means that we are forced to choose between matching the curve to our general expectations or our very local expectations, however, we are unable to do both.

Kernel weighted local polynomial fitting

We previously discussed the R command `ksmooth`, which implements the Nadaraya-Watson kernel density regression function; it is a fast and simple way to identify trends in data with no a-priori knowledge or assumptions about the algebraic form of those trends. However, if we wish to do kernel smoothing regression that allows us to incorporate specific expectations about the relationship between the two variables for particular ranges of values, we will need to turn to the `locpoly` command in the `KernSmooth` package.

The `locpoly` command extends traditional kernel regression; rather than simply using a weighted mean of values as it is done in `ksmooth`, it uses kernel density weighted local polynomial regression. We will discuss polynomial regression further in this chapter but for now, we will point out that polynomial regression is basically like linear regression, except that you fit a curve with quadratic, cubic, or higher power terms. Typically, quadratic polynomials are used in kernel weighted regression but we could use linear terms or even zero-order terms, which would be identical to the traditional Nadaraya-Watson estimator.

A practical advantage that `locpoly` provides is that it allows us to assign bandwidths locally along the range of values of the variables that we are examining. In essence, we wish to be sensitive to height differences between years in the first two decades of life because we think that height differences here represent a real phenomenon, and we wish to be insensitive to differences in height between people of various ages for those beyond 20 years because we suspect that this largely reflects random errors. In kernel density estimation, this is achieved by adjusting the bandwidth, so we need a way to assign different bandwidths to different ages, which we can do with the `locpoly` command, which also uses fixed window bandwidths. This is shown by the following code:

```
library(KernSmooth)
plot(age, height, xlab = 'Age', ylab = 'Height', main = 'Height vs
Age', col = 'gray', pch = 16)
bandwidth.vals <- c(rep(1, 20), rep(5, 30))
smooth.height <- locpoly(age, height, gridsize = 50, bandwidth =
bandwidth.vals)
lines(smooth.height, col = 'red')
```

The `locpoly` command takes a few additional arguments that are not used in `ksmooth`, which we take advantage of here. In particular, we no longer specify a single bandwidth to be used over the entire range of *x* values but can now declare bandwidths to be as wide or narrow as we would like over the range of x values. The `gridsize` argument tells R how many equally spaced points the kernel estimation will be performed at; we must have a vector of bandwidths with the same length as the `gridsize` argument, in this case 50. We set the bandwidth of the first 20 points as one, and the bandwidth of the last 30 points as zero, effectively being very sensitive to changes in height at early ages and relatively insensitive at later ages. The curve that this gives us is still a little jagged but overall it appears to capture what we would likely regard as the salient features of the dataset: an increasing height in the first 15 to 20 years of life, followed by a rapid plateau in height, and a slight loss of height in later years.

A wider bandwidth effectively increases the sample size for kernel estimation at any given point. Therefore, it is also worth examining the number of individuals at each point, as can be done with the `hexbin` command, mentioned in the tip given prior to setting local bandwidths. In this case, the density of individuals represented on the left-hand side of the plot is relatively high but if there were relatively few individuals, it is not clear whether this would have worked as well.

Optimal bandwidth selection

So far, we have been tinkering with bandwidth values to get a desired curve—a perfectly reasonable approach to exploring relationships in data but an approach that hardly seems scientific. While this approach to understanding relationships in data is more often used in science than many researchers would care to admit, it is still nice to have a more systematic method to choose an optimal bandwidth.

There have been a number of bandwidth selection methods described over the past few decades, one of which currently is a plug-in bandwidth estimator, which seeks to minimize the mean squared error. The `KernSmooth` package contains a function for providing an optimal bandwidth based on the plug-in estimator, which can be done with the `dpill` function. This function allows us to estimate either a single optimal bandwidth for the entire region for which regression is being done or different bandwidths for different regions. An alternative approach to select the optimal bandwidth is based on cross-validation, which can be done using the `npregbw` function in the `np` package.

Using `dpill` from the `KernSmooth` package, as follows:

```
h <- dpill(age, height, gridsize = 80)
plot(age, height, xlab = 'Age', ylab = 'Height', main = 'Height vs
Age', col = 'gray', pch = 16)
smooth.height <- locpoly(age, height, bandwidth = h, gridsize = 80,
kernel = 'normal')
lines(smooth.height, col = 'red')
```

The result is shown in the following plot:

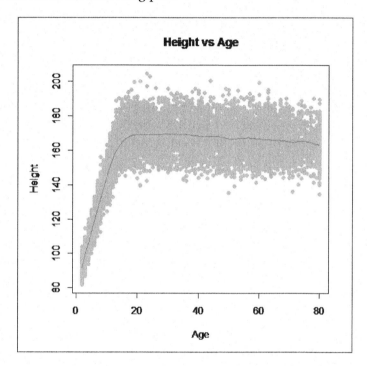

This does not give a perfectly smooth line but appears to adequately capture the trends in the data that we would expect to see, and it took no tinkering on our part to constrain the data to our preconceived notions.

Using cross-validation to select the optimal bandwidth is much more computationally intensive. As such, we will demonstrate it on a smaller subsample of this dataset in a subsequent section.

A practical scientific application of kernel regression

Thus far, we have used kernel smoothing regression only to visually explore and describe data rather than to address any specific scientific questions. Some might argue that this is how kernel smoothing is designed to be used, but nevertheless we will attempt to use kernel density regression to answer a particular question: At what age does growth slow down?

Operationally, this question is a matter of the second derivative of the function of height versus age. The first derivative of this function is the velocity of growth (for example, how much a person grows each year), and the second derivative is the acceleration in growth. What we are interested in is the age at which growth is decelerating the most. Since we know that men and women tend to hit puberty at different ages, we should probably separate them out and check if the growth of women slows down at a younger age than the growth of men. Luckily, the `locpoly` command supports this operation. We specify with the `drv` argument that we are interested in the second derivative (that is, acceleration):

```
> smooth.height.2.males <- locpoly(age[gender ==1], height[gender ==
1], drv = 2, bandwidth = h, gridsize = 80, kernel = 'normal')
> smooth.height.2.males$x[smooth.height.2.males$y == min(smooth.
height.2.males$y)]
[1] 13.8481
> smooth.height.2.females <- locpoly(age[gender ==2], height[gender ==
2], drv = 2, bandwidth = h, gridsize = 80, kernel = 'normal')
> smooth.height.2.females$x[smooth.height.2.females$y == min(smooth.
height.2.females$y)]
[1] 11.87342
```

These results suggest that women do, in fact, have their growth slow down at a younger age than men, as we expected.

Like point-wise regression, weighted regression can be used for exploratory analyses, albeit with a weighting function that allows some smoothing of the noise in the data. The addition of this weighting function also allows us to gain some insights into the relationship in the data beyond simple plotting.

Locally weighted polynomial regression and the loess function

In the previous section, we discussed methods to fit nonlinear data but the methods that we discussed are applicable only in cases in which we wish to model the relationship between two variables. In real data analysis, we often wish to model the relationship between a larger number of variables or model an outcome as a function of a number of predictors. For this, the `ksmooth()` and `locpoly()` functions simply won't do as they are limited to comparing only two variables. However, as we will see, R has a built-in function, `loess`, which is able to support kernel regression in multiple dimensions.

The `loess` command has a number of distinct differences between the kernel smoothing methods described earlier. Chiefly, `loess` uses a bandwidth based on nearest neighbors rather than a fixed bandwidth.

While we focus here on the `loess` command, R also contains a similar function, `lowess`, which is the predecessor to `loess` and does not support multiple predictor variables. The `loess` command can model up to four predictor variables and handle a Guaussian or rectangular kernel. Alternatively, `lowess` can only handle a single predictor variable and only supports a tricubic kernel.

We can model weight as a function of height and age. We will do this modeling here in the same manner as we declare a linear regression model (in this case only on males), as follows:

```
male.weight <- weight[gender == 1]
male.age <- age[gender == 1]
male.height <- height[gender == 1]
weight.fit <- loess(male.weight ~ male.age * male.height, span = 1,
family = 'gaussian')
```

We can then use the model named `weight.fit`, which we created to estimate the expected weight of a person for a given age and height. However, unlike linear regression, which gives us a simple formula that we can compute by hand, knowing only a few coefficients, we will have to rely on the software to give us predictions for a potentially highly nonlinear model. To do this, we use the `predict` command and then plot the surface created but before we can do this, we must give new values to `predict` for use. By looking at the `fit.vals` object, we can get the raw estimated values for each age and height, as follows:

```
age.vals <- seq(from = 2, to = 85, by = 1)
height.vals <- seq(from =80, to = 200, by = 1)
predicted.weight <- predict(weight.fit, newdata = expand.grid(male.age
= age.vals, male.height = height.vals))
persp(age.vals, height.vals, predicted.weight, theta = 40, xlab =
'Age', ylab = 'Height', zlab = 'Weight')
```

The result is as shown in the following plot:

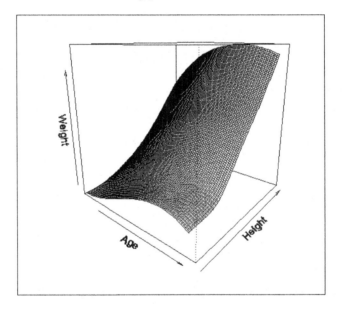

We can adjust the view on the plot to see the effects of multiple dimensions by changing the theta argument of the `persp` command. In this case, a value of 40 seems to work well.

Generally, in science, we want to know more than the estimate of a value; we also want to have a confidence interval telling us the potential range of values within a given probability window (often 95 percent). The `loess` command is not able to do this with multiple predictors but the `npreg` command from the `np` package does have this capability.

Nonparametric methods with the np package

A very powerful R package, which is able to perform most of the functions mentioned earlier plus some others, has been developed and titled np. This package offers many powerful functions but some users might find it inconvenient to use because of the computationally intensive nature of many of the functions contained within it.

Nonlinear quantile regression

We have so far attempted to fit a curve or surface to data points to either understand the basic trend in the data or come up with a general estimate of a dependent variable based on one or two independent variables. However, what if we want to create regression curves to figure out where a member of the population ranks in comparison to others within the population? This kind of task is routinely carried out with height and weight data in the form of pediatric growth charts that are used to monitor development during routine visits to the pediatrician. The basic idea is that instead of fitting one curve to a dataset, multiple curves, each representing a particular quantile, can be fit. We will use the npqreg command from the np package to do this.

First, we will create a data frame of only those within a certain age (from age 2 to 10 in this case) and place them in a new data frame, as follows:

```
detach(body.measures)
juveniles <- which(body.measures$age %in% c(2:10))
body.measures.juveniles.1 <- body.measures[juveniles,]
```

The npqreg command works best with data that has been ordered, so we will sort the data frame by year of age and store this in a new data frame, which we will use for the data analysis.

```
attach(body.measures.juveniles.1)
body.measures.juveniles.2 <- body.measures.juveniles.1[order(age),]
detach(body.measures.juveniles.1)
attach(body.measures.juveniles.2)
```

Now, we can use the body measures from this data frame to generate quantile curves for the 10th, 25th, 50th, 75th, and 90th percentiles and plot them. First, we will calculate the optimal bandwidth and then compute the quantile curves. These steps can be computationally intensive, which is why for this demonstration, we are restricting the age to those from two to ten:

```
library(np)
bw.est <- npcdistbw(formula=height~age)
```

```
qreg.10th <- npqreg(bws=bw.est, tau=0.1)
qreg.25th <- npqreg(bws=bw.est, tau=0.25)
qreg.50th <- npqreg(bws=bw.est, tau=0.5)
qreg.75th <- npqreg(bws=bw.est, tau=0.75)
qreg.90th <- npqreg(bws=bw.est, tau=0.9)
```

We can now plot the results, as follows:

```
plot(height ~ age, type = 'n', xlab = 'Age', ylab = 'Height', main =
'Quantiles of Age for Height',xaxp = c(2,10,(10-2)), yaxp = c(80,160,
(160-80)/10))
abline(h=seq(80,160, 10), v=2:10, col='gray', lty=3)
lines(qreg.10th$quantile ~ age)
lines(qreg.25th$quantile ~ age)
lines(qreg.50th$quantile ~ age)
lines(qreg.75th$quantile ~ age)
lines(qreg.90th$quantile ~ age)
```

The result is as shown in the following plot:

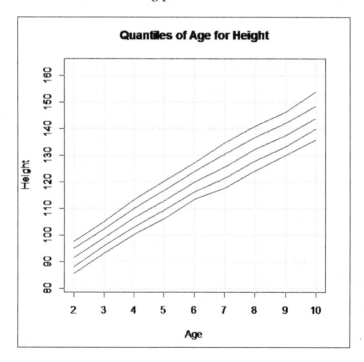

The previous diagram shows the curves representing the 10th, 25th, 50th, 75th, and 90th percentiles of height at each year of age. This could be repeated for a larger range of ages for a picture that highlights the nonlinear nature of this relationship at the cost of significantly increased computational intensity.

Summary

In this chapter, we reviewed applications of nonlinear methods in R using parametric and nonparametric methods for both theory-driven and exploratory analyses. As we reviewed, R has many excellent built-in functions for this, namely, `nls`, `lm`, `ksmooth`, and `loess`. There are additional functions available in a number of packages including `KernSmooth` and `np`. The np package is possibly the most capable of all packages discussed in this chapter but it offers this flexibility at the cost of high computational (and syntactic) resources, limiting its use in quickly exploring relationships in data.

In the subsequent chapters, we will focus on linear methods, first by reviewing linear algebra. This will be followed by two chapters on topics which make heavy use of linear algebra for model-based statistical analysis.

5

Linear Algebra

Linear algebra has been described as the mathematics of computer science, and this chapter will be a bit different from prior chapters. Prior chapters discussed topics such as regression and statistical significance tests, and techniques that can directly be applied to a dataset to produce a solution of interest. A single linear algebra technique in isolation rarely provides a solution of interest to a substantive researcher. However, many numerical analysis techniques rely on linear algebra and matrix operations, making them an important part of scientific computing.

In this chapter, we will discuss the following topics:

- Matrix properties
- Mathematical operations on matrices
- Matrix inversion
- Solving linear systems
- Eigenvalues and eigenvectors
- LU decomposition
- Singular value decomposition of a matrix
- Choleski decomposition of a matrix
- Outer products
- Applications of linear algebra using R

Matrices and linear algebra

In mathematics, matrices are simply an organized table of numbers. The reason they are used is because scientists and mathematicians have found that some numerical problems (generally systems of equations) can be solved algorithmically when the data placed into the problem is organized this way. In mathematics, a row or column of a matrix is termed a "vector", though R has a vector data structure that is not the same thing as the row or column of a matrix. The numbers characterizing a vector in mathematics are thought of as the endpoint of that vector with vector's origin at the origin of the coordinate system (this is what we term a "vector" mathematically, but it is really a point).

While the term "matrix" is often used to refer to a rectangular arrangement for string data (that is, a table), we must be much more cautious with our use of the term in numeric computation since R has more than one way to store composite variables.

Matrices in R

While data analysts often load a dataset from an external file into a data frame, which looks like a matrix at first glance, a matrix has a number of defining features, mentioned as follows:

- Matrices can store the data of only a single data type (for example, we can't mix floating point numbers and categorical data in a single matrix)
- Matrices are more memory-efficient in R
- Data frames allow us to call values by the name of the variable, but they are a special instance of the list rather than a matrix
- Matrix operations tend to require a matrix as input and do not allow data frames
- R's matrix operations are often one hundred times faster than data frame operations

To convert a data frame into a matrix, we use the `as.matrix` function, which will require that all data elements be of the same data type.

Vectors in R

A vector data structure in R means something slightly different than a vector data structure in mathematics. In mathematics, a vector can either be a column vector or a row vector, but in R, a vector has no dimensions. Let's take a look at the following examples:

```
> a <- c(1,2,3,4)
```

```
> b <- matrix(a, nrow = 1)
> a
[1] 1 2 3 4
> b
     [,1] [,2] [,3] [,4]
[1,]    1    2    3    4
```

As we can see, both a and b store the same values, but R recognizes columns and rows for b, something that it does not do for a. However, if we were to apply a in a linear algebraic operation, R would treat it as a column vector.

Matrix notation

We typically refer to a matrix as an *m x n* data structure with *m* rows and *n* columns. There a few different kinds of matrices that we will define, as follows:

- **Rectangular**: Arguably, all matrices are some type of a rectangular matrix. The matrix command defines a square matrix with the number of specified rows and columns. To create a two-row matrix filled with the numbers 1 to 24, we will use the following code:

  ```
  matrix(c(1:24), nrow = 2)
  ```

  Alternatively, we can also specify the number of columns as follows:

  ```
  matrix(c(1:24), ncol = 12)
  ```

- **Square**: This is a rectangular matrix in which *m* is equal to *n*. Many commonly used matrix operations can only be done on a square matrix.

- **Diagonal**: This is a square matrix in which all elements are zero, except for the elements along the diagonal. R has a special function to create diagonal matrices, in which we specify the values to the diagonal, and the number of rows and columns. R will apply this command even if column and row dimensions do not match, as follows:

  ```
  diag(c(1:3), 3, 3)
  ```

- **Triangular**: The elements either above the diagonal or below the diagonal (but not necessarily including the diagonal) are all equal to zero. There are upper and lower triangular matrices that refer to whether the non-zero side is the upper or lower side, respectively. We will cover triangular matrices in detail in the *Triangular matrices* section in this chapter, shortly.

- **Symmetric**: This is a matrix in which each (*m*, *n*) element is equal to the corresponding (*n*, *m*) element (that is, reversing the rows and columns of the matrix will yield the same matrix).

- **Identity**: This is a diagonal matrix in which the diagonal is filled with 1s. Any matrix multiplied by its identity matrix will be equal to the original matrix (that is, multiplying a matrix by its identity matrix is like multiplying a number by 1). An identity matrix can be easily created in R, using the `diag()` function and passing only the dimensions to it as follows:

```
diag(5)
```

- **Vector**: Mathematically speaking, this is a matrix with either a width of one or a height of one, termed column matrix and row matrix, respectively. In R, a vector can be created either as a one-dimensional matrix or using the R's `c()` function, which will coerce all elements to be of the same data type.

- **Sparse matrix**: This term refers to a matrix that is mostly composed of zeros. Alternatively, a dense matrix is mostly filled with values. These matrices are commonly used as design matrices for mathematical functions, which will be explained in further detail in the following sections.

The physical functioning dataset

This chapter will use data from the **National Health and Nutrition Examination Survey (NHANES)**. This survey collects data in two year cycles for about 10,000 civilian community-dwelling Americans and is available on the CDC website at `http://www.cdc.gov/nchs/nhanes/nhanes_questionnaires.htm`. The cleaned dataset that we will use in this chapter is available on the Internet at `http://scholar.harvard.edu/gerrard/mastering-scientific-computation-r`. Please see the terms of use at the CDC's website. We will start by loading the dataset and creating a matrix from the data frame:

```
phys.func <- read.csv('phys_func.txt')[,c(-1)]
phys.func.mat <-  as.matrix(phys.func)
```

This dataset includes cleaned data from the years 2003 to 2010 with all missing values removed. Answers that were not missing but answered as unknown or refused have also been removed. Survey respondents are asked how much difficulty they have with the following 20 items (questions are paraphrased here):

- Managing money
- Walking for a quarter of a mile
- Walking up 10 steps
- Stooping, crouching, or kneeling
- Lifting or carrying 10 pounds
- Doing chores around the house

- Preparing meals
- Walking from one room to another
- Standing up from a chair
- Getting in or out of bed
- Eating
- Dressing
- Standing for two hours
- Sitting for two hours
- Reaching up overhead
- Grasping small objects
- Going out to spectator events
- Participating in social activities
- Relaxing at home
- Pushing or pulling large objects

Respondents give an answer between 1 and 5, with higher responses indicating more difficulty. As expected, most Americans expressed no difficulty in performing these activities.

Basic matrix operations

It is important to first point out that computational operations can be done on both whole matrices, termed "matrixwise operations", and on the individual elements of a matrix, termed "element-wise operations". Matrix addition or subtraction is simply a matter of the addition of, or subtraction from, each individual value in a matrix to the value in the corresponding location in another matrix, so matrixwise and element-wise operations are the same. However, matrix multiplication is different from element-wise multiplication of elements within a matrix.

Let's start by creating a correlation matrix of our physical functioning data and creating an abbreviated raw data matrix:

```
cor.mat <- matrix(cor(phys.func), ncol = 20)
phys.brief.mat <- as.matrix(phys.func[c(1:30),])
```

This dataset is categorical rather than ordinal and is far from being normally distributed, but as we will discuss in this chapter, on the common factor model, this may still be a legitimate way to handle the data.

We will now go over a few basic matrix operations with the two matrices stored as `cor.mat` and `phys.mat`, which are the correlation matrix and the first 10 observations in the raw data (stored as a matrix rather than a data frame), respectively. It is worth noting that `cor.mat` has the same height and width of 20, so it is a square matrix, while `phys.mat` has a height of 30 and width of 20, making it a rectangular matrix.

Element-wise matrix operations

The topics that will be covered in this section are matrix subtraction, matrix addition, and matrix sweep.

Matrix subtraction

Matrix addition is element-wise subtraction. We can use a simple operator to transform the values of a matrix by adding to each element individually. We can subtract the same value to or from each element of the matrix as follows:

```
phys.brief.mat   1
```

Matrix addition

We can add each element of the matrix to the corresponding element of a different matrix:

```
phys.brief.mat + matrix(rnorm(600), ncol = 20)
```

We can also divide (or multiply) a matrix by the standard deviation of the entire matrix:

```
phys.brief.mat / sd(phys.brief.mat)
```

Matrix sweep

What if we want to divide each column by the column standard deviation and subtract the respective column mean from each individual element? To do this, we either need to do some coding to perform operations on individual columns or use R's built-in functions.

R's sweep function will "sweep out" a value or summary statistic from a matrix. This particular function can be confusing, but in summary, we will tell R about the matrix we want to do the sweeping on; whether we want to apply the sweep to columns or rows, the statistic or value we want to sweep out, and how we want to sweep things out. For example, if we want to sweep out the mean of each column by subtracting the column mean from each element of a matrix, we will do the following:

```
mean.phys <- apply(phys.brief.mat, 2, mean)
phys.sweep.1 <- sweep(phys.brief.mat, 2, mean.phys, '-')
```

We can then divide each element in each column by the standard deviation of the column:

```
sd.phys <- apply(phys.sweep.1, 2, sd)
phys.sweep.2 <- sweep(phys.sweep.1, 2, sd.phys, '/')
#The zeroes will give one variable NaN responses
```

We actually did things the hard way here. This type of rescaling of matrices is done so often that R has actually a built-in command:

```
phys.scaled <- scale(phys.brief.mat, center = TRUE, scale = TRUE)
```

Likewise, column means can be calculated with the built-in function:

```
colMeans(phys.brief.mat)
```

We can see that this gives us essentially the exact same answer as the two-step sweep process we did previously, by performing an element-wise division (a number divided by itself is 1):

```
phys.sweep.2 / phys.scaled
```

Basic matrixwise operations

In the previous section, we reviewed how to apply an operation individually to each element of the matrix as if the matrix elements existed outside it. Here, we will go over the operations that involve the matrix as a whole.

Transposition

One of the simplest matrix operations is transposition, which switches columns and rows of a matrix, as follows:

$$\text{transpose}\left(\begin{bmatrix} a & b & c \\ d & e & f \end{bmatrix}\right) = \begin{bmatrix} a & d \\ b & e \\ c & f \end{bmatrix}$$

This can be easily performed in R using the following code:

```
t(phys.mat)
```

 The transposition of a matrix A is often denoted as A^T or as A'.

Matrix multiplication

To perform matrix multiplication with two matrices A and B, we multiply each element of each row in matrix A by each element of each column in matrix B, yielding a matrix with a height equal to matrix A's height and width equal to matrix B's width. The number of rows in A must match the number of columns in B. Unlike multiplication of two numbers, matrix multiplication is not commutative. The importance of this is that matrix multiplication allows us to decompose systems of linear equations into matrices.

Suppose, we have a system of three equations as follows:

$$ax_1 + bx_2 + cx_3 = 0$$
$$dx_1 + ex_2 + fx_3 = 0$$
$$gx_1 + hx_2 + ix_3 = 0$$

Then, we could rewrite this as the product of two matrices as follows:

$$\begin{bmatrix} a & b & c \\ d & e & f \\ g & h & i \end{bmatrix}\begin{bmatrix} x_1 \\ x_2 \\ x_3 \end{bmatrix} = 0$$

To perform matrix multiplication, we use the special matrix multiplier binary operator `%*%`. A toy example to demonstrate the non-commutativity of matrix multiplication is as follows:

```
A <- matrix(c(rep(2,3), rep(5,3)), ncol = 2, byrow = FALSE)
B <- matrix(c(1:16), nrow = 2, byrow = TRUE)
C <- matrix(1, ncol = 2, nrow =3 , byrow = FALSE)
A %*% B
B %*% A
C %*% A
A %*% t(C)
```

The second and third multiplication should give errors because A has more columns than B has rows. Matrix C, which is a perfectly valid matrix, cannot be multiplied by matrix A either because of the mismatch between rows and columns. This mismatch between rows and columns is called **non-conformable arguments** in R. The final multiplication does work because of the transposition of matrix C.

Multiplying square matrices for social networks

Let's say that we have a social networking site where some members follow others (and nobody follows themselves). We can represent this network as a matrix, with a value of one in the position where a person follows another person. For example, in the matrix describing six people in the following figure, we would say that person **1** is followed by persons **2**, **3**, and **5** because there is a 1 in the second, third, and fifth columns of the first row. We would say that person **2** is only followed by person **1** and follows everyone else except person **3**:

We can recreate this matrix in R as follows:

```
small.network <- matrix(c(0,1,1,0,1,0,1,0,1,0,0,0,1,0,0,1,0,1, 0, 1,
0, 0, 0, 1, 0, 1, 0, 1, 0, 0, 0, 1, 0, 0, 1, 0), nrow = 6, byrow =
TRUE)
```

We can take the sum of individual rows to figure out who is the most influential in this network because a sum of rows is simply the total number of followers a person has:

```
apply(small.network, 1, sum)
```

This suggests that persons **1** and **3** are equally influential, both with total counts of three, and persons **2**, **5**, and **6** are all equally influential with counts of two. However, we must consider that a person in a social network may be influential if they have second degree followers (that is their followers are followed). Conveniently, to determine how many second degree followers a person has, we simply have to multiply the matrix by itself:

```
> apply((small.network %*% small.network), 1, sum)
[1] 7 6 7 4 4 4
```

This tells us that person **2** is actually more influential than persons **5** and **6** when second degree relationships are considered. If we simply add the original matrix to the squared matrix, we can get the total number of first or second degree relationships:

```
apply((small.network %*% small.network + small.network), 1, sum)
```

Real social networks, of course, have much larger graphs. Just to demonstrate that R can handle much larger matrices, we will use a bigger example with 1,000 people (for which we will simulate some data):

```
set.seed(51)
social.network.mat <- matrix(sample(c(0,1), 1000000, replace = TRUE,
prob = c(0.7, 0.3)), ncol = 1000)
diag(social.network.mat)<-0
```

When simulating random data, is there a way to make R give the same results each time?

The set.seed function allows the same result to be displayed each time random data is simulated. R will then generate pseudorandom data based on the given seed. If the same seed is used, the same pseudorandom data will be produced.

Next, determine first degree relationships:

```
influence.1 <- apply(social.network.mat, 1, sum)
```

Compute the matrix of second degree relationships:

```
second.degree.mat <- social.network.mat %*% social.network.mat
influence.2 <- apply(second.degree.mat, 1, sum)
```

Compute the total influence in first or second degree relationships:

```
influence.1.2 <- apply(social.network.mat + second.degree.mat, 1, sum)
```

Many online social networks will have millions of people making these graphs much larger, but even on my modest laptop, R handles these computations in seconds. Additionally, to find third degree relationships, we simply have to raise the matrix to the third power.

Can we make our R code look more like the matrix formulas that we are likely to encounter in journals and textbooks?

We use the `apply` command with the sum function, which many R users are likely familiar with, but this is not a standard mathematical notation. We can use matrix multiplication to sum the rows as well, which is typically how this operation is expressed in the quantitative literature. Let's take a look at the following example:

$$\begin{bmatrix} a_{11} & \cdots & a_{1j} \\ \vdots & \ddots & \vdots \\ a_{i1} & \cdots & a_{ij} \end{bmatrix}\begin{bmatrix} 1 \\ \vdots \\ 1 \end{bmatrix} = \begin{bmatrix} \sum a_{11} & \cdots & a_{ij} \\ & \vdots & \\ \sum a_{i1} & \cdots & a_{ij} \end{bmatrix}$$

We simply need to create a vector of ones with as many rows as our matrix has columns and post multiply the matrix by this vector:

```
(social.network.mat + second.degree.mat) %*% rep(1, 1000)
```

Outer products

In linear algebra, the outer product is classically applied to two vectors and produces a matrix with as many rows as the length of the first vector and as many columns as the length of the second vector. The elements in the matrix are produced by multiplying the corresponding elements in the two vectors together. The outer product is defined as follows:

$$\begin{bmatrix} x_1 \\ \vdots \\ x_m \end{bmatrix}\begin{bmatrix} y_1 & \cdots & y_n \end{bmatrix} = \begin{bmatrix} x_1 y_1 & \cdots & x_1 y_n \\ \vdots & \ddots & \vdots \\ x_m y_1 & \cdots & x_m y_n \end{bmatrix}$$

For example, if we have two vectors, we can compute outer products in R using the `outer()` command:

```
x<- c(1:3)
y<- c(4:6)
outer(x, y)
```

Alternatively, we can also compute the outer product as follows:

```
x %o% y
```

However, the outer command is actually much more flexible than this. It does not simply apply the multiplication operator but can actually apply any function to the elements of the vectors. The outer product in R is defined as follows:

$$
\text{Outer}\left(\begin{bmatrix} x_1 \\ \vdots \\ x_m \end{bmatrix}, \begin{bmatrix} y_1 & \cdots & y_n \end{bmatrix}, f(z)\right) = \begin{bmatrix} f(x_1 y_1) & \cdots & f(x_1 y_n) \\ \vdots & \ddots & \vdots \\ f(x_m y_1) & \cdots & f(x_m y_n) \end{bmatrix}
$$

To apply this, we simply have to pass a function rather than let R default to multiplication:

```
outer(x, y, FUN = '+')
```

Using sparse matrices in matrix multiplication

We can use matrix multiplication to transform datasets as follows:

```
> M <- matrix(rep(1, 9), nrow = 3)
> N <- diag(c(1:3), nrow = 3)
> P <- matrix(rep(c(1:3),3), nrow = 3)
> Q <- matrix(1, nrow = 3)
> M
     [,1] [,2] [,3]
[1,]    1    1    1
[2,]    1    1    1
[3,]    1    1    1
> N
     [,1] [,2] [,3]
[1,]    1    0    0
[2,]    0    2    0
[3,]    0    0    3
> P
     [,1] [,2] [,3]
[1,]    1    1    1
```

```
[2,]    2    2    2
[3,]    3    3    3
> Q
       [,1]
[1,]    1
[2,]    1
[3,]    1
```

Postmultiplying a matrix M by a diagonal matrix N is equivalent to multiplying the values in each column of M, by the corresponding value along the diagonal of N:

```
M %*% N
```

Premultiplying a matrix M by a diagonal matrix N is equivalent to multiplying the values in each row of M by the corresponding value along the diagonal of N:

```
N %*% M
```

Postmultiplying a matrix by a column vector of 1s yields the sum of each row:

```
P %*% Q
```

We can obtain the total score of each person on our physical functioning index using matrix multiplication. First, we will create a matrix of all of our physical functioning observations:

```
phys.func.mat <-  as.matrix(phys.func)
```

The following code will give us the total score for each person on the entire physical functioning measure:

```
total.scores <- phys.func.mat %*% matrix(rep(1, 20), nrow = 20)
```

If we look at the items on this physical function, they appear to cover different kinds of activities. Some are concerned with mobility while others are concerned with cognition. Let's say that this measure, which consists of three different domains, is composed of the following items (previously published research actually does suggest this):

- **Cognition or social function**: This contains items A, Q, R, and S (columns 1, 17, 18, and 19)

- **Lower extremity (leg or mobility) activities**: This contains items B, C, D, H, I, J, M, and N (columns 2, 3, 4, 8, 9, 10, 13, and 14)

- **Upper extremity (arm and hand) activities**: This contains items E, F, G, K, L, O, P, and T (columns 5, 6, 7, 11, 12, 15, 16, and 20)

We want to create a new matrix with three columns, each of which has the score of a particular domain. To do this, we simply multiply the raw data matrix, `phys.func.mat` (which has 20 columns), by a design matrix. This design matrix will be a sparse matrix that will have three columns (one for each domain) and 20 rows (one for each item). Each row will contain a 1 in the column corresponding to the domain in which that item belongs:

```
design.matrix <- matrix(rep(0, 60), nrow = 20)
#Place 1s for the cognitive domain
design.matrix[c(1,17,18,19), 1] <- 1
# Place 1s for the lower extremity domain
design.matrix[c(2,3,4,8,9,10,13,14), 2] <- 1
# Place 1s for the upper extremity domain
design.matrix[c(5, 6, 7, 11, 12, 15, 16, 20), 3] <- 1
total.scores <- phys.func.mat %*% design.matrix
summary(total.scores)
```

The notion of a design matrix is frequently used in linear algebra to assign group membership.

Matrix inversion

There is no such thing as matrix division, but matrix inversion is something close to it. Only square matrices can be inverted, and not all square matrices can be inverted. When a matrix is multiplied by its inverse, it produces an identity matrix; hence, the analogy for division.

Inversion is defined as follows:

$$A = \begin{bmatrix} a_{1i} & \cdots & a_{1j} \\ \vdots & \ddots & \vdots \\ a_{i1} & \cdots & a_{ii} \end{bmatrix}$$

$$A^{-1} = \mathrm{Inverse}(A)$$

$$AA^{-1} \begin{bmatrix} 1 & \cdots & 0 \\ \vdots & \ddots & \vdots \\ 0 & \cdots & 1 \end{bmatrix}$$

To invert a matrix in R, we simply use the `solve()` command (we will see a more general use for this command in the following sections):

```
solve(cor.mat)
cor.mat %*% solve(cor.mat)
```

Solving systems of linear equations

We can use R to solve a large system of linear equations with linear algebra. For example, say that we have the following set of linear equations:

$$12x_1 + 41x_2 + \cdots + 46x_1 0 = 1$$
$$49x_1 + 45x_2 + \cdots + 85x_1 0 = 2$$
$$\vdots$$
$$73x_1 + 84x_2 + \cdots + 8x_1 0 = 10$$

This involves 10 unknowns and 10 equations. While this is solvable by hand, it is quite tedious. Instead, we can solve it in R by decomposing the system of equations into three matrices: **C**, **X**, and **Y**:

$$C = \begin{bmatrix} 12 & \cdots & 46 \\ \vdots & \ddots & \vdots \\ 73 & \cdots & 8 \end{bmatrix} \quad X = \begin{bmatrix} x_1 \\ \vdots \\ x_{10} \end{bmatrix} \quad Y = \begin{bmatrix} y_1 \\ \vdots \\ y_{10} \end{bmatrix}$$

$$CX = Y$$

If we simply divide **Y** by **C**, we can get the matrix of **X** values. However, since there is no matrix division, we will instead have to rely on multiplication by the inverse of **C**:

$$X = C^{-1}Y$$

The coefficients to be placed in matrix **C** are available in the `coefficients_matrix.txt` file, in which columns 2 to 11 give the coefficients, and column 12 gives the **Y** values:

```
Y <- as.matrix(read.csv('coefficients_matrix.csv')[,12] )
C <- as.matrix(read.csv('coefficients_matrix.csv')[,c(2:11)])
X <- solve(C) %*% Y
X
```

In fact, R automates this process for us by passing two arguments to the `solve` command:

```
solve(C, Y)
```

For those who wish to experiment, we can simulate coefficients for very large systems of equations with many (for example, 1,000) unknowns. As can be seen, R can do these computations extremely quickly:

```
C.2 <- matrix(sample(c(1:100), 1000000, replace = TRUE), nrow = 1000)
Y.2 <- matrix(sample(c(1:1000), 1000, replace = TRUE), nrow = 1000)
solve(C.2, Y.2)
```

Determinants

Only square matrices have a determinant. This can be used to test whether the vectors in the matrix are linearly independent of one another, which means that no vector can be written as a combination of other vectors. If the vectors are linearly dependent then there are two important consequences:

- There is redundancy of information
- The matrix cannot be inverted

The determinant of a matrix in R can be found with the `det()` function:

```
det(cor.mat)
```

The fact that a determinant is not equal to zero implies that the 20 vectors in the `cor.mat` matrix are linearly independent (and therefore this matrix can be inverted).

Triangular matrices

The `tri.mat` function in R can be used to create a triangular matrix. This function returns a matrix of true or false values, corresponding to the upper or lower triangle. The following commands return a lower triangular matrix of the `cor.mat` matrix:

```
triangle.matrix <- cor.mat
triangle.mat[upper.tri(triangle.matrix)] <-
triangle.matrix
```

Here, we use `upper.tri` to identify the elements of the matrix that we wish to set to NA. In the case of this correlation matrix, the upper and lower triangles are identical, so retaining only half of the matrix makes sense.

We will also further discuss the decomposition of a square matrix into an upper and lower triangular matrix.

Matrix decomposition

Matrix decomposition is the matrix equivalent to algebraic factorization. In this section, we will discuss methods that break a single matrix into the product of two or more smaller matrices.

QR decomposition

QR decomposition is a decomposition that breaks a matrix **M** into two different matrices, **Q** and **R**, such that **M** is equal to **QR**. **Q** is an orthogonal matrix (a matrix in which the inverse of the matrix is equal to its transposition), and **R** is an upper triangular matrix. Here, we demonstrate QR factorization in R on R's internal trees dataset using the `qr` command:

```
> data(trees)
> head(trees)
  Girth Height Volume
1   8.3     70   10.3
2   8.6     65   10.3
3   8.8     63   10.2
4  10.5     72   16.4
5  10.7     81   18.8
6  10.8     83   19.7

> trees.qr <- qr(trees[,c(2:3)])
```

We recover the **Q** and **R** matrices with the `qr.Q` and `qr.R` commands, respectively. If we multiply these together, we see that we get our starting dataset as follows:

```
> Q <- qr.Q(trees.qr)
> R <- qr.R(trees.qr)
> head(Q%*%R)
      Height Volume
[1,]      70   10.3
[2,]      65   10.3
[3,]      63   10.2
[4,]      72   16.4
[5,]      81   18.8
[6,]      83   19.7
```

The most common use of QR factorization is to find numerically stable solutions to linear least squares regression. Let's say that we have a matrix of linear predictors **X**, and a vector of predicted data **Y**, to which we wish to fit a linear regression with regression coefficients stored in a vector **B**.

In fact, R's `lm` function uses QR factorization, as we demonstrate in the following code, and stores the results in an object called `qr` from which we can retrieve an **R** and a **Q** matrix as mentioned previously:

```
> trees.lm <- lm(trees$Volume ~ trees$Girth + trees$Height)
> names(trees.lm)
 [1] "coefficients"  "residuals"     "effects"       "rank"
"fitted.values" "assign"        "qr"            "df.residual"
 [9] "xlevels"       "call"          "terms"         "model"
> Q.2 <- qr.Q(trees.lm$qr)
> R.2 <- qr.R(trees.lm$qr)
```

Notably, this QR decomposition was only done on a matrix with values containing `trees$Girth` and `trees$Height`; whereas previously, our QR decomposition was done on the entire matrix. To get our regression coefficients, we can apply the formula:

$$B = R^{-1}Q^TY$$

In R, using the previous formula, we can develop the following code:

```
> solve(R.2) %*% t(Q.2) %*% trees$Volume
                    [,1]
(Intercept)  -57.9876589
trees$Girth    4.7081605
trees$Height   0.3392512
```

Calling the regression coefficients directly can be achieved as follows:

```
> trees.lm
Call:
lm(formula = trees$Volume ~ trees$Girth + trees$Height)
Coefficients:
  (Intercept)    trees$Girth  trees$Height
     -57.9877         4.7082        0.3393
```

As we can see, they match. It might be interesting to look at the matrix that we get when multiplying our **Q** and **R** matrices, as follows:

```
> head(Q.2%*%R.2)
      (Intercept) trees$Girth trees$Height
[1,]            1         8.3           70
[2,]            1         8.6           65
[3,]            1         8.8           63
[4,]            1        10.5           72
[5,]            1        10.7           81
[6,]            1        10.8           83
```

We see that instead of having the expected two columns, it has three. This is because the first column filled with 1s was added by R prior to doing the QR decomposition. The coefficient for this column of 1s is the intercept term in the regression.

Eigenvalue decomposition

An eigenvalue decomposition can only be done on a square matrix. This decomposition yields a matrix in which each column is termed an eigenvector and each eigenvector has a corresponding eigenvalue.

The eigenvalue decomposition of a matrix decomposes a matrix into the product of three other matrices:

- A matrix of so-called "eigenvectors", a matrix defined as V, in which each column is one eigenvector
- A diagonal matrix of the eigenvalues corresponding to each eigenvector, a matrix denoted as L^2
- The transpose of the matrix of eigenvalues, denoted V^T

Expressed mathematically for a given matrix A as follows:

$$A = VL^2V^T$$

These eigenvectors have important properties that make them relevant:

- These eigenvectors are orthogonal to one another (that is, at 90 degrees or uncorrelated).
- The original matrix postmultiplied by one of its eigenvectors is equal to that eigenvector premultiplied by its corresponding eigenvalue. Stated in another way, postmultiplying a matrix by one of its eigenvectors rescales that eigenvector, changing its length but not its direction. The magnitude of this rescaling is the eigenvalue. Because of this directional invariance, eigenvectors are often referred to as "characteristic roots".

To find eigenvectors and eigenvalues in R, we can use the `eigen()` function. This function returns a list with a vector containing the eigenvalues ordered from the highest to lowest and a matrix containing the eigenvectors corresponding to each eigenvalue. For example, we can find the eigenvalues and eigenvectors of the correlation matrix for the physical functioning data:

```
eigen(cor.mat)$values
eigen(cor.mat)$vectors
```

We can demonstrate the property that a matrix postmultiplied by one of its eigenvalues yields a scalar transformation of that eigenvalue. Here, we use the largest eigenvalue and its corresponding eigenvector:

```
cor.mat %*% eigen(cor.mat)$vectors[,1]
eigen(cor.mat)$values[1] * eigen(cor.mat)$vectors[,1]
```

These two vectors should have the same values. Note that one of these commands uses element-wise rather than matrixwise multiplication.

Lower upper decomposition

The lower upper decomposition is also termed **LU decomposition**. The idea of LU decomposition is to factor a matrix A into two triangle matrices, a lower (L) and an upper (U) triangle matrix:

$$A = LU$$

By breaking a matrix into two triangular matrices, we can reduce the computational demands of many numerical problems. However, finding the LU decomposition itself comes at a computational cost. As such, this can be used in iterative or repeated computational procedures in which A does not change, such as finding the inverse of a matrix or solving a system of linear equations repeatedly, in which the coefficients of the equations do not change between repetitions In such cases, we incur the cost of the LU decomposition only once, but reap the benefits of the computationally easier operation on the decomposed products repeatedly.

To perform LU decomposition in R, we can use the `lu()` function in the `Matrix` package. This does not only perform a simple LU decomposition, but may also rearrange (termed "permuting") the entries of the matrix to avoid zero entries. Applying `lu()` to a matrix will return an object that is not very useable by itself but can be passed to the `expand()` function to provide both the upper and lower matrix.

An example with matrix **C** is given in the following code:

```
library(Matrix)
lu.mat <- expand(lu(C))
lower.mat <- lu.mat$L
upper.mat <- lu.mat$U
p.mat <- lu.mat$P
```

To get the original matrix **C**, we perform matrix multiplication on the **P**, **L**, and **U** matrices, where **P** is the permutation matrix:

```
p.mat %*% lower.mat %*% upper.mat
```

If we do not include the permutation matrix, then we would arrive at a matrix with the same elements as our original matrix but ordered differently.

Cholesky decomposition

Cholesky decomposition is another matrix factorization that can only be computed on square matrices. The basic idea is once again to decompose a matrix **M** into the product of two triangle matrices — one upper triangle matrix **U** and the transposition of this upper triangle matrix, U^T. Similar to the LU decomposition, the use of this method is typically to reduce the computational burden of solving large systems of equations.

In R, this is done with the `chol()` function, which returns only the upper triangle matrix:

```
chol(cor.mat)
```

To reconstruct the original matrix, simply premultiply the result of the `chol()` function by its transpose:

```
t(chol(cor.mat)) %*% chol(cor.mat)
```

Singular value decomposition

Singular value decomposition can be performed on square or rectangular matrices. The idea is to decompose a matrix M, with n columns into n "blocks" of information. Each block is composed of a matrix U, the transpose of a matrix V, and one of the n singular values d:

$$M = U_1 d_1 V_1^T + \cdots + U_n d_n V_n^T$$

When the singular value decomposition is done in R, the result returned is the matrix U, the matrix V, the individual values of d, and the singular values.

The practical use in this is that we can look at the size of each singular value, and if a particular singular value is negligible, then data can be summarized leaving out the block containing that singular value. This can be used as a data compression method or as a noise reduction method. In *Chapter 6, Principal Component Analysis and the Common Factor Model*, we will discuss singular value decomposition on covariance matrices as a data reduction tool.

Let's see how singular value decomposition can be used as a data compression method. Let's create a matrix that represents the picture of a cross composed of zeros and ones. A picture could be converted to a matrix as follows, but there is a file format known as "portable bitmap format" that does use text file representation as given in the following code:

```
cross.mat <- matrix(
  c(
    0, 0, 0, 1, 1, 0, 0, 0,
    0, 0, 0, 1, 1, 0, 0, 0,
    0, 0, 0, 1, 1, 0, 0, 0,
    1, 1, 1, 1, 1, 1, 1, 1,
    1, 1, 1, 1, 1, 1, 1, 1,
    1, 1, 1, 1, 1, 1, 1, 1,
    1, 1, 1, 1, 1, 1, 1, 1,
    0, 0, 0, 1, 1, 0, 0, 0,
    0, 0, 0, 1, 1, 0, 0, 0,
    0, 0, 0, 1, 1, 0, 0, 0
  ),
byrow = TRUE, nrow = 10)
```

We can then apply the singular value decomposition, which will give us eight "blocks" represented as eight column vectors in the **U** and **V** matrices and eight values in the **d** vector:

```
cross.svd <- svd(cross.mat)
```

To inspect the size of each singular value, we look at **d**:

```
cross.svd$d
```

As we can see, the last six singular values are negligible, so we will recreate the image from the first two singular values and first two column vectors of **U** and **V**:

```
cross.svd$u[,c(1,2)] %*% diag(cross.svd$d[c(1,2)]) %*% t(cross.svd$v[,
c(1,2)])
```

This gives us the recreated cross from compressed data. The previous code gives us something that looks like a mess because we estimate the original matrix rather than reproducing exactly. However, if we round up to an integer value, then we reproduce the original matrix:

```
round(cross.svd$u[,c(1,2)] %*% diag(cross.svd$d[c(1,2)]) %*% t(cross.
svd$v[, c(1,2)]), 0)
```

The original `cross.mat` had 80 (8*10) data points. Our compressed data based on singular value decomposition contained 20 values from matrix **u**, 20 values from matrix **v**, and 2 values from vector **d** or a total of 42 values ((2*10)+(2*10)+2). Thus, we were able to compress the data to something nearly half as large.

 If we are working with an image with only two colors, we can recreate the original image exactly by rounding to an integer value. However, if our matrix represented a gray scale image where the numeric value represented the color intensity of the gray, then we would get a close but not completely faithful recreation of the original image.

What if we wanted to clean up the image? Let's create a new cross with a speck of dust on the picture as follows:

```
cross.mat <- matrix(
  c(
     0, 0, 0, 1, 1, 0, 0, 0,
     1, 0, 0, 1, 1, 0, 0, 0,
     0, 0, 0, 1, 1, 0, 0, 0,
     1, 1, 1, 1, 1, 1, 1, 1,
     1, 1, 1, 1, 1, 1, 1, 1,
     1, 1, 1, 1, 1, 1, 1, 1,
     1, 1, 1, 1, 1, 1, 1, 1,
     0, 0, 0, 1, 1, 0, 0, 0,
     0, 0, 0, 1, 1, 0, 0, 0,
     0, 0, 0, 1, 1, 0, 0, 0
  )
,byrow = TRUE, nrow = 10)
```

Notice the value of 1 at position (2, 1) in the previous code, which is our speck of dust. Next, we recreate our cross based on the same idea:

```
cross.svd <- svd(cross.mat)
round(cross.svd.2$u[,c(1,2)] %*% diag(cross.svd.2$d[c(1,2)]) %*%
t(cross.svd.2$v[, c(1,2)]), 0)
```

Voila! The speck of dust is gone.

Applications

We have shown some uses of linear algebra in this chapter, but for the most part, linear algebra techniques derive practical use from the ways in which they are combined both with each other and other functions. As such, this section is included to show how linear algebra and matrix operations can be applied for substantive use.

Rasch analysis using linear algebra and a paired comparisons matrix

In recent decades, a statistical technique termed "Rasch analysis" has become increasingly popular in psychology, education, and healthcare. This is attributed to the Danish statistician, Georg Rasch, who published it in the 1960s. The basic idea is that a scale (for example, an academic test, a measure of a psychological trait, or a physical functioning measure) represents a one-dimensional latent trait, which can be represented as a number line with an arbitrary zero point. We can plot individuals along this line based on their ability. Individuals with higher abilities on the latent trait are plotted at higher values. We can also plot items on this line ordered by difficulty, with more difficult items placed at high-valued locations on the line. A formula based on logistic regression tells us the probability of a person with given ability giving an affirmative answer (or a getting a correct answer) to an item with a given difficulty.

The probability of a person with a particular ability giving an affirmative response is given as follows:

$$P = \frac{e^{\theta - b}}{1 + e^{\theta - b}}$$

In this formula, P is the probability of an affirmative response to the item, e is the base of the natural logarithm, θ is the person's ability, and b is the item's difficulty.

The difficulty of an item is equal to the ability level of a person who has a 50 percent chance of giving an affirmative answer to the item. Both the person's ability θ and the item's difficulty b are not directly observed but must be estimated based on the data obtained from responses on the scale.

A tremendous amount has been written both in textbooks and psychometrics journals, but generally speaking, the question that people wish to answer with Rasch analysis is what the difficulty of each item is.

We will transform our physical functioning data into binary data to indicate some difficulty versus no difficulty and apply Rasch analysis to figure out which items are the most difficult. We will perform Rasch analysis on the lower extremity domain only.

We will begin by using matrix multiplication to create a new matrix with just the lower extremity items:

```
lower.extremity.mat <- phys.func.mat[,c(2,3,4,8,9,10,13,14)]
```

We will then convert this matrix of ordinal data to a matrix of binary data as follows:

```
lower.extremity.binary <- replace(lower.extremity.mat, which(lower.
extremity.mat %in% c(2:5)), 0)
```

In `lower.extremity.binary`, individuals who have no difficulty doing a task are given a value of 1 and individuals who have difficulty are given a value of 0.

 In the original data, higher scores meant more difficulty, but in this binary data frame, we have coded the data to be the opposite for the purpose of easily interpreting the results.

Thus, the latent trait that we are interested in now is the ability to perform tasks using the lower extremities without difficulty.

There are many ways to statistically estimate the item difficulties in the Rasch model, but the method that we will use here is based on a paired comparison's matrix. The overall scheme is as follows:

1. Count the number of individuals able to perform an item without difficulty and compare that to the number of individuals able to do the other seen items without difficulty. Populate a matrix R of raw comparison data:

$$R = \begin{bmatrix} r_{11} & \cdots & r_{1j} \\ \vdots & \ddots & \vdots \\ r_{i1} & \cdots & r_{ij} \end{bmatrix}$$

   In the preceding diagram, r_{ij} is the number of people who score a 1 on item i and 0 on item j.

   The R code to create the paired comparisons matrix is as follows:

```
create.paired.comparisons <- function (input.matrix) {
  n.items <- ncol(input.matrix)
  output.matrix <- matrix(0, nrow = n.items, ncol = n.items)
  for (i in 1:n.items) {
    for (j in 1:n.items) {
       output.matrix[i, j] <- length(which(input.matrix[,i] -
input.matrix[,j] > 0))
    }
  }
  return(output.matrix)
}
R <- create.paired.comparisons(lower.extremity.binary)
R
```

2. Create a matrix D as follows:

$$d_{ij} = \frac{r_{ji}}{r_{ij}}$$

3. The corresponding R code is as follows:

```
D <- t(R) / R
diag(D) <- rep(1, 8)
D
```

4. Take the natural logarithm of each element in **D**:

```
ln.D <- log(D, exp(1))
```

5. Find the mean of each row as follows:

```
(ln.D %*% matrix(rep(1, 8), nrow = 8)) / 8
```

The final command shows us that the locations for each item are as follows:

No.	Item	Location
B	Walking for a quarter mile	0.854
C	Walking up 10 steps	-0.169
D	Stooping, crouching, kneeling	2.076
H	Walking from one room to another	-3.561
I	Standing up from a chair	-0.440
J	Getting in or out of bed	-0.761
M	Standing for 2 hours	1.936
N	Sitting for 2 hours	0.065

These results suggest that the easiest mobility item on this scale is item B, and the most difficult is item D. Thus, if a person has only a little difficulty with use of their legs (due to arthritis or other impairments), they might report problems with stooping, crouching, or kneeling, but if they report problems with simply walking between rooms, we would expect that they have a high degree of impairment and are likely to have difficulty with every other item on this scale.

There are a number of other methods to estimate the parameters of the Rasch model with implementations of them in various R packages. The eRm package is one of the numerous available packages, which offer a full suite of functions for both applying the Rasch model and testing model fit. The answers obtained in the previous example can be compared to those obtained from the RM() command in the eRM package:

```
library(eRM)
RM(lower.extremity.binary)
```

The units in which these difficulties are expressed are often called "logits". They have no meaning outside of the scale to which they are being applied, and the zero point is arbitrary, so it is perfectly acceptable to add or subtract (but not multiply or divide) any number to them.

Calculating Cronbach's alpha

Earlier, we went over the Rasch analysis, which is a part of a psychometric approach termed **item response theory** (**IRT**). However, long before there was IRT, there was **classical test theory** (**CTT**), which was concerned with estimating or measuring "true scores". The underlying idea of CTT posited that on a test is *Observed Score = True Score + Error*.

Therefore, much of the classical test theory is concerned with determining how much of a person's observed score is due to the true score. One important metric for this that is still in heavy use today (in spite of arguments that it has outlived its usefulness) is Cronbach's coefficient alpha. The basic idea underlying internal consistency reliability (and CTT in general) is that the score on a subgroup of items should be correlated with the score on the rest of the test. In the case of alpha, the subgroups of items that are examined are split halves, such that alpha is equal to the average split-half reliability for all possible splits of items. Conveniently, an algebraic formula to compute alpha has been developed so that analysts do not actually have to determine all split half correlations and average them.

The formula for Cronbach's alpha is:

$$\alpha = \frac{k}{k-1}\left(1 - \frac{\sum s_i^2}{s_t^2}\right)$$

In the preceding formula, α is a Cronbach's alpha, k is the number of items, s_i^2 is a variance of item i, and s_i^2 is a variance of total test scores.

Here, we will use matrix operations in R to compute alpha for the correlation matrix of the NHANES physical functioning measure.

1. First, compute the total score for each domain for each person as follows:

    ```
    domain.totals <- phys.func.mat %*% design.matrix
    ```

    The total score variance for any domain is the diagonal of the covariance matrix of total scores:

    ```
    tot.score.var <- diag(cov(domain.totals))
    ```

2. We then find the sum variance of each item for each scale and convert it to a row vector:

```
item.var <- diag(cov(phys.func.mat))
item.var <- matrix(item.var, ncol = 20)
```

3. We then post multiply it by our design matrix to obtain total item variances on each domain:

```
item.var.tot <- item.var %*% design.matrix
```

4. We can calculate the number of items in each domain using our design matrix:

```
n <- matrix(1, ncol = 20) %*% design.matrix
```

5. Finally, we put everything in the formula for alpha:

```
alpha <- (n / (n-1)) * (1 - (item.var.tot / tot.score.var))
alpha
```

This is the raw alpha. The standardized alpha can be obtained by performing these operations on the correlations rather than covariances.

Image compression using direct cosine transform

Earlier, we saw how SVD can be used to compress a matrix that is representative of data. Here, we will use another decomposition method to decompose an image into spectral features, which we can use for image compression. We will do this with the discrete cosine transform (DCT) of a square matrix. The DCT is one of a variety of transformation functions that transforms a signal expressed in terms of location to one expressed in terms of frequency. In the case of the DCT, this is done by decomposing a set of discrete values into a series of cosine functions.

Importing an image into R

Before we can start working with an image, we have to import the image, which we will do using the png package. We will import the picture as an array and examine its dimensions as follows:

```
> library(png)
> picture <- readPNG('landscape.png')
> dim(picture)
[1] 1536 2048    3
```

The first two dimensions give the pixel dimensions of the image, and the third dimension gives the number of color layers. This array has two important features in its dimensions. The first is that the third dimension is three, which indicates that even though this is a picture of a landscape that has been converted to shades of gray, it is still stored as a three-color PNG file, with a red, green, and blue layer. However, each color layer has identical values in this matrix. The second notable feature is that the pixel dimensions of the image are divisible by eight. This is important because we will base our image compression example on the JPEG standard for image compression in the following section, which decomposes an image into 8 pixel squares; image padding is needed if the number of pixels on a side is not divisible by eight.

Here, we create an array composed of just the first color layer and then use R's image command to view the array as a graphic. We transpose the array and reverse the counting of rows to place the image in the correct orientation. We also tell it to plot intensity values using grayscale rather than color, as shown in the following code:

```
picture.1 <- picture[,,1]
image(t(picture.1)[,nrow(picture.1):1], col = gray(seq(0,1, length.out
= 256)))
```

We can see the following screenshot imported into R plotted on a graphics device:

The compression technique

We will start with describing the basic image compression technique and show the corresponding R code further. The following are the basic steps in our image compression:

1. Break an image into 64 (8*8) block of pixels, which in our case means 8*8 submatrices or subarrays.

2. Convert each 8*8 block into an 8*8 block of frequencies (that is, coefficients for cosine terms). This is done using a transformation matrix **T**, which we will see further.

3. Discard the frequencies of least importance in each 8*8 block and keep only those of the most importance, which we do with a quantization matrix **Q**.

Decompression is simply a reversal of the first two steps (we can't undiscard lost data). In the end, we will lose some of the data but hopefully not enough to be visually noticeable, which is similar to what we did with SVD previously.

Creating the transformation and quantization matrices

To perform the DCT, we will first need to compute a transformation matrix T, which we will later use in the actual image transformation. More detailed treatment of the underlying theory is present in many signal processing textbooks but here, we will skip to presenting the needed formulas. We will assume that T is a square matrix with N rows and columns, denoted by i and j, respectively, with the numbering of i and j starting at 0. The formula is shown as follows:

$$T = \begin{cases} \dfrac{1}{\sqrt{N}} & \text{if } i = 0 \\ \sqrt{\dfrac{2}{N}} \cos\left(\dfrac{(2j+i)i\pi}{2N} \right) & \text{if } i > 0 \end{cases}$$

The quantization matrix **Q** will be based on a predeveloped quantization table, which in this case will be a quantization table provided by the independent JPEG group. This is the most commonly used table, but others are available, and some companies have patented methods for the ad hoc creation of quantization tables based on the image being compressed. The basic quantization table is shown as follows:

16	11	10	16	24	40	51	60
12	12	14	19	26	58	60	55

14	13	16	24	40	57	69	56
14	17	22	29	51	87	80	62
18	22	37	59	68	109	103	77
24	35	55	64	81	104	113	92
49	64	78	87	103	121	120	101
72	92	95	98	112	100	103	99

A quality level between 0 and 100 can be created, and the matrix shown in the previous table produces a compression at a quality level of 50. Additional quantization matrices can be created as scalar multiples of the quantization table based on the image quality desired with higher levels corresponding to higher quality. This table has smaller values at the top-left corner and larger values towards the bottom-right corner. As we will see in a moment, this is an important part of compression.

Putting the matrices together for image compression

To transform the original 8*8 matrix R to the discrete cosine transformed matrix D, we simply use matrix multiplication:

$$D = TRT'$$

Here, T' is the transposition of T.

The compressed matrix C is created by the element-wise division of D, by Q rounded to the nearest integer value:

$$C_{i,j} = D_{i,j} / Q_{i,j}$$

The most important frequencies in the matrix tend to congregate towards the top-left corner of D. Since Q has small values in the top-left corner and large values in the bottom-right corner, the division followed by rounding will mean that those values in the top-left corner will be retained as integers while those in the bottom-right corner will be rounded to zero and discarded.

To reverse the quantization of the image, we perform element-wise multiplication of C by Q:

$$D_{i,j} = C_{i,j} / Q_{i,j}$$

Since we rounded some of the values of C in the compression process, this D matrix will be slightly different than the D matrix we started with.

We then perform the opposite matrix multiplication to get R:

$$R = T'DT$$

DCT in R

We will now implement the procedures described earlier in R code. The first thing that we will do is convert our array of pixel values from 0 to 1 to an array of 256 integer pixel values from -128 to 127, as shown in the following code:

```
picture.1.256 <- round(picture.1 * 255 -128)
```

Our compression method relies on rounding to integer values, so some type of transformation to integer values is crucial.

Then, we will write a function that can calculate the values of the matrix **T**, for any desired size:

```
create.dct.matrix <- function(n) {
  output.matrix <- matrix(0, nrow = n, ncol = n)
  for (i in 1:n) {
    for (j in 1:n) {
      if (i == 1) {output.matrix[i,j] <- 1/sqrt(n) }
      if (i > 1) {
        output.matrix[i,j] <-
          sqrt(2 / n) * cos( (2*(j-1) +1)*(i-1)*pi / (2* n))
      }
    }
  }
  return(output.matrix)
}
```

The formula to compute the elements of the quantization matrix assumes that matrix rows and columns are numbered starting with 0, but R numbers start with 1, which we must account for in our code.

We will simply define the basic quantization matrix as follows:

```
quant.matrix <- matrix(
  c(
  16,11,10,16,24,40,51,60,
  12,12,14,19,26,58,60,55,
  14,13,16,24,40,57,69,56,
  14,17,22,29,51,87,80,62,
```

```
18,22,37,59,68,109,103,77,
24,35,55,64,81,104,113,92,
49,64,78,87,103,121,120,101,
72,92,95,98,112,100,103,99
),
byrow = TRUE,
nrow = 8, ncol = 8
)
```

We will then give R a compression ratio for the desired quality as follows:

```
compression.ratio <- 50
```

Now, we will compute the Q matrix as a scalar multiple of the basic quantization table based on our desired compression ratio, and we will create a matrix T for *n* equal to 8, as shown:

```
Q <- round(quant.matrix * (100-compression.ratio)/50)
T <- create.dct.matrix(8)
```

Finally, we will create the function that breaks the original image into 8*8 subimages, performs the DCT, and does the compression:

```
dct.compress <- function(input.matrix) {
  input.row <- nrow(input.matrix)
  input.col <- ncol(input.matrix)
  output.matrix <- matrix(0, nrow = input.row, ncol = input.col)
  working.row <- c(1:8)
  while (max(working.row) <= input.row) {
    working.col  <- c(1:8)
    while (max(working.col) <= input.col) {
      output.matrix[working.row, working.col] <-
      (T %*% input.matrix[working.row, working.col] %*% t(T))/Q
      working.col <- working.col + 8
    }
    working.row <- working.row + 8
  }
  return(output.matrix)
}
```

Now, let's actually compress our image using the following function:

```
picture.compressed <- dct.compress(picture.1.256)
```

This is transformed and compressed image (if appropriately encoded, the abundance of zeros will require less storage space). If we want to see what the image looks like, we can plot it using the following code:

```
image(t(picture.compressed)[,nrow(picture.compressed):1], col =
gray(seq(1,0, length.out = 2)))
```

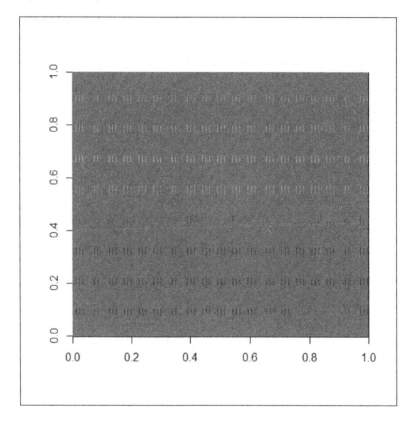

Now, this compression technique is useless if we can't recreate the original image, so we will create a function to reverse what our compression function did:

```
decompress.image <- function(input.matrix) {
  input.row <- nrow(input.matrix)
  input.col <- ncol(input.matrix)
  output.matrix <- matrix(0, nrow = input.row, ncol = input.col)
  working.row <- c(1:8)
  while (max(working.row) <= input.row) {
    working.col <- c(1:8)
    while (max(working.col) <= input.col) {
```

```
        output.matrix[working.row, working.col] <-
        (t(T) %*% (Q * input.matrix[working.row, working.col]) %*% T)
        working.col <- working.col + 8
    }
    working.row <- working.row + 8
  }
  return(output.matrix)
}
```

Let's now apply our decompression function and plot the result to see how faithfully our original image was recreated:

```
picture.decompressed <- decompress.image(picture.compressed)
image(t(picture.decompressed)[,nrow(picture.decompressed):1], col =
gray(seq(0,1, length.out = 256)))
```

The result of the function is as shown in the following figure:

We see that the original image is pretty well preserved. It may be interesting to try lower values for a compression ratio other than 50 to see how well the original image is preserved with more and more compression.

Summary

In this chapter, we covered linear algebra techniques in R. Unlike many of the prior chapters, many of the methods covered in this chapter do not produce an interesting result that has a substantive interpretation. Rather, these methods can be used to build numerical algorithms as shown in the final two examples. We covered linear algebra operations, including transposition, inversion, matrix multiplication, and a number of matrix transformations. We then went on to explore how these methods can be applied in Rasch analysis, internal consistency, and image compression. The subsequent chapters will focus on linear algebra's use in dealing with covariance matrices to perform principal component analysis, factor analysis, and structural equation modeling.

6

Principal Component Analysis and the Common Factor Model

The previous chapter explored linear algebra and matrix operations. This chapter can best be characterized as concerned with the linear algebra of covariance and correlation matrices. **Principal component analysis (PCA)** and **factor analysis (FA)** are two classic methods of identifying structures in the correlations of datasets. Despite the fact that they are concerned with covariances and correlations, many statisticians have very limited experience with these methods, because they make heavy use not only of statistics, but also of linear algebra; therefore, they straddle the realms of both statistics and engineering.

In this chapter, the following topics will be discussed:

- A primer on correlation and covariance structures
- Principle component analysis
- Basic exploratory factor analysis
- Advanced exploratory factor analysis

A primer on correlation and covariance structures

In the case of both PCA and FA, it is worth taking a moment to review some basic mathematical properties of covariances and correlations. Covariance is a measure of the linear codependence of two variables. Correlation is the covariance divided by the product of the standard deviation of the two variables. Thus, the correlation is a scaled covariance. In this chapter, we will be placing these covariances or correlations into matrices, called **covariance matrices** or **correlation matrices**.

The correlation matrix is a square matrix that has as many rows (and as many columns) as there are variables. Each element of the matrix represents the correlation between two variables. For example, in a dataset with three variables, A, B, and C, the correlation matrix would be as follows:

$$\begin{bmatrix} 1 & \mathrm{cor}(A,B) & \mathrm{cor}(A,C) \\ \mathrm{cor}(B,A) & 1 & \mathrm{cor}(B,C) \\ \mathrm{cor}(C,A) & \mathrm{cor}(C,B) & 1 \end{bmatrix}$$

The diagonals are all **1** because the correlation of a variable with itself is 1. In a covariance matrix, the variances of the variables fall along the diagonal.

Datasets used in this chapter

We will use a few datasets in this chapter, which will cover a wide range of topics. What they have in common is that they are all multidimensional; as a result, the techniques of this chapter are easy to implement. For convenience, all datasets are available online at http://scholar.harvard.edu/gerrard/mastering-scientific-computation-r. The following are some of the datasets:

- **Red wine**: This is a dataset of red wine properties. This dataset contains the chemical properties of the wine as well as the wine quality score. This dataset comes from the paper *P. Cortez, A. Cerdeira, F. Almeida, T. Matos, and J. Reis. Modeling wine preferences by data mining from physicochemical properties. In Decision Support Systems, Elsevier, 47(4):547-553, 2009.* It was downloaded from the University of California Irvine Machine Learning Repository at http://archive.ics.uci.edu/ml/.

- **Abalone**: This is a dataset of abalone measurements. The measurements are concerned largely with sizes and weights of various parts of the abalone. This dataset comes from the University of California Irvine Machine Learning Repository available at `http://archive.ics.uci.edu/ml/`.

- **Physical functioning**: We used this dataset in the previous chapter. For full details, refer to *Chapter 5, Linear Algebra*. To summarize, the survey respondents are asked how much difficulty they have with 20 items related to functional independence.

All **UC Irvine Machine Learning Repository** datasets come from Kevin Bache and Moshe Lichman (2013). The UCI Machine Learning Repository is available at `http://archive.ics.uci.edu/ml`. *Irvine, CA: University of California, School of Information and Computer Science.*

Principal component analysis and total variance

Simply put, PCA is a tool that enables dimension reduction of data. While this sounds simple enough, let's discuss in a bit more detail. If we start with a dataset that has a large number of variables, say 100, then the question may arise as to whether we really need all 100 variables or if there is some redundancy in the data such that it can be summarized with fewer variables. In this case, redundancy does not mean complete duplication of a measurement but rather a significant amount of overlap.

We will get to some real data in a moment, but for now, let's assume the voting results from senate bills in the United States. Each bill gets voted on by up to 100 senators (some may abstain), and we want to get an idea of how each bill was received by the voting members of the senate. There are two political parties in the United States, Democratic and Republican, and there may be a lot of redundancy in voting. In fact, ample research shows that in general, members of Congress tend to vote with the rest of their party, suggesting that such redundancy does exist. If this is the case, then we can keep only a small portion of the data and be mostly accurate (though sometimes wrong) at figuring out how a bill was received by members of Congress.

There are a number of dimension reduction techniques, but PCA is one of the most commonly used techniques.

Understanding the basics of PCA

The basic idea of PCA is to figure out whether the data represented in multiple dimensions can be effectively modeled with fewer dimensions. PCA actually returns the same number of dimensions that we started with, but it tells us whether most of the information is loading along the first few dimensions with a little additional information provided by recording data for additional dimensions. This is probably best explained with an example using simulated data.

First, simulate data for two variables, such that one variable is strongly related to the other:

```
set.seed(20)
x <- sample(c(0:100), replace = TRUE, 1000)
y <- x + sample(c(-10:10), replace = TRUE, 1000)
plot(y ~ x)
```

The result is shown in the following plot:

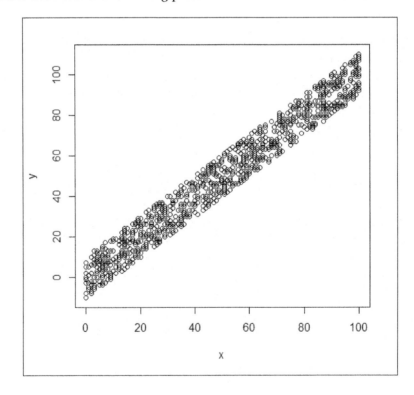

As can be seen in the preceding plot, we have actually plotted a fuzzy line. We are using two dimensions to locate points on this line, but if we reduced this to only a single dimension by rotating our axes, we would not lose much information regarding where on the line each point is located. The trick is figuring out the rotation that gives us only one dimension, something that is simple in this two-dimensional, well-behaved dataset, but more difficult in multidimensional and less well-behaved data. This is where PCA comes in; it rotates the axes giving us a new set of axes with just as many dimensions, but it captures as much of the variance as possible on the first dimension, as much of the remaining variance as possible on the second dimension, and so on. In this way, the first few of our newly created dimensions will explain as much of the data as possible. If they explain enough, then perhaps the following dimensions are not needed.

Mathematically, PCA works by taking an eigenvalue decomposition (see *Chapter 5, Linear Algebra*) of the covariance or the correlation matrix, where the eigenvalues represent the total variance explained by the corresponding eigenvector (or principal component), or by performing a singular value decomposition on the raw data. It does matter whether correlations or covariances are used in the eigenvalue method, and we may need to scale the data prior to performing an SVD-based PCA. We will discuss this further in the section *Scaled versus unscaled PCA*.

What is the difference between `princomp` **and** `prcomp` **in R?**

There are two R functions (in the base R software) for performing PCA: `prcomp` and `princomp`. They differ particularly in how they go about performing PCA. Where `princomp` does an eigenvalue decomposition on the covariance (or correlation) matrix, `prcomp` performs a singular value decomposition on the raw data. These two commands differ slightly in output, and `prcomp` is considered to provide a better numerical estimate.

We can apply R's `prcomp` function, which performs PCA and summarizes the results as follows:

```
>pca.sample <- prcomp(matrix(c(x,y), ncol =2))
>summary(pca.sample)

Importance of components:
                          PC1      PC2
Standard deviation      42.3675  4.31650
Proportion of Variance   0.9897  0.01027
Cumulative Proportion    0.9897  1.00000
```

This shows that almost 99 percent of the variance is explained by the first newly created dimension (called a **principal component**).

As indicated earlier, PCA just rotates the axes. This suggests that we should be able to use the results of a PCA to see how our data can be plotted on this new set of axes, and in fact this can be done easily. The object returned by `prcomp` contains a matrix of loadings:

```
pca.sample$rotation
> pca.sample$rotation
           PC1         PC2
[1,] -0.6983965  0.7157111
[2,] -0.7157111 -0.6983965
> pca.sample <- prcomp(matrix(c(x,y), ncol =2))
> rotation.matrix <- -pca.sample$rotation
```

In this case, the loadings are mostly negative, which is completely arbitrary, so we reverse the sign before saving it into a new matrix, the name of which hints at what can be done with it. We now multiply it with the rotation matrix, and we get a new set of coordinates, which represent how each value in the original data matrix can be projected onto our new coordinate system:

```
rotated.data <- matrix(c(x,y), ncol = 2) %*% rotation.matrix
```

Now, if we plot this rotated data, we will see something that looks a lot like our original plot of the data; only here, we have rotated the axes as shown in the following plot:

```
plot(rotated.data[,1], rotated.data[,2], xlim = c(0, 150), ylim = c(-
75, 75))
```

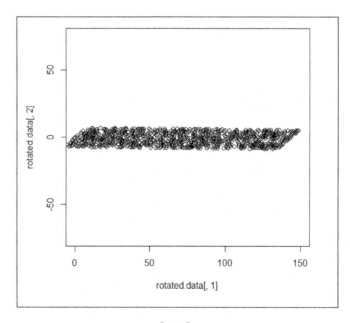

Compare the previous plot with the one before it to see that this is simply a rotation of the original data onto new axes. Notice that the new horizontal axis has points from 0 to almost 150, whereas the old horizontal axis only went as high as 100. This is because the new horizontal axis is really a hypotenuse passing through the cloud of data points, and the hypotenuse of a right triangle with two legs of length 100 is about 141.

How does PCA relate to SVD?

As we discussed in *Chapter 5, Linear Algebra*, a singular value decomposition decomposes a matrix M into two matrices U and V, and a vector of singular values D (see *Chapter 5, Linear Algebra*, for further elaboration):

$M=UDV^T$

Multiplying just the upper matrix U by the diagonal matrix D, for which the diagonal values are given by the vector of the singular value D, will project the data onto the new coordinates in the same way as multiplying the original data with the rotation matrix. For example, we could perform the rotation that we achieved with R's `prcomp` command the following way with the `svd` command:

```
svd.sample <- svd(matrix(c(x,y), ncol = 2))
manual.rotation <- svd.sample$u %*% -diag(svd.sample$d)
plot(manual.rotation[,1], manual.rotation[,2], xlim = c(0, 150), ylim
= c(-75, 75))
```

The result is shown in the following plot:

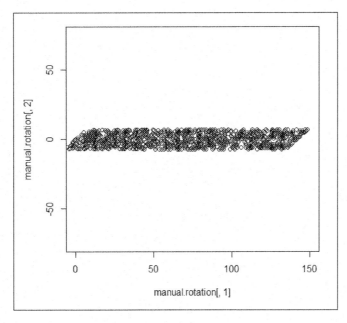

Scaled versus unscaled PCA

Previously, we have discussed the fact that a correlation is a scaled covariance. It is important to point out here that scaling of the data can make a big difference. Both eigenvalue decomposition and SVD attempt to tell us the direction of data of a matrix point. We will encounter a problem in datasets that have variables placed on different scales. In such data sets, eigenvalue decomposition on the covariances or SVD on the raw data will tend to give the illusion that the data is aligned in the direction of the variables with largest values. This is a problem if some variables have large values only because they are expressed in small units (for example, expressing a length in millimeters rather than meters will multiply a length value by 1,000). These large values mean large variances, and PCA attempts to rotate the first component in the direction of the largest variance. Thus, if variables are measured on very different scales, then it is necessary to somehow scale the variables (typically to a variance of one). This is best seen with some examples.

Let's load the wine dataset, as follows:

```
red.wine <- read.csv('winequality-red.txt')
```

Now, we will take an eigenvalue decomposition of the covariance matrix ignoring the last variable, followed by an eigenvalue decomposition of the correlation matrix (this is close to what R does in the `princomp` command):

```
wine.eigen.cov <- eigen(cov(red.wine[,-12]))
wine.eigen.cor <- eigen(cor(red.wine[,-12]))
```

Now, let's look at the proportion of variance explained by each principal component in the two different eigenvalue decompositions. We will compute the proportion of variance explained by dividing each eigenvalue by the sum of eigenvalues:

```
> wine.eigen.cov$values / sum(wine.eigen.cov$values)
 [1] 9.465770e-01 4.836830e-02 2.589172e-03 1.518968e-03
 [5] 8.735540e-04 3.456072e-05 1.936276e-05 9.472781e-06
 [9] 8.413766e-06 1.214728e-06 4.687628e-10
> wine.eigen.cor$values / sum(wine.eigen.cor$values)
 [1] 0.281739313 0.175082699 0.140958499 0.110293866 0.087208370
 [6] 0.059964388 0.053071929 0.038450609 0.031331102 0.016484833
[11] 0.005414392
```

It can be seen that there is a stark difference between the two datasets. Based on the covariance matrix, the first principal component explains almost 95 percent of the variance, whereas using the correlation matrix method, the first principal component does not even explain 30 percent of the variance. The reason is because some variables (for example, those related to sulfur dioxide) are expressed in units that provide much bigger numbers than the other variables.

This can be a problem when using R's `prcomp` command if we are not careful:

```
wine.prcomp <- prcomp(red.wine[,-12])
wine.prcomp.scaled <- prcomp(red.wine[,-12], scale = TRUE)
summary(wine.prcomp)
summary(wine.prcomp.scaled)
```

The output is as shown in the following screenshot:

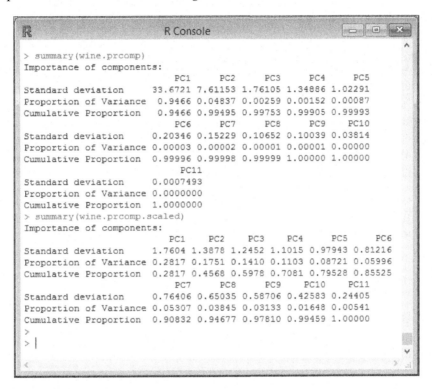

The unscaled version of this PCA gives us a misleading result because one particular variable, sulfur dioxide, has a very large absolute variance, which is a consequence of the units it is measured in. `PC1` is essentially the sulfur dioxide variable. This is akin to measuring most variables in meters and one variable in centimeters; centimeters are smaller than meters, so variances expressed in terms of centimeters will be numerically larger. By adding the `scale = TRUE` argument, we are telling R to rescale all variables to unit variance. If variables are not expressed on the same or at least similar scales, rescaling is needed.

There are a number of key points to keep in mind with PCA:

- PCA retains the same number of dimensions in the data but rotates the axes in the direction of the data
- PCA attempts to account for all of the variance in variables
- Variables on very different scales may need to be rescaled
- The principle components created in PCA do not have to mean anything substantive

PCA for dimension reduction

Thus far, we have discussed the mathematical properties of PCA but not actually discussed how it can be used. In short, PCA is a technique that allows us to interpret observations from a multidimensional dataset in terms of fewer dimensions. Here, we will use a dataset examining the chemical properties of red wine to demonstrate PCA in R. We will use commands from R's `FactoMineR` package, which is based on SVD and has numerous utilities for interpreting the results of PCA.

While PCA has been described as a dimension reduction technique, an application for it may not be immediately obvious. To demonstrate its use, let's look at the abalone dataset that consists of a variety of measurements on abalone:

```
abalone <- read.csv('abalone.txt')
library(FactoMineR)
abalone.pca <- PCA(abalone[, c(-1)])
```

The PCA command produces a **variables factor map** that plots as vectors to show how each original variable falls on the rotated axes produced by PCA, as shown in the following diagram:

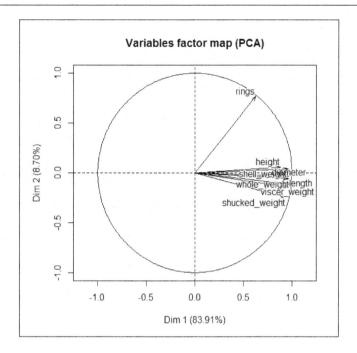

The preceding figure only shows two dimensions; so it is of limited use when many dimensions are retained but very useful in cases where one or two dimensions capture most of the variance. It appears that nearly all of the individual measurements of an abalone can be captured on a single dimension. From a practical standpoint, this suggests that most of these abalone traits are really just slight variants of a single underlying trait—**size**, which as we can see captures nearly 84 percent of the variance in all of the measurements.

PCA to summarize wine properties

The abalone example demonstrates how PCA can arrive at a nice and simple solution for a dataset. Unfortunately, most real-world datasets are not so conveniently categorized. Let's return to the red wine dataset for an example of this. First, let's just look at the correlation matrix of the red wine data, usually a good first step before engaging in PCA. R's `cor` command applied to a data frame will give a correlation matrix:

```
cor(red.wine)
```

We won't get into the details of wine chemistry and oenology here, but some high correlations are expected. For example, citric acid is one of the fixed acids in wine, so we would expect a high correlation here. However, we see a mix of high and low correlations, which means that there may be some structure to this data consisting of more than one dimension, but fewer than the total number of wine measurements. Let's perform a PCA on this dataset now:

```
wine.pca <- PCA(red.wine, quanti.sup = 12)
```

By declaring `quanti.sup = 12`, we are telling the PCA command not to use the 12th variable, which is quality in the construction of the new dimensions. However, we are asking the PCA command to estimate the parameters for this variable on the newly created dimensions, which is shown in the following figure:

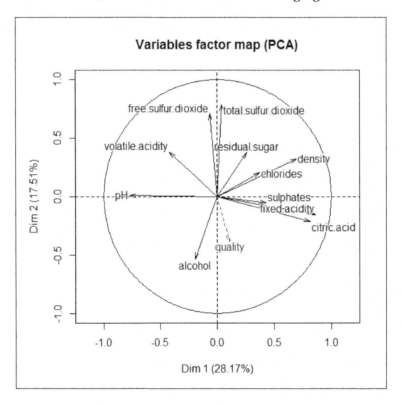

The preceding graphic produced gives us a hint of what we are getting into with our attempts at dimension reduction, and this is much more representative of common datasets seen in the real world. Let's dig into the `wine.pca` object to try to make sense of things:

```
summary(wine.pca)
```

Let's have a look at the following screenshot:

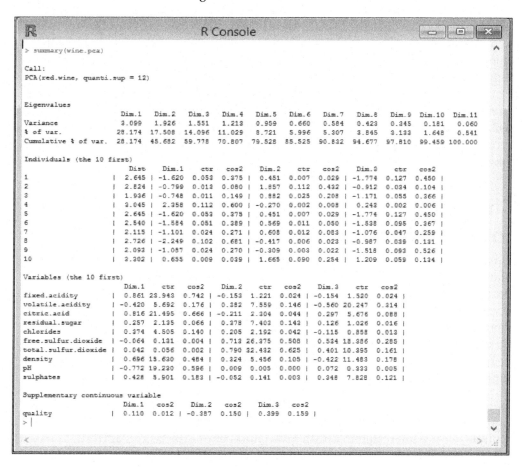

The preceding screenshot summarizes the eigenvalue decomposition, shows how to plot the individual wines on the rotated axes, and provides a summary of the variables. We will discuss each of these individually here.

The eigenvalues are from an eigenvalue decomposition of a correlation matrix (although SVD was actually used). The sum of these eigenvalues will be the total number of variables, in this case 11. The proportion of variance explained by a particular principal component (that is, rotated new dimension) is simply the ratio of that eigenvalue to the total number of variables. The importance of this is that once an eigenvalue is less than one, the principal component associated with that eigenvalue explains less of the variance than a single original variable. We will discuss this in a bit more detail in the next section.

The individual information and variable information simply provides the data to plot individual and original variables along the new rotated axes. By default, this data is provided for only the first three principal components. There are a number of columns shown in the preceding screenshot. The first column denoted by **Dim** refers to the coordinate of each variable on each principal component. The second column denoted by **ctr** provides the contribution of that coordinate to the creation of that dimension. The quality variable has no contribution column, because it did not contribute to the creation of the principal components. The final column, named **cos2**, provides the squared cosine. The closer the squared cosine is to 1 (or the greater it is), the better that variable is projected onto the axis and the closer that variable is linked to that principal component.

Choosing the number of principal components to retain

As we discussed earlier, PCA (regardless of which R command is used) simply rotates the axes in the direction of the data, but there are as many principal components as there are original variables. The question then is how PCA can be used as a dimension reduction technique if it returns the same number of dimensions that we started with. As we have already touched upon here, the key is to choose only as many principal components as are important and ignore the rest. This then leaves the question as to how we decide on how many principal components are important.

There are a number of possible ways to go about choosing the number of principal components to retain. Qualitative methods include choosing based on theory (for example, we are interested in only a given number of dimensions apriori), or based on looking at the principal components and keeping those that we can substantively find meaning in. The two most commonly used quantitative methods include the **Kaiser-Guttman** rule and the **Screen** test.

The Kaiser-Guttman rule simply states that principal components with an eigenvalue greater than one should be retained. The rationale for this is that principal components with eigenvalues less than one explain less of the total variance than a single original variable does on average. Based on this rule, we should keep four principal components in the PCA of the red wine data. The screen test simply plots the eigenvalues (or the proportion of variance) as a function of principal components. If there is a leveling off in the plot, then those principal components are regarded as unnecessary. The code to plot the graph is shown as follows:

```
plot(wine.pca$eig$eigenvalue, type = 'b', xlab = 'Principal
Component', ylab = 'Eigenvalue', main = 'Eigenvalues of Principal
Components')
```

The result is as shown in the following plot:

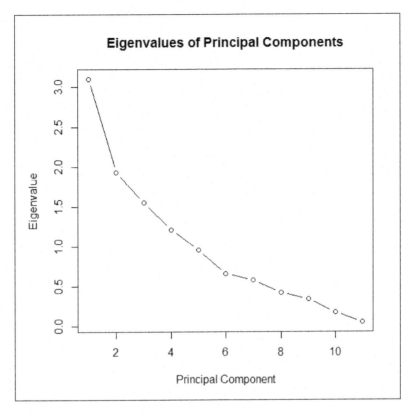

As can be seen in the preceding plot, the leveling off is not nice, so by scree criteria we would not really be able to determine an appropriate threshold of principal components to include for the red wine dataset. In comparison, let's look at what the scree plot shows for the abalone PCA:

```
plot(abalone.pca$eig$eigenvalue, type = 'b', xlab = 'Principal
Component', ylab = 'Eigenvalue', main = 'Eigenvalues of Principal
Components')
```

The result is shown in the following scree plot:

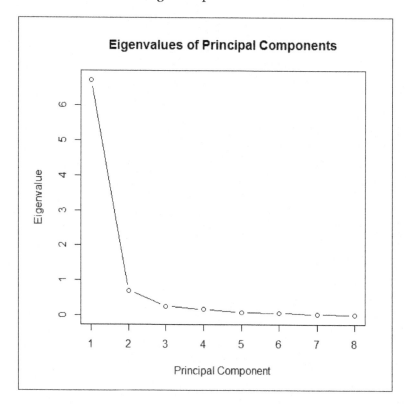

In the preceding figure, the scree plot for abalone largely levels off starting at the second principal component and definitely by the third. As such, by scree plot criteria, we would keep one or at most two dimensions in the PCA of the abalone dataset.

An important limitation of the Kaiser-Guttman rule is related to the fact that the components in PCA do not necessarily have to have any meaning. For example, if we apply PCA to 20 simulated uncorrelated random variables, the Kaiser-Guttman rule will probably reveal that we should retain a large number of components, despite the fact that no meaningful correlation structure actually exists. Run the following R code to see a demonstration of this:

```
simulated.data <- matrix(sample(1:100, 20000, replace
= TRUE), ncol = 20)
summary(PCA(simulated.data))
```

Let's return to the wine PCA to discuss an interpretation of the PCA results. We will attempt to make sense of four dimensions, explaining nearly 71 percent of the variance. So, we will print the summary of the PCA results again telling R that we want the coordinates, contribution, and squared cosine for four dimensions rather than the default three:

```
summary(wine.pca, ncp = 4, )
```

The results are shown in the following screenshot:

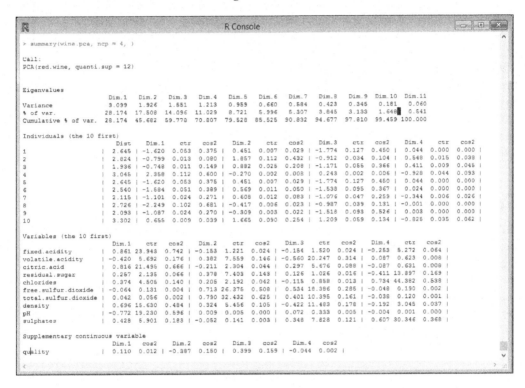

There is no guarantee of substantive meaning in these four components, but by examination of the loadings and contribution of the variables to each, a convention to describe them can be (and this is very subjective):

- Complexity (something that acids are thought to impact)
- Sulfite burden
- Yeastiness
- Grapiness

Bear in mind that the complexity dimension by the very nature of PCA will capture more variance than any subsequent components, so this interpretation also implies that complexity is the foremost aspect of wine to consider, followed by sulfite burden, yeastiness, and finally grapiness. An important consideration is whether this classification scheme makes sense.

 It is critical to remember that both the selection of the number of components to be retained as well as the interpretation of the components are not strictly matters of quantitative analysis; instead, they require some substantive understanding of the topic at hand and sometimes, subjective judgment of the researcher.

Now, the ultimate question is: **How good is the wine?** There was the wine quality variable, which we included as a supplementary variable, and as we can see in the output, it has a low-squared cosine with all four principal components. Thus, while our four principal components explain slightly more than 70 percent of the variance, quality is not strongly tied to any one of them. Maybe there really is something artistic and magical about wine not explained in simple chemistry.

Formative constructs using PCA

Let's delve into another example using PCA that will be instructive when compared to factor analysis later on in the *Exploratory factor analysis and reflective constructs* section. We will return to the physical functioning dataset used earlier in this book. Here we will discuss the notions of formative and reflective constructs. See the following diagram (paying close attention to the arrow directions) for a visual representation of the differences. A formative construct is one in which a general trait is composed of a number of very specific traits as shown in the diagram. The arrows pointing towards the construct indicate that the construct is derived from the traits.

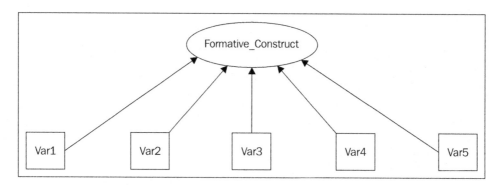

Alternately, a reflexive construct is one in which a general trait is thought to underlie and cause specific traits, as shown in the following diagram. The arrows pointing away from the construct are designed to reflect the fact that the construct drives the traits, and the specific traits are merely manifestations of this construct:

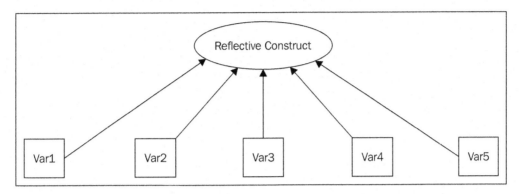

PCA is often considered a method of modeling formative constructs. Later on in this chapter, we will discuss factor analysis, which models reflective constructs.

The physical functioning dataset collects data on the ability of individuals to engage in 20 ADLs and IADLs. Taken together, we would expect that the way a person scores on this would be some sort of a measure of functional independence with ADLs and IADLs. Unfortunately, reporting the scores for all 20 items for each individual is tedious, so we wish to use some sort of a summed score or multiple summed scores to summarize a person's functional status. The question is whether this can legitimately be done. Does it make sense to add standing to walking? There is one more question: **What are we trying to achieve by creating summary scores?** The answer to this question lies in what we seek to measure with this scale. If we assume that a person should be able to do these 20 things independently to be truly independent, then we are assuming that functional independence is in some sense defined by the abilities to perform these 20 items, and we have a formative construct. Alternately, if we assume that the abilities to perform these 20 items simply serve as manifestations of an underlying trait of functional independence, then we have a reflective construct in mind. Statistically, this is the difference between a fixed effects and random effects model, respectively.

We will start here with the idea that we are attempting to use these 20 items to model a formative construct, and we will use PCA for this. We will apply PCA on the physical functioning dataset and look at the variance explained in the PCA:

```
> phys.func <- read.csv('phys_func.txt')[,c(-1)]
> phys.func.pca <- PCA(phys.func)
> summary(phys.func.pca)

Call:
PCA(phys.func)


Eigenvalues
```

	Dim.1	Dim.2	Dim.3	Dim.4	Dim.5
Variance	6.423	1.574	1.286	1.094	0.988
% of var.	32.113	7.869	6.428	5.470	4.939
Cumulative % of var.	32.113	39.983	46.410	51.880	56.818
	Dim.6	Dim.7	Dim.8	Dim.9	Dim.10
Variance	0.865	0.800	0.738	0.699	0.657
% of var.	4.323	4.001	3.689	3.494	3.287
Cumulative % of var.	61.142	65.143	68.832	72.326	75.613
	Dim.11	Dim.12	Dim.13	Dim.14	Dim.15
Variance	0.643	0.560	0.523	0.510	0.485
% of var.	3.213	2.802	2.613	2.552	2.425
Cumulative % of var.	78.826	81.628	84.241	86.793	89.218
	Dim.16	Dim.17	Dim.18	Dim.19	Dim.20
Variance	0.467	0.454	0.440	0.416	0.380
% of var.	2.333	2.271	2.200	2.080	1.899
Cumulative % of var.	91.551	93.821	96.021	98.101	100.000

We can see that the first component explains more than four times as much of the variance as any other single component, and four components are needed to explain the majority of the variance. This suggests that there may be a more simple summary interpretation than inspecting all 20 variables for each subject.

We can also plot the results of the scree plot as follows:

```
plot(phys.func.pca$eig$eigenvalue, type = 'b', xlab = 'Principal
Component', ylab = 'Eigenvalue', main = 'Eigenvalues of Principal
Components')
```

The result is as shown in the following scree plot:

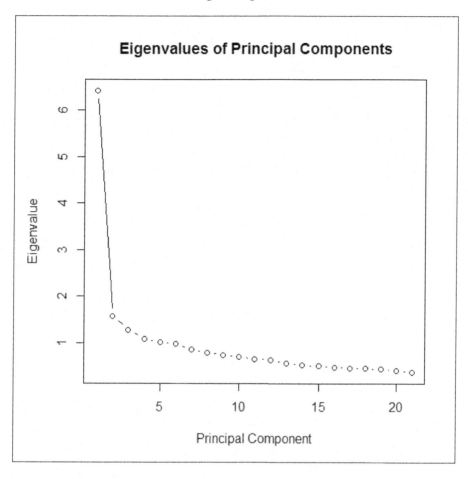

The first question is whether we should simply treat physical functioning as a uni-dimensional scale (that is, reduce 20 dimensions to one) or whether we should treat physical functioning as being multidimensional. Based on the Kaiser-Guttman rule, we should retain four components. Based on the screenshot, it is less clear how many components are worth retaining. Looking very closely at the preceding graph, it appears that there are two plateaus: one that starts after the third component and another that starts after the sixth component. Thus, we should probably retain three components based on scree criteria. However, there is also the problem of the interpretation of the components. Let's try to make sense of a three to four component model by looking at the squared cosines. Remember that these reflect how well a variable is projected onto an axis, so if it is not well projected, then it is not helpful to use that axis to measure the variable:

```
> phys.func.cos <- phys.func.pca$var$cos2
> phys.func.cos[ phys.func.cos < 0.2 ] <- NA
> phys.func.cos
```

	Dim.1	Dim.2	Dim.3	Dim.4	Dim.5
PFQ061A	NA	NA	0.2180148	NA	NA
PFQ061B	0.3425603	NA	NA	NA	NA
PFQ061C	0.3197294	NA	NA	NA	NA
PFQ061D	0.3846285	NA	NA	NA	NA
PFQ061E	0.4029381	NA	NA	NA	NA
PFQ061F	0.3407052	NA	NA	NA	NA
PFQ061G	NA	NA	0.3237579	NA	NA
PFQ061H	0.2748247	NA	NA	NA	0.2984617
PFQ061I	0.4465091	NA	NA	NA	NA
PFQ061J	0.4352429	NA	NA	NA	NA
PFQ061K	NA	0.2953024	NA	NA	NA
PFQ061L	0.3623138	NA	NA	NA	NA
PFQ061M	0.4776348	NA	NA	NA	NA
PFQ061N	0.3667740	NA	NA	NA	NA
PFQ061O	0.3354625	NA	NA	NA	NA
PFQ061P	0.2383867	NA	NA	NA	NA
PFQ061Q	0.3746035	NA	NA	NA	NA
PFQ061R	0.3054978	NA	NA	NA	NA
PFQ061S	NA	NA	NA	0.2773378	NA
PFQ061T	0.4540454	NA	NA	NA	NA

We have set a relatively low threshold of 0.2 for a squared cosine, and we see that most of the variables meet this criterion for the first component, but most fail to meet this criterion for subsequent components. All items meet this criterion for one component when we include four components, but two components have only a single item. As we can see, the items that have a low projection on the first component do not really relate to mobility, whereas those that meet our 0.2 criterion do. Based on this data, we may simply want to consider this outcome measure as being composed of a single dimension that is concerned with physical mobility and exclude the five items from our scoring of the test that do not project well onto this dimension.

In the following sections, we will revisit this as a reflective construct yielding more interpretable results.

What kind of commonly encountered constructs are regarded as formative?

The analysis that we did begins to touch on concepts of psychometrics, which is a field that rarely models formative constructs since it is usually concerned with observable manifestations of invisible psychological processes (for example, reflective constructs). Socio-economic status is one of the few well accepted formative constructs in the psychological and social science canon.

Exploratory factor analysis and reflective constructs

The PCA method that we have discussed so far models all of the variance of the variables to which it is applied. An alternative approach, which is often confused with PCA, is to model only the common variance: an approach called factor analysis (FA). In this chapter, we will discuss **exploratory factor analysis (EFA)**.

Familiarizing yourself with the basic terms

The following are the basic terminologies that you need to be aware of:

- **Latent trait or common factor**: This is an unobserved variable that explains some or all of the variance in observed variables.

- **Path coefficient**: This is the correlation coefficient between a latent trait and an observed variable.

- **Communality**: This refers to the square of a path coefficient in a single factor model.

- **Uniqueness**: Computationally, this is simply one minus the communality of an observed variable. (If a covariance matrix is used, it is equal to variance minus one.)

- **Observed**: This is used to describe matrices and values that are obtained by direct measure or calculations on directly observed values.

- **Implied**: This is used to describe matrices and values that are not observed but estimated to be consistent with other values.

- **Orthogonal factor structure**: We have already seen that PCA treats all of the original variables as being plotted on dimensions at 90 degrees to one another (that is, uncorrelated dimensions) and attempts to account for correlations that really do exist by rotating the coordinate space. Factor analysis that treats the factors as being represented by coordinates at 90 degrees to one another yields an orthogonal factor solution.

- **Oblique factor structure**: This refers to a factor analysis solution in which the factors can be thought of as axes that are not perpendicular to one another and are actually correlated.

Matrices of interest

The following is a list of the matrices that you should familiarize yourself with:

- **Reduced correlation matrix**: This is represented here as R_r; this is the correlation matrix of observed variables with the "1s" along the diagonal replaced by the communalities corresponding to the observed variables.

- **Implied correlation matrix**: This is represented here as R_{imp}; this is the correlation matrix implied by the factor analysis solution.

- **Residual correlation matrix**: This is denoted as R_{resid}. This is the matrix obtained when the implied correlation matrix is subtracted from the observed correlation matrix. The diagonal of this matrix contains the uniqueness values.

- **Factor pattern matrix**: This is represented as **P**. This is a matrix in which factors are represented as columns and observed variables as rows. There should be more observed variables than factors, so this matrix should be taller than it is wide. Each element in the matrix is the path coefficient corresponding to the respective factor and observed variable.

- **Factor correlation matrix**: This is represented as **F**. This is the correlation matrix of the factors with each other. In the case of a single factor model, this is simply a single value "1". In the case of an orthogonal factor structure, this is a diagonal matrix of "1s".

- **Uniqueness matrix**: This is a diagonal matrix, represented as **U**, with individual uniqueness values of each observed variable.

Expressing factor analysis in a matrix model

In matrix representation terms, we can relate the previously mentioned matrices as follows (P' is the transposition of P):

$$R_r = PFP'$$

$$R_{imp} = PFP' + UU$$

Arriving at a factor analysis solution is then a matter of solving for the elements of these matrices.

Basic EFA and concepts of covariance algebra

EFA assumes that the observed variables can be explained by some unobserved variables, also called latent variables, which are statistically modeled as a source of common variance.

If we look at the following diagram, it depicts a **Trait** that is a common source of variance to five observed variables, **A** through **E**. In this diagram, the arrows represent correlations between the observed variables and the latent trait as well as the path coefficients:

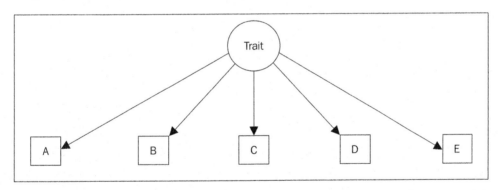

The rules of covariance algebra give us the following formula:

$$cov(A, B) = cov(A, Trait) \times cov(B, Trait)$$

$$cov(A, C) = cov(A, Trait) \times cov(C, Trait)$$

Based on these rules, EFA tries to estimate the path coefficients using some type of statistical estimation method that achieves the best fit, since we are not able to directly calculate these correlations.

Concepts of EFA estimation

To understand the basic idea of how this can be done for a single factor and introduce some concepts, we will start with a very old method of factor estimation, known as the centroid method. This method has largely been supplanted by new computerized methods but serves well to demonstrate the basic idea of factor analysis.

For the single factor model, we will call the path coefficients by the small letter version of the capital representing the observed trait (for example, $cor(A, trait) = a$). Let's assume that we can place the products of all path coefficients with each other into a square matrix, which is called the reduced correlation matrix R_r:

$$R_r = \begin{bmatrix} a^2 & ab & ac & ad & ae \\ ba & b^2 & bc & bd & be \\ ca & cb & c^2 & cd & ce \\ da & db & dc & d^2 & de \\ ea & eb & ec & ed & e^2 \end{bmatrix}$$

We do not know the values of the path coefficients a, b, c, d, or e. (After all, it is these values that we are trying to estimate.) However, because of the rules of covariance algebra, we know:

$$ab = cor(A,B)$$

Thus, while we do not know the values of any of the path coefficients, we are able to estimate the product of these coefficients simply by calculating the correlations between the observed variables associated with these path correlations. It is only the communalities along the diagonal that we are unable to calculate and must come up with some initial estimates.

There are a number of possible methods to generate initial communality estimates:

- Just use "1s".
- Use the highest value off of the diagonal in the same row (or column).
- Use squared multiple correlations (SMCs). These are found by inverting the correlation matrix and subtracting the reciprocals of the values along the diagonal from one. This is the most computationally intensive of the three methods, but generally the best of the three as well.

The greater the number of variables involved, the lesser the importance of the initial estimates of the communalities. This is because when there are more observed variables, the size of the matrix increases dramatically, and the larger a matrix is, the smaller the proportion of elements that fall on the diagonal.

The centroid method

To give the mathematical background of the centroid method, we start with the reduced correlation matrix. To emphasize that the diagonal has merely initial estimates of communalities, we use the 0 subscript, as shown in the following matrix:

$$R_r = \begin{bmatrix} a_0^2 & ab & ac & ad & ae \\ ba & b_0^2 & bc & bd & be \\ ca & cb & c_0^2 & cd & ce \\ da & db & dc & d_0^2 & de \\ ea & eb & ec & ed & e_0^2 \end{bmatrix}$$

We then sum each row (or each column, since this is a symmetric matrix) to get the following matrix. Here we achieve the sum of rows by post-multiplying the reduced correlation matrix by a column matrix of 1s as shown in the following matrix:

$$\begin{bmatrix} a_0^2 & ab & ac & ad & ae \\ ba & b_0^2 & bc & bd & be \\ ca & cb & c_0^2 & cd & ce \\ da & db & dc & d_0^2 & de \\ ea & eb & ec & ed & e_0^2 \end{bmatrix} \begin{bmatrix} 1 \\ 1 \\ 1 \\ 1 \\ 1 \end{bmatrix} = \begin{bmatrix} \sum row_a \\ \sum row_b \\ \sum row_c \\ \sum row_d \\ \sum row_e \end{bmatrix}$$

We then sum all elements of this matrix of row sums to get the sum of all elements in the reduced correlation matrix, and we take the square root of the total as shown in the following formula:

$$\sqrt{\text{Total}} = \sqrt{\sum \begin{bmatrix} \sum row_a \\ \sum row_b \\ \sum row_c \\ \sum row_d \\ \sum row_e \end{bmatrix}}$$

We then divide the sum of each row by the square root of the total to create path coefficient estimates:

$$P = \begin{bmatrix} a \\ b \\ c \\ d \\ e \end{bmatrix} = \frac{1}{\sqrt{\text{Total}}} \begin{bmatrix} \sum row_a \\ \sum row_b \\ \sum row_c \\ \sum row_d \\ \sum row_e \end{bmatrix}$$

If we wish to obtain better path coefficient estimates, we repeat this procedure multiple times by substituting the squared path coefficient estimates for the initial communality estimates.

Since this is a single factor, the matrix *F* is simply a 1. Using these solutions, we can now solve for *U*:

$$R_{imp} - PFP' = UU$$

And for the residual correlation matrix:

$$R_{obs} - R_{imp} = R_{resid}$$

Now, we will execute the same steps using R. We start with a single factor model from the physical functioning dataset, and pick just the items that we think are related to the leg function:

```
le.matrix <- as.matrix(phys.func[,c(2,3,4,8,9,10,13,14)])
```

When coming up with a numerical solution, we need initial estimates for the communalities. We then use the simplest possible reduced correlation matrix. We will use "1" for simplicity as initial estimates for communalities (that is, we use the observed correlation matrix as the reduced correlation matrix) as depicted in the following funtion:

```
le.cor <- cor(le.matrix)
le.cor.reduced <- le.cor
```

Following this step, we sum the rows (or the columns), and from these row sums, we create a sum of all values in the matrix. Path coefficient estimates are equal to the row sums divided by the square root of the total sum of all values in the matrix:

```
row.sums <- le.cor.reduced %*% matrix(rep(1, 8), nrow = 8)
total.sum <- sum(row.sums)
sqrt.total <- sqrt(total.sum)

row.sums / sqrt.total
```

Now, if we recall, our initial communality estimates were just "1". The communalities are simply the path coefficients squared. Therefore, if we like, we can use our solutions for path estimates to create a new reduced correlation matrix, and submit this new reduced correlation matrix to the centroid method all over again. We could do this repeatedly until the path coefficient estimates change minimally with each additional iteration.

An important limitation of the centroid method is that it assumes that all observed variables are correlated in the same direction (for example, all positive) with the latent trait.

Multiple actors

Earlier in this chapter, we went through the basic idea of estimating a path coefficient for a single common factor, but EFA is used not for a single factor but for multiple underlying factors, as depicted in the following figure:

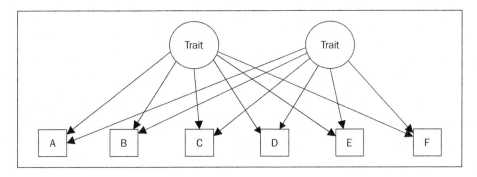

Here we see that there are two traits and six observed variables with both unobserved traits assuming to have some (potentially almost zero) correlation with each of the observed variables and with each other (arrows not shown for this). Here we will use a small letter followed by a number to indicate the path. For example, a_1 is the path coefficient from **Trait-1** to **A**.

The centroid method described earlier only extracts a single factor. If we want to extract multiple factors, we have to do this one at a time, subjecting residual matrices to the centroid method repeatedly. Since this is not a typically used method with modern computers, we will not go through this tedious exercise, but rather skip to a commonly used method that can extract multiple factors.

Direct factor extraction by principal axis factoring

Rather than iteratively factoring out residual matrices, we can directly extract the desired number of factors using **principal axis factoring (PAF)**.

We start with our reduced correlation matrix. We then perform an eigenvalue decomposition of the reduced correlation matrix, yielding eigenvalues, **L**, rank ordered from small to large, and a matrix of corresponding eigenvalues, **V**. If we wish to compute a two-factor solution, we post-multiply the matrix of the first two eigenvectors by a diagonal matrix containing the first two eigvenvalues.

Performing principal axis factoring in R

We will now go through the basic steps of how PAF can be performed in R. We will be demonstrating this with multiple factors, so we will use the full physical functioning dataset. First, we obtain the correlation matrix using the following code:

```
phys.cor <- cor(phys.func)
```

Then, we create a reduced correlation matrix using squared multiple correlations:

```
reduce.cor.mat <- function(cor.mat) {
  inverted.cor.mat <- solve(cor.mat)
  reduced.cor.mat <- cor.mat
  diag(reduced.cor.mat) <- 1 - (1/diag(inverted.cor.mat))

  return(reduced.cor.mat)
}


phys.cor.reduced <- reduce.cor.mat(phys.cor)
```

Finally, we perform the PAF:

```
paf.method <- function(reduced.matrix, nfactor) {
  row.count <- nrow(reduced.matrix)
  eigen.r <- eigen(reduced.matrix, symmetric = TRUE)
  V <- eigen.r$vectors[,c(1:nfactor)]
  L <- diag(sqrt(eigen.r$values[c(1:nfactor)]), nrow = nfactor)

  return((V %*% L))
}


path.coef <- paf.method(phys.cor.reduced, 3)
```

You may find that all loadings on a factor are negative. There is nothing wrong with reversing the sign on a factor loading so long as the relative signs of factors remain consistent (that is, the sign reversal has to be applied consistently to path coefficients). It is important to note that all observed variables have a loading on all extracted factors.

Depending on our goals, this can be the end of our factor analysis, but generally researchers seek to find a simpler structure by rotating the factor structure in a similar manner as PCA rotates axes.

Other factor extraction methods

Principal axis factoring is likely the oldest commonly used method of factor extraction, and it is probably still the most commonly used. It does not make distributional assumptions, and in the case of normally distributed data gives pretty similar estimates as methods that do make distributional assumptions. Maximum likelihood estimation is being used increasingly and is considered numerically superior on datasets that are close to multivariate normally distributed. This method assumes that the dataset is normally distributed and maximizes the (usually log) likelihood function based on a normal distribution. It is relatively robust to mild or moderate deviations from this assumption. Minimum residual factoring seeks to minimize the residual correlations off the diagonal and gives similar estimates as maximum likelihood, while being robust to poorly behaved matrices.

Factor rotation

The final step in most factor analyses is factor rotation. The goal of this step is to determine whether the cloud of data can be represented by a simpler set of coordinates by rotating the axes of the factors. Rotation should increase the number of near zero coefficients in the factor pattern matrix. All observed variables will still have a loading on all of the factors, but ideally, observed variables will show substantially higher loadings on a single particular factor than on other factors once this is completed.

Broadly speaking, there are two approaches to factor rotation: orthogonal and oblique. Orthogonal rotations are still the most commonly used methods, and many regard them as producing easier to interpret solutions. However, oblique rotations are thought to provide more of a real-world estimate. It is also worth noting that single factor models cannot be rotated.

There are many different factor analysis methods, but here we will delve into just four: two orthogonal and two oblique rotations.

Orthogonal factor rotation methods

In this section, we will discuss the commonly used orthogonal factor rotation methods. These rotation methods produce factors that have no correlation, which is why they are thought to be easier to interpret. The downside is that many of the constructs we think of in the real world are in fact correlated.

Quartimax rotation

Quartimax rotation attempts to satisfy the criteria of maximizing the sum of all values in the factor pattern matrix raised to the fourth power:

$$\max = \sum_{j=1}^{f} \sum_{i=1}^{v} p_{ij}^4$$

Here, P_{ij} is the element in i^{th} row and j^{th} column of the factor pattern matrix P (in which variables are represented by rows and factors by columns). The number of variables is denoted by v which is also the number of rows in P. The number of factors is denoted by f, which is also the number of columns in P.

Raising a number to the fourth power has the effect of exaggerating the differences between large and small numbers, so the quartimax criterion will be better met in a factor loading matrix with very large loadings and very small loadings than in one with many moderate-sized loadings. Notably, this rotation simply maximizes this very simple criterion without regard for whether the higher loadings are well distributed among factors or all load onto a single factor.

Varimax rotation

The varimax rotation subtracts a term summing over squared elements of rows and columns. Its criterion is to find a rotation fitting the following formula:

$$\max = \sum_{j=1}^{f}\sum_{i=1}^{v} p_{ij}^4 - \frac{1}{v}\sum_{j=1}^{f}\left(\sum_{i=1}^{v} p_{ij}^4\right)^2$$

The effect of this is to favor rotations in which large loadings are distributed over those with large loadings falling on a single (or relatively few) factors.

Varimax is probably the most widely used factor rotation method.

Oblique rotations

We saw that orthogonal transformations attempt to maximize a transformation of the sums of factor loadings. Oblique rotations do the opposite; they minimize such sums.

Oblimin rotation

Oblimin rotation seeks to minimize the following criteria:

$$\min = \sum_{x,y}\left(\sum_{i=1}^{v} p_x^2 p_y^2 \sum_{i=1}^{v} p_x^2 \sum_{i=1}^{v} p_y^2\right)$$

Here, (x,y) represents a pair of variables, and the summation is done for all variable pairs.

Promax rotation

Promax is an oblique rotation that starts with varimax and then rotates the varimax to an oblique solution. It takes the factor loadings in the promax solution, raises them to a high power to bring small loadings close to zero, and then attempts a rotation that makes the closest loadings to zero equal to zero.

Factor rotation in R

A package that fits many different rotations has been developed, known as GPA rotation. It is available in languages outside of R as well. Notably, it uses a method that can be applied to almost any rotation criterion, so the package offers functions of not only common rotations but some obscure ones as well. For example:

```
> library(GPArotation)
> rotated.structure <- oblimin(path.coef)
> rotated.structure
Oblique rotation method Oblimin Quartimin converged.
Loadings:
          [,1]      [,2]       [,3]
 [1,]  -0.0013   0.06999   3.58e-01
 [2,]  -0.6804  -0.10073   4.18e-02
 [3,]  -0.6434  -0.04880  -1.12e-02
 [4,]  -0.6764   0.06330  -1.20e-01
 [5,]  -0.4324   0.11336   2.17e-01
 [6,]  -0.2496   0.06544   4.82e-01
 [7,]   0.0446   0.06167   5.50e-01
 [8,]  -0.2300   0.31230   5.50e-02
 [9,]  -0.4410   0.34663  -6.06e-02
[10,]  -0.4072   0.41199  -1.13e-01
[11,]   0.1783   0.58615   1.36e-01
[12,]  -0.0698   0.56071   1.03e-01
[13,]  -0.6842  -0.01633   1.11e-01
[14,]  -0.4586   0.20304  -6.44e-03
[15,]  -0.2744   0.37031  -9.65e-05
[16,]   0.0308   0.60407   7.37e-03
[17,]  -0.2598   0.22145   2.99e-01
[18,]  -0.1519   0.29464   2.58e-01
[19,]  -0.0840   0.38490   2.30e-02
[20,]  -0.5786   0.00746   2.10e-01
```

```
Rotating matrix:
        [,1]    [,2]    [,3]
[1,]   0.627  -0.397  -0.202
[2,]   1.017   0.855   0.414
[3,]  -0.025  -0.748   1.001


Phi:
        [,1]    [,2]    [,3]
[1,]   1.000  -0.519  -0.356
[2,]  -0.519   1.000   0.374
[3,]  -0.356   0.374   1.000
```

The object produced by this command has a number of important matrices including the new factor loading matrix produced by the rotation, the correlation matrix of the factors, and the rotation matrix (post-multiplication of the original factor pattern matrix with any of the previously mentioned matrices gives the new factor loading matrix).

The question then is how to interpret these factors. The factor loading matrix shows that all 20 observed items load on all three factors (as is typical of EFA), but the loadings are pretty low on some factors. As such, we can interpret what each factor means by those items that load sufficiently heavily on it. What constitutes "sufficiently heavy" loading is far from clear. One of the most commonly used criteria is that the item should have a loading of at least 0.4. However, other criteria exist that require that an item load substantially more on a single factor than any other factor. In general, it is probably best to use some judgment rather than rigid criteria.

Here, we will reprint the loading matrix replacing all those values less than 0.3 with NA for ease of examination:

```
> loading.matrix <- rotated.structure$loadings
> loading.matrix[ abs(loading.matrix) < 0.3] <- NA
> loading.matrix
            [,1]        [,2]        [,3]
 [1,]         NA          NA   0.3582315
 [2,]  -0.6804255         NA          NA
 [3,]  -0.6434025         NA          NA
 [4,]  -0.6763837         NA          NA
 [5,]  -0.4324032         NA          NA
 [6,]         NA          NA   0.4824759
 [7,]         NA          NA   0.5499046
 [8,]         NA   0.3123046          NA
 [9,]  -0.4410473  0.3466325          NA
[10,]  -0.4071513  0.4119939          NA
```

```
[11,]        NA 0.5861508       NA
[12,]        NA 0.5607121       NA
[13,] -0.6842129       NA       NA
[14,] -0.4585589       NA       NA
[15,]        NA 0.3703143       NA
[16,]        NA 0.6040669       NA
[17,]        NA       NA       NA
[18,]        NA       NA       NA
[19,]        NA 0.3848953       NA
[20,] -0.5785879       NA       NA
>
```

Based on these results, it appears that we have a first factor dealing with gross motor function, a second factor dealing mostly with fine motor function, and a third factor concerned with household management. The two items concerned with recreation (rows 18 and 19) fall on none of these factors. Appropriately, the factor correlation matrix suggests that the factors we interpret as fine and gross motor are more highly correlated with each other than with the household management factor.

Advanced EFA with the psych package

We have gone through the basic conceptual and computational ideas underlying EFA in R. As we discussed earlier, to get good estimates, multiple iterations of these computations are needed until some criteria indicating that an optimal solution has been achieved. An excellent package that bundles much of the work we have done earlier into convenient commands is the psych package. We will now go over how to use this package, including calling some of the advanced features that it offers.

We will continue to use the physical functioning dataset here. Our question at hand is whether a few common sources of variance are able to explain the responses to the 20 items. We saw that a three-factor solution is likely most appropriate (or maybe a four-factor solution, but we will stick with three here). For serious exploratory work, it is often ideal to split off a development and validation dataset, but we will skip that step here.

We also do one more thing here. We are working with ordinal data and treating it like it is continuous. Now we will explicitly account for the fact that it is ordinal rather than continuous. We will use polychoric correlations here to create our correlation matrix. The polychoric correlation assumes that the data is ordinal but represents some continuous underlying phenomena that have simply been binned into discrete ordered categories. The polychoric correlation attempts to estimate a correlation with this assumption and calculate the threshold at which the discretization occurs.

Let's start by finding the polychoric correlations:

```
library(psych)
fit.efa.prep <- polychoric(phys.func, polycor = TRUE)
```

We then take the correlation matrix from these polychoric correlations and place it into our factor analysis:

```
> fit.efa.3 <- fa(fit.efa.prep$rho, nfac = 3, rotate = 'promax')
> fit.efa.3
Factor Analysis using method =   minres
Call: fa(r = fit.efa.prep$rho, nfactors = 3, rotate = "promax")
Standardized loadings (pattern matrix) based upon correlation matrix
          MR1    MR3    MR2    h2   u2 com
PFQ061A -0.13   0.72  -0.09 0.33 0.67 1.1
PFQ061B  0.88   0.09  -0.27 0.62 0.38 1.2
PFQ061C  0.88   0.00  -0.19 0.59 0.41 1.1
PFQ061D  0.96  -0.27   0.03 0.65 0.35 1.2
PFQ061E  0.49   0.22   0.10 0.55 0.45 1.5
PFQ061F  0.35   0.46   0.04 0.62 0.38 1.9
PFQ061G -0.23   0.81   0.10 0.54 0.46 1.2
PFQ061H  0.52   0.31   0.05 0.67 0.33 1.7
PFQ061I  0.64   0.03   0.20 0.65 0.35 1.2
PFQ061J  0.60   0.01   0.28 0.66 0.34 1.4
PFQ061K -0.24   0.08   0.98 0.78 0.22 1.1
PFQ061L  0.17   0.17   0.56 0.67 0.33 1.4
PFQ061M  0.77   0.09  -0.06 0.63 0.37 1.0
PFQ061N  0.58   0.13   0.05 0.51 0.49 1.1
PFQ061O  0.38   0.01   0.40 0.52 0.48 2.0
PFQ061P  0.01  -0.07   0.85 0.65 0.35 1.0
PFQ061Q  0.26   0.69  -0.04 0.74 0.26 1.3
PFQ061R  0.13   0.74  -0.01 0.69 0.31 1.1
PFQ061S  0.12   0.51   0.14 0.49 0.51 1.3
PFQ061T  0.66   0.16  -0.01 0.60 0.40 1.1

                      MR1   MR3   MR2
SS loadings          6.09  3.55  2.57
Proportion Var       0.30  0.18  0.13
Cumulative Var       0.30  0.48  0.61
Proportion Explained 0.50  0.29  0.21
Cumulative Proportion 0.50 0.79  1.00

 With factor correlations of
      MR1   MR3   MR2
```

```
MR1 1.00 0.71 0.67
MR3 0.71 1.00 0.68
MR2 0.67 0.68 1.00

Mean item complexity =  1.3
Test of the hypothesis that 3 factors are sufficient.

The degrees of freedom for the null model are  190  and the objective
function was  15.46
The degrees of freedom for the model are 133  and the objective
function was  2.09

The root mean square of the residuals (RMSR) is  0.04
The df corrected root mean square of the residuals is  0.05

Fit based upon off diagonal values = 0.99
Measures of factor score adequacy
                                               MR1  MR3  MR2
Correlation of scores with factors            0.97 0.95 0.95
Multiple R square of scores with factors      0.94 0.90 0.90
Minimum correlation of possible factor scores 0.89 0.80 0.81
```

There are a number of matrices that we can see in the `fit.efa.3` object. The first is the factor pattern matrix, which contains the factor loadings. To the right of this are two columns, namely `h2` and `u2`, the communality and uniqueness estimates for each item respectively. The two values should sum to one. The greater the communality, the more the total variance of an item is explained by the common factors. The next matrix informs us how much of the variance is explained both by the individual factors and by the whole EFA model. Then there is the matrix with the correlations between the common factors, which is not present for orthogonal solutions.

Let's start by looking at the communalities in the `h2` column. Low communalities suggest that the latent variables do not explain the data well. The communality is computed as the sum of the squared factor loadings of the unrotated factor solution. They tell us how much of the variance of each observed variable is explained by all factors. The communalities are relatively high with the exception of item A, so we are a little suspicious of how well this item is explained even by all three factors together, but for now we will keep all items.

Let's now look at the loadings. Remember that these loadings indicate how these items relate to some underlying unobserved variables that are causing the observed data. However, we have to try to make sense of what these unobserved factors actually are.

Item A (concerned with money management) loads heavily on MR3. Items Q, R, and S also load heavily on this factor. These items appear to be concerned with cognition and social engagement, requiring a few physical demands. Items B, C, D, E, H, I, and T all load heavily on MR1. These items require leg use and are concerned with mobility. Items K, L, O, and P load fairly heavily onto MR2. These are items that tend to require hand use, suggesting that this is an arm or hand function factor. It is worth pointing out that item O loads almost as heavily on MR1, suggesting that some component of mobility is needed to reach overhead. This may be because reaching overhead requires good torso control, which is also needed to walk around and do basic mobility skills. Let me emphasize that this interpretation of the results is made based on a researcher's substantive understanding of the items rather than the statistical analysis alone.

There is some additional information provided, but I will bring your attention to the fit measures in particular. These are a bigger deal in confirmatory factor analysis (discussed in the next chapter), but in summary, these give us some sense of how well the model explains the data. There is more disagreement than agreement on which fit measures for use and how to interpret it. However, three of the commonly used measures are **Root Mean Square Residual (RMSR)**, **Root Mean Square Error of Approximation (RMSEA)**, and the **Tucker-Lewis Index (TLI)**. We would see all three of these if we did not use polychoric correlations, but in this case we see only RMSR. An acceptable fit is usually thought to be indicated by an RMSR less than 0.08, RMSEA less than 0.06, and TLI greater than 0.95 (some would accept greater than 0.90 as adequate).

Now that we have made sense of the factors and the model fit, let's look at the internal consistency reliability. The basic idea of internal consistency is to look at the proportion of variance in scale scores accounted for by the latent variables. In the previous chapter, we touched on this topic discussing how to calculate Cronbach's alpha. Coefficient alpha is the most widely used measure of internal consistency, but for multidimensional scales, McDonald's Omega (of which there are a few) is generally considered better. Let's use psych's omega function to examine internal consistency reliability:

```
omega(fit.efa.prep$rho, nfac = 3, rotate = 'promax')

Omega
Call: omega(m = fit.efa.prep$rho, nfactors = 3, rotate = "promax")
Alpha:                    0.95
G.6:                      0.97
Omega Hierarchical:       0.83
Omega H asymptotic:       0.86
Omega Total               0.96
```

We simply show the beginning of the output from this function, which shows a number of internal consistency reliability coefficients including Cronbach's alpha, Guttman's lambda 6, omega hierarchical, omega asymptotic, and omega total. Cronbach's alpha is the classic split half reliability (discussed in further detail under the applications section of *Chapter 5, Linear Algebra*). Guttman's lambda 6, while rarely used nowadays, is the squared multiple correlation of the item with the other items.

We will focus on omega hierarchical, omega asymptotic, and omega total here. Omega assumes that a multifactor scale has both specific factors onto which only some items load and a general factor onto which all items load. Omega hierarchical gives us the proportion of variance in scaled scores explained by the general factor. Omega asymptotic is the estimated omega hierarchical for a test with the same structure and infinite length (reliability tends to increase with test length). Omega total is the total reliability of a test including that attributable to both the general factor and the factors onto which not all items load.

Before we look at these reliability coefficients, it may be worth looking back at the results of the `fa` function. We see that there are sizeable correlations between the factors, 0.67 to 0.71. If these correlations were low (for example, 0.2), then it would be questionable as to whether omega hierarchical should even be examined given that low correlations between the factors would suggest the non-existence of a general factor that explains scores well.

We can see from these results that omega hierarchical is relatively good (0.83), suggesting that a general factor explains a large proportion of the variance in the scale scores.

Summary

In this chapter, we have reviewed the application of linear algebra to covariance and correlation matrices. We have shown in R how to use PCA to account for total variance in a set of variables and how to use EFA to model common variance among these variables. We have also discussed how these methods relate to formative and reflective constructs. Notably, EFA refers to a set of numerical methods, rather than referring to an analysis intent; but as we have shown here, EFA has significant applicability in exploratory analyses. In the next chapter, we will delve into confirmatory factor analysis (CFA), which models covariance or correlation structures without rotations.

7
Structural Equation Modeling and Confirmatory Factor Analysis

In this chapter, we will discuss the fundamental ideas underlying structural equation modeling, which are often overlooked in other books discussing **structural equation modeling (SEM)** in R, and then delve into how SEM is done in R. We will then discuss two R packages, OpenMx and lavaan. We can directly apply our discussion of the linear algebra underlying SEM using OpenMx. Because of this, we will go over OpenMx first. We will then discuss lavaan, which is probably more user friendly because it sweeps the matrices and linear algebra representations under the rug so that they are invisible unless the user really goes looking for them. Both packages continue to be developed and there will always be some features better supported in one of these packages than in the other.

The previous chapter introduced quantitative techniques that apply linear algebra to correlation or covariance matrices to gain some insight into the correlation or covariance structure of a large dataset. This chapter will continue this theme, discussing SEM and a common application of SEM, **Confirmatory Factor Analysis (CFA)**.

In this chapter, we will discuss the following topics:

- The basic ideas of SEM
- The matrix representation of structural equation models
- Model fitting and estimation methods
- OpenMx
- Lavaan

Datasets

We will use three datasets in this chapter, which are discussed in the following sections to give you an idea of their content.

Political democracy

This is a dataset included in the lavaan package. This is a classic dataset for use in SEM. It contains variables concerned with political freedom movements and economic development in 1960 and 1965, as follows:

- **x1**: This variable is for per capita gross national product in 1960
- **x2**: This variable is for per per capita energy consumption in 1960
- **x3**: This variable is for proportion of the labor force in the industry in 1960
- **y1**: This variable is for ratings of the freedom of the press in 1960
- **y2**: This variable is for freedom of political opposition in 1960
- **y3**: This variable is for fairness of elections in 1960
- **y4**: This variable is for legislature effectiveness in 1960
- **y5**: This variable is for freedom of political opposition in 1965
- **y6**: This variable is for freedom of political opposition in 1965
- **y7**: This variable is for fairness of elections in 1965
- **y8**: This variable is for legislature effectiveness in 1965

Physical functioning dataset

This is the **National Health and Nutrition Examination Survey (NHANES)** physical functioning dataset used in prior chapters. For the purpose of this chapter, it is worth noting that this is a dataset of complete data that has 20 ordinal categorical items concerned with how much difficulty a person faces during basic self-care tasks.

Holzinger-Swineford 1939 dataset

This is another classic dataset of structural equation modeling. We will use the data from the lavaan package (though other packages in R contain the same dataset). It has basic demographic data on students and nine items concerned with mental abilities.

We will simply look at the following variables from this dataset:

- **x1**: This variable is for visual perception
- **x2**: This variable is for cubes
- **x3**: This variable is for lozenges
- **x4**: This variable is for paragraph comprehension
- **x5**: This variable is for sentence completion
- **x6**: This variable is for word meaning
- **x7**: This variable is for speeding addition
- **x8**: This variable is for speeding counting of dots
- **x9**: This variable is for speeding discrimination between straight and curved capitals

It is hypothesized that three domains of intellectual function, visual, textual, and speed, account for the responses of individuals to the nine items. We will apply such a model here.

The basic ideas of SEM

In the previous chapter, we went over the concepts of path coefficients and covariance algebra. In reality, these terms, though used for exploratory factor analysis, come from the tradition of SEM. **Exploratory factor analysis (EFA)** simply attempted to model covariance structure based on identifying common sources of variance. Alternatively, SEM attempts to use covariance to model many, very explicit relationships between variables. Like EFA, SEM can incorporate both observed and unobserved variables, but unlike EFA, SEM does not necessarily need to have unobserved variables. In SEM, the relationships between variables can be represented as a series of paths, whether those variables are observed or latent. The correlation between any two variables is a path coefficient. Each observed variable will also have some residual correlation, and residual correlations may be correlated with one another, something that is not allowed in EFA.

Components of an SEM model

The following is a list of the components of an SEM model:

- **Observed variable**: This is a variable for which we directly collect data that goes into model estimation.

- **Latent variable**: This is a variable that we do not observe but theorize to exist and behave in a certain way. We use observed data and theorized model constraints to estimate quantitative relationships between observed and unobserved variables, and possibly relationships among unobserved variables themselves.

- **Path**: This is a theorized relationship between two variables. Paths are thought of as going from a causal variable to a caused variable. In some cases, a path can go in both the directions.

- **Residual**: This is the portion of the data not explained by the causal paths in the model.

- **Covariance algebra**: These are a set of mathematical tricks describing how covariances behave algebraically. They are as follows:

$$\text{Cov}(\text{Constant}, X_1) = 0$$

$$\text{Cov}(\text{Constant} * X_1, X_2) = \text{Constant} * \text{Cov}(X_1, X_2)$$

$$\text{Cov}(X_1 + X_2, X_3) = \text{Cov}(X_1, X_3) + \text{Cov}(X_2, X_3)$$

In the previous chapter, we described the common factor that the model has relying on the relationship in the following figure:

$$\text{Cov}(X_1, X_2) = \text{Cov}(X_1, F) * \text{Cov}(X_2, F)$$

In the preceding formula, F is a common underlying factor. This is a really special case. SEM allows for an extension of this basic idea to more complex models in which the observed variables can themselves be connected as we will see further in this chapter. This also calls for different estimation methods.

Path diagram

The most typical method to represent an SEM model is with a path diagram. These diagrams use boxes and arrows to represent proposed causal relationships and a set of standard graphical elements have been proposed to represent models.

- **Observed variable**: This is represented with a rectangular box.

- **Latent variable**: This is represented with an elliptical box.

- **Causal path**: This is represented with a straight arrow. The arrow points from causal to effect. A double-headed arrow is also allowed.

- **Residual or correlation**: This is represented with a two-headed curved arrow. If both arrow heads point to the same variable, it is a residual variance. If they point to two different variables, they show a correlated error term. See the figures related to the political economy of SEM as an example in the next sections.

Matrix representation of SEM

We saw path diagrams that allow for a conceptual representation of causal effects. However, to allow for computational solutions to SEM models based on data, a number of statisticians have developed different matrix representations of SEM models. There are numerous such representations, the most common of which are the LISREL model or the simple **reticular action model** (**RAM**). We will discuss two SEM packages in R here: the lavaan package and OpenMx. There is an older package called "sem", which was the first R package available on CRAN to perform SEM, which we will not actually discuss.

The lavaan package does not use any of the common matrix representations (though it uses something close to LISREL). OpenMx uses the RAM by default in its internal representation of path diagrams, but OpenMx also allows the user to customize a matrix representation. Various matrix representations largely achieve the same thing but differ in how they must be multiplied or added together to achieve this. We will review the RAM model here for its simplicity, but other matrix representations can also be used. The exercise of looking at matrix representations is not just academic, but will highlight what is meant by some of the ways that structural equation modelers describe as relationships in models.

The reticular action model (RAM)

All SEM models are trying to solve an implied covariance matrix, C. Each of the linear algebra representations of an SEM model expresses an implied covariance matrix in terms of matrices with model coefficients. The RAM expresses this implied covariance matrix in terms of three matrices, which we will call A, S, and F. The three matrices are described as follows:

- **A**: This is an asymmetric square matrix of paths. It has as many rows (and columns) as there are variables in the model. Model paths are represented as moving from the variable corresponding to the column to the variable corresponding to the row. When a path does not lead from one variable to another, it has a value of 0 in the matrix.

- **S**: This is a symmetric matrix that contains covariances (or correlations) and residual variances. This is also a square matrix with the same dimensions as A. Along the diagonal are the residual variances of variables. If there are covariances between variables not explained by the causal paths (given in A), then these are, in essence, residual covariances and are expressed in off-diagonal elements. The residual variance terms on the diagonal are special cases of residual covariance (covariance of a variable with itself). Since covariance works both ways, if the $i*j$ element of a matrix is filled, then the $j*i$ element must be filled too. If a correlation (that is standardized covariance) matrix is used, then both of these values will be the same.

- **F**: This is a matrix that "filters" out the observed variables. This is a variant of the identity matrix. This matrix has as many columns as there are variables in the model and as many rows as there are observed variables. A value of 1 occupies the corresponding row and column for the observed variables, and a value of 0 for all other terms in the matrix. Thus, there should be exactly one "1" in every row and exactly one "1" in each column that corresponds to an observed variable.

A final important matrix is an identity matrix I, which has as many rows and columns as total variables.

The McArdle McDonald equation shown in the following figure relates the earlier mentioned matrices to the implied covariance matrix:

$$C = F(I-A)^{-1} S(I-A)^{-1'} F$$

Here, the superscript $^{-1}$ denotes matrix inversion, and the ` denotes matrix transposition. (See *Chapter 5, Linear Algebra*, for matrix operations.)

The goal of SEM software is to solve unconstrained parameters in these matrices. We will discuss this in a bit more detail in the next section coupled with an example.

An example of SEM specification

A classic set of data to demonstrate SEM is a model of political democracy. In essence, this model attempts to relate the economic functioning of a country to the democratic functioning of its government. Conceptually, the idea of this model is that economic development at a particular time (whatever that means) drives democratic functioning of a government at the same time. Both economic development and democratic effectiveness at a particular time drive democratic effectiveness at a later point in time. Now, economic development and democratic functioning are not something that can be measured, so we must figure out some good manifestations that we can measure, such as employment rates or perceptions of freedom (which even if subjective, can at least be measured via a survey).

The following figure, taken from `http://www.jstatsoft.org/v48/i02/paper`, displays the theorized manner underlying the relationships of the variables:

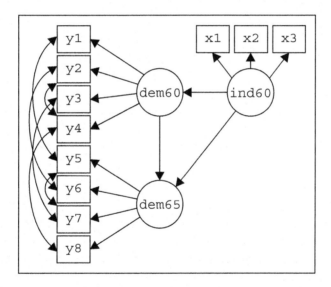

The preceding figure uses the classic notation of circles for latent (unobserved) variables and rectangles for observed variables. Democratic functioning and economic functioning are modeled as latent variables, each with a number of observed variables, which are manifestations of the underlying latent variable.

The following figure has been marked with three rectangles and one ellipse:

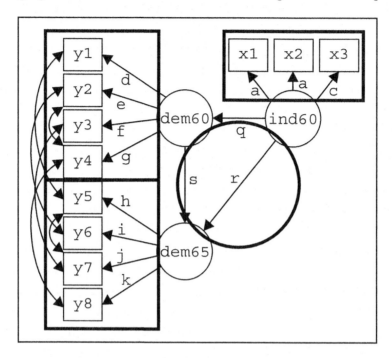

These rectangles and ellipse break the model into measurement components and structural components, respectively. In the previous model, **x1**, **x2**, and **x3** are manifestations of economic independence in 1960, while **y1**, **y2**, **y3**, and **y4**, and **y5**, **y6**, **y7**, and **y8** are manifestations of democratic functioning in 1960 and 1965, respectively. The paths have also been labeled with letters so as to make matrix representation straightforward. (Letters m, n, o, and p have been deliberately excluded.) We should also point out that while it is not explicitly shown, there are residual (that is not explained by causal paths) variances for all variables. There are some paths with curved arrows that indicate a correlation between these residual terms (that is residual covariance).

It is considered important to assess the validity of a measurement model of a latent variable prior to studying the relationships between the latent variables (that is the structural component of the model).

We will now move on to place the previous model in matrices of the RAM model. Rows and columns have been named with their respective variables in the model for ease of following the matrix. The first matrix is the implied covariance matrix, as shown in the following matrix:

$$C = \begin{array}{c} \\ x_1 \\ x_2 \\ \vdots \\ y_7 \\ y_8 \end{array} \begin{array}{ccccc} x_1 & x_2 & \cdots & y_7 & y_8 \\ \left(\begin{array}{ccccc} \mathrm{Var}(x_1) & \mathrm{Cov}(x_1,x_2) & \cdots & \mathrm{Cov}(x_1,y_7) & \mathrm{Cov}(x_1,y_8) \\ \mathrm{Cov}(x_2,x_1) & \mathrm{Var}(x_2) & & \mathrm{Cov}(x_2,y_7) & \mathrm{Cov}(x_2,y_8) \\ \vdots & & \ddots & & \vdots \\ \mathrm{Cov}(y_7,x_1) & \mathrm{Cov}(y_7,x_2) & & \mathrm{Var}(y_7) & \mathrm{Cov}(y_7,y_8) \\ \mathrm{Cov}(y_8,x_1) & \mathrm{Cov}(y_8,x_2) & \cdots & \mathrm{Cov}(y_8,y_7) & \mathrm{Var}(y_8) \end{array} \right) \end{array}$$

The next matrix is the matrix of causal paths A, which is shown in the following figure:

$$A = \begin{array}{c} \\ x_1 \\ x_2 \\ x_3 \\ y_1 \\ y_2 \\ \vdots \\ y_{10} \\ ind_{60} \\ dem_{60} \\ dem_{65} \end{array} \begin{array}{cccccccc} x_1 & x_2 & \cdots & y_{10} & ind_{60} & dem_{60} & dem_{65} \\ \left(\begin{array}{ccccccc} 0 & 0 & \cdots & 0 & a & 0 & 0 \\ 0 & 0 & \cdots & 0 & b & 0 & 0 \\ 0 & 0 & \cdots & 0 & c & 0 & 0 \\ 0 & 0 & \cdots & 0 & 0 & d & 0 \\ 0 & 0 & \cdots & 0 & 0 & e & 0 \\ \vdots & \vdots & & \vdots & \vdots & \vdots & \vdots \\ 0 & 0 & \cdots & 0 & 0 & 0 & 0 \\ 0 & 0 & \cdots & 0 & 0 & 0 & 0 \\ 0 & 0 & \cdots & 0 & q & 0 & 0 \\ 0 & 0 & \cdots & 0 & r & s & 0 \end{array} \right) \end{array}$$

To avoid an excessively large (13 x 13) matrix, not all paths are illustrated. As can be seen in the preceding matrix, path A going from *ind60* to *x1* is placed in the appropriate column and row.

Then, we move on to the residual variances and covariance matrix S, which is given in the following figure:

$$
S = \begin{array}{c}
\\ x_1 \\ x_2 \\ x_3 \\ y_1 \\ y_2 \\ \vdots \\ y_5 \\ y_6 \\ \vdots \\ dem_{65}
\end{array}
\begin{array}{ccccccccccc}
x_1 & x_2 & x_3 & y_1 & y_2 & \cdots & y_5 & y_6 & \cdots & dem_{65} \\
\begin{pmatrix} \delta_{x1} & 0 & 0 & 0 & 0 & \cdots & 0 & a & 0 & 0 \\
0 & \delta_{x2} & 0 & 0 & 0 & \cdots & 0 & b & 0 & 0 \\
0 & 0 & \delta_{x3} & 0 & 0 & \cdots & 0 & c & 0 & 0 \\
0 & 0 & 0 & \delta_{y1} & 0 & \cdots & \delta_{y5,y1} & 0 & 0 & 0 \\
0 & 0 & 0 & 0 & \delta_{y2} & \cdots & 0 & \delta_{y6,y2} & 0 & 0 \\
\vdots & \vdots & \vdots & \vdots & \vdots & \ddots & \vdots & \vdots & \ddots & \vdots \\
0 & 0 & 0 & \delta_{y1,y5} & 0 & \cdots & \delta_{y5} & 0 & 0 & 0 \\
0 & 0 & 0 & 0 & \delta_{y2,y6} & \cdots & 0 & \delta_{y6} & 0 & 0 \\
\vdots & \vdots & \vdots & \vdots & \vdots & \cdots & 0 & 0 & \ddots & \vdots \\
0 & 0 & 0 & 0 & 0 & \cdots & 0 & 0 & 0 & \epsilon_{dem65} \end{pmatrix}
\end{array}
$$

Here, the letter δ is used to denote a residual (that is unexplained by the causal paths) covariance for observed variables. The letter ⊡ is used to denote residual covariances among latent variables. Along the diagonal are the residual covariances of a variable with itself (that is the residual variance).

Finally, the filter of observed variables F is shown in the following figure:

$$
F = \begin{array}{c}
\\ x_1 \\ x_2 \\ x_3 \\ y_1 \\ y_2 \\ \vdots \\ y_{10}
\end{array}
\begin{array}{cccccccccc}
x_1 & x_2 & x_3 & y_1 & y_2 & \cdots & y_{10} & ind_{60} & dem_{60} & dem_{65} \\
\begin{pmatrix} 1 & 0 & 0 & 0 & 0 & \cdots & 0 & 0 & 0 & 0 \\
0 & 1 & 1 & 1 & 1 & \cdots & 1 & 1 & 1 & 1 \\
0 & 0 & 0 & 0 & 0 & \cdots & 0 & 0 & 0 & 0 \\
0 & 0 & 0 & 0 & 0 & \cdots & 0 & 0 & 0 & 0 \\
0 & 0 & 0 & 0 & 0 & \cdots & 0 & 0 & 0 & 0 \\
\vdots & \vdots & \vdots & \vdots & \vdots & \ddots & \vdots & \vdots & \vdots & \vdots \\
0 & 0 & 0 & 0 & 0 & \cdots & 0 & 0 & 0 & 0 \end{pmatrix}
\end{array}
$$

In the preceding matrix, there are 1s along the diagonal of only those variables that are observed (hence, the 0s for the last three latent variables).

Something to note here is that the RAM matrix representation does not separate the measurement model from the structural model. By looking at the matrices, one can tell what the measurement and structural models are from a combination of the filter matrix and the matrix of causal paths, but this takes some work and is far from obvious without the path diagram. The LISREL matrix instead uses a few additional matrices and separates out the measurement and structural models.

Something to note is that this matrix representation with explicit modeling of variances and covariances allows us to do some things not feasible in exploratory factor analysis. The first thing is that we can define a particular structural model. This is in stark contrast to EFA, which simply assumes that all latent variables are either correlated or uncorrelated. Additionally, we can constrain path coefficients to be equal. For example, if we wanted to test a model where the causal paths from *ind60* to *x1*, *x2*, and *x3* were equal, we would simply substitute a single variable representing each of these paths in the *A* matrix. Finally, we can allow variables to be correlated, something not allowed in typical EFA techniques. A final, somewhat obvious difference, is that CFA requires us to prioritize explicitly define which variables have paths between them. However, this is actually not quite as defining a distinction as one might think; EFA has a type of rotation in which paths are prioritize described, known as target rotation.

An example in R

We went over the matrix representation of SEM models in theory. Now, we will show how this can be practically done in R using the RAM matrix specifications mentioned earlier. We will use the political democracy dataset available in the lavaan package for this example. Notably, this dataset is ordered such that the first eight columns are the y variables and the last three are the x variables. Let's take a look at the following example:

```
library(lavaan)
data(PoliticalDemocracy)
```

We will create the covariance matrix of this dataset, as follows:

```
pd.cov <- cov(PoliticalDemocracy)
```

Now, we will create each of our matrices A, S, F, and I. In a real SEM example, we would iteratively create new A and S matrices in an attempt to find the best values to match the implied to the observed covariance matrix. Think of this as starting values for the matrices. In this case, we will choose starting values that pretty closely match a final solution, so that we do not have to iterate through dozens of times to find a good solution. Remember that we have 11 observed and three unobserved variables for a total of 14 variables.

First, let's take a look at the A matrix of paths, which is a matrix of *14*14*:

```
mat.A <- matrix(
  c(0, 0, 0, 0, 0, 0, 0, 0, 0, 0, 0, 0, 1,   0,
    0, 0, 0, 0, 0, 0, 0, 0, 0, 0, 0, 0, 1,   0,
    0, 0, 0, 0, 0, 0, 0, 0, 0, 0, 0, 0, 1,   0,
    0, 0, 0, 0, 0, 0, 0, 0, 0, 0, 0, 0, 1,   0,
    0, 0, 0, 0, 0, 0, 0, 0, 0, 0, 0, 0, 0,   1,
    0, 0, 0, 0, 0, 0, 0, 0, 0, 0, 0, 0, 0,   1,
    0, 0, 0, 0, 0, 0, 0, 0, 0, 0, 0, 0, 0,   1,
    0, 0, 0, 0, 0, 0, 0, 0, 0, 0, 0, 0, 0,   1,
    0, 0, 0, 0, 0, 0, 0, 0, 0, 0, 0, 1, 0,   0,
    0, 0, 0, 0, 0, 0, 0, 0, 0, 0, 0, 2, 0,   0,
    0, 0, 0, 0, 0, 0, 0, 0, 0, 0, 0, 2, 0,   0,
    0, 0, 0, 0, 0, 0, 0, 0, 0, 0, 0, 0, 0,   0,
    0, 0, 0, 0, 0, 0, 0, 0, 0, 0, 0,1.5,0,   0,
    0, 0, 0, 0, 0, 0, 0, 0, 0, 0, 0,0.5,0.5,0
  ), nrow = 14, byrow = TRUE
)
```

Then, let's take a look at the S matrix of residual variances or covariances, which is also a matrix of *14*14*:

```
mat.S <- matrix(
  c(2, 0, 0, 0,.5, 0, 0, 0, 0, 0, 0, 0, 0, 0,
    0, 7, 0, 1, 0, 2, 0, 0, 0, 0, 0, 0, 0, 0,
    0, 0, 5, 0, 0, 0, 1, 0, 0, 0, 0, 0, 0, 0,
    0, 1, 0, 3, 0, 0, 0,.5, 0, 0, 0, 0, 0, 0,
   .5, 0, 0, 0, 2, 0, 0, 0, 0, 0, 0, 0, 0, 0,
    0, 2, 0, 0, 0, 5, 0, 1, 0, 0, 0, 0, 0, 0,
    0, 0, 1, 0, 0, 0, 3, 0, 0, 0, 0, 0, 0, 0,
    0, 0, 0,.5, 0, 1, 0, 3, 0, 0, 0, 0, 0, 0,
    0, 0, 0, 0, 0, 0, 0, 0,.1, 0, 0, 0, 0, 0,
    0, 0, 0, 0, 0, 0, 0, 0, 0,.1, 0, 0, 0, 0,
    0, 0, 0, 0, 0, 0, 0, 0, 0, 0,.5, 0, 0, 0,
    0, 0, 0, 0, 0, 0, 0, 0, 0, 0, 0,.5, 0, 0,
    0, 0, 0, 0, 0, 0, 0, 0, 0, 0, 0, 0, 4, 0,
    0, 0, 0, 0, 0, 0, 0, 0, 0, 0, 0, 0, 0,.2
  ), nrow = 14, byrow = TRUE
)
```

Next, let's take a look at the filter matrix, which selects the observed variables is a matrix of *11*14*:

```
mat.F <- matrix(
  c(1, 0, 0, 0, 0, 0, 0, 0, 0, 0, 0, 0, 0, 0,
    0, 1, 0, 0, 0, 0, 0, 0, 0, 0, 0, 0, 0, 0,
    0, 0, 1, 0, 0, 0, 0, 0, 0, 0, 0, 0, 0, 0,
    0, 0, 0, 1, 0, 0, 0, 0, 0, 0, 0, 0, 0, 0,
    0, 0, 0, 0, 1, 0, 0, 0, 0, 0, 0, 0, 0, 0,
    0, 0, 0, 0, 0, 1, 0, 0, 0, 0, 0, 0, 0, 0,
    0, 0, 0, 0, 0, 0, 1, 0, 0, 0, 0, 0, 0, 0,
    0, 0, 0, 0, 0, 0, 0, 1, 0, 0, 0, 0, 0, 0,
    0, 0, 0, 0, 0, 0, 0, 0, 1, 0, 0, 0, 0, 0,
    0, 0, 0, 0, 0, 0, 0, 0, 0, 1, 0, 0, 0, 0,
    0, 0, 0, 0, 0, 0, 0, 0, 0, 0, 1, 0, 0, 0
  ), nrow = 11, byrow = TRUE
)
```
Finally the 14 x 14 identity matrix:
```
mat.I <- diag(rep(1, 14), nrow = 14)
```

We can write a function that will perform all of the matrix operations of the McArdle McDonald equation (variables have a 0 in the name), as follows:

```
RAM.implied.covariance <- function(A.0, S.0, F.0, I.0) {
  implied.covariance <- F.0 %*% solve(I.0-A.0) %*% S.0 %*%
t(solve(I.0-A.0)) %*% t(F.0)
  return(implied.covariance)
}
```

And, finally, we can estimate an implied covariance matrix based on our starting A and S matrices, which is shown in the following matrix rounded to 2 decimal places:

```
> round(RAM.implied.covariance(mat.A, mat.S, mat.F, mat.I), 2)
        [,1]   [,2]   [,3] [,4] [,5] [,6] [,7] [,8] [,9] [,10] [,11]
 [1,]  7.12   5.12   5.12 5.12 3.44 2.94 2.94 2.94 0.75  1.50  1.50
 [2,]  5.12  12.12   5.12 6.12 2.94 4.94 2.94 2.94 0.75  1.50  1.50
 [3,]  5.12   5.12  10.12 5.12 2.94 2.94 3.94 2.94 0.75  1.50  1.50
 [4,]  5.12   6.12   5.12 8.12 2.94 2.94 2.94 3.44 0.75  1.50  1.50
 [5,]  3.44   2.94   2.94 2.94 3.98 1.98 1.98 1.98 0.63  1.25  1.25
 [6,]  2.94   4.94   2.94 2.94 1.98 6.98 1.98 2.98 0.63  1.25  1.25
 [7,]  2.94   2.94   3.94 2.94 1.98 1.98 4.98 1.98 0.63  1.25  1.25
 [8,]  2.94   2.94   2.94 3.44 1.98 2.98 1.98 4.98 0.63  1.25  1.25
 [9,]  0.75   0.75   0.75 0.75 0.63 0.63 0.63 0.63 0.60  1.00  1.00
[10,]  1.50   1.50   1.50 1.50 1.25 1.25 1.25 1.25 1.00  2.10  2.00
[11,]  1.50   1.50   1.50 1.50 1.25 1.25 1.25 1.25 1.00  2.00  2.50
```

Compare the preceding matrix to the observed covariance matrix as follows:

```
> round(pd.cov, 2)
      y1    y2    y3    y4   y5    y6    y7    y8   x1   x2   x3
y1  6.88  6.25  5.84  6.09 5.06  5.75  5.81  5.67 0.73 1.27 0.91
y2  6.25 15.58  5.84  9.51 5.60  9.39  7.54  7.76 0.62 1.49 1.17
y3  5.84  5.84 10.76  6.69 4.94  4.73  7.01  5.64 0.79 1.55 1.04
y4  6.09  9.51  6.69 11.22 5.70  7.44  7.49  8.01 1.15 2.24 1.84
y5  5.06  5.60  4.94  5.70 6.83  4.98  5.82  5.34 1.08 2.06 1.58
y6  5.75  9.39  4.73  7.44 4.98 11.38  6.75  8.25 0.85 1.81 1.57
y7  5.81  7.54  7.01  7.49 5.82  6.75 10.80  7.59 0.94 2.00 1.63
y8  5.67  7.76  5.64  8.01 5.34  8.25  7.59 10.53 1.10 2.23 1.69
x1  0.73  0.62  0.79  1.15 1.08  0.85  0.94  1.10 0.54 0.99 0.82
x2  1.27  1.49  1.55  2.24 2.06  1.81  2.00  2.23 0.99 2.28 1.81
x3  0.91  1.17  1.04  1.84 1.58  1.57  1.63  1.69 0.82 1.81 1.98
```

As we can see, it is pretty close. Can we improve it? Yes, but it will take some trial and error with new values in the A (and subsequently the S) matrix. This is what optimizers do in statistical software, and the R packages that we described here do just that. Notably, there are actually an infinite number of possible solutions for many SEM models, so some constraining of values is often needed. In this case, we would want to constrain a few particular path values. In this case, constraining one path going from each of the latent variables to a manifest variable will do the trick.

How important are the starting values that I choose?

The choice of starting values is a bit of a problem. In SEM software, poor starting values can fail to converge to good solutions; a problem that you will likely run into as you do more and more SEM. Additionally, search routines that seek to optimize or fit the object can get stuck in local maxima and minima. Even SEM programs that choose the starting values for you also occasionally suffer from this problem. When you obtain SEM results that don't make sense, choosing new starting values can often yield a much better solution.

A couple of other points worth noting here are that these matrices are relatively large. There is the key step of matrix inversion, which will become more computationally intensive as more variables are included in the SEM model.

SEM model fitting and estimation methods

In an earlier section, we mentioned that to ultimately find a good solution, software has to use trial and error to come up with an implied covariance matrix that matches the observed covariance matrix as well as possible. The question is what does "as well as possible" mean? The answer to this is that the software must try to minimize some particular criterion, usually some sort of discrepancy function. Just what that criterion is depends on the estimation method used. The most commonly used estimation methods in SEM include:

- Ordinary least squares (OLS) also called unweighted least squares
- Generalized least squares (GLS)
- Maximum likelihood (ML)

There are a number of other estimation methods as well, some of which can be done in R, but here we will stick with describing the most common ones. In general, OLS is the simplest and computationally cheapest estimation method. GLS is computationally more demanding, and ML is computationally more intensive. We will see why this is, as we discuss the details of these estimation methods.

Any SEM estimation method seeks to estimate model parameters that recreate the observed covariance matrix as well as possible. To evaluate how closely an implied covariance matrix matches an observed covariance matrix, we need a discrepancy function. If we assume multivariate normality of the observed variables, the following function can be used to assess discrepancy:

$$\text{Discrepancy} = \frac{1}{2}\,\text{tr}\,((R - C)V)^2$$

In the preceding figure, R is the observed covariance matrix, C is the implied covariance matrix, and V is a weight matrix.

The *tr* function refers to the trace function, which sums the elements of the main diagonal.

The choice of V varies based on the SEM estimation method:

- For OLS, $V = I$
- For GLS, $V = R^{-1}$

In the case of an ML estimation, we seek to minimize one of a number of similar criteria to describe ML, as follows:

$$\ln|C| - \ln|R| + trRC^{-1} - n$$

In the preceding figure, n is the number of variables.

There are a couple of points worth noting here. GLS estimation inverts the observed correlation matrix, something computationally demanding with large matrices, but something that must only be done once. Alternatively, ML requires inversion of the implied covariance matrix, which changes with each iteration. Thus, each iteration requires the computationally demanding step of matrix inversion. With modern fast computers, this difference may not be noticeable, but with large SEM models, this might start to be quite time-consuming.

Assessing SEM model fit

The final question in an SEM model is how well the model explains the data. This is answered with the use of SEM measures of fit. Most of these measures are based on a chi-squared distribution. The fit criteria for GLS and ML (as well as a number of other estimation procedures such as asymptotic distribution-free methods) multiplied by *N-1* is approximately chi-square distributed. Here, the capital *N* represents the number of observations in the dataset, as opposed to lower case *n*, which gives the number of variables. We compute degrees of freedom as the difference between the number of estimated parameters and the number of known covariances (that is, the total number of values in one triangle of an observed covariance matrix).

This gives way to the first test statistic for SEM models, a chi-squared significance level comparing our chi-square value to some minimum chi-square threshold to achieve statistical significance.

As with conventional chi-square testing, a chi-square value that is higher than some minimal threshold will reject the null hypothesis. Most experimental science features such as rejection supports the hypothesis of the experiment. This is not the case in SEM, where the null hypothesis is that the model fits the data. Thus, a non-significant chi-square is an indicator of model fit, whereas a significant chi-square rejects model fit. A notable limitation of this is that a greater sample size, greater *N*, will increase the chi-square value and will therefore increase the power to reject model fit. Thus, using conventional chi-squared testing will tend to support models developed in small samples and reject models developed in large samples.

The choice an interpretation of fit measures is a contentious one in SEM literature. However, as can be seen, chi-square has limitations. As such, other model fit criteria were developed that do not penalize models that fit in large samples (some may penalize models fit to small samples though). There are over a dozen indices, but the most common fit indices and interpretation information are as follows:

- **Comparative fit index**: In this index, a higher value is better. Conventionally, a value of greater than 0.9 was considered an indicator of good model fit, but some might argue that a value of at least 0.95 is needed. This is relatively sample size insensitive.

- **Root mean square error of approximation**: A value of under 0.08 (smaller is better) is often considered necessary to achieve model fit. However, this fit measure is quite sample size sensitive, penalizing small sample studies.

- **Tucker-Lewis index** (Non-normed fit index): This is interpreted in a similar manner as the comparative fit index. Also, this is not very sample size sensitive.

- **Standardized root mean square residual**: In this index, a lower value is better. A value of 0.06 or less is considered needed for model fit. Also, this may penalize small samples.

In the next section, we will show you how to actually fit SEM models in R and how to evaluate fit using fit measures.

Using OpenMx and matrix specification of an SEM

We went through the basic principles of SEM and discussed the basic computational approach by which this can be achieved. SEM remains an active area of research (with an entire journal devoted to it, *Structural Equation Modeling*), so there are many additional peculiarities, but rather than delving into all of them, we will start by delving into actually fitting an SEM model in R.

OpenMx is not in the CRAN repository, but it is easily obtainable from the OpenMx website, by typing the following in R:

```
source('http://openmx.psyc.virginia.edu/getOpenMx.R')"
```

Summarizing the OpenMx approach

In this example, we will use OpenMx by specifying matrices as mentioned earlier. To fit an OpenMx model, we need to first specify the model and then tell the software to attempt to fit the model. Model specification involves four components:

- Specifying the model matrices; this has two parts:
    - ○ Declare starting values for the estimation
    - ○ Declaring which values can be estimated and which are fixed

- Telling OpenMx the algebraic relationship of the matrices that should produce an implied covariance matrix

- Giving an instruction for the model fitting criterion

- Providing a source of data

The R commands that correspond to each of these steps are:

- `mxMatrix`
- `mxAlgebra`
- `mxMLObjective`
- `mxData`

We will then pass the objects created with each of these commands to create an SEM model using `mxModel`.

Explaining an entire example

First, to make things simple, we will store the FALSE and TRUE logical values in single letter variables, which will be convenient when we have matrices full of TRUE and FALSE values as follows:

```
F <- FALSE
T <- TRUE
```

Specifying the model matrices

Specifying matrices is done with the mxMatrix function, which returns an MxMatrix object. (Note that the object starts with a capital "M" while the function starts with a lowercase "m.") Specifying an MxMatrix is much like specifying a regular R matrix, but MxMatrices has some additional components. The most notable difference is that there are actually two different matrices used to create an MxMatrix. The first is a matrix of starting values, and the second is a matrix that tells which starting values are free to be estimated and which are not. If a starting value is not freely estimable, then it is a fixed constant. Since the actual starting values that we choose do not really matter too much in this case, we will just pick one as a starting value for all parameters that we would like to be estimated. Let's take a look at the following example:

```
mx.A <- mxMatrix(
  type = "Full",
  nrow=14,
  ncol=14,

  #Provide the Starting Values
  values = c(
    0, 0, 0, 0, 0, 0, 0, 0, 0, 0, 0, 0, 1, 0,
    0, 0, 0, 0, 0, 0, 0, 0, 0, 0, 0, 0, 1, 0,
    0, 0, 0, 0, 0, 0, 0, 0, 0, 0, 0, 0, 1, 0,
    0, 0, 0, 0, 0, 0, 0, 0, 0, 0, 0, 0, 1, 0,
    0, 0, 0, 0, 0, 0, 0, 0, 0, 0, 0, 0, 0, 1,
    0, 0, 0, 0, 0, 0, 0, 0, 0, 0, 0, 0, 0, 1,
    0, 0, 0, 0, 0, 0, 0, 0, 0, 0, 0, 0, 0, 1,
    0, 0, 0, 0, 0, 0, 0, 0, 0, 0, 0, 0, 0, 1,
    0, 0, 0, 0, 0, 0, 0, 0, 0, 0, 0, 1, 0, 0,
    0, 0, 0, 0, 0, 0, 0, 0, 0, 0, 0, 1, 0, 0,
    0, 0, 0, 0, 0, 0, 0, 0, 0, 0, 0, 1, 0, 0,
    0, 0, 0, 0, 0, 0, 0, 0, 0, 0, 0, 0, 0, 0,
    0, 0, 0, 0, 0, 0, 0, 0, 0, 0, 0, 1, 0, 0,
    0, 0, 0, 0, 0, 0, 0, 0, 0, 0, 0, 1, 1, 0
  ),
```

```
#Tell R which values are free to be estimated
free = c(
  F,  F,  F,  F,  F,  F,  F,  F,  F,  F,  F,  F,  F,  F,
  F,  F,  F,  F,  F,  F,  F,  F,  F,  F,  F,  F,  T,  F,
  F,  F,  F,  F,  F,  F,  F,  F,  F,  F,  F,  F,  T,  F,
  F,  F,  F,  F,  F,  F,  F,  F,  F,  F,  F,  F,  T,  F,
  F,  F,  F,  F,  F,  F,  F,  F,  F,  F,  F,  F,  F,  F,
  F,  F,  F,  F,  F,  F,  F,  F,  F,  F,  F,  F,  F,  T,
  F,  F,  F,  F,  F,  F,  F,  F,  F,  F,  F,  F,  F,  T,
  F,  F,  F,  F,  F,  F,  F,  F,  F,  F,  F,  F,  F,  T,
  F,  F,  F,  F,  F,  F,  F,  F,  F,  F,  F,  F,  F,  F,
  F,  F,  F,  F,  F,  F,  F,  F,  F,  F,  F,  T,  F,  F,
  F,  F,  F,  F,  F,  F,  F,  F,  F,  F,  F,  T,  F,  F,
  F,  F,  F,  F,  F,  F,  F,  F,  F,  F,  F,  F,  F,  F,
  F,  F,  F,  F,  F,  F,  F,  F,  F,  F,  F,  T,  F,  F,
  F,  F,  F,  F,  F,  F,  F,  F,  F,  F,  F,  T,  T,  F
  ),
  byrow=TRUE,

  #Provide a matrix name that will be used in model fitting
  name="A",
)
```

We will now apply this same technique to the S matrix. Here, we will create two S matrices, S1 and S2. They differ simply in the starting values that they supply. We will later try to fit an SEM model using one matrix, and then the other to address problems with the first one. The difference is that S1 uses starting variances of 1 in the diagonal, and S2 uses starting variances of 5. Here, we will use the "symm" matrix type, which is a symmetric matrix. We could use the "full" matrix type, but by using "symm", we are saved from typing all of the symmetric values in the upper half of the matrix. Let's take a look at the following matrix:

```
mx.S1 <- mxMatrix("Symm", nrow=14, ncol=14,
  values = c(
    1,
    0, 1,
    0, 0, 1,
    0, 1, 0, 1,
    1, 0, 0, 0, 1,
    0, 1, 0, 0, 0, 1,
    0, 0, 1, 0, 0, 0, 1,
    0, 0, 0, 1, 0, 1, 0, 1,
    0, 0, 0, 0, 0, 0, 0, 0, 1,
    0, 0, 0, 0, 0, 0, 0, 0, 0, 1,
    0, 0, 0, 0, 0, 0, 0, 0, 0, 0, 1,
```

```
        0, 0, 0, 0, 0, 0, 0, 0, 0, 0, 0, 1,
        0, 0, 0, 0, 0, 0, 0, 0, 0, 0, 0, 0, 1,
        0, 0, 0, 0, 0, 0, 0, 0, 0, 0, 0, 0, 0, 1
    ),

    free = c(
    T,
    F, T,
    F, F, T,
    F, T, F, T,
    T, F, F, F, T,
    F, T, F, F, F, T,
    F, F, T, F, F, F, T,
    F, F, F, T, F, T, F, T,
    F, F, F, F, F, F, F, F, T,
    F, F, F, F, F, F, F, F, F, T,
    F, F, F, F, F, F, F, F, F, F, T,
    F, F, F, F, F, F, F, F, F, F, F, T,
    F, F, F, F, F, F, F, F, F, F, F, F, T,
    F, F, F, F, F, F, F, F, F, F, F, F, F, T
    ),
    byrow=TRUE,
    name="S"
)


#The alternative, S2 matrix:
mx.S2 <- mxMatrix("Symm", nrow=14, ncol=14,
    values = c(
        5,
        0, 5,
        0, 0, 5,
        0, 1, 0, 5,
        1, 0, 0, 0, 5,
        0, 1, 0, 0, 0, 5,
        0, 0, 1, 0, 0, 0, 5,
        0, 0, 0, 1, 0, 1, 0, 5,
        0, 0, 0, 0, 0, 0, 0, 0, 5,
        0, 0, 0, 0, 0, 0, 0, 0, 0, 5,
        0, 0, 0, 0, 0, 0, 0, 0, 0, 0, 5,
        0, 0, 0, 0, 0, 0, 0, 0, 0, 0, 0, 5,
        0, 0, 0, 0, 0, 0, 0, 0, 0, 0, 0, 0, 5,
        0, 0, 0, 0, 0, 0, 0, 0, 0, 0, 0, 0, 0, 5
    ),
```

```
        free = c(
        T,
        F,  T,
        F,  F,  T,
        F,  T,  F,  T,
        T,  F,  F,  F,  T,
        F,  T,  F,  F,  F,  T,
        F,  F,  T,  F,  F,  F,  T,
        F,  F,  F,  T,  F,  T,  F,  T,
        F,  F,  F,  F,  F,  F,  F,  F,  T,
        F,  F,  F,  F,  F,  F,  F,  F,  F,  T,
        F,  F,  F,  F,  F,  F,  F,  F,  F,  F,  T,
        F,  F,  F,  F,  F,  F,  F,  F,  F,  F,  F,  T,
        F,  F,  F,  F,  F,  F,  F,  F,  F,  F,  F,  F,  T,
        F,  F,  F,  F,  F,  F,  F,  F,  F,  F,  F,  F,  F,  T
        ),
    byrow=TRUE,
    name="S"
)
mx.Filter <- mxMatrix("Full", nrow=11, ncol=14,
    values= c(
            1,  0,  0,  0,  0,  0,  0,  0,  0,  0,  0,  0,  0,  0,
            0,  1,  0,  0,  0,  0,  0,  0,  0,  0,  0,  0,  0,  0,
            0,  0,  1,  0,  0,  0,  0,  0,  0,  0,  0,  0,  0,  0,
            0,  0,  0,  1,  0,  0,  0,  0,  0,  0,  0,  0,  0,  0,
            0,  0,  0,  0,  1,  0,  0,  0,  0,  0,  0,  0,  0,  0,
            0,  0,  0,  0,  0,  1,  0,  0,  0,  0,  0,  0,  0,  0,
            0,  0,  0,  0,  0,  0,  1,  0,  0,  0,  0,  0,  0,  0,
            0,  0,  0,  0,  0,  0,  0,  1,  0,  0,  0,  0,  0,  0,
            0,  0,  0,  0,  0,  0,  0,  0,  1,  0,  0,  0,  0,  0,
            0,  0,  0,  0,  0,  0,  0,  0,  0,  1,  0,  0,  0,  0,
            0,  0,  0,  0,  0,  0,  0,  0,  0,  0,  1,  0,  0,  0
            ),
        free=FALSE,
        name="Filter",
        byrow = TRUE
)
```

And finally, we will create our identity and filter matrices the same way, as follows:

```
mx.I <- mxMatrix("Full", nrow=14, ncol=14,
    values= c(
        1, 0, 0, 0, 0, 0, 0, 0, 0, 0, 0, 0, 0, 0,
        0, 1, 0, 0, 0, 0, 0, 0, 0, 0, 0, 0, 0, 0,
        0, 0, 1, 0, 0, 0, 0, 0, 0, 0, 0, 0, 0, 0,
        0, 0, 0, 1, 0, 0, 0, 0, 0, 0, 0, 0, 0, 0,
        0, 0, 0, 0, 1, 0, 0, 0, 0, 0, 0, 0, 0, 0,
        0, 0, 0, 0, 0, 1, 0, 0, 0, 0, 0, 0, 0, 0,
        0, 0, 0, 0, 0, 0, 1, 0, 0, 0, 0, 0, 0, 0,
        0, 0, 0, 0, 0, 0, 0, 1, 0, 0, 0, 0, 0, 0,
        0, 0, 0, 0, 0, 0, 0, 0, 1, 0, 0, 0, 0, 0,
        0, 0, 0, 0, 0, 0, 0, 0, 0, 1, 0, 0, 0, 0,
        0, 0, 0, 0, 0, 0, 0, 0, 0, 0, 1, 0, 0, 0,
        0, 0, 0, 0, 0, 0, 0, 0, 0, 0, 0, 1, 0, 0,
        0, 0, 0, 0, 0, 0, 0, 0, 0, 0, 0, 0, 1, 0,
        0, 0, 0, 0, 0, 0, 0, 0, 0, 0, 0, 0, 0, 1
    ),
    free=FALSE,
    byrow = TRUE,
    name="I"
)
```

Fitting the model

Now, it is time to declare the model that we would like to fit using the `mxModel` command. This part includes steps 2 through step 4 mentioned earlier. Here, we will tell `mxModel` which matrices to use. We will then use the `mxAlgegra` command to tell R how the matrices should be combined to reproduce the implied covariance matrix. We will tell R to use ML estimation with the `mxMLObjective` command, and we will tell it to apply the estimation to a particular matrix algebra, which we named "C". This is simply the right-hand side of the McArdle McDonald equation. Finally, we will tell R where to get the data to use in model fitting using the following code:

```
factorModel.1 <- mxModel("Political Democracy Model",

    #Model Matrices
    mx.A,
    mx.S1,
    mx.Filter,
    mx.I,
```

```
  #Model Fitting Instructions
  mxAlgebra(Filter %*% solve(I-A) %*% S %*% t(solve(I - A)) %*%
  t(Filter), name="C"),
        mxMLObjective("C", dimnames = names(PoliticalDemocracy)),

  #Data to fit
  mxData(cov(PoliticalDemocracy), type="cov", numObs=75)
)
```

Now, let's tell R to fit the model and summarize the results using `mxRun`, as follows:

```
summary(mxRun(factorModel.1))
Running Political Democracy Model
Error in summary(mxRun(factorModel.1)) :
  error in evaluating the argument 'object' in selecting a method for
  function 'summary': Error: The job for model 'Political Democracy
  Model' exited abnormally with the error message: Expected covariance
  matrix is non-positive-definite.
```

Uh oh! We got an error message telling us that the expected covariance matrix is not positive definite. Our observed covariance matrix is positive definite but the implied covariance matrix (at least at first) is not. This is an effect of the fact that if we multiply our starting value matrices together as specified by the McArdle McDonald equation, we get a starting implied covariance matrix. If we perform an eigenvalue decomposition of this starting implied covariance matrix, then we will find that the last eigenvalue is negative. This means a negative variance does not make much sense, and this is what "not positive definite" refers to. The good news is that this is simply our starting values, so we can fix this if we modify our starting values. In this case, we can choose values of five along the diagonal of the S matrix, and get a positive definite starting implied covariance matrix. We can rerun this using the `mx.S2` matrix specified earlier and the software will proceed as follows:

```
#Rerun with a positive definite matrix

factorModel.2 <- mxModel("Political Democracy Model",

  #Model Matrices
  mx.A,
  mx.S2,
  mx.Filter,
  mx.I,

  #Model Fitting Instructions
  mxAlgebra(Filter %*% solve(I-A) %*% S %*% t(solve(I - A)) %*%
  t(Filter), name="C"),
```

```
    mxMLObjective("C", dimnames = names(PoliticalDemocracy)),

  #Data to fit
  mxData(cov(PoliticalDemocracy), type="cov", numObs=75)
)


  summary(mxRun(factorModel.2))
```

This should provide a solution. As can be seen from the previous code, the parameters solved in the model are returned as matrix components. Just like we had to figure out how to go from paths to matrices, we now have to figure out how to go from matrices to paths (the reverse problem). In the following screenshot, we show just the first few free parameters:

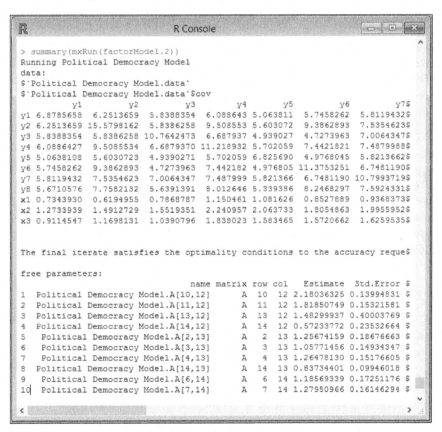

The preceding screenshot tells us that the parameter estimated in the position of the tenth row and twelfth column in the matrix A is 2.18. This corresponds to a path from the twelfth variable in the A matrix *ind60*, to the 10th variable in the matrix *x2*. Thus, the path coefficient from *ind60* to *x2* is 2.18.

There are a few other pieces of information here. The first one tells us that the model has not converged but is "Mx status Green." This means that the model was still converging when it stopped running (that is, it did not converge), but an optimal solution was still found and therefore, the results are likely reliable. Model fit information is also provided suggesting a pretty good model fit with CFI of 0.99 and RMSEA of 0.032.

This was a fair amount of work, and creating model matrices by hand from path diagrams can be quite tedious. For this reason, SEM fitting programs have generally adopted the ability to fit SEM by declaring paths rather than model matrices. OpenMx has the ability to allow declaration by paths, but applying model matrices has a few advantages. Principally, we get under the hood of SEM fitting. If we step back, we can see that OpenMx actually did very little for us that is specific to SEM. We told OpenMx how we wanted matrices multiplied together and which parameters of the matrix were free to be estimated. Instead of using the RAM specification, we could have passed the matrices of the LISREL or Bentler-Weeks models with the corresponding algebra methods to recreate an implied covariance matrix. This means that if we are trying to come up with our matrix specification, reproduce prior research, or apply a new SEM matrix specification method published in the literature, OpenMx gives us the power to do it. Also, for educators wishing to teach the underlying mathematical ideas of SEM, OpenMx is a very powerful tool.

Fitting SEM models using lavaan

If we were to describe OpenMx as the SEM equivalent of having a well-stocked pantry and full kitchen to create whatever you want, and you have the time and know how to do it, we might regard lavaan as a large freezer full of prepackaged microwavable dinners. It does not allow quite as much flexibility as OpenMx because it sweeps much of the work that we did by hand in OpenMx under the rug. Lavaan does use an internal matrix representation, but the user never has to see it. It is this sweeping under the rug that makes lavaan generally much easier to use. It is worth adding that the list of prepackaged features that are built into lavaan with minimal additional programming challenge many commercial SEM packages.

The lavaan syntax

The key to describing lavaan models is the model syntax, as follows:

- X =~ Y: Y is a manifestation of the latent variable X

- Y ~ X: Y is regressed on X

- Y ~~ X: The covariance between Y and X can be estimated

- Y ~ 1: This estimates the intercept for Y (implicitly requires mean structure)
- Y | a*t1 + b*t2: Y has two thresholds that is a and b
- Y ~ a * X: Y is regressed on X with coefficient a
- Y ~ start(a) * X: Y is regressed on X; the starting value used for estimation is a

It may not be evident at first, but this model description language actually makes lavaan quite powerful. Wherever you have seen a or b in the previous examples, a variable or constant can be used in their place. The beauty of this is that multiple parameters can be constrained to be equal simply by assigning a single parameter name to them.

Using lavaan, we can fit a factor analysis model to our physical functioning dataset with only a few lines of code. We will use the physical functioning dataset described in the previous chapter, as follows:

```
phys.func.data <- read.csv('phys_func.csv')[-1]
names(phys.func.data) <- LETTERS[1:20]
```

R has a built-in vector named LETTERS, which contains all of the capital letters of the English alphabet. The lower case vector letters contains the lowercase alphabet.

We will then describe our model using the lavaan syntax. Here, we have a model of three latent variables, our factors, and each of them has manifest variables. Let's take a look at the following example:

```
model.definition.1 <- '
   #Factors
     Cognitive =~ A + Q + R + S
     Legs =~ B + C + D + H + I + J + M + N
     Arms =~ E + F+ G + K +L + O + P + T

   #Correlations Between Factors
     Cognitive ~~ Legs
     Cognitive ~~ Arms
     Legs ~~ Arms
'
```

We then tell lavaan to fit the model as follows:

```
fit.phys.func <- cfa(model.definition.1, data=phys.func.data, ordered
= c('A','B', 'C','D', 'E','F','G', 'H','I','J', 'K', 'L','M','N',
'O','P','Q','R', 'S', 'T'))
```

In the previous code, we add an `ordered` `=` argument, which tells lavaan that some variables are ordinal in nature. In response, lavaan estimates polychoric correlations for these variables. Polychoric correlations assume that we binned a continuous variable into discrete categories, and attempts to explicitly model correlations assuming that there is some continuous underlying variable. Part of this requires finding thresholds (placed on an arbitrary scale) between each categorical response. (for example, threshold 1 falls between the response of 1 and 2, and so on). By telling lavaan to treat some variables as categorical, lavaan will also know to use a special estimation method. Lavaan will use diagonally weighted least squares, which does not assume normality and uses the diagonals of the polychoric correlation matrix for weights in the discrepancy function.

With five response options, it is questionable as to whether polychoric correlations are truly needed. Some analysts might argue that with many response options, the data can be treated as continuous, but here we use this method to show off lavaan's capabilities.

All SEM models in lavaan use the `lavaan` command. Here, we use the `cfa` command, which is one of a number of wrapper functions for the `lavaan` command. Others include `sem` and `growth`. These commands differ in the default options passed to the `lavaan` command. (For full details, see the package documentation.)

Summarizing the data, we can see the loadings of each item on the factor as well as the factor intercorrelations. We can also see the thresholds between each category from the polychoric correlations as follows:

```
summary(fit.phys.func)
```

We can also assess things such as model fit using the `fitMeasures` command, which has most of the popularly used fit measures and even a few obscure ones. Here, we tell lavaan to simply extract three measures of model fit as follows:

```
fitMeasures(fit.phys.func, c('rmsea', 'cfi', 'srmr'))
```

Collectively, these measures suggest adequate model fit. It is worth noting here that the interpretation of fit measures largely comes from studies using maximum likelihood estimation, and there is some debate as to how well these generalize other fitting methods.

The lavaan package also has the capability to use other estimators that treat the data as truly continuous in nature. For this, a particular dataset is far from multivariate normal distributed, so an estimator such as ML is appropriate to use. However, if we wanted to do so, the syntax would be as follows:

```
fit.phys.func.ML <- cfa(model.definition.1, data=phys.func.data,
  estimator = 'ML')
```

Comparing OpenMx to lavaan

It can be seen that lavaan has a much simpler syntax that allows to rapidly model basic SEM models. However, we were a bit unfair to OpenMx because we used a path model specification for lavaan and a matrix specification for OpenMx. The truth is that OpenMx is still probably a bit wordier than lavaan, but let's apply a path model specification in each to do a fair head-to-head comparison.

We will use the famous Holzinger-Swineford 1939 dataset here from the lavaan package to do our modeling, as follows:

```
hs.dat <- HolzingerSwineford1939
```

We will create a new dataset with a shorter name so that we don't have to keep typing `HozlingerSwineford1939`.

Explaining an example in lavaan

We will learn to fit the Holzinger-Swineford model in this section. We will start by specifying the SEM model using the `lavaan model` syntax:

```
hs.model.lavaan <- '
  visual  =~ x1 + x2 + x3
  textual =~ x4 + x5 + x6
  speed   =~ x7 + x8 + x9

  visual  ~~ textual
  visual  ~~ speed
  textual ~~ speed
'

fit.hs.lavaan <- cfa(hs.model.lavaan, data=hs.dat, std.lv = TRUE)
summary(fit.hs.lavaan)
```

Here, we add the `std.lv` argument to the fit function, which fixes the variance of the latent variables to 1. We do this instead of constraining the first factor loading on each variable to 1.

Only the model coefficients are included for ease of viewing in this book. The result is shown in the following model:

```
> summary(fit.hs.lavaan)
...
```

	Estimate	Std.err	Z-value	P(>|z|)
Latent variables:				
visual =~				
x1	0.900	0.081	11.127	0.000
x2	0.498	0.077	6.429	0.000
x3	0.656	0.074	8.817	0.000
textual =~				
x4	0.990	0.057	17.474	0.000
x5	1.102	0.063	17.576	0.000
x6	0.917	0.054	17.082	0.000
speed =~				
x7	0.619	0.070	8.903	0.000
x8	0.731	0.066	11.090	0.000
x9	0.670	0.065	10.305	0.000
Covariances:				
visual ~~				
textual	0.459	0.064	7.189	0.000
speed	0.471	0.073	6.461	0.000
textual ~~				
speed	0.283	0.069	4.117	0.000

Let's compare these results with a model fit in OpenMx using the same dataset and SEM model.

Explaining an example in OpenMx

The OpenMx syntax for path specification is substantially longer and more explicit. Let's take a look at the following model:

```
hs.model.open.mx <- mxModel("Holzinger Swineford",
    type="RAM",
        manifestVars = names(hs.dat)[7:15],
    latentVars = c('visual', 'textual', 'speed'),
```

```
# Create paths from latent to observed variables
mxPath(
      from = 'visual',
      to = c('x1', 'x2', 'x3'),
  free = c(TRUE, TRUE, TRUE),
  values = 1
  ),

mxPath(
      from = 'textual',
      to = c('x4', 'x5', 'x6'),
      free = c(TRUE, TRUE, TRUE),
      values = 1
      ),

mxPath(
  from = 'speed',
  to = c('x7', 'x8', 'x9'),
  free = c(TRUE, TRUE, TRUE),
  values = 1
      ),

# Create covariances among latent variables
mxPath(
  from = 'visual',
  to = 'textual',
  arrows=2,
  free=TRUE
      ),

mxPath(
      from = 'visual',
      to = 'speed',
      arrows=2,
      free=TRUE
      ),

mxPath(
      from = 'textual',
      to = 'speed',
      arrows=2,
      free=TRUE
      ),
```

```
#Create residual variance terms for the latent variables
mxPath(
   from= c('visual', 'textual', 'speed'),
   arrows=2,

   #Here we are fixing the latent variances to 1
   #These two lines are like st.lv = TRUE in lavaan
   free=c(FALSE,FALSE,FALSE),
   values=1
),

   #Create residual variance terms
   mxPath(
from= c('x1', 'x2', 'x3', 'x4', 'x5', 'x6', 'x7', 'x8', 'x9'),
   arrows=2,
),

   mxData(
      observed=cov(hs.dat[,c(7:15)]),
      type="cov",
      numObs=301
   )
)
```

```
fit.hs.open.mx <- mxRun(hs.model.open.mx)
summary(fit.hs.open.mx)
```

Here are the results of the OpenMx model fit, which look very similar to lavaan's. This gives a long output. For ease of viewing, only the most relevant parts of the output are included in the following model (the last column that R prints giving the standard error of estimates is also not shown here):

```
> summary(fit.hs.open.mx)
...

free parameters:
                          name matrix      row      col  Estimate  Std.
Error
1    Holzinger Swineford.A[1,10]     A       x1   visual 0.9011177
2    Holzinger Swineford.A[2,10]     A       x2   visual 0.4987688
3    Holzinger Swineford.A[3,10]     A       x3   visual 0.6572487
4    Holzinger Swineford.A[4,11]     A       x4  textual 0.9913408
```

5	Holzinger Swineford.A[5,11]	A	x5	textual	1.1034381
6	Holzinger Swineford.A[6,11]	A	x6	textual	0.9181265
7	Holzinger Swineford.A[7,12]	A	x7	speed	0.6205055
8	Holzinger Swineford.A[8,12]	A	x8	speed	0.7321655
9	Holzinger Swineford.A[9,12]	A	x9	speed	0.6710954
10	Holzinger Swineford.S[1,1]	S	x1	x1	0.5508846
11	Holzinger Swineford.S[2,2]	S	x2	x2	1.1376195
12	Holzinger Swineford.S[3,3]	S	x3	x3	0.8471385
13	Holzinger Swineford.S[4,4]	S	x4	x4	0.3724102
14	Holzinger Swineford.S[5,5]	S	x5	x5	0.4477426
15	Holzinger Swineford.S[6,6]	S	x6	x6	0.3573899
16	Holzinger Swineford.S[7,7]	S	x7	x7	0.8020562
17	Holzinger Swineford.S[8,8]	S	x8	x8	0.4893230
18	Holzinger Swineford.S[9,9]	S	x9	x9	0.5680182
19	Holzinger Swineford.S[10,11]	S	visual	textual	0.4585093
20	Holzinger Swineford.S[10,12]	S	visual	speed	0.4705348
21	Holzinger Swineford.S[11,12]	S	textual	speed	0.2829848

In summary, the results agree quite closely. For example, looking at the coefficient for the path going from the latent variable visual to the observed variable *x1*, lavaan gives an estimate of 0.900 while OpenMx computes a value of 0.901.

Summary

The lavaan package is user friendly, pretty powerful, and constantly adding new features. Alternatively, OpenMx has a steeper learning curve but tremendous flexibility in what it can do. Thus, lavaan is a bit like a large freezer full of prepackaged microwavable dinners, whereas OpenMx is like a well-stocked pantry with no prepared foods but a full kitchen that will let you prepare it if you have the time and the know-how. To run a quick analysis, it is tough to beat the simplicity of lavaan, especially given its wide range of capabilities. For large complex models, OpenMx may be a better choice. The methods covered here are useful to analyze statistical relationships when one has all of the data from events that have already occurred. In the next chapter, we will cover an entirely different set of approaches that are focused on modeling what can occur.

8
Simulations

Simulations are often used in advanced scientific modeling to make predictions and even to simulate the experimental design of an experiment. So this chapter will show you how to perform basic sample simulations and how to use simulations to answer statistical problems. You will also learn how to use R to generate random numbers, and how to simulate random variables from several common probability distributions. Then, we will show you how simulations can be used to evaluate integrals.

In this chapter, we will cover the following topics:

- Basic sample simulations in R
- Pseudorandom numbers
- Monte Carlo simulation
- Monte Carlo integration
- Rejection sampling
- Importance sampling
- Simulating physical systems

Basic sample simulations in R

We already showed you the basics of generating random variables from common probability distributions in *Chapter 2, Statistical Methods with R*. For example, to simulate four numbers from a normal distribution with a mean of 10 and standard deviation of 3, we use the rnorm() function with the mean and sd arguments set to 10 and 3, respectively:

```
> rnorm(4, mean=10, sd=3)
[1]  9.546714  8.600795 14.344557 11.669767
```

Similarly, we can simulate 10 numbers from a Poisson distribution with a lambda of 3 with `rpois(10, lambda=3)`. A table showing the function names for the most common distributions is available in *Chapter 2, Statistical Methods with R.*

We can also select random variables from a predetermined vector using the `sample()` function. This function allows you to randomly select a specified number of elements with the `size` argument from a vector, with or without replacing the values taken with the `replace` argument set to `TRUE` or `FALSE`, respectively. For example, if we wanted to obtain five random numbers from 1 to 100 without any duplicates, we would use the `sample()` function with the `replace` argument set to `FALSE`. Let's take a look at the following example:

```
> sample(1:100, size=5, replace=FALSE)
[1] 83 79  3 11 55
```

Now let's say that we wanted to simulate data from throwing a dice six times. We could use the `sample()` function with size equal to 6, and set `replace` to `TRUE` because it is possible to draw the same number more than once, as follows:

```
> sample(1:6, size=6, replace=TRUE)
[1] 6 2 1 4 5 2
```

We can also use the sample function with character vectors as we saw in *Chapter 3, Linear Models.*

```
> fruits <- c("apple", "orange", "strawberry", "lemon", "clementine")
> sample(fruits, size=2, replace=T)
[1] "orange" "apple"
```

Pseudorandom numbers

Now, we will show you how to simulate random numbers, or more accurately called pseudorandom numbers, because as you will see, unlike true random numbers, which truly can't be predicted, these numbers can be predicted using random number generator algorithms. Let's review how to generate a series of pseudorandom numbers from 0 to 1. One of the simplest methods is to simulate independent uniform random variables using a multiplicative congruential pseudorandom number generator. Since there are many different methods used to generate pseudorandom numbers, let's consider the following example of a simple multiplicative congruential pseudorandom number generator that can be used to simulate random variables. Let m be a large prime integer and k be another integer less than 10, preferably close to the square root of m. We can generate pseudorandom numbers by applying the following formula:

$$x_{i+1} = kx_i \, mod\,(m)$$

In the preceding formula, *i = 0, 1, 2, 3, ... , n*.

Now let's apply the previous formula to generate six pseudorandom numbers. Before we begin, we need to set the seed, which in this equation corresponds to x_i when $i = 0$. Ideally, we should set the seed x_0 to any value between *1* and *m*. Then, once the seed has been chosen, we can generate each pseudorandom number with the previous equation. To translate this mathematical equation into a function, we can run the `getRandomNbs()` function that we write in R as follows:

```
> getRandomNbs <- function(n, m, seed){
# create a numeric vector to store the numbers
pseudorandom.numbers <- numeric(n)

# set k near square root of m
k = round(sqrt(m)) -2

# use a for loop to generate the numbers
for(i in 1:n){
seed <- (k*seed) %% m
pseudorandom.numbers[i] <-seed/m
}
return(pseudorandom.numbers)
}
```

Now let's use our function to generate five pseudorandom variables, as shown in the following code, with the seed set to `27000` and `334753` as our large prime integer. You can verify that 334,753 is a prime number at `http://www.onlineconversion.com/prime.htm`.

```
> getRandomNbs(5, 334753, 27000)
[1] 0.5387913 0.8825731 0.2446909 0.1866272 0.6838684
```

When writing your own pseudorandom number generator, it is important to make sure that the numbers generated follow a uniform distribution and that these values are independent of each other. We can test that the pseudorandom numbers generated with the `getRandomNbs(5, 334753, 27000)` function follow a uniform distribution using a Chi-square test. Instead of the `chisq.test()` function available in R, we will use the `rng.chisq()` function that was specifically written to test random number generators for uniformity. To add this function to your R session, enter the following code:

```
> rng.chisq <- function(x, m) {
Obs <- trunc(m*x)/m
 Obs <- table(Obs)
 p <- rep(1,m)/m
```

```
Exp <- length(x)*p
chisq <- sum((Obs-Exp)^2/Exp)
pvalue <- 1-pchisq(chisq, m-1)
results <- list(test.statistic=chisq, p.value=pvalue, df=m-1)
return(results)
}
```

In the `rng.chisq()` function, x is the output from a pseudorandom number generator, where the output is in the `[0, 1]` interval and m is the number of subintervals to use for the Chi-square test. To test our random number generator for uniformity, we will use our `getRandomNb()` function to simulate 1,000 pseudorandom variables, and use the `rng.chisq()` function to test for uniformity using five subintervals for the test. Let's take a look at this in the following lines of code:

```
> v <- getRandomNbs(1000, 334753, 27000)
> rng.chisq(v, m=5)
$test.statistic
[1] 2.9

$p.value
[1] 0.5746972

$df
[1] 4
```

Since our p value is large, we don't have sufficient evidence to reject the null hypothesis that our random variables follow a uniform distribution. Next, we want to make sure that the pseudorandom numbers generated are independent of each other. A simple way we can test whether the values we generated are truly random is to plot a lag plot with the `lag.plot()` function. Random data should not show any underlying structure in the lag plot. To inspect our random numbers for independency, let's plot the lag plot for the 1,000 pseudorandom numbers we generated with the `getRandomNb()` function as follows:

```
> lag.plot(v)
```

The result is shown in the following plot:

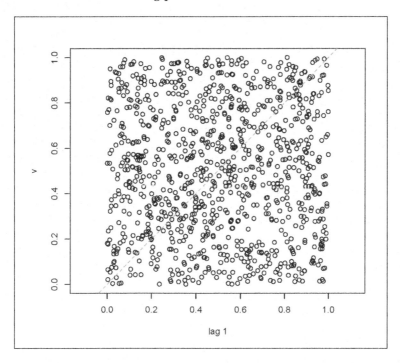

Overall, the data looks randomly distributed. There are more formal ways to test for independence that are beyond the scope of this book, but if you are interested in learning more on the topic, we suggest you read about **Spectral Tests** at http://en.wikipedia.org/wiki/Spectral_test.

The runif() function

Instead of generating your own pseudorandom number generator, you can use the runif() function to generate random numbers from the uniform distribution that lies between the intervals *a* and *b*, where *min* = *a* and *max* = *b*. The runif() function selects a seed internally and uses a different formula than the one we used in our getRandomNbs() function to generate pseudorandom numbers. Let's take a look at this in the following example:

```
> runif(n=5, min=0, max=1)
[1] 0.4562942 0.1861085 0.4779453 0.6313259 0.9768385
```

Each time you run the `runif()` function, R will select a different seed. So if you would like to use a specific seed throughout your session, then you can set the seed using the `set.seed()` function. By setting the seed, you will be able to generate a sequence of numbers that look random, but you will be able to reproduce them when you call the `set.seed()` function with the same seed. Here is an example to illustrate this point.

First, let's generate three pseudorandom numbers without setting the seed as follows:

```
> runif(3)
[1]  0.9744210 0.4709912 0.1204069
```

Now generate three pseudorandom numbers after setting the seed to 27000 as follows:

```
> set.seed(27000)
> runif(3)
[1]  0.5522500 0.5538553 0.4528518
```

Now generate three more random numbers as follows:

```
> runif(3)
[1]  0.6177212 0.4572295 0.4544682
```

Notice you do not get the same numbers from the previous run. To get the same three numbers from the time you set the seed to 27000, you will need to rerun the `set.seed(27000)` function before entering `runif(3)` as follows:

```
> set.seed(27000)
> runif(3)
[1]  0.5522500 0.5538553 0.4528518
```

Let's generate five random numbers, as follows:

```
> runif(5)
[1]  0.6177212 0.4572295 0.4544682 0.9808293 0.5509730
```

You will also notice that the next string of numbers has the same first three numbers after the second command following the `set.seed()` from above. Now, say we wanted to continue from the three numbers that were initially generated after setting the seed to 27000. All we need to do is enter `set.seed(27000)` and then `runif(5)` as follows:

```
> set.seed(27000)
> runif(5)
[1]  0.5522500 0.5538553 0.4528518 0.6177212 0.4572295
```

As you can see, we get the same first three numbers as we got when we ran `runif(3)` after setting the seed to `27000` because, similar to the `getRandomNbs()` function that we wrote, the `runif()` function uses a random number generation algorithm. Therefore, by setting the seed, you will obtain a predefined sequence of numbers. Hence, we refer to these values as pseudorandom numbers because they can be predicted using a specific algorithm, though they appear random to the untrained eye.

We just showed you how to generate random numbers using predefined set seeds so that you can regenerate the same random numbers in a latter session to make your script reproducible for others. However, what if you don't want to use a preselected seed in your script but you still want to be able to reproduce the data in a later session? You can save the state of the random number generator of your session stored in the global environment variable `.Random.seed` in a new object that you use to reset the `.Random.seed` variable at a later point in your script. Let's go through an example to illustrate this point.

First, we generate five random numbers to create the `.Random.seed` variable because when you start a new session, this variable doesn't exist until you generate random numbers for the first time. Let's take a look at this in the following code:

```
> runif(5)
[1] 0.49442371 0.48252765 0.44946379 0.96708434 0.04600508
```

Next, we save the state of the current random number generator in a separate object, as shown in the following code. This will allow us to save the seeds used for the subsequent simulations:

```
> saved.seed <- .Random.seed
```

Now, we can simulate other numbers as follows:

```
> runif(5)
[1] 0.41319284 0.57805579 0.11691655 0.09548216 0.75445132
> runif(2)
[1] 0.04699241 0.82974142
```

Now, say we want to regenerate the same numbers after the first time we saved the state of the random number generator. All we need to do is update the `.Random.seed` variable with the `saved.seed` variable, as shown in the following code, and rerun the commands that we ran earlier:

```
>.Random.seed <- saved.seed

# Rerun the commands from earlier
> runif(5)
[1] 0.41319284 0.57805579 0.11691655 0.09548216 0.75445132
> runif(2)
[1] 0.04699241 0.82974142
```

As you can see, you get the same values you obtained earlier because R reuses the same sequence of seeds saved in the original `.Random.seed` variable. However, it is important to specify that the same data will be resimulated in the same R session, but since the seed was not set with the `set.seed()` function before we saved the `.Random.seed` variable, you will not get the same values if you were to run the code in a new R session. This is because the starting seed will be taken from that session, which is different each time you start a new R session. Therefore, a better way to save the state of the random number generator would be to set the seed first with the `set.seed()` function. This way, the pseudorandom numbers you generate will be reproducible in other R sessions as follows:

```
> set.seed(245)
> .Random.seed <- saved.seed
> runif(5)
[1] 0.92701730 0.48499598 0.23385692 0.67666045 0.02424925
> runif(2)
[1] 0.2860802 0.9330553
> .Random.seed <- saved.seed
> runif(5)
[1] 0.92701730 0.48499598 0.23385692 0.67666045 0.02424925
> runif(2)
[1] 0.2860802 0.9330553
```

When writing a function to check or restore seed values to the `.Random.seed` variable, it is important to remember that we need to inspect or change the variable in the global environment and not just the local variable. To retrieve and assign values to global environment variables in R, we need to use the `get()` and `assign()` functions. For example, let's write a function that will return 10 random numbers using a user-defined seed, and then reset the state of the random number generator by restoring the `.Random.seed` variable to its original value set in the global environment. Let's take a look at this in the following example:

```
returnRandomNbs <- function(n, a, b){

# By default we assume the .Random.seed variable was not set in the
global environment
seed.found   <- FALSE
if (exists(".Random.seed"))  {
saved.seed <- get(".Random.seed", .GlobalEnv)
seed.found <- TRUE
}
v <- runif(n, min=a, max=b)
if(seed.found) {
assign(".Random.seed", saved.seed, .GlobalEnv)
}
```

```
return(v)

}
```

Now we can set the seed and run our function as follows:

```
> set.seed(753)
> returnRandomNbs(10, 0, 2)
 [1] 1.0074840 1.7143867 1.0060674 1.0500559 0.6218600 0.3472834
0.7659655 1.1762890 0.7091655 0.6026619
> returnRandomNbs(10, 0, 2)
 [1] 1.0074840 1.7143867 1.0060674 1.0500559 0.6218600 0.3472834
0.7659655 1.1762890 0.7091655 0.6026619
> returnRandomNbs(10, 0, 2)
 [1] 1.0074840 1.7143867 1.0060674 1.0500559 0.6218600 0.3472834
0.7659655 1.1762890 0.7091655 0.6026619
```

Notice that our function will always return the same values because the seed is always reset to the initial random number generator state, which is `set.seed(753)`:

```
> runif(10, 0, 2)
 [1] 1.0074840 1.7143867 1.0060674 1.0500559 0.6218600 0.3472834
0.7659655 1.1762890 0.7091655 0.6026619
```

Now the next time we run the `runif()` function, a different seed will be used as follows:

```
> runif(10, 0, 2)
 [1] 1.7727796 0.1779565 0.4772016 0.3180717 0.7163699 0.1385670
0.3976083 1.1769520 1.5818106 0.8082054
> runif(10, 0, 2)
 [1] 0.4378311 0.5187945 0.6013744 1.5483450 1.0333229 1.2363457
1.8626718 0.5275801 0.2906055 0.8752832
```

Bernoulli random variables

We can also simulate other random variables such as **Bernoulli random variables**. A Bernoulli trial has only two possible outcomes, that is, pass or fail. We can simulate guessing the right answer on a test using the `runif()` function. For example, let's simulate what score a high school student would get if he guessed all 30 questions on the test when the probability of getting the answer right answer is 0.25. Let's take a look at this in the following function:

```
> set.seed(23457)
```

Since each question can be considered as an independent Bernoulli trial, we can use the `runif()` function to simulate the student's answer to each question as follows:

```
> guessed.correctly <- runif(30)
```

If the number is less than 0.25, the student guesses correctly because the probability that a uniform random variable is less than 0.25 is exactly 0.25. Let's take a look at the results in the following code:

```
>   table(guessed.correctly < 0.25)

FALSE   TRUE
   24      6
```

As you can see, the simulated high school student score would be 6 divided by 30, or 20 percent.

Alternatively, we could use the `rbern()` function to simulate the number of questions the student would answer correctly by using the p argument to specify the probability of success, or in this case, that he guesses the correct answer. The `rbern()` function returns 1 for success with the probability (p) defined by the p argument, and 0 for failure with the probability of $1 - p$. Therefore, a value of 1 means he answered correctly, and 0 means he did not. Let's take a look at the following code:

```
> set.seed(23457)
> guessed.correctly <- rbern(n=30, p=.25)
> guessed.correctly
 [1] 1 0 0 0 0 0 0 1 0 0 0 0 0 0 0 1 0 1 0 0 1 0 0 0 0 0 1 0 0 0
```

Now, we can total the number of correctly answered questions as follows:

```
> sum(guessed.correctly)
[1] 6
```

Binomial random variables

We can also use the `rbinom()` function to simulate Binomial random variables. The Bernoulli distribution is the success of one trial, whereas the Binomial distribution represents the sum of all the successes of repeated Bernoulli trials. For example, we could have used the `rbinom()` function to simulate the number of questions the student guessed correctly by setting the size argument to 1 to specify one trial, as follows:

```
> set.seed(23457)
> rbinom(n=30, size=1, p=.25)
 [1] 1 0 0 0 0 0 0 1 0 0 0 0 0 0 0 1 0 1 0 0 1 0 0 0 0 0 1 0 0 0
```

Now let's simulate the number of cracked beer bottles per hour in a manufacturing plant that produces 100 bottles an hour if the probability that a bottle cracks is 0.05. If the plant is open 10 hours a day, we can simulate the number of cracked beer bottles each hour with the `rbinom()` function as follows:

```
> set.seed(23457)
> rbinom(n=10, size=100, p=0.05)
 [1] 7 4 6 4 5 1 6 8 5 5
```

Poisson random variables

Poisson random variables are often used to model count data that occurs in an interval of time by simulating the total number of counts. For example, we could simulate the number of shower-related injuries in the United States for the next 15 years using the `rpois()` function. We will assume there are approximately 43,600 cases per year. Let's take a look at the following function:

```
> rpois(15, 43600)
 [1] 43700 43476 43770 43928 43546 43443 43512 43627 43637 43795 43778
43799 43400 43959 43870
```

Exponential random variables

Exponential random variables are often used to simulate situations that model the time until something happens. For example, if we assume the mean time to failure of a computer is 6 years, we can simulate the lifetime of 25 computers in a classroom using the `rexp()` function. In this case, we would set the rate argument to `1/6`, where *rate = 1/mean time to failure*. Let's take a look at the following function:

```
> set.seed(453)
> computer.lifetime <- rexp(25, 1/6)
```

We can plot a histogram of these results with a theoretical density curve using the `dexp()` function as follows:

```
> hist(computer.lifetime, probability=TRUE, col="gray",
main="Exponential curve for computers with a mean time to failure of 6
years", cex.lab=1.5, cex.main=1.5)
```

We can add the theoretical density curve to the histogram plot with the `curve` function, with the `add` argument set to TRUE, as follows:

```
> curve(dexp(x, 1/6), add=T)
```

The result is shown in the following plot:

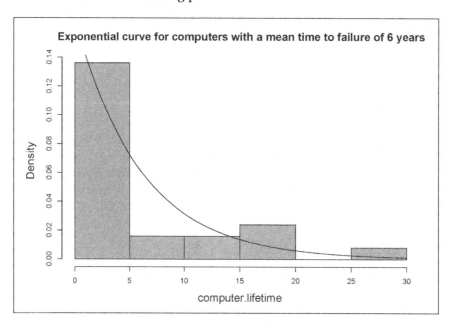

Monte Carlo simulations

An important part of statistical analysis is to be able to evaluate expectations of random variables. However, under certain circumstances, it is not feasible to apply a deterministic algorithm or difficult to obtain a closed-form expression. In other words, it is difficult or impossible to express the relationship between the explanatory and response variables under analytical terms using a finite number of elementary functions such as constants, exponents, n roots, and logarithms. A practical way to solve these problems is to use Monte Carlo methods, which are a broad class of computational algorithms that rely on repeated random sampling of quantities to approximate the distribution of an unknown probability distribution.

Methods based on Monte Carlo are used to approximate the properties of random variables. For example, to estimate *mean* = $E(X)$ of a distribution using the Monte Carlo method, we generate m independent and identically distributed copies of X, namely $X1, ..., Xm$, and use the sample means $\overline{X}m = (1/m) \sum X_i$ as an estimate for the true mean. This is because for large m values, the sample mean $\overline{X}m$ gives a good approximation for $E(X)$ in accordance with the law of large numbers. The law of large numbers predicts that as the sample size approaches infinity, the center of the $\overline{X}m$ distribution becomes very close to the population mean. Therefore, as m grows larger, the average of the results from a large number of trials will be close to the expected value. The law of large numbers also tells us that the density histogram of many independent samples is close to the density of the underlying distribution.

Central limit theorem

The central limit theorem tells us that, as the sample size tends to approach infinity, the distribution of $\overline{X}m$ resembles a normal distribution. This is also true for any type of random variables. For example, we will simulate 10,000 random samples from an exponential distribution with a rate of 0.4 as follows:

```
> set.seed(983)
> x.exp <- rexp(10000, rate=0.4)
> hist(x.exp, probability=TRUE, col=gray(0.8), main="", cex.axis=1.2,
cex.lab=1.5)
```

Now let's calculate the mean and standard deviation of this sample distribution using the following function:

```
> mean(x.exp)
[1] 2.518002
> sd(x.exp)
[1] 2.492727
```

The result is shown in the following plot:

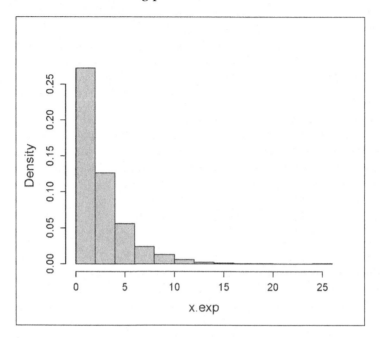

As expected, the distribution of the actual random variables is not normal, but let's see what happens when we plot the mean of 500 sample distributions from 100 random exponential variables with a rate of 0.4.

First, we will generate a numeric vector to store the 500 sample means as follows:

```
> x.exp.means <- numeric(500)
```

Then, we will use a `for` loop to calculate the mean for each simulation as follows:

```
> for (i in 1:500) {
  x.exp.means[i] <- mean(rexp(100, 0.4))
}
```

Now let's plot the distribution of the means as follows:

```
> hist(x.exp.means, probability=TRUE, col=gray(0.8), main="", cex.
axis=1.2, cex.lab=1.5)
```

The result is shown in the following plot:

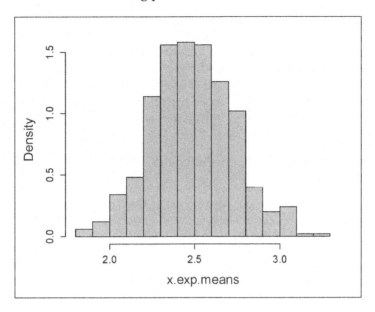

Notice how the distribution more closely resembles a normal distribution. From the central limit theorem, we also know that the standard deviation (σ_m) of the approximately normally distributed sample means is related to the standard deviation of the population (σ) by the following equation:

$$\sigma_m = \sigma / \sqrt{n}$$

Now, let's calculate the mean and standard deviation of the sample distribution of the x.exp.means attribute, as follows:

```
> mean(x.exp.means)
[1] 2.486572
> sd(x.exp.means)
[1] 0.2389426
```

In this example, the population mean and standard deviation for the distribution is 2.5. We can calculate σ_m by applying the equation in R as follows:

```
> 2.5/sqrt(100)
[1] 0.25
```

So from our example, you can see that our sample mean and standard deviation we calculated using a Monte Carlo method is very similar to the theoretical values. You could apply this method to random variables from any other distribution.

Now let's use this Monte Carlo method to solve an actual problem. For example, let's assume a desktop will fail if either the motherboard or hard drive fails. The mean time to failure of the motherboard is 8 years and the hard drive is 4 years. We can estimate the mean and variance of the time to failure by simulating random exponential variables for the time to failure for each component and applying the central limit theory.

First, let's simulate the time for the motherboard and hard drive to fail for 10,000 computers as follows:

```
> motherboard.fail <- rexp(10000, rate=1/8)
> hard.drive.fail <- rexp(10000, rate=1/6)
```

Then, let's plot the results as follows:

```
> par(mfrow=c(1,2))

> hist(motherboard.fail, probability=TRUE, col=gray(0.8),
main="Simulated motherboard time to failure", cex.axis=1.2, cex.
lab=1.5)

> hist(hard.drive.fail, probability=TRUE, col=gray(0.8),
main="Simulated hard drive time to failure", cex.axis=1.2, cex.
lab=1.5)
```

The result is shown in the following plot:

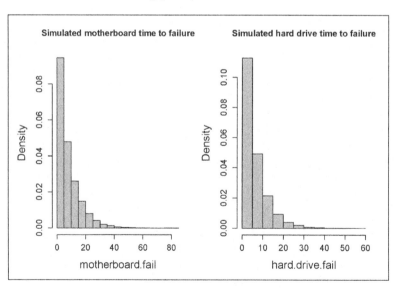

Since each index of the `motherboard.fail` and `hard.drive.fail` vectors contains the time to failure for each component of the same computer in our simulation, we can determine the number of times the computer failed by taking the time to failure of the first component that failed by taking the index of that component. Let's take a look at this in the following code:

```
# The ind object stores the index of the computers where the
motherboards failed first.

> ind <- (hard.drive.fail - motherboard.fail) > 0
```

Now we can get the number of times each computer failed by applying the index information as follows:

```
# !ind tells us the index of the computers in which the hard drive
failed first

> computer.fail <- c(motherboard.fail[ind], hard.drive.fail[!ind])
```

Next, we can estimate the mean and variance of the time for each computer to fail as follows:

```
> mean(computer.fail)
[1] 3.411752
> var(computer.fail)
[1] 12.00455
```

Therefore, from our preceding example, we can say that the average time for a computer to fail is 3.4 years with a variance of 12.0.

Using the mc2d package

You may also want to consider using the `mc2d` package for Monte Carlo simulations. The package allows you to perform one-dimensional and two-dimensional Monte Carlo simulations. This package was originally designed for quantitative risk analysis in the food domain, but the methods and functions can be applied to a variety of situations. For more general information about the package, you can consult the CRAN page available at http://cran.at.r-project.org/web/packages/mc2d/index.html. You can also download the package at this website or install it directly in R using the `install.packages()` function, as follows:

```
> install.packages("mc2d")
```

Briefly, we will go through some examples based on the `mc2d` documentation to illustrate how to use the functions available in this package to perform Monte Carlo simulations. For more details, go to http://cran.r-project.org/web/packages/mc2d/vignettes/docmcEnglish.pdf.

One-dimensional Monte Carlo simulation

One-dimensional (or first-order) Monte Carlo simulation is a sampling method that uses a set of random numbers as inputs to evaluate how random variations in the parameters affect the sensitivity, performance, or reliability of the system that is being modeled. For example, let's consider the following model to assess the risk of getting cancer from drinking water contaminated with high levels of arsenic after excess dumping from agricultural and industrial practices in a town. Here are the assumptions we make to model the data:

- The mean concentration of arsenic in the drinking water of this town is 12 parts per billion (ppb) instead of the maximum recommended dose 10 ppb

- The inhabitants that exclusively drink tap water represent 43.2 percent, inhabitants who drink a mixture of tap and bottled spring water represent 22.6 percent, and those who only drink bottled spring water represent 34.2 percent

- An individual will reduce their exposure to arsenic to one third if they drink a mixture of tap and bottled water, and one fifth if they drink bottled water exclusively

- The variability in the amount of water an individual drinks can be described by an inverse Gaussian distribution with a mean equal to 6 and shape equal to 6

- The arsenic ingested follows a Poisson distribution

- The overall probability of getting cancer (P) from ingesting arsenic is a dose-response relationship described by a one-hit model, where the probability of getting cancer each time the individual consumes arsenic is 0.0013

- There are no uncertainties in our model

This information can be summarized as follows:

arsenic.conc = 12

drinking.habit = empirical.distribution ({1, 1/3, 1/5}, {0.432, 0.226, 0.342})

tap.water.drank = invgauss.distribution (mean=6, shape=60)

arsenic.consumed = Poisson.distribution(arsenic.conc × arsenic.exposure × arsenic.consumed)

prob.per.hit = 0.0013

$P = 1 - (1 - prob.per.hit)^n$

Now that we've laid out the problem and the variables needed to model the situation, we can use Monte Carlo simulation to determine the risk of developing cancer due to increased arsenic levels in the water supply of this town. We will use the mc2d package to perform the Monte Carlo simulations needed to help solve this problem.

Load the packages for the analysis using the following function:

```
> library("statmod")
> library("mc2d")
```

Set the default number of simulations as follows:

```
> ndvar(1001)
[1] 1001
> arsenic.conc <- 12
```

Use the rempiricalD() function to generate random numbers that will constitute the empirical distribution for the water drinking habits of the 1,001 individuals. We use the mcstoc() function to generate the Monte Carlo node (mcnode) associated with the variable needed to create the Monte Carlo (mc) object later. Let's take a look at the following code:

```
> drinking.habit <- mcstoc(func=rempiricalD, values=c(1,1/3,1/5),
prob=c(0.432, 0.226, 0.342))
```

Use the rinvgauss() function as part of the statmod library to generate the random numbers from the inverse Gaussian distribution to model the amount of water drank as follows:

```
> tap.water.drank <- mcstoc(rinvgauss, mean=6, shape=60)
```

Calculate the arsenic exposure for each simulated individual as follows:

```
> arsenic.exposure <- arsenic.conc * drinking.habit * tap.water.drank
```

Use the rpois() function to generate random numbers using the simulated mean arsenic exposures (lambda), as follows:

```
> arsenic.dose <- mcstoc(rpois, lambda=arsenic.exposure)
```

Calculate the risk from the overall probability of getting cancer from ingesting arsenic as follows:

```
> prob.per.hit <- 0.0013
> risk <- 1 - (1 - prob.per.hit)^arsenic.dose
```

Finally, we use the `mc ()` function to combine all the `mcnode` objects into a single (Monte Carlo) `mc` object to analyze the Monte Carlo simulation results as follows:

```
> As1 <- mc(drinking.habit, tap.water.drank, arsenic.exposure,
arsenic.dose, risk)

> summary(As1)
drinking.habit :
        mean      sd Min 2.5% 25%    50% 75% 97.5% Max   nsv Na's
NoUnc 0.583 0.373 0.2   0.2 0.2  0.333   1     1   1 1001      0

tap.water.drank :
        mean   sd  Min 2.5%  25%  50%   75% 97.5%  Max   nsv Na's
NoUnc 6.03  1.9 2.38 3.17 4.67 5.76  7.02  10.4 16.9 1001      0

arsenic.exposure :
        mean sd  Min 2.5%  25%  50%   75% 97.5% Max   nsv Na's
NoUnc 42.2 31 6.03 8.82 15.7 28.8 65.2    110  203 1001      0

arsenic.dose :
        mean    sd Min 2.5% 25% 50% 75% 97.5% Max   nsv Na's
NoUnc 42.2 31.7   3    7  16  30  64   109 220 1001      0

risk :
          mean      sd     Min    2.5%     25%     50%      75% 97.5%    Max
nsv Na's
NoUnc 0.0526 0.0383 0.00389 0.00906 0.0206 0.0383 0.0799 0.132 0.249
1001      0
```

The risk summary (the last row of the previous code) informs us that the probability of getting cancer from arsenic exposure in this town is 0.0526 or 5 percent.

Two-dimensional Monte Carlo simulation

In the previous example, we assumed that there were no uncertainties in our model. However, that might not always be the case. To take into account the variability in the model, we can apply a two-dimensional (or second-order) Monte Carlo simulation. It is considered a two-dimensional simulation because it uses one dimension to account for the variability and the other for the uncertainty in the parameters used for the evaluation. In this case, the variability and uncertainty distributions are simulated separately. To implement the 2D Monte Carlo method, the mc2d package uses the mcnode objects, which are arrays of *nsv* × *nsu* × *nvariates* dimensions, where *nsv* represents the dimensions of variability, *nsu* represents the dimensions of uncertainty, and *nvariates* represents the number of variates. Each mcnode is associated with a particular variable, as we saw earlier when we used the mcstoc() function to generate the drinking.habit, tap.water.drank, and arsenic.dose objects. There are four types of nodes that we can create, which are given in the following code:

- V for variability, which are arrays of *nsv* × *1* × *nvariates* dimensions
- U for uncertainty, which are arrays of *1* × *nsu* × *nvariates* dimensions
- VU for variability and uncertainty, which are arrays of *nsv* × *nsu* × *nvariates* dimensions
- 0 for neither variability nor uncertainty, which are arrays of *1* × *1* × *nvariates* dimensions

We can specify the type of node to be built using the type argument in the mcstoc() function. By default, this argument was set to "V" in our one-dimensional Monte Carlo simulation. You can find more details on the mcnode object using the help(mcnode) function.

Now, let's go back to our previous example and apply the two-dimensional Monte Carlo simulation method to estimate the risk of getting cancer after ingesting arsenic from the town's tap water, if we can't make the assumption that there are no uncertainties in our models. For example, let's say we don't know the exact concentration of arsenic in the town's drinking water but know that the uncertainty of the estimate can be represented by a normal distribution with a mean equal to 2 and standard deviation of 0, and that the probability of getting cancer each time the individual consumes arsenic is not exactly 0.0013, but can be represented by a uniform distribution between 0.00001 and 0.0017. Using this information, we can make the following modifications to our model:

arsenic.conc ~ normal.distribution(12, mean=2, sd=0.5)

drinking.habit ~ empirical.distribution({1, 1/3, 1/5}, {0.432, 0.226, 0.342})

tap.water.drank ~ invgauss.distribution(mean=6, shape=60)

arsenic.consumed ~ Poisson.distribution(arsenic.conc × arsenic.exposure × arsenic.consumed)

prob.per.hit ~ uniform.distribution(min=0.00001, max=0.0017)

$P = 1 - (1 - prob.per.hit)^n$

In the revised model, `arsenic.conc` and `prob.per.hit` objects are represented by uncertainty distributions, and `drinking.habit` and `tap.water.drank` are represented by variability distributions.

Let's go over the steps to estimate the risk of developing cancer due to increased arsenic levels in the town's water supply, as follows:

```
> set.seed(223)
```

First, we set the number of iterations in the uncertainty and variability dimension with the `ndunc()` and `ndvar()` functions, respectively, as follows:

```
> ndunc(101)
[1] 101
> ndvar(1001)
[1] 1001
```

Then, we use the `rnorm()` function to generate the random variables to model the uncertainty associated with the arsenic concentration. We use the `mcstoc()` function to generate the `mcnode` object with `type="U"`, since the distribution represents uncertainty in the `arsenic.conc` parameter, as follows:

```
> arsenic.conc <- mcstoc(rnorm, type="U", mean=2, sd=0.5)
```

Now, we can repeat the same steps as before with the exception that we also specify the `mcnode` type.

Since the `drinking.habit` and `tap.water.drank` parameters are associated with variability only, we set the `type` to variability, or `V`, in the `mcstoc()` function as follows:

```
> drinking.habit <- mcstoc(func=rempiricalD,type ="V",
values=c(1,1/3,1/5), prob=c(0.432, 0.226, 0.342))

> tap.water.drank <- mcstoc(rinvgauss, type ="V", mean=6, shape=60)
```

Then, we calculate the arsenic exposure for each simulated individual as follows:

```
> arsenic.exposure <- arsenic.conc * drinking.habit * tap.water.drank
```

Since `arsenic.consumed` is a function of `arsenic.conc`, `drinking.habit`, and `tap.water.drank`, we need to take into account both the variability (in the first dimension) and uncertainty (in the second dimension) of this parameter. Hence, we set the `type` to variability and uncertainty, or `"VU"`, in the `mcstoc()` function as follows:

```
> arsenic.dose <- mcstoc(rpois, type="VU", lambda=arsenic.exposure)
```

Since the `prob.per.hit` parameter is associated with uncertainty, we set the `type` to uncertainty, or `"U"`, in the `mcstoc()` function as follows:

```
> prob.per.hit <- mcstoc(runif, type="U", min=0.00001, max=0.0017)
```

Calculate the risk from the overall probability of getting cancer from ingesting arsenic as follows:

```
> risk <- 1 - (1 - prob.per.hit)^arsenic.dose
```

Finally, we create an `mc` object to analyze the results as follows:

```
> As1 <- mc(arsenic.conc, drinking.habit, tap.water.drank, arsenic.
exposure, arsenic.dose, prob.per.hit, risk)
```

We can use the `print()` function to summarize the results and conditions used to build the `mcnode` object as follows:

```
# We use digits=2 to specify the number of minimum significant digits

> print(As1, digits=2) #output truncated, outm removed
              node     mode nsv nsu nva variate      min      mean
median      max Nas type
1      arsenic.conc numeric   1 101   1       1 5.41e-01 2.034117
2.090518  3.2362   0    U
2    drinking.habit numeric 1001   1   1       1 2.00e-01 0.568165
0.333333  1.0000   0    V
3  tap.water.drank numeric 1001   1   1       1 2.08e+00 5.959144
5.648943 16.5622   0    V
4 arsenic.exposure numeric 1001 101   1       1 2.24e-01 6.979608
4.463318 47.0704   0   VU
5      arsenic.dose numeric 1001 101   1       1 0.00e+00 6.983324
5.000000 53.0000   0   VU
6      prob.per.hit numeric   1 101   1       1 1.21e-05 0.000923
0.000977  0.0017   0    U
7              risk numeric 1001 101   1       1 0.00e+00 0.006373
0.003651  0.0739   0   VU
```

We can get additional statistical information for each variable using the `summary()` function as follows:

```
> summary(As1)
arsenic.conc :
        NoVar
median 2.091
mean   2.034
2.5%   0.918
97.5%  2.857

drinking.habit :
        mean   sd Min 2.5% 25%   50% 75% 97.5% Max  nsv Na's
NoUnc 0.568 0.37 0.2  0.2 0.2 0.333   1     1   1 1001    0

tap.water.drank :
        mean   sd  Min 2.5%  25%  50%  75% 97.5%  Max  nsv Na's
NoUnc 5.96 1.87 2.08 3.17 4.62 5.65 6.99  10.2 16.6 1001    0

arsenic.exposure :
        mean   sd  Min  2.5%  25%  50%   75% 97.5%  Max  nsv Na's
```

```
median 7.17 5.51 0.868 1.499 2.72 4.49 11.03 19.40 30.4 1001    0
mean   6.98 5.36 0.844 1.458 2.65 4.37 10.73 18.88 29.6 1001    0
2.5%   3.15 2.42 0.381 0.658 1.19 1.97  4.84  8.52 13.4 1001    0
97.5%  9.80 7.52 1.186 2.048 3.72 6.14 15.07 26.52 41.6 1001    0


arsenic.dose :
       mean   sd Min  2.5%  25%  50%   75% 97.5%  Max  nsv Na's
median 7.17 6.16   0 0.000 2.00 5.00 11.0  22.0 36.0 1001    0
mean   6.98 5.99   0 0.139 2.35 4.88 10.7  21.4 34.9 1001    0
2.5%   3.13 3.02   0 0.000 1.00 2.00  5.0  11.0 18.0 1001    0
97.5%  9.97 8.29   0 1.000 3.50 7.00 15.5  29.5 51.0 1001    0


prob.per.hit :
          NoVar
median 9.77e-04
mean   9.23e-04
2.5%   6.15e-05
97.5%  1.66e-03


risk :
          mean       sd Min      2.5%       25%       50%       75%
97.5%     Max   nsv Na's
median 0.005865 0.004900   0 0.000000 0.001972 0.003932 0.008702
0.01733 0.02974 1001    0
mean   0.006373 0.005441   0 0.000124 0.002158 0.004504 0.009719
0.01944 0.03168 1001    0
2.5%   0.000484 0.000405   0 0.000000 0.000108 0.000331 0.000723
0.00144 0.00226 1001    0
97.5%  0.013516 0.011443   0 0.001396 0.004754 0.009488 0.020378
0.04084 0.06840 1001    0
```

As you can see, when taking into account the uncertainty in certain parameters of the model, the risk of getting cancer from the arsenic levels in this town's water supply decreases to 0.006373 or 0.6 percent. As you can see, in this model, the uncertainty is taken into account, since the confidence interval of the mean [0.04 percent, 1.3 percent] is much lower than the precedent case, which makes sense as the expected value for prob.per.hit is much lower than in the deterministic case.

Additional mc2d functions

The mc2d package has a lot of other useful functions to help perform and analyze Monte Carlo simulations in R. We will highlight a few here, but I deeply encourage you to read more about the package and its features in the mc2d documentation at http://cran.r-project.org/web/packages/mc2d/vignettes/docmcEnglish.pdf.

The mcprobtree() function

The mcprobtree() function allows you to build an mcnode object of a mixture distribution of variability and/or uncertainty. For example, suppose we were 85 percent sure that the mean concentration of the arsenic concentration in the town's water supply followed a normal distribution with a mean equal to 12 and standard deviation equal to 0.5, and the other 15 percent sure that the mean concentration followed a uniform distribution with a minimum value of 10 and maximum value of 12.7. In this case, we could simulate each possibility separately and then combine the two using the mcprobtree() function.

We create two separate mcnode objects representing the uncertainty associated with the arsenic concentration, as follows:

```
> arsenic.conc1 <- mcstoc(rnorm, type="U", mean=12, sd=0.5)
> arsenic.conc2 <-  mcstoc(runif, type="U", min=10, max=12.7)
```

Since we know the probability that the mean arsenic concentration will fall under arsenic.conc1 85 percent of the time and under arsenic.conc2 15 percent of the time, we can determine when it falls in either distribution using the rbern() function to simulate random Bernoulli variables if we assume that a value of "1" means the concentration came from arsenic.conc1 and "0" means it came from arsenic.conc2. Then, use the mcprobtree() function to create the mcnode object for the arsenic.conc parameter, as follows:

```
> arsenic.distr <- mcstoc(rbern, type="U", prob=0.85)

> arsenic.conc <- mcprobtree(arsenic.distr, list("0"=arsenic.
conc1,"1"=arsenic.conc2), type="U")
```

The cornode() function

The cornode() function is used to specify a correlation between two or more variables. More specifically, it builds a rank correlation structure between the mcnode objects using the **Iman and Connover** method. For example, suppose there was a study that showed that there is 50 percent correlation between an individual's water drinking habit and the amount of water he consumes. We can include this relationship in our risk estimation with the cornode() function by setting target=0.5, as follows:

```
> cornode(drinking.habit, tap.water.drank, target=0.5, result=TRUE,
seed=223)

output Rank Correlation per variates
variates: 1
[1] 1.0000000 0.4728949 0.4728949 1.0000000
$drinking.habit
  node     mode  nsv nsu nva variate min  mean  median max Nas type outm
1    x  numeric 1001   1   1       1 0.2 0.568  0.333    1   0    V each


$tap.water.drank
  node     mode  nsv nsu nva variate  min mean median  max Nas type
outm
1    x  numeric 1001   1   1       1 2.08 5.96   5.65 16.6   0    V
each
```

 Note that the `result` argument allows us to include the output rank correlation per variates in the printed output.

The mcmodel() function

Instead of going through all the steps we went through to generate our `As1` model in our two-dimensional Monte Carlo simulation example, we could have done it all in one step using the `mcmodel()` function as follows:

```
modelAs1 <- mcmodel({
arsenic.conc <- mcstoc(rnorm, type="U", mean=2, sd=0.5)

drinking.habit <- mcstoc(func=rempiricalD,type ="V",
values=c(1,1/3,1/5), prob=c(0.432, 0.226, 0.342))

tap.water.drank <- mcstoc(rinvgauss, type ="V", mean=6, shape=60)

arsenic.exposure <- arsenic.conc * drinking.habit * tap.water.drank

arsenic.dose <- mcstoc(rpois, type="VU", lambda=arsenic.exposure)

prob.per.hit <- mcstoc(runif, type="U", min=0.00001, max=0.0017)

risk <- 1 - (1 - prob.per.hit)^arsenic.dose
mc(arsenic.conc, drinking.habit, tap.water.drank, arsenic.exposure,
arsenic.dose, prob.per.hit, risk)

})
```

Note that our code must be written within the { } brackets and end with an mc() function.

The evalmcmod() function

Once we have generated our mcmodel object with the mcmodel() function, we can evaluate our model with the evalmcmod() function. We specify the number of simulations for the variability dimension with the nsv argument and the number of simulations in the uncertainty dimension with the nsu argument. We can also specify the seed with the seed argument as follows:

```
> As1 <- evalmcmod(modelAs1, nsv=1001, nsu=101, seed=223)
> print(As1)
             node     mode  nsv nsu nva variate      min      mean
median     max Nas type outm
1      arsenic.conc numeric    1 101   1       1 5.41e-01 2.034117
2.090518  3.2362   0    U each
2    drinking.habit numeric 1001   1   1       1 2.00e-01 0.568165
0.333333  1.0000   0    V each
3   tap.water.drank numeric 1001   1   1       1 2.08e+00 5.959144
5.648943 16.5622   0    V each
4  arsenic.exposure numeric 1001 101   1       1 2.24e-01 6.979608
4.463318 47.0704   0   VU each
5      arsenic.dose numeric 1001 101   1       1 0.00e+00 6.983324
5.000000 53.0000   0   VU each
6      prob.per.hit numeric    1 101   1       1 1.21e-05 0.000923
0.000977  0.0017   0    U each
7              risk numeric 1001 101   1       1 0.00e+00 0.006373
0.003651  0.0739   0   VU each
```

This is also useful in cases where we want to try a different number of simulations in the dimensions of variability and uncertainty. Just bear in mind that the more simulations you run in both dimensions, the longer it will take for your program to run. So, for your first test, you might want to limit nsv to 1000 and nsu to 100 to have an idea of what the results look like before running nsv and nsu at much higher numbers, as given in the following code:

```
> As2 <- evalmcmod(modelAs1, nsv=100, nsu=10, seed=223)
> As3 <- evalmcmod(modelAs1, nsv=1000, nsu=100, seed=223)
> As4 <- evalmcmod(modelAs1, nsv=10000, nsu=1000, seed=223)
```

Data visualization

You can use the hist() function to visualize the histograms for the different parameters that make up an mc object as follows:

```
> hist(As1)
```

The result is shown in the following plot:

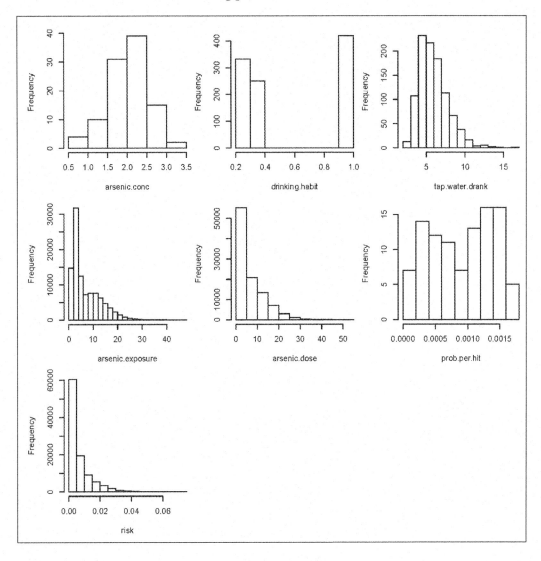

Note that in the most recent version (0.1-15) of the `mc2d` package, the uncertainty and variability distributions are collapsed for "VU" type `mcnode` objects.

You can also use the `plot()` function to visualize the cumulative empirical distribution for your results as follows:

```
> plot(As1)
```

The result is shown in the following plot:

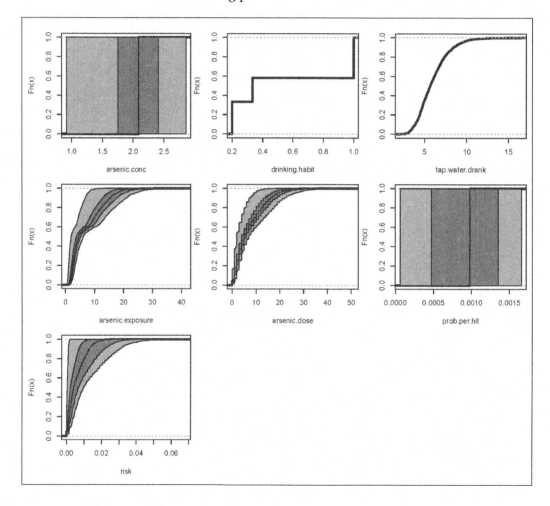

You can also use the `hist()` and `plot()` functions for individual `mcnode` objects. For example, we could plot a histogram of the `prob.per.hit` object as given in the following code:

```
> hist(prob.per.hit)
```

The result is shown in the following plot:

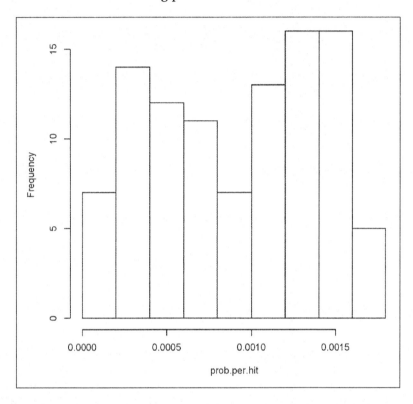

We could also plot the `risk` `mcnode` object using the `plot()` function as follows:

```
> plot(risk)
```

The result is shown in the following plot:

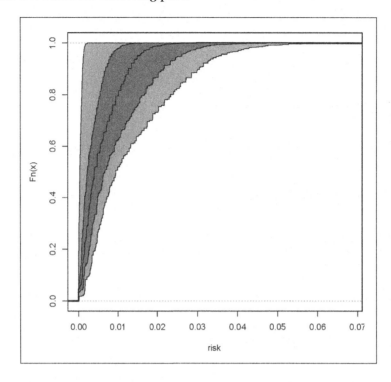

Multivariate nodes

If you go back to our example estimating the risk of developing cancer due to increased arsenic levels in the town's water supply, you will realize that all the variables in our model were univariates. However, the mc2d package also allows us to perform Monte Carlo simulation on multivariate data by specifying the number of variates with nvariates in the mcstoc() function. This is particularly useful for multivariate distributions including **Dirichlet** distribution and **multinomial or multivariate normal** distribution. Let's take a look at the following code:

```
> parameter1 <- mcstoc(rdirichlet, type="VU", nvariates=4,
alpha=c(1,4,5,7))

> parameter1
   node    mode  nsv nsu nva variate      min    mean median    max Nas
type outm
1     x numeric 1001 101   4       1 4.08e-07 0.0586 0.0423  0.530   0
VU each
2     x numeric 1001 101   4       2 8.53e-03 0.2351 0.2244  0.758   0
VU each
```

```
3     x numeric 1001 101    4           3 2.13e-02 0.2943 0.2858 0.805   0
VU each
4     x numeric 1001 101    4           4 4.64e-02 0.4120 0.4081 0.869   0
VU each


> mcstoc(rmultinomial,type="VU", nvariates=4, size=100,
prob=parameter1)
   node     mode  nsv nsu nva variate min   mean median max Nas type outm
1     x numeric 1001 101    4       1   0   5.88      4  55   0   VU each
2     x numeric 1001 101    4       2   0  23.59     22  80   0   VU each
3     x numeric 1001 101    4       3   0  29.36     28  86   0   VU each
4     x numeric 1001 101    4       4   2  41.17     41  91   0   VU each
```

You may also require multivariate nodes when you want to test two separate situations. Going back to the example of assessing the risk of developing cancer due to increased arsenic levels in the town's water supply, let's say we want to test both models for the uncertainty associated with the mean arsenic concentration separately. We will use the `arsenic.conc1` and `arsenic.conc2` mcnode objects we created earlier in the *The mcprobtree() function* section.

To create a bivariate mcnode for the arsenic concentration, we will use the `mcdata()` function that is similar to the `mcstoc()` function, except that it allows you to create a mcnode object from vectors, arrays, or mcnodes instead of random variable generating functions. Let's take a look at this in the following code:

```
> arsenic.conc <- mcdata(c(arsenic.conc1, arsenic.conc2), type="U",
nvariates=2)
```

Let's use the `mcmodel()` function to create the `mc` object to assess the risk of getting cancer from ingesting arsenic from the town's water supply in both situations, bearing in mind that the `arsenic.conc` parameter should be written in the same way as the previous code. Let's take a look at this in the following code:

```
> modelAs1.Bivariate <- mcmodel({

arsenic.conc <- mcdata(c(arsenic.conc1, arsenic.conc2), type="U",
nvariates=2)

drinking.habit <- mcstoc(func=rempiricalD,type ="V",
values=c(1,1/3,1/5), prob=c(0.432, 0.226, 0.342))

tap.water.drank <- mcstoc(rinvgauss, type ="V", mean=6, shape=60)

arsenic.exposure <- arsenic.conc * drinking.habit * tap.water.drank
```

```
arsenic.dose <- mcstoc(rpois, type="VU", lambda=arsenic.exposure,
nvariates=2)

prob.per.hit <- mcstoc(runif, type="U", min=0.00001, max=0.0017)

risk <- 1 - (1 - prob.per.hit)^arsenic.dose

mc(arsenic.conc, arsenic.dose, risk)

})

> As1.Bivariate <- evalmcmod(modelAs1.Bivariate, nsv=1001, nsu=101,
seed=223)

> print(As1.Bivariate)
          node    mode  nsv nsu nva variate   min    mean   median
max Nas type outm
1 arsenic.conc numeric    1 101   2       1  11.2 12.0821 12.0505
13.423   0    U each
2 arsenic.conc numeric    1 101   2       2  10.0 11.3572 11.2740
12.632   0    U each
3 arsenic.dose numeric 1001 101   2       1   0.0 41.2056 27.0000
214.000  0   VU each
4 arsenic.dose numeric 1001 101   2       2   0.0 38.7404 26.0000
204.000  0   VU each
5         risk numeric 1001 101   2       1   0.0  0.0344  0.0210
0.303    0   VU each
6         risk numeric 1001 101   2       2   0.0  0.0323  0.0196
0.272    0   VU each

> summary(As1.Bivariate)

arsenic.conc :
[[1]]
       NoVar
median  12.1
mean    12.1
2.5%    11.3
97.5%   12.9


[[2]]
       NoVar
median  11.3
mean    11.4
2.5%    10.1
```

```
97.5%    12.5


arsenic.dose :
[[1]]
       mean   sd Min 2.5%  25%  50%  75% 97.5% Max  nsv Na's
median 41.2 31.9 3.0 7.00 15.0 27.0 64.0   116 181 1001    0
mean   41.2 32.0 2.6 6.97 15.6 27.3 63.7   116 181 1001    0
2.5%   38.6 29.9 0.5 6.00 14.5 26.0 59.5   109 164 1001    0
97.5%  44.0 34.0 4.0 8.00 17.0 29.5 68.0   124 206 1001    0


[[2]]
       mean   sd  Min 2.5%  25%  50% 75% 97.5% Max  nsv Na's
median 38.5 30.0 2.00 6.00 14.0 26.0  60   109 169 1001    0
mean   38.7 30.1 2.13 6.41 14.6 25.8  60   109 169 1001    0
2.5%   34.2 26.7 0.00 5.00 13.0 23.0  53    98 142 1001    0
97.5%  42.9 33.2 4.00 8.00 16.0 29.0  67   121 198 1001    0



risk :
[[1]]
          mean      sd      Min     2.5%     25%      50%      75%
97.5%    Max  nsv Na's
median 0.03352 0.0253 1.84e-03 0.005909 0.01286 0.02258 0.05185
0.09198 0.1477 1001    0
mean   0.03437 0.0259 2.22e-03 0.006047 0.01336 0.02329 0.05323
0.09407 0.1422 1001    0
2.5%   0.00269 0.0021 1.71e-05 0.000438 0.00101 0.00179 0.00411
0.00765 0.0112 1001    0
97.5%  0.06503 0.0485 5.88e-03 0.011723 0.02519 0.04428 0.10102
0.17740 0.2706 1001    0


[[2]]
          mean      sd     Min     2.5%      25%      50%      75%
97.5%    Max  nsv Na's
median 0.03396 0.02557 0.00162 0.005210 0.013199 0.02265 0.05255
0.09183 0.1345 1001    0
mean   0.03229 0.02439 0.00184 0.005484 0.012487 0.02199 0.05009
0.08863 0.1328 1001    0
2.5%   0.00252 0.00196 0.00000 0.000426 0.000949 0.00167 0.00392
0.00716 0.0112 1001    0
97.5%  0.06178 0.04635 0.00490 0.011360 0.023585 0.04270 0.09702
0.16840 0.2488 1001    0
```

Using this approach, we can easily evaluate the effects of both situations for the uncertainty associated with the estimate for the mean arsenic concentration present in the town's water supply. As you can see, the risk associated with the situation represented by `arsenic.conc1` is 0.03437 with a confidence interval of [0.00269, 0.06503], and the situation represented by `arsenic.conc2` is 0.03229 with a confidence interval of [0.00252, 0.06503]. As you can see, the values are quite close with over-lapping confidence intervals, and so the estimated risk does not significantly differ between the two situations tested.

Monte Carlo integration

Solving integrals is an important mathematical concept related to areas and other quantities modeled by a function. Informally, a definite integral is defined as the signed area of the region outlined by the function *f* of a real variable *x* between *a* and *b*. Let's consider a simple function that is integrable between the interval *[a, b]* defined by the integral:

$$F(x) = \int_a^x f(t)\,dt$$

The Monte Carlo integration method relies on the law of large numbers to approximate the integral using the **Mean Value theorem** for integrals. If *f(x)* is continuous on the *[a, b]* interval, then there must exist a value *u* in *[a, b]* such that we can apply the following formula:

$$\frac{F(b) - F(a)}{b - a} = F'(u)$$

This formula can be rewritten as follows:

$$F(b) - F(a) = F'(c)(b - a)$$

Since the fundamental theorem of calculus implies $F'(x) = f(x)$, we can rewrite the equation as follows:

$$\int_a^b f(t)\,dt = f(c)(b - a)$$

The preceding formula is the **first mean value theorem**, where *f(c)* is the average value of *f(x)* on the [a, b] interval. Since we can use Monte Carlo simulation to obtain the average value of *f(x)* on the [a, b] interval, we can write the sample mean as follows:

$$E\left[f\left(U_i\right)\right] = \int_a^b f\left(u\right)\frac{1}{b-a}du$$

In the preceding formula, $E\left[f\left(U_i\right)\right]$ is the sample mean of the simulated distribution of independent uniform random variables U_1, U_2, ..., *Un* on the interval [a, b]. This formula can be rewritten as follows:

$$\int_a^b f\left(u\right)du = \left(b-a\right)*E\left[f\left(U_i\right)\right]$$

Therefore, the integer can be approximated by *b* – *a* times the sample mean of our simulated distribution on the [a, b] interval. Now, let's apply this method to approximate the integral for $\int_0^4 x^2 dx$ as follows:

```
> u <- runif(100000, min=0, max=4)
> mean(u^2)*(4-0)
[1] 21.34383
```

Let's check the solution using the `integrate()` function in R. The `integrate` function allows us to calculate the integral by adaptive quadrature of functions of one variable over a finite or infinite interval. To use this function, we must first define *f(x)* and save it in the `integrand` object as follows:

```
> integrand <- function(x) {x^2}
```

Then, we use the `integrate()` function with our `integrand` function and set the interval [a, b] and lower and upper limit with the `lower` and `upper` arguments, respectively, as follows:

```
> integrate(integrand, lower = 0, upper = 4)
21.33333 with absolute error < 2.4e-13
```

When we solve the integral, the exact answer is as follows:

$$f\left(x\right) = x^2$$

$$\int f\left(x\right)dx = \frac{x^3}{3}$$

$$\int_0^4 f(x)\,dx = \frac{4^3}{3} = \frac{64}{3} = 21.33333$$

Now, let's solve the integral $\int_3^6 \cos(x)\,dx$ using both methods.

Using the Monte Carlo method, we can write the following code:

```
> u <- runif(100000, min=3, max=6)
> mean(cos(u))*(6-3)
[1] -0.4214223
```

Using the `integrate()` function, we can write the following code:

```
> integrand <- function(x) {cos(x)}
> integrate(integrand, lower=3, upper=6)
-0.4205355 with absolute error < 2.1e-14
```

The exact solution is given in the following formula:

$$f(x) = \cos(x)$$

$$\int f(x)\,dx = \sin(x)$$

$$\int_3^6 f(x)\,dx = \sin(6) - \sin(3) = -0.4205355$$

As you can see, the solution we obtained using the Monte Carlo method (-0.4214223) is quite close to those obtained using the `integrate()` function and by solving the integral by hand (-0.4205355).

Multiple integration

We can also use the Monte Carlo method to find the approximate solution to multiple integrals. Multiple integrals are the generalization of definite integrals of two or more real variables. For example, we could approximate the value of a double integral as follows:

$$\int_0^1 \int_0^1 f(x,y)\,dx\,dy$$

Using Monte Carlo simulation, we can create a large set of independent uniform random variables, with x defined as $U_1, U_2, ..., U_n$ and y defined as $V_1, V_2, ..., V_n$, and then take the average of the two sample means; since the law of large numbers implies the following formula:

$$\lim_{n \to \infty} \sum_{i=1}^{n} \frac{f(U_i, V_i)}{n} = \int_0^1 \int_0^1 f(x, y) \, dx \, dy$$

For example, let's approximate the integral for $\int_0^1 \int_0^1 \sin(x + y)$:

```
#By default min=0 and max=1 in the runif()
> U <- runif(100000)
> V <- runif(100000)
> mean(sin(U + V))
[1] 0.7723399
```

Now let's adapt this approach to approximate the integral of $\int_3^7 \int_1^5 \sin(x + y) \, dx \, dy$ as follows:

```
> U <- runif(100000, min=3, max=7)
> V <- runif(100000, min=1, max=5)
> UV.mean <- mean(sin(U+V))
```

Next, we need to compensate for the joint density of U and V by multiplying with *(7 – 3)(5 – 1)* or 16, as follows:

```
> UV.mean*16
[1] 3.235
```

More generally, we could say for $\int_a^b \int_c^d f(x, y) \, dx \, dy$, we need to multiply the average of the sample means by *(b – a)(d – c)*.

Let's test our solution using the `adaptIntegrate()` function from the `cubature` package, which is an extension of the basic `integrate()` function in R. You can install the package as follows:

```
> install.packages("cubature")
```

Load the library using the following function:

```
> library("cubature")
```

To define the separate variables such as x and y, the adaptIntegrate() function requires that you use a vector, in this case x, and specify a separate index for each variable as follows:

```
> f <- function(x) { sin(x[1]+ x[2]) }
> adaptIntegrate(f, lowerLimit = c(3, 1), upperLimit = c(7, 5))
$integral
[1] 3.272092

$error
[1] 3.16107e-05

# full output truncated
```

As you can see, the estimate we got by applying the Monte Carlo method (3.235) was very close to the value we obtained using the adaptIntegrate() function (3.272092).

Other density functions

So far, we have showed you how to estimate integrals by simulating independent random variables from the uniform distribution. We used the uniform density defined as $f(u) = 1/(b - a)$ to estimate our integrals. To approximate $\int_0^4 x^2 dx$, we run the following lines of code:

```
> u <- runif(100000, min=0, max=4)
> mean(u^2)*(4-0)
[1] 21.34182
```

However, if the density of X is $h(x)$, then we can also write the sample mean as follows:

$$E\left[\frac{f(X)}{h(X)}\right] = \int \left[\frac{f(x)}{h(x)}\right] h(x) dx = \int f(x) dx$$

Therefore, we can approximate the integral by the sample averages of $\dfrac{f(X)}{h(X)}$. So we can also estimate the integral as follows:

```
> mean(u^2/dunif(u, min=0, max=4))
[1] 21.34182
```

Now let's apply this method to estimate the integral $\int_1^\pi e^x dx$:

```
> u <- runif(100000, min=1, max=pi)
> mean(exp(u)/dunif(u, min=1, max=pi))
[1] 20.42738
```

Instead of using the uniform distribution for Monte Carlo integration, we can also use other distributions. For example, let's estimate the integral $\int_1^\infty e^x dx$ using the `rexp()` function to simulate random variables from the exponential distribution.

First, we need to rewrite the integral in a form so that we can use the default settings for the `rexp()` function as follows:

$$\int_1^\infty e^{-x} dx = \int_1^\infty e^{-(x+1)} dx$$

Let's take a look at this in the following lines of code:

```
> u <- rexp(10000)
> mean(exp(-(u+1))/dexp(u))
[1] 0.3678794
```

Now let's check the solution with the `integrate()` function as follows:

```
> f <- function(x) { exp(-x) }
> integrate(f, lower=1, upper=Inf)
0.3678794 with absolute error < 2.1e-05
```

Monte Carlo integration is only successful when the ratio of $f(X)/h(X)$ converges. So try to pick $h(x)$, which will keep the ratio roughly constant and avoid situations where $g(x)/f(x)$ can be arbitrarily large.

Rejection sampling

So far, we have showed you how to simulate data from well-defined distributions. However, you may also wish to simulate data from an unknown distribution. The first method we will show you to simulate random variables is through **rejection sampling**. This method is based on the idea that if you want to sample a random variable from a target distribution, you just have to sample the region under the curve of its density function. For example, let's consider a triangle distribution defined by the following density function:

$$f(x) = |x < 2||2 - x|$$

First, let's plot the function in R by creating a `triangle()` function, as follows:

```
> triangle <- function(x) {(abs(x) < 2) * (2 - abs(x))}
```

Now, let's create a vector *x* to contain the *x* values and plot the values as follows:

```
> x<-seq(from=-3,to=3,by=0.001)
> plot(x, triangle(x), type = "l", ylim = c(0,2), ylab =
as.character("f(x)=(|x < 2|)(2-|x|)"), cex.lab=1.3)
```

The result is shown in the following plot:

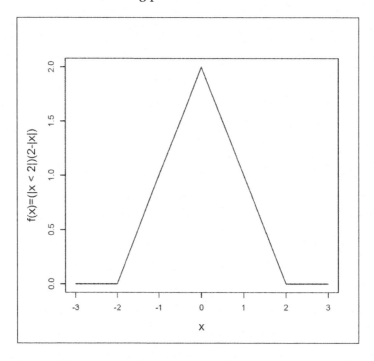

Now if we would like to generate pseudorandom variables from this triangular function, we just have to select points that fall below the curve. To simplify the process, we could draw a rectangle in which the triangle will be fully contained in that rectangle. To illustrate this point, let's write a `rectangle()` function and plot a rectangle onto our triangle distribution as follows:

```
> rectangle <- function(x) {(abs(x) < 2) * 2 }
> lines(x, rectangle(x), lty = 2)
```

The result is shown in the following plot:

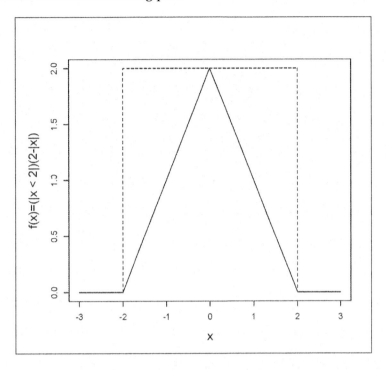

The preceding plot shows us that a subset of uniformly distributed points in this rectangle will be uniformly distributed in the triangle density region. We can simulate values from this rectangle by considering it as a uniform continuous distribution on the interval *[-2, 2]*. Therefore, a strategy to get random variables from the triangular region is to simulate random variables from the rectangular region using the uniform distribution `runif()` function and then reject values that are not part of the triangular region. Let's plot the region from which we want to reject the value using the following code:

```
#To produce shaded dark gray area on the curve
> y1 <- triangle(x)
> y2 <- rectangle(x)
> polygon(c(x,rev(x)),c(y2,rev(y1)),col="darkgray")
```

The result is shown in the following plot:

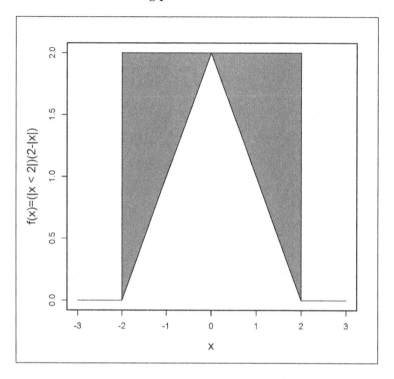

Since the triangular region occupies half the area of the rectangle, we expect 50 percent of the values simulated in the rectangular region to be present in the triangular region. So let's first simulate points in the rectangle where the coordinates will be (Rect1[i], Rect2[i]):

```
# For the x coordinates, which are between -2 and 2
> Rect1 <- runif(100000, min=-2, max=2)

 # For the y coordinates, which are between 0 and 2
> Rect2 <- runif(100000, min=0, max=2)
```

Now let's remove all points that are part of the shaded area and store the remaining values in tri.random, as follows:

```
tri.random <- Rect1[Rect2 < (abs(Rect1) < 2) * (2 - abs(Rect1)))]
```

The `tri.random` code contains the *x* values for all the points present in the triangular region. We can check our assumption that 50 percent of our simulated points were maintained by checking the length of `tri.random` using the `length()` function. Since we simulated 100,000 points, we expect 50,000 points to remain:

```
> length(tri.random)
[1] 50176
```

As expected, we retained approximately 50.2 percent of the points.

Essentially, we use the density *g* of a well-characterized distribution to generate random variables from the unknown distribution with density *f* so long as $f(x) \leq kg(x)$ for all values of *x*, where *k* is a normalizing constant. Therefore, we can obtain a sample *X* from *f* by:

- Generating a sample *Y* from *g* using the density function *g(x)*
- Generating a random number *U* from the uniform distribution on *[0, 1]*
- If $U \leq f(Y)/cg(Y)$, we accept the value of *Y* as a sample *X* from *f*

We can rewrite the conditional statement in the last point as $U*c*g(Y) \leq f(Y)$. Hence, when *g(x)* is uniform, we can simplify the `if` statement to $cU < f(Y)$ because the density of the uniform distribution on *[1, 0]* is 1.

To illustrate these steps, let's apply rejection sampling to simulate values from a beta distribution with `shape1=2` and `shape2=2`.

First, let's plot the beta distribution using the following code to have an idea of what it looks like:

```
> curve(dbeta(x, shape1=2, shape2=2), cex.lab=1.4)
```

The result is shown in the following plot:

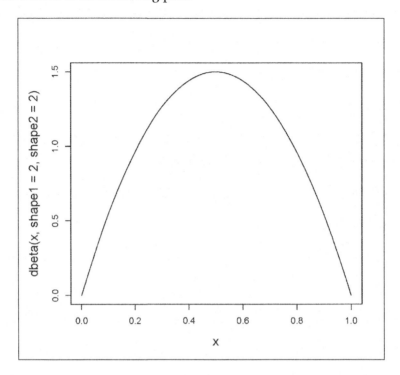

Since the values on the y-axis of our beta distribution function don't go over 1.5, we will set our constant to 1.5 as follows:

```
> c <- 1.5
```

Now we will simulate values from $g(x)$, which in this case is a uniform distribution, as follows:

```
> Y <- runif(300,min=0,max=1)
```

Then, we will simulate U values for the uniform distribution on the interval *[0, 1]* as given in the following code:

```
> u <- runif(300,min=0,max=1)
```

We determine which points are below our region of interest defined by our beta distribution by testing if $U*c*g(Y) \leq f(Y)$ as follows:

```
> below <- which(c*u*dunif(Y,min=0,max=1) <= dbeta(Y,2,2))
```

Since our density function is uniform, we can also write the function as follows:

```
below <- which(M*u <= dbeta(r,2,2))
```

We finish by plotting the beta curve with the points we simulated. The points we accepted are marked as "+" and those we rejected are marked as "-", as given in the following code:

```
> curve(dbeta(x,2,2),from=0,to=1,ylim=c(0,c), cex.lab=1.4)
> points(Y[below],c*u[below],pch="+")
> points(Y[-below],c*u[-below],pch="-")
```

The result is shown in the following plot:

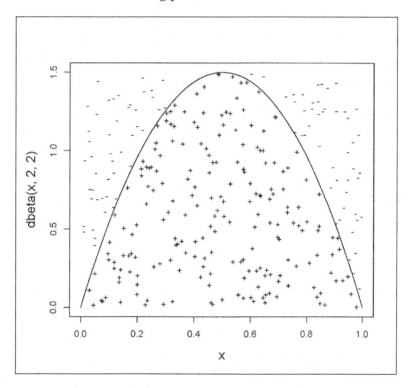

Alternatively, you could plot a histogram of Y[below] with the hist() function as follows:

```
> hist(Y[below])
#Plot not shown
```

Importance sampling

Importance sampling is a method to study one distribution while sampling from another. Essentially, it performs biased sampling to generate pseudorandom numbers more sparingly. For example, instead of taking the points from a uniform distribution, the points are chosen from a distribution that concentrates the points in the region of interest of the function being integrated, thus focusing on the most important samples. The formula for the integrand can be written as follows:

$$\int_a^b f(x)\,dx = \int_a^b \frac{f}{g}(x)g(x)\,dx = \int_a^b \frac{f}{g}(x)\,dG(x)$$

To perform importance sampling, we need to do the following:

- Generate n random numbers ($x1, x2, ..., xi$) approximately $g(x)$
- Introduce weights $f(x)/g(x)$ and estimate the integrand as

$$\int_a^b \frac{f}{g}(x)g(x)\,dx = E\left[\frac{f(x)}{g(x)}\right], \text{ where } x \text{ is approximately equal to } g$$

- Compute the Monte Carlo estimate for the integrand as follows:

$$\frac{1}{n}\sum_{i=1}^n \frac{f(x)}{g(x)}, where\ X_1, X_2, ..., X_n \sim g$$

For example, let's estimate the integral $\int_0^1 e^x$ using this method.

Using the truncated exponential sampling distribution ($\lambda = 0.65$) truncated at $T = 1$, we can write:

$$g(x) = \frac{\lambda e^{-\lambda x}}{1-e^{-T\lambda}}, where\ x \in (0,1)$$

$$f(x) = e^{-x}$$

Hence, $\frac{f(x)}{g(x)}$ becomes $\dfrac{e^{-x}}{0.7e^{-0.65x}/\left(1-e^{-1*0.65}\right)}$ and the integral can be estimated

as $\frac{1}{n}\sum_{i=1}^n \frac{f(x)}{g(x)}$.

Now implement this in R as follows:

```
> set.seed(23564)
> n <- 100000
> T   <- 1
> lambda <- 0.65
> Rand.num <- runif(n,0,1)*(1-exp(-T*lambda))
> x = -log(1-Rand.num)/lambda
> f<-exp(-x)
> g<-lambda*exp(-lambda*x)/(1-exp(-T*lambda))
> fg<-f/g
> sum(fg)/n
[1] 0.6320664
```

Now let's see what we get using the standard Monte Carlo integration:

```
> set.seed(23564)
> X <- runif(100000, 0, 1)
> Y <- exp(-X)
> mean(Y)
[1] 0.6319162
```

Although both methods produce similar results, the estimate using the importance method is much closer to the true value of $1-e^{-1} \approx 0.63212$. Let's compare the variance of the two sample distributions using the following lines of code:

```
# Importance Sampling
> var(fg)
[1] 0.003894969
#Standard Monte Carlo Integration
> var(Y)
[1] 0.03267516
```

As you can see, we achieve a much better estimation using the importance sampling method; we obtain 8.4 times less variance than with simple Monte Carlo integration.

Simulating physical systems

As a brief introduction to simulating physical systems, we will show you how to simulate **Brownian motion** in R. In physics, Brownian motion is defined as the random movement of particles suspended in liquid or gas caused by the collision of these particles in its surrounding medium. As a result, Brownian motion can be seen as a stochastic process continuous in time. We can simulate this process by successively adding random variables from a normal distribution, where the total number of normal random variables to be simulated represents the total number of discrete time intervals. For example, let's plot Brownian motion in one dimension using 10,000 discrete time intervals as follows:

```
> motion <- rnorm(10000, 0, 1)
> motion <- cumsum(motion)

> plot(motion, type="l", main="Brownian Motion in 1-Dimension",
xlab="time", ylab="displacement")
```

The result is shown in the following plot:

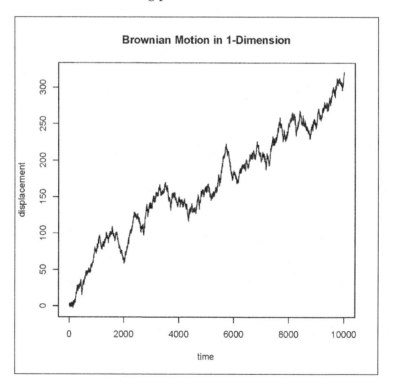

Alternatively, we could plot simple Brownian motion in two dimensions by simulating the distance for each coordinate separately, as follows:

```
> x.dist <- rnorm(10000, 0, 1)
> y.dist <- rnorm(10000, 0, 1)
> x.dist <- cumsum(x.dist)
> y.dist <- cumsum(y.dist)

> plot(x.dist, y.dist, type="l", main="Brownian Motion in
2-Dimensions", xlab="time", ylab="displacement")
```

The result is shown in the following plot:

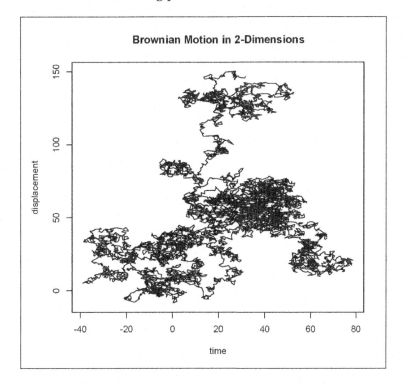

These are just two simple examples, but it does show you how simulating random variables from well-characterized distributions can be used to model physical systems.

Summary

In this chapter, you learned how to perform basic simulations. We showed you how to generate pseudorandom numbers from a variety of common probability distributions. We also showed you how to perform Monte Carlo simulations including an overview of the `mc2d` package, and how it can be used to perform one- and two-dimensional Monte Carlo simulations in risk analysis. We also showed you how Monte Carlo methods can be applied to estimate integrals. Next, we demonstrated how importance sampling can be used to improve integral estimates. Then, we showed you how to generate random variables from unknown distributions using the rejection sampling method. Finally, we briefly showed you how simulation can be used to model physical systems by looking at Brownian motion in one- and two-dimensions. Now that you are familiar with the generation of random variables and Monte Carlo simulations, we are ready to move on to the next chapter, where we will show you how to perform numerical optimization.

9
Optimization

Often, in scientific computing, we are required to find the value of x for which a function $f(x)$ will attain a maximum or minimum value. In other words, we want to maximize or minimize $f(x)$. This process is termed as **numerical optimization** and can be summarized as follows:

$$\min_{x \in \mathbb{R}^n} f(x) \quad subject\,to \begin{cases} zi(x) = 0, & i \in N \\ zi(x) \geq 0, & i \in M \end{cases}$$

In the preceding formula, x represents a vector of variables also known as the unknowns or parameters, f is the function of x we want to maximize or minimize known as the objective function, z_i is the constraint functions that x must fulfill, and N and M are sets of indices. Optimization problems are used in mathematics, finance, and computer science to find the best solution from all feasible solutions. We can simplify maximization optimization problems to minimization problems by remembering that the maximum of $f(x)$ is essentially the minimum of $-f(x)$. Therefore, to maximize the function f, we simply need to minimize f. In this chapter, you will learn different methods and functions used to perform numerical optimization in R.

In this chapter, we will cover the following topics:

- The golden section search method
- The Newton-Raphson method
- The Nelder-Mead simplex method
- Other methods with the `optim()` function
- Linear programming
- Integer-restricted optimization
- Unrestricted variables with the `lp()` function
- Quadratic programming

Let's start by minimizing the following function:

$$f(x) = |x - 2.5| + (x - 1)^2$$

In the preceding example, the function *f* has no constraints, so we can select variables within its full range freely. To solve this problem, we will apply the golden section search method, which is a one-dimensional unconstrained optimization method.

One-dimensional optimization

One-dimensional unconstrained optimization is used to minimize the function of the type $f(x) \to \min \ x \in \mathbb{R}$. The golden section search method is a zero-line search method used to solve functions of the type $f(x) \to \min \ a \le x \le b$. This method uses the values of the objective function *f* and not their derivatives, making this type of solution best applicable to minimize the $f(x) = |x - 2.5| + (x - 1)^2$ function since *f(x)* is not differentiable at *x* = 2.5.

The golden section search method

The golden section search method uses an interval reduction strategy independent of the number of iterations, where the ratio between the sizes of two consecutive intervals is constant and makes use of the golden ratio ϕ. The golden ratio is defined algebraically as follows:

$$\frac{a+b}{a} = \frac{a}{b} = \phi \quad with \ a > b > 0$$

Here, $\phi = \dfrac{1 + \sqrt{5}}{2}$.

Basically, it is an iterative method that minimizes the function by:

- Defining an interval *[a, b]* that contains the minimizer.
- Shrinking the interval into progressively smaller intervals *[a', b']* that still contain the minimizer.
- Repeating the second step until the difference between *b' – a'* is small enough based on a pre-set tolerance.
- Using the midpoint of that interval as an estimate for the true minimizer, which is calculated as *(a' + b')/2*. The maximum error for this minimizer becomes *(b' – a')/2*.

Let's take a look at the following steps to perform the Golden search method to initialize f(x):

1. To apply the previous points to minimize the function, we will write a function that will pick two points on the *[a, b]* interval defined as *x1* and *x2*, where *x1 < x2*.

2. Then, we calculate *f(x1)* and *f(x2)*. If *f(x1) > f(x2)*, then the minimizer must be to the right of *x1*. Conversely, if *f(x1) < f(x2)*, then the minimizer must be to the left of *x2*.

3. Consequently, the minimizer will be in the interval *[x1, b]* if the former is true and in the interval *[a, x2]* if the latter is true.

4. To take advantage of certain properties of the golden ratio, we will set *x1* and *x2* as follows:

$$x_1 = b - (b-a)/\phi$$
$$x_2 = a + (b-a)/\phi$$

5. Here is how we justify the equation for *x2*. After the first iteration of the golden search method, *a* will be replaced with *a' = x1* and the next value for *x1* will be *x1'*:

$$x_1' = b - \frac{b-a'}{\phi}$$
$$x_1' = b - \frac{b-x_1}{\phi}$$

6. Now we can replace *x1* in the formula by $b-(b-a)/\phi$, which yields the following formula:

$$x_1' = b - \frac{b-a}{\phi^2}$$

7. One of the properties of the golden ratio is as follows:

$$\frac{1}{\phi^2} = 1 - \frac{1}{\phi}$$

8. So we can substitute $\dfrac{1}{\phi^2}$ by $1-\dfrac{1}{\phi}$, and by applying simple algebra, we can write:

$$x_1' = b - (b-a)\left(\frac{1}{\phi^2}\right)$$

$$x_1' = b - (b-a)\left(1 - \frac{1}{\phi}\right)$$

$$x_1' = b - \left((b-a) - \frac{(b-a)}{\phi}\right)$$

$$x_1' = b - b + a + \frac{b-a}{\phi}$$

$$x_1' = a + \frac{b-a}{\phi}$$

Since $x_1' = x_2$, we can write $x_2 = a + (b-a)/\phi$.

9. Now, to translate these steps into an R function, we can use the following function to find the minimizer:

$$f(x) = |x - 2.5| + (x-1)^2$$

10. We start by defining our function, which we will call `golden.method()`, and set arguments to specify the pre-set the tolerance and initial values for *a* and *b*. By default, let's set the tolerance value to 0.000001 as given in the following code:

```
golden.method <- function(f, a, b, tolerance=0.000001){

  # store the golden ratio in the object psi
  psi <- (1 + sqrt(5))/2

  #Calculate value for x1 and x2 using the formulas we defined
  x1 <- b - (b - a)/psi
  x2 <- a + (b - a)/psi

  #Find the value for f(x1) and f(x2)
```

```
    fx1 <- f(x1)
    fx2 <- f(x2)

# Repeat test for the minimizer while the absolute difference
# between b and a is greater than the set threshold

    while(abs(b-a) > tolerance){

    # Use an if statement to test if the minimizer is to the
    # left of x2 else it is to the right of x1

      if(fx2 > fx1){

        # Since the minimizer is to the left of x2, we can re-
      # use x2 for b' (defined b in loop)

          b <- x2

        # We can reuse x1 for x2 for the next iteration of loop

          x2 <- x1

        # Since we re-use x1 for x2 we can use the value stored
        # in fx1 for fx2

          fx2 <- fx1

        # Now we calculate a new value for x1 and f(x1) to test
        # in the next iteration of the loop

          x1 <- b - (b - a)/psi

          fx1 <- f(x1)

      } else {

        # Similarly, since the minimizer is to the right of x1,
        # we can re-use the value x1 for a

          a <- x1

        # We can re-use x2 for x1 in the next iteration of the loop

          x1 <- x2
```

```
        fx1 <- fx2

        # We calculate a new value for x2 and f(x2) to test in
        # the next iteration of the loop

        x2 <- a + (b - a)/psi
        fx2 <- f(x2)


    }
}


    # When the absolute difference between b and a is below our
    # set threshold, we can use the midpoint of the final
    # [a', b'] interval as an estimate for the true minimize

    minimizer <- (a + b)/2
    max.error <- (b - a)/2

    #return the minimizer and the maximum error in a list

    results <- list(minimizer=minimizer, maximum.error=max.error)

    return(results)
}
```

Now let's give our `golden.method()` function a try with $f(x) = |x - 2.5| + (x-1)^2$.

First, let's take a look at the curve for $f(x)$ using the `curve()` function to help determine the best [a, b] interval to start from in our `golden.method()` function, as follows:

```
# Define the function f
> f <- function(x) {
    abs(x - 2.5) + (x - 1)^2
}

#Plot the curve
> curve(f, from=0, to=5)
```

The result is shown in the following plot:

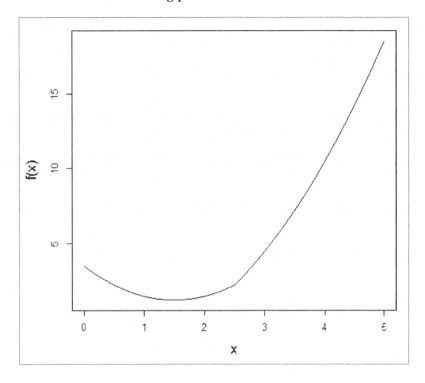

From the previous plot, it seems that the minimizer is located between **1** and **3**, so we will set `a=1` and `b=3` in our `golden.method()` function, as follows:

```
> golden.method(f, a=1, b=3)
$minimizer
[1] 1.5

$maximum.error
[1] 3.321874e-07
```

You can also add the minimizer to the graph as follows:

```
> curve(f, from=0, to=5, cex.lab=1.5)
> res <- golden.method(f, a=1, b=3)
> points(res$minimizer, f(res$minimizer))
```

The result is shown in the following plot:

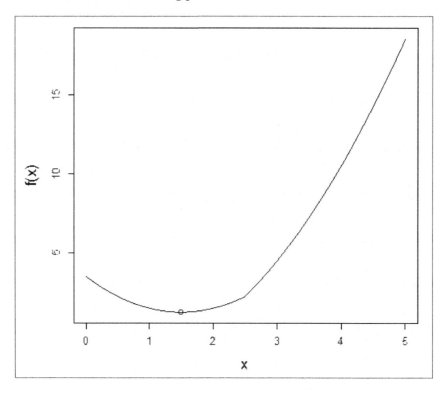

Now let's use the `golden.method()` function to maximize
$g(x) = |x - 2.5| - |x - 1| - |x - 0.5|$ using the following lines of code:

```
# Define the function f
> g <- function(x) {
   abs(x-2.5) - abs(x -1) - abs(x -0.5)
}

#Plot the curve
> curve(g, from=-10, to=10)
```

The result is shown in the following plot:

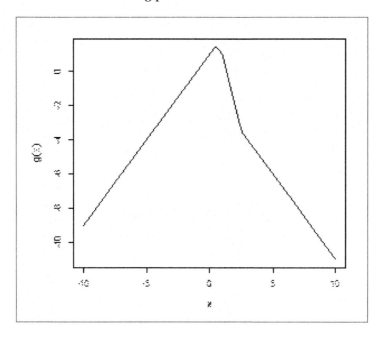

Now, to maximize $g(x)$, we simply need to minimize $-g(x)$ by creating a function to calculate negative g and use it as input into our `golden.method()` function. Let's take a look at this in the following lines of code:

```
> h <- function(x) {
  -g(x)
}

# We know from the curve the minimizer is between [-5, 5]
> golden.method(h, a=-5, b=5)
$minimizer
[1] 0.4999999

$maximum.error
[1] 3.92094e-07
```

> In the previous example, we had to write a new function that calculates
> `-g(x)`, because if we write `golden.method(-g, a=-5, b=5)`, we will
> get `Error in -g : invalid argument to unary operator`.

The optimize() function

Instead of using the `golden.method()` function we defined, we could also use the built-in `optimize()` function. This function uses a combination of the golden search method and successive parabolic interpolation, which we will not go into detail about here. Nevertheless, we will show you how to use the function to minimize our first example, $f(x) = |x - 2.5| + (x - 1)^2$, with the `optimize()` function. Let's take a look at this in following lines of code:

```
> f <- function(x) {

abs(x - 2.5) + (x - 1)^2
}
```

Then, we use the optimize function using the `interval` argument to define *a* and *b* and the `tol` argument to set the tolerance. Let's take a look at this in the following lines of code:

```
> optimize(f, interval=c(1, 3), tol=0.000001)
$minimum
[1] 1.5

$objective
[1] 1.25
```

As you can see, we get the same answer as before, that is, 1.5. The function also returns `$objective`, which corresponds to the value of *f(x)* at that point. We could have also defined the interval with the `lower` and `upper` arguments instead as follows:

```
> optimize(f, lower=1, upper=3, tol=0.000001)
$minimum
[1] 1.5

$objective
[1] 1.25
```

Another useful feature of the `optimize()` function is its ability to directly maximize a function without the user needing to specify the negative of the function, like we did earlier. Instead, you just need to specify `maximum=TRUE` when you use the `optimize` function. Let's use the `optimize` function to maximize $g(x) = |x - 2.5| - |x - 1| - |x - 0.5|$ from our earlier example. Let's take a look at this in the following lines of code:

```
> g <- function(x) {
    abs(x-2.5) - abs(x -1) - abs(x -0.5)
  }
```

```
> optimize(g, lower=-5, upper=5, tol=0.000001, maximum=TRUE)
$maximum
[1]  0.5

$objective
[1]  1.5
```

The Newton-Raphson method

The Newton-Raphson method is a derivative-based numerical method used to solve one-dimensional optimization problems. By using an initial point and the derivative information of the `objective` function, you can obtain the minimum for $f(x)$. It uses linear approximation to solve the root of the equation. Given that $f(x)$ is a convex function, otherwise known as a "well-behaved" function, and r is the root of the equation $f(x) = 0$, we can estimate the true root r with $x0$, where $r = x0 + h$ and h is the measure of how far $x0$ is from r. If h is very small and near 0, we can use a Taylor series approximation to solve the equation as follows:

$$0 = f(r) = f(x_0 + h) \approx f(x_0) + hf'(x_0)$$

$$h \approx -\frac{f(x_0)}{f'(x_0)}$$

Therefore, $r = x0 + h$ can be approximated as follows:

$$r \approx x_0 - \frac{f(x_0)}{f'(x_0)}$$

This approximation can be done with a potentially better estimate for r being $x1$ defined as follows:

$$x_1 = x_0 - \frac{f(x_0)}{f'(x_0)}$$

If we repeat this process multiple times, the subsequent estimates for r will be defined as follows:

$$x_{n+1} = x_n - \frac{f(x_n)}{f'(x_n)}$$

This process will be repeated until $f(x_n)$ is near 0 or a pre-set tolerance ε such that $|f(x_n)| < \varepsilon$. Therefore, as long as the minimizer for $f(x)$ is in the interval $[a, b]$ and not a or b and satisfies $f'(x) = 0$, we can find the minimizer of $f(x)$ using this approach by using the following formula:

$$x_{n+1} = x_n - \frac{f'(x_n)}{f''(x_n)}$$

However, we must also check that the value we find is actually a minimizer of the function and not just a maximizer or a point of inflection. So, to guarantee that our solution is a minimizer, we check whether $f''(x) > 0$.

Now let's use the Newton-Raphson method to minimize the function $f(x) = e^{-x^2} + x^3$.

The first derivative of $f(x)$ is as follows:

$$f'(x) = \frac{d(f(x))}{dx} = 3x^2 - 2xe^{-x^2}$$

The second derivative of $f(x)$ is as follows:

$$f''(x) = \frac{d^2(f(x))}{dx^2} = 4x^2e^{-x^2} - 2e^{-x^2} + 6x$$

Before we begin, we will plot the function to determine the best initial estimate for $x0$. Let's take a look at this in the following lines of code:

```
> f <- function(x) {
  exp(-x^2) + x^3
}
> curve(f, from=-1, to=4)
```

The result is shown in the following plot:

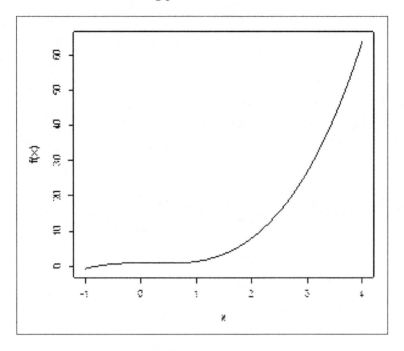

From the curve, a reasonable estimate for *x0* is 1. Now, we will write a function to implement the Newton-Raphson method to minimize the function.

We include the N argument to define the maximum number of iterations we should run, which we default to 100, as follows:

```
newton.method <- function(f, ff, fff, x0, tol=0.000001, N=100){

  # We start the counter at 1

  i <- 1

  # We create a vector to store the estimates and values for
  # f(x), f'(x) and f''(x)

  estimates <- numeric(N)
   fvalue <- numeric(N)
   ffvalue <- numeric(N)
```

```
      fffvalue <- numeric(N)

    while(i <= N){

        # We use the Newton-Raphson formula to estimate the
        # minimizer

      x1 <- x0 - ff(x0)/fff(x0)

        # We store the estimates and values for f(x), f'(x) and
        # f''(x)

      estimates[i] <- x1
       fvalue[i] <- f(x1)
       ffvalue[i] <- ff(x1)
       fffvalue[i] <- fff(x1)

        # We update the counter

      i <- i + 1

        # We break from the loop if we reach below our pre-set
        # tolerance

      if(abs(x0 - x1) < tol) break

        # Before the next iteration of the loop we replace x0 with
        # the value x1

      x0 <- x1

    }

    # We return a dataframe  of all the estimates and values for
    # the first & second derivative

  estimates <- estimates[1:(i-1)]
   fvalue <- fvalue[1:(i-1)]
   ffvalue <- ffvalue[1:(i-1)]
   fffvalue <- fffvalue[1:(i-1)]

  df <- as.data.frame(cbind(estimates, fvalue, ffvalue,   fffvalue))

  return(df)

}
```

Now, let's use the function we wrote to minimize our function stored in `f`. First, we need to create a function for $f'(x)$ and $f''(x)$, which we will store in `fp` and `fpp`, respectively.

For the first derivative $f'(x) = 3x^2 - 2xe^{-x^2}$, we use the following lines of code:

```
fp <- function(x) {
   3*x^2 - 2*x*exp(-x^2)
}
```

For the second derivative $f''(x) = 4x^2e^{-x^2} - 2e^{-x^2} + 6x$, we use the following lines of code:

```
fpp <- function(x) {
   4*x^2*exp(-x^2 )- 2*exp(-x^2 )+ 6*x
}
```

Next, we use the `newton.method()` function with `x0=1` using `f`, `fp`, and `fpp`, as follows:

```
> newton.method(f, fp, fpp, x0=1)
  estimates    fvalue        ffvalue fffvalue
1 0.6638477 0.9361433   4.675900e-01 3.830410
2 0.5417746 0.9046560   7.262741e-02 2.634812
3 0.5142100 0.9036205   3.761765e-03 2.361857
4 0.5126173 0.9036175   1.255900e-05 2.346086
5 0.5126120 0.9036175   1.418679e-10 2.346033
6 0.5126120 0.9036175  -1.110223e-16 2.346033
```

From the output, we can see that our minimum is 0.5126120, and since $f''(x)$ is positive, we can conclude that it is a local minimum. We can check our solution with the `optimize()` function in the *[0, 2]* interval as follows:

```
> optimize(f, interval=c(0, 2), tol=0.000001)
$minimum
[1] 0.5126119

$objective
[1] 0.9036175
```

As you can see, we get a pretty close value of 0.5126120 compared to 0.5126119 using the `optimize()` function.

There is also a Newton-Raphson function, (), which is part of the spuRs package. Let's use it to minimize the function as follows:

```
> install.packages("spuRs")
> library("spuRs")
```

To be able to use the newtonraphson() function to minimize our equation, we need to create a function that will return the value for $f'(x)$ and $f''(x)$ in a vector as the fftn argument.

Since we need to apply the Newton-Raphson method on the $f'(x)$ and $f''(x)$ function, we store these values in separate variables that we will combine in a results vector to return to the newtonraphson() function. Let's write the ftn argument function and call it minimizer.ftn() as follows:

```
minimizer.ftn <- function(x){
   ffvalue <- 3*x^2 - 2*x*exp(-x^2)
   fffvalue <- 4*x^2*exp(-x^2 )- 2*exp(-x^2 )+ 6*x
   results <- c(ffvalue, fffvalue)
   return(results)

}
```

Now we run the analysis setting x0=1 for our initial estimate and tol=0.000001 for our pre-set tolerance as follows:

```
> newtonraphson(minimizer.ftn, x0=1, tol=0.000001)
At iteration 1 value of x is: 0.6638477
At iteration 2 value of x is: 0.5417746
At iteration 3 value of x is: 0.51421
At iteration 4 value of x is: 0.5126173
At iteration 5 value of x is: 0.512612
Algorithm converged
[1] 0.512612
```

We get almost the same answer as with our newton.method() function.

The Nelder-Mead simplex method

An alternative derivative-free approach to the Newton-Raphson method is the
Nelder-Mead simplex method. It is a nonlinear optimization technique to minimize
an objective function in multiple dimensions. By default, the `optim()` function,
which is part of the basic functions in R, uses the Nelder-Mead simplex method to
minimize your function of choice. Let's use the `optim()` function with its default
settings to solve $f(x) = e^{-x^2} + x^3$. To set the initial estimate $x0$ in the `optim()`
function, we use the `par` argument. In this case, we set `par` to 1 as follows:

```
> f <- function(x) {
  exp(-x^2) + x^3
  }

> optim(par=1, fn=f)
$par
[1] 0.5126953

$value
[1] 0.9036175

$counts
function gradient
      26       NA

$convergence
[1] 0

$message
NULL

Warning message:
In optim(1, f) : one-dimensional optimization by Nelder-Mead is
unreliable:
use "Brent" or optimize() directly
```

From the output, you will notice that the minimizer is given in `$par`. You will also
notice that there is a warning message to use the Brent method or `optimize()`
function directly since it yields more accurate results. We can apply the Brent
method directly by specifying `method="Brent"` and the *[a, b]* interval with the
`upper` and `lower` arguments, as follows:

```
> optim(1, f, method="Brent", lower=0, upper=2)
$par
[1] 0.512612

$value
```

```
[1]  0.9036175

$counts
function gradient
        NA       NA

$convergence
[1]  0

$message
NULL
```

As you can see, we get the same value we found earlier with the Brent method compared to the Nelder-Mead method. However, it is worth mentioning that the Nelder-Mead approach is a heuristic search method that is preferentially used to solve problems that can't easily be solved with other methods.

The Nelder-Mead method is also used to solve multidimensional problems. For example, let's minimize the rosenbrock function, which is defined as follows:

$$f(x, y) = (1-x)^2 + 100(y - x^2)^2$$

First, we store the function in an object called rosenbrock.f, as follows:

```
> rosenbrock.f <- function(x1,y1) {
  (1-x1)^2 + 100*(y1 - x1^2)^2
  }
```

Then, we can plot the function as follows:

1. First, we define the x and y values to plot:

    ```
    > x <- seq(-3, 3, by=0.2)
    > y <- seq(-2, 3, by=0.2)
    ```

2. Then, we obtain the outer product of the x and y vectors using the outer() function as follows:

    ```
    > z <- outer(x, y, rosenbrock.f)
    ```

3. Next, we plot the function using the persp() function as follows:

    ```
    >persp(x,y,z,phi=40,theta=40,col="turquoise",shade=.000001,ticktyp
    e="detailed", cex.lab=1.5, zlab="")
    ```

The result is shown in the following plot:

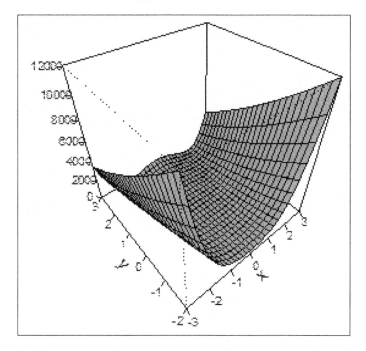

One of the properties of the Rosenbrock function is that it is always positive except when $y = x^2$ and $x = 1$, where it is 0; so, *(1, 1)* is a minimum for this function. Let's see how close we get to the minimum using the Nelder-Mead method with the optim() function.

To be able to use the optim() function, we need to rewrite rosenbrock.f so that *x* and *y* are respectively stored in the first and second index of a single vector x as follows:

```
> rosenbrock.f2 <- function(x) {
  (1-x[1])^2 + 100*(x[2]-x[1]^2)^2
}
```

Now we can use the optim() function to minimize the Rosenbrock function. This time, we must specify coordinates *(x0, y0)* for the initial estimate of the minimizer using a vector for the $par argument. In this case, we will guess (0.7, 0.7) for the initial values of the parameters to be optimized as follows:

```
> optim(par=c(0.7,0.7), rosenbrock.f2)
$par
[1] 1.000065 1.000120

$value
```

```
[1] 1.499038e-08

$counts
function gradient
      71       NA

$convergence
[1] 0

$message
NULL
```

As you can see, we get values pretty close to `(1, 1)`. If we set the initial parameters to `(1.5, 1.5)`, we get similar results as follows:

```
> optim(par=c(1.5,1.5), rosenbrock.f2)
$par
[1] 0.9995667 0.9991578

$value
[1] 2.463013e-07
# Output truncated here
```

It is also recommended that you check out the `neldermead` package if you are interested in applying variants of the Nelder-Mead method for your optimization problems. The `neldermead` package provides you with the opportunity to manage settings specific to the Nelder-Mead method such as the method to compute the initial simplex, that is, the specific termination criteria. The `neldermead` package also allows you to apply the fixed shape simplex method of Spendley, Hext, and Himsworth, the variable shape simplex method of Nelder and Mead, and the Box complex method. You can read more on this package at `http://cran.r-project.org/web/packages/neldermead/vignettes/neldermead_manual.pdf`.

More optim() features

The `optim()` function allows you to use a variety of methods to minimize functions, which are given in the following table:

The optim() function method name	Full method name
"Nelder-Mead"	Nelder and Mead
"BFGS"	Broyden, Fletcher, Goldfarb, and Shanno
"CG"	Conjugate gradient

The optim() function method name	Full method name
"L-BFGS-B"	Limited-memory BFGS
"SANN"	Simulated annealing
"Brent"	Brent

For example, we could minimize the Rosenbrock function using the **simulated annealing** method by setting method="SANN". The simulated annealing method is a stochastic global optimization method that can also be used for non-differentiable functions. It performs random jumps around the starting point to explore its vicinity and progressively narrows the jumps around a point until it finds the minimum. Since its output depends on the random number generator, you will get slightly different values each time you run the method, unless you set the seed first to reproduce the data at a later point. Let's take a look at the following lines of code:

```
> set.seed(267)

> optim(par=c(0.7,0.7), rosenbrock.f2, method="SANN")
$par
[1] 1.019317 1.039894

$value
[1] 0.000451745

#Output truncated
```

The optim() function also allows you to apply quasi-Newton methods to solve your optimization problems. For example, let's use the **Broyden–Fletcher–Goldfarb–Shanno (BFGS)** algorithm method to solve $f(x) = (x-2)^2 + (y-1)^2$.

First, let's plot the function using the lattice package instead of the persp() function as follows:

```
# We store the function f(x, y) in h using the first index
# for x and the second index for y

h <- function(x){
  (x[1]-2)^2 + (x[2] -1)^2
}

# We get values for x[1] and x[2] and store them in separate vectors

> x1 <- seq(-4, 4, by=0.5)
```

```
> x2 <- seq(-4, 4, by=0.5)

#We use the expand.grid() to create a matrix from all combinations of
both vectors

> mat <- as.matrix(expand.grid(x1, x2))

# We rename the columns to x1 and x2
> colnames(mat) <- c(«x1», «x2»)

# Calculate f(x, y) and store in z by applying the function
# h on the matrix by row

> z <- apply(mat, 1, h)

# We create a date frame containing x1, x2 and z

> df <- data.frame(mat, z)

# We load the lattice package and use wireframe function to plot

> library(lattice)
> wireframe(z ~ x1 * x2 , data=df, shade = TRUE, scales = list(arrows
= FALSE), screen = list(z = -35, x = -50))
```

The result is shown in the following plot:

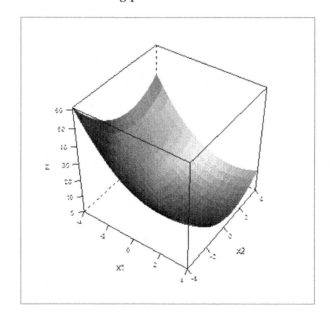

If you prefer to plot the function using the `persp()` function, use the following lines of code:

```
# Script to use to plot f(x, y) with the persp() function
> hfn <- function(x, y){
  (x-2)^2 + (y -1)^2
  }
> x <- seq(-5, 5, by=0.2)
> y <- seq(-5, 5, by=0.2)
> z <- outer(x, y, hfn)


> persp(x,y,z,phi=35,theta=50,col="purple",shade=.00000001,
ticktype="detailed")

# Plot not shown
```

From this plot, we can use $(0, 0)$ for the initial parameters in the `optim()` function. This method does not require that the Hessian matrix of second derivatives be calculated directly. Instead, the Hessian matrix is approximated using rank-one updates obtained from approximate gradient evaluations. The `optim()` function allows us to return a numerically differentiated Hessian matrix with `hessian=TRUE` and supply a function to return the gradient with `gr`. For simplicity, we will leave the default setting `gr=NULL`, which uses a finite-difference approximation for the gradient. Let's apply these conditions to minimize the function as follows:

```
> optim(par=c(0,0), h, method="BFGS", hessian = T)
$par
[1] 2 1

$value
[1] 6.357135e-26

$counts
function gradient
       9        3

$convergence
[1] 0

$message
NULL

$hessian
     [,1] [,2]
[1,]    2    0
[2,]    0    2
```

As expected, the minimizer is (2, 1).

Linear programming

Linear programming is used to minimize or maximize a function subject to constraints when both the objective function and the constraints can be expressed as linear equations or inequalities. More generally, these optimization problems can be expressed as follows:

$$\min_{x_1, x_2, \ldots, x_n} L(x) = c_1 x_1 + c_2 x_2 + c_n x_n$$

The preceding formula is subject to the following constraints:

$$a_{11} x_1 + a_{12} x_2 + \cdots + a_{1n} x_n \geq b_1$$
$$a_{21} x_1 + a_{22} x_2 + \cdots + a_{2n} x_n \geq b_2$$
$$a_{m1} x_1 + a_{m2} x_2 + \cdots + a_{mn} x_n \geq b_m$$

It is also subject to the non-negativity constraint $x_1 \geq 0$, $x_2 \geq 0$, ..., $x_n \geq 0$. In other words, we are interested in finding the values for the decision variables $x_1, x_2, \ldots, x_n$, which minimize the objective function $L(x)$ subject to the constraints and non-negative conditions. The opposite of this is also true to maximize a linear program, as follows:

$$\max_{x_1, x_2, \ldots, x_n} L(x) = c_1 x_1 + c_2 x_2 + c_n x_n$$

The preceding formula is subject to the following constraints:

$$a_{11} x_1 + a_{12} x_2 + \cdots a_{1n} x_n \leq b_1$$
$$a_{21} x_1 + a_{22} x_2 + \cdots + a_{2n} x_n \leq b_2$$
$$a_{m1} x_1 + a_{m2} x_2 + \cdots + a_{mn} x_n \leq b_m$$

It is also subject to the non-negativity constraint $x_1 \geq 0$, $x_2 \geq 0$, ..., $x_n \geq 0$.

R has a few packages and functions available to help solve linear programming problems. We will go over a few examples to show you how to use these functions to set up and solve linear programs. Let's start by solving the following problem:

$$\min L = 4x_1 + 7x_2$$

The preceding equation is subject to the following constraints:

$$x_1 + x_2 \geq 4$$
$$x_1 + 2x_2 \geq 6$$
$$\overline{}$$
$$x_1 \geq 0$$
$$x_2 \geq 0$$

Firstly, we will plot and solve this problem using the `lpSolveAPI` package as follows:

```
> install.packages("lpSolveAPI")
> library("lpSolveAPI")
```

Next, we will create an `lpSolve` linear program model object with two constraints and two decision variables with the `make.lp()` function as follows:

```
> lp1 <- make.lp(2, 2)
```

Then, we will build the model column-wise using the `set.column()` function for each decision variable using a vector with a_{11} to a_{m1} for x_1 (column 1) and a_{12} to a_{m2} for x_2 (column 2) as given in the following lines of code:

```
> set.column(lp1, 1, c(1, 1))
> set.column(lp1, 2, c(1, 2))
```

Now let's set the objective function using the `set.objfn()` function and a vector with c_1 and c_2, and the constraint type with the `set.constr.type()` function for each inequality in a vector as follows:

```
> set.objfn(lp1, c(4, 7))
> set.constr.type(lp1, rep(">=", 2))
```

Lastly, we set the values to the right-hand side of the constraint inequalities using the set.rhs() function, as given in the following code, using a vector with b_1 and b_2:

```
> set.rhs(lp1, c(4, 6))
```

We can see an overview of our model by entering lp1 as follows:

```
> lp1
Model name:
                C1      C2
Minimize        4       7
R1              1       1    >=    4
R2              1       2    >=    6
Kind          Std     Std
Type         Real    Real
Upper         Inf     Inf
Lower           0       0
```

As you can see, the upper and lower bounds are automatically set to ∞ and 0 by default, so we are ready to solve the problem. We will show you how to change the default settings later. We can plot the model using the plot() function as follows:

```
> plot(lp1)
```

The result is shown in the following plot:

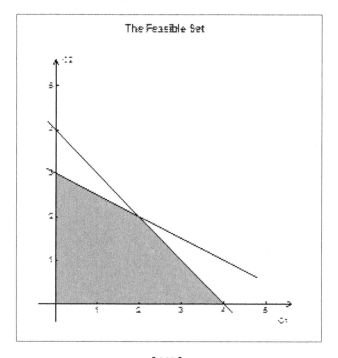

The plot() function only plots linear program models with real, non-negative decision variables that do not have a finite upper bound. See ?plot.lpExtPtr for more information.

In the previous plot, the region in gray shows the values for when neither constraints are satisfied. It seems like the solution to our problem is (2, 2), but let's go through the necessary steps to validate the solution. First, we can double-check our linear program that we entered by saving the model to a file that we will call model1.lp with the write.lp() function as follows:

```
> write.lp(lp1,'model1.lp',type='lp')
```

If you open the file in a text editor, you will see the following lines:

```
/* Objective function */
min: +4 C1 +7 C2;

/* Constraints */
+C1 +C2 >= 4;
+C1 +2 C2 >= 6;
```

The preceding lines match our objective function $\min L = 4x_1 + 7x_2$ and inequalities as follows:

$$x_1 + x_2 \geq 4$$
$$x_1 + 2x_2 \geq 6$$

Next, we check whether an optimal solution has been found for our linear program with the solve() function as follows:

```
> solve(lp1)
[1] 0
```

Since this is a generic function in R, we need to go to the help page with ?solve.lpExtPtr to be able to know what 0 means, as follows:

```
> ?solve.lpExtPtr
# [...]
Status Codes

0:   "optimal solution found"
```

```
1:    "the model is sub-optimal"
2:    "the model is infeasible"
3:    "the model is unbounded"
4:    "the model is degenerate"
5:    "numerical failure encountered"
6:    "process aborted"
7:    "timeout"
9:    "the model was solved by presolve"
10:    "the branch and bound routine failed"
11:    "the branch and bound was stopped because of a break-at-first or
break-at-value"
12:    "a feasible branch and bound solution was found"
13:    "no feasible branch and bound solution was found"
# Output truncated
```

We can get the values for x_1 and x_2 with the `get.variables()` function and the minimum value of the objective function with the `get.objective()` function as follows:

```
> get.variables(lp1)
[1] 2 2
> get.objective(lp1)
[1] 22
```

Alternatively, we could have used the `lp()` function from the `lpSolve` package as follows:

```
> install.packages("lpSolve")
> library(lpSolve)
> lp.ex1 <- lp(objective.in=c(4, 7), const.mat=matrix(c(1,1,1,2),
nrow=2), const.rhs=c(4, 6), const.dir=rep(">=", 2))
```

As you will notice, we specify the c_1 and c_2 values for the objective function with the `objective.in` argument, the values for the columns as a matrix with the `const.mat` argument, the constants to the right-hand side of the constraint formulas with the `const.rhs` argument, and the constraint types with the `const.dir` argument.

To check whether the problem is solved, we simply need to enter the model `lp.ex1` object generated from the `lp()` function in R as follows:

```
> lp.ex1
Success: the objective function is 22
```

The `lp.ex1` object is actually a list of multiple elements including the `$solution` numeric vector containing the values for x_1 and x_2, which we access with `lp.ex1$solution` as follows:

```
> lp.ex1$solution
[1] 2 2
```

Integer-restricted optimization

We can also solve integer-restricted linear programs with the `lpSolveAPI` and `lpSolve` packages. Consider the following example; a company produces laptops and tablets. The profit for the laptops is 52 dollars per laptop and 82 dollars per tablet. Due to production capacity, no more than 100 laptops and 170 tablets can be made per day. The company has a private contract that requires them to produce at least 65 laptops and 92 tablets. If the company only wants to make at most 200 units per day, how many laptops and tablets should they produce to maximize profits? Let's set up the problem as an objective function and inequalities.

Let *x1* be the number of laptops to be produced and *x2* be the number of tablets to be produced. We will use the following formula to solve this problem:

$$\max L = 50x_1 + 82x_2$$

The constraints are as follows:

$$x_1 + x_2 \leq 200$$
$$65 \leq x_1 \leq 100$$
$$92 \leq x_2 \leq 170$$

These inequalities can be entered into a `lpSolveAPI` model as follows:

```
> lp2 <- make.lp(1, 2)

> set.column(lp2, 1, c(1))
> set.column(lp2, 2, c(1))

> set.objfn(lp2, c(50, 82))
> set.constr.type(lp2, c("<="))

> set.rhs(lp2, c(200))
```

Set the boundaries for both decision variables as follows:

```
> set.bounds(lp2, lower = c(65, 92), columns = c(1, 2))
> set.bounds(lp2, upper = c(100, 170), columns = c(1, 2))
```

Since x_1 and x_2 are necessary integers, we need to set the type to `"integer"` as follows:

```
> set.type(lp2, 1, "integer")
> set.type(lp2, 2, "integer")
```

 You can also set the type to `"binary"` for binary decision variables, which will automatically set the type to `integer` with `lower=0` and `upper=1`.

We can view a summary of the model by entering `lp2` as follows:

```
> lp2
Model name:
            C1    C2
Minimize    50    82
R1           1     1  <=  200
Kind       Std   Std
Type       Int   Int
Upper      100   170
Lower       65     0
```

Since we want to maximize the objective function, we need to set the objective direction with the `lp.control()` function and the `sense` argument as follows:

```
> lp.control(lp2,sense='max')

# Output not shown
```

We can check our model by saving `lp2` in a file that we can view in a text editor as follows:

```
> write.lp(lp2,'model2.lp',type='lp')

/* Objective function */
max: +50 C1 +82 C2;

/* Constraints */
+C1 +C2 <= 200;

/* Variable bounds */
```

```
65 <= C1 <= 100;
92 <= C2 <= 170;

/* Integer definitions */
int C1,C2;
```

As you can see, everything is in order and the objective function direction is set to max. Now, to check whether we can solve the linear program with solve(lp2):

```
> solve(lp2)
[1] 0
```

Since we can solve the problem, we can print the values for the decision variable and the maximum value as follows:

```
> get.variables(lp2)
[1]   65 135
> get.objective(lp2)
[1] 14320
```

Similarly, we can solve this linear program using the lp() function including the direction argument set to "max" and specifying the integer-restricted decision variables in a vector with the int.vec argument. To more easily conceptualize the const.mat argument, we will rewrite the constraint inequalities as follows:

$$x_1 + x_2 \leq 200$$
$$x_1 + 0x_2 \geq 65$$
$$x_1 + 0x_2 \leq 100$$
$$0x_1 + x_2 \geq 92$$
$$0x_1 + x_2 \leq 170$$

So, const.mat will be matrix(c(1,1,1,0,0,1,0,0,1,1), nrow=5) as follows:

```
> lp.ex2 <- lp(objective.in=c(50, 82), const.mat=matrix
(c(1,1,1,0,0,1,0,0,1,1), nrow=5), const.rhs=c(200, 65, 100, 92, 170),
const.dir=c("<=", ">=", "<=", ">=", "<="), direction="max", int.
vec=c(1, 2))
```

We can get the optimal solution as follows:

```
> lp.ex2
Success: the objective function is 14320

> lp.ex2$solution
[1]   65 135
```

Unrestricted variables

The `lp()` function is set up to solve linear programs for decision variables that satisfy the non-negativity constraints $x_1 \geq 0$, $x_2 \geq 0$, ..., $x_n \geq 0$. One way to overcome this limitation is to replace the unrestricted decision variables x_z with the difference between two non-negative decision variables $x_z = x_n - x_{n+1}$.

For example, let's minimize the following linear program:

$$\min L = 3x_1 + 4x_2$$

The preceding equation is subject to the following constraints:

$$x_1 + 2x_2 \leq 14$$
$$3x_1 - x_2 \geq 0$$
$$x_1 - x_2 \leq 2$$
$$x_1 \geq 0$$

However, x_2 is unrestricted in sign. To solve this problem, we will replace x_2 with $x_3 - x_4$, where $x_3 \geq 0$ and $x_4 \geq 0$, and rewrite the objective function and constraint inequalities as follows:

$$\min L = 3x_1 + 4x_3 - 4x_4$$
$$x_1 + 2x_3 - 2x_4 \leq 14$$
$$3x_1 - x_3 + x_4 \geq 0$$
$$x_1 - x_3 + x_4 \leq 2$$

We can now solve the problem as follows:

```
> lp.ex3 <- lp(objective.in=c(3, 4, -4), const.mat=matrix
(c(1,3,1,2,-1,-1,-2,1,1), nrow=3), const.rhs=c(14, 0, 2), const.
dir=c("<=", ">=", "<="), direction="min")

> lp.ex3
Success: the objective function is -8

> lp.ex3$solution
[1] 0 0 2
```

The optimal solution is therefore $x_3 - x_1$ and $x_2 = x_3 - x_4$, which means that $x_2 = 0 - 2 = -2$.

Quadratic programming

Quadratic programming is an optimization problem where the objective function is quadratic and the constraint functions are linear. We can solve quadratic programs in R using the `solve.QP()` function part of the `quadprog` package. Quadratic programs are often expressed in the form of the following equation:

$$\min_{\beta} \frac{1}{2}\beta^T G\beta - d^T\beta$$

The preceding equation is subject to the following constraints:

$$A_i^T \beta = b_i, \quad i \in N$$
$$A_i^T \beta \geq b, \quad i \in M$$

However, the `solve.QP()` function requires that your quadratic program be written in the standard form:

$$\min_{\beta} \frac{1}{2}\beta^T G\beta - d^T\beta$$

The preceding equation is subject to the following constraint:

$$A^T \beta \geq b$$

In the preceding constraint, ^{T} is the mathematical symbol for transpose (matrix A, but with its rows swapped for columns), β is a vector of p unknowns, G is a positive definite symmetric $p \times p$ matrix, d is a vector of length p, A is a $p \times c$ matrix, and b is a vector with the length of the number of constraints c. For example, let's solve the following quadratic program:

$$\min x_1^2 + 2x_2^2 + x_3^2 - x_1 - x_2 + 5x_3$$

The preceding equation is subject to the following constraints:

$$x_1 + x_3 \leq 1$$
$$x_1 \geq 5$$
$$x_2 \leq 0$$

First, we install the package and load it as follows:

```
> install.packages("quadprog")
> library("quadprog")
```

To view a list of the arguments for the `solve.QP()` function, we can consult the help page as follows:

```
> help(solve.QP)
```

Briefly, the function and arguments are `solve.QP(Dmat, dvec, Amat, bvec, meq=0,` and `factorized=FALSE)`.

For the data matrix in the quadratic function to be minimized, we will create a QP object as follows:

```
> QP <- 2*diag(c(1, 2, 4))
> QP
     [,1] [,2] [,3]
[1,]    2    0    0
[2,]    0    4    0
[3,]    0    0    8
```

For the d vector appearing in the quadratic function to be minimized, we will create an object d as follows:

```
> d <- c(-1, -1, 5)
```

For the matrix A defining the constraints, we will create an A object, which we will transpose later with the t() function. To better see how we create the matrix, we can rewrite the constraint inequalities as follows:

$$-x_1 + 0x_2 - x_3 \geq -1$$
$$x_1 + 0x_2 + 0x_3 \geq 5$$
$$0x_1 - x_2 + 0x_3 \geq 0$$

Let's take a look at the following lines of code:

```
> A <- matrix(c(-1, 1, 0, 0, 0, -1, -1, 0, 0), nrow=3)
> A
     [,1] [,2] [,3]
[1,]   -1    0   -1
[2,]    1    0    0
[3,]    0   -1    0
```

Lastly, we will create the b vector for the values on the right-hand side of the constraint inequalities as follows:

```
> b <- c(-1, 5, 0)
```

We can now use the solve.QP() function to solve the quadratic program and print the solution as follows:

```
> qp1 <- solve.QP(QP, -d, t(A), b)

> qp1$solution
[1]  5  0 -4
```

We can also print the value of the quadratic function at the solution with $value as follows:

```
> qp1$value
[1] 64
```

General non-linear optimization

You may be interested in solving general non-linear optimization problems where the constraints are not linear. The `solnp()` function from the `Rsolnp` package allows you to solve general non-linear programming problems. For example, say we wanted to minimize the $f(x, y) = 4x - 2y$ function subject to the constraint $x^2 + y^2 = 41$.

First, we install and load the package as follows:

```
> install.packages("Rsolnp")
> library("Rsolnp")

# We also suggest taking a look at the help page for the function
arguments and restriction
> help(solnp)
```

Then, we store our function to minimize f as follows:

```
> f <- function(x){
    4*x[1] - 2*x[2]
}
```

We need to store our constraint function in a separate object as follows:

```
> ctr <- function(x){
    x[1]^2 + x[2]^2
}
```

Next, we store the value on the right-hand side of the constraint equation in a separate object as follows:

```
> constraints <- c(41)
```

Then, we store the initial parameters for x_0 and y_0 in x0 as follows:

```
> x0 <- c(1, 1)
```

We are ready to solve the problem with the `solnp()` function. We use `eqfun` for the constraint function and `eqB` for the constraint as follows:

```
> gnlp1 <- solnp(x0, fun = f, eqfun = ctr, eqB = constraints)

Iter: 1 fn: 4.8490    Pars:    7.97483 13.52517
Iter: 2 fn: -89.3900    Pars:   -13.15464   18.38573
Iter: 3 fn: -75.5164    Pars:   -17.70654    2.34511
```

```
Iter: 4 fn: -50.6915    Pars:   -9.26314  6.81945
Iter: 5 fn: -34.8293    Pars:   -7.33659  2.74148
Iter: 6 fn: -29.4963    Pars:   -5.79341  3.16135
Iter: 7 fn: -28.6698    Pars:   -5.74107  2.85273
Iter: 8 fn: -28.6358    Pars:   -5.72713  2.86361
Iter: 9 fn: -28.6356    Pars:   -5.72713  2.86356
Iter: 10 fn: -28.6356   Pars:   -5.72713  2.86356
solnp--> Completed in 10 iterations
```

We can obtain the values for *x* and *y* that minimize the function with $par as follows:

```
> gnlp1$par
[1] -5.727129   2.863564
```

Now let's say we wanted to minimize $f(x, y) = 4x - 2y$ subject to the constraint $x^2 + y^2 \leq 45$. All we need to do is use `ineqfun` for the constraint function and set the `ineqLB` argument's lower boundary to 0 and the `ineqUB` argument to 45 in the `solnp()` function. For simplicity, we will set the initial parameters to (-5, 5) as follows:

```
> x0 <- c(-5, -5)
> gnlp2 <- solnp(x0, fun = f, ineqfun = ctr, ineqLB = c(0),
ineqUB=c(45))

Iter: 1 fn: -13.6535    Pars:   -5.44225 -4.05775
Iter: 2 fn: -19.9098    Pars:   -6.33853 -2.72215
Iter: 3 fn: -27.9987    Pars:   -7.16312 -0.32691
Iter: 4 fn: -32.6786    Pars:   -6.85051  2.63826
Iter: 5 fn: -30.2915    Pars:   -6.02704  3.09169
Iter: 6 fn: -30.0031    Pars:   -6.00113  2.99927
Iter: 7 fn: -30.0000    Pars:   -6.00000  3.00000
Iter: 8 fn: -30.0000    Pars:   -6.00000  3.00000
Iter: 9 fn: -30.0000    Pars:   -6.00000  3.00000
solnp--> Completed in 9 iterations
> gnlp2$par
[1] -6   3
```

Other optimization packages

There are a lot more packages available to solve optimization problems in R. Here is a short table summary of the packages or functions that will help you pick the best package and/or function for your optimization problem:

	Linear Objective	Quadratic Objective	Non-linear Objective	Heuristic Approachs
No contraints, Box constraints			optim optimize nlminb	DEoptim rgenoud NMOF
Linear constraints		quadprog LowRankQP	constrOptim	
Linear, integer constraints	Boot lpSolve lpSolveAPI linprog limSolve			
Quadratic constraints		Rcplex Rmosek		
Semi-definite	Rcsdp			
Non-linear constraints			Rsolnp	

You can also go to http://cran.rproject.org/web/views/ Optimization.html to visit the Optimization and Mathematical Programming web page for a more complete and up-to-date list of the packages available to solve optimization problems.

Summary

Hopefully, throughout this chapter, you learned a variety of methods and techniques to optimize a variety of functions. We covered how to use a wide range of R packages and functions to set up, solve, and visualize different optimization problems, so you should be ready to give your own minimization and maximization problems a try. Now that you are much more familiar with R and its packages for scientific computing, we are ready to move on to our last chapter, which will teach you to clean up and manage your data for efficient programming and analysis in R.

10

Advanced Data Management

When we discuss data analysis, we usually think of the operations performed on data that yield new insights about whatever phenomena the data reflect. However, as a prelude to doing such operations, it is better to clean up the data that we start with and wrangle it into an analyzable form. Unfortunately, such wrangling typically occupies at least as much time as (if not more than) the actual analysis in most real world projects. Thus, data management is probably one of the most useful skills in data analysis, and it is given ample coverage in books on database programming, but little coverage in most texts on R.

Data wrangling is a term that is applied to activities that make data more usable by changing their form, but not their meaning. Data wrangling may involve reformatting data, mapping data from one data model to another, or converting data into more consumable forms. Such data wrangling activities make it easier to submit data to a database or repository, load data into analysis software, publish it to the Internet, compare datasets, or otherwise make data more accessible, usable, and shareable in different settings.

In this chapter, we will discuss the following topics:

- Cleaning up datasets
- Pattern matching
- Floating point operations and numerical data types
- Memory management
- Missing data and multiple imputation

We will focus on data types, data structures, and messy data in this chapter. While this is usually not considered the exciting part of data analysis, this is where most data analysts will likely spend the majority of their time, unless they are fortunate to have extremely well curated datasets to work with.

Cleaning datasets in R

The first step in any data analysis is preparing the data for the analysis. The rest of this chapter will mostly deal with this topic, but here we will review some basic considerations and R techniques. The most important part of any data analysis is to know the dataset and to have some idea of how each of the variables in the dataset was created.

For a basic overview, we will use the pumpkin dataset, which is short and artificial. Have a look at all of the following data in it:

```
pumpkins <- read.csv('messy_pumpkins.txt', stringsAsFactors = FALSE)
> pumpkins
         weight       location
1           2.3         europe
2         2.4kg        Europee
3       3.1 kg            USA
4  2700 grams  United States
5            24           U.S.
```

> When loading data frames, R's default behavior is to treat strings as categorical factors rather than as literal strings. This is usually the desired behavior of a dataset with consistently denoted factors but a problem if the same factors have been denoted with different strings. If we wish to treat the strings as strings, we can pass the `stringsAsFactors = FALSE` command in the `read.csv` command.

As can be seen from the previous data, the weights are written in different ways and in different units. The locations don't have consistency, and there is misspelling. This is hopefully messier than most datasets that you will have to work with, but this is the kind of problem that is frequently encountered in large datasets, especially when good efforts are not made to ensure high quality data entry up front.

Notably, the 24 seen in the fifth row is a very different number than the rest of the values, and has no units attached. Do we assume it is kilograms and someone left out the decimal point when entering the data? Do we ignore it as completely unreliable? This is not a statistical question but a substantive one. Here we will assume that a decimal point was actually ignored and it is in kilograms.

String processing and pattern matching

Pattern matching is concerned with identifying patterns of characters in strings, and has a long history in computer programming outside of its use in R. The simplest kind of pattern matching would be to ask whether a given character is equal to a value or a group of values, which would be a simple program to write in nearly any language, but it would also have very limited functionality. A bigger problem is dealing with patterns of characters; for example, uppercase alphabet characters, numerals, and so on. A language for describing patterns of string characters has been identified and adopted in many languages including R, called **regular expressions**, which the grep family of R functions is based on. We will first discuss these functions and then delve into using regular expressions.

The grep family of functions includes a number of similar functions for identifying and replacing patterns of text. The most commonly used functions are as follows:

- grep: This function is used to find strings that match a given character pattern. It takes a vector of strings as input and produces a vector of indices of those strings in the vector that match the given pattern.

- grepl: This function is used to find strings that match a given character pattern, but differs from grep in the output. This function takes a vector of strings as input and produces a vector of logical values telling which elements of the original vector match the pattern.

- sub: This function searches for a character pattern in a string and then replaces it with another string of text. It only makes this replacement in the first matching pattern it finds.

- gsub: This function searches for a character pattern in a string and then replaces it with another string of text. As opposed to sub, this function makes the replacement in all available matches.

There is one more function that is potentially quite useful that does not require strict pattern matching:

- agrep: This function tells which elements of a vector of strings closely match a given pattern. It takes as input a vector of strings and returns a vector of indices reporting which elements of the input vector match the pattern. Rather than using strict matching, it will allow for close matches. Closeness is determined by the number of insertions, deletions, or substations that have to be made to achieve a perfect match.

Regular expressions

Regular expressions can contain literal characters or symbolic representations of characters, but what makes them powerful are metacharacters, character classes, and sequences.

For letters or words, we can just use the literal string representation. For example, locate the letter `"k"` in the following code:

```
> pumpkins$weight[grep(pattern = "k", pumpkins$weight)]
[1] "2.4kg"  "3.1 kg"
```

To find particular letter sequences, we can simply use their literal string representation, but for those characters that have a symbolic meaning in regular expressions, we have to escape them with the \\ prefix.

Most punctuation marks cannot be used as literal characters, because regular expressions have a particular meaning to these. If we try to find cells with a `"."` without keeping this in mind, things go astray:

```
> pumpkins$weight[grep(pattern = ".", pumpkins$weight)]
[1] "2.3"        "2.4kg"       "3.1 kg"      "2700 grams" "24"
```

The cell containing `"2700 grams"` has no `"."` yet gets included.

If we want to search for a `"."`, we need to escape `"."` with `"\\"`. The correct way to do this would be as follows:

```
> pumpkins$weight[grep(pattern = "\\.", pumpkins$weight)]
[1] "2.3"    "2.4kg"  "3.1 kg"
```

It is also worth mentioning that some characters that would normally be interpreted literally are given a special meaning by adding `"\\"` in front of them. For example, `"d"` would be literally interpreted in a regular expression as `"d"`, but `"\\d"` would be interpreted as a digit.

> There are multiple standards for regular expressions, and different languages may handle regular expressions slightly differently. Perl regular expressions are allowed in R in many commands by passing the `perl = TRUE` argument to most functions in the `grep` family.

The following table gives the meaning of metacharacters and sequences. This is not a comprehensive list, and regular expressions can differ depending on context and the language being used. Some commonly used regular expressions in R are shown in the following table, though the list is not comprehensive:

Metacharacters	Match meaning
.	This character means any character.
$	This character means end of line.
?	This character means zero or one of the previous character.
*	This character means zero or more of the previous character.
+	This character means one or more of the previous character.
^	This character means line beginning if it is outside of the [ ] operator, and if it is inside the [ ] operator, then it means negate the following character class.
|	This character means an or operator.
[ ]	This character means character class described within brackets.
{ }	This character means number of times the preceding pattern should be present for a positive match. (The ?, *, and + metacharacters mentioned previously are shortcuts for this expression.)
\\d	This character means a digit.
\\D	This character means a non-digit character.
\\s	This character means a space character.
\\S	This character means a non-space character.
\\w	This character means an alphanumeric character.
\\W	This character means a non-alphanumeric character.

Now, let's look at how some of these can be used. We already saw an example of the " . " metacharacter earlier in this chapter.

To look for at least one zero, we can use the following code:

```
> pumpkins$weight[grep(pattern = "0+", pumpkins$weight)]
[1] "2700 grams"
```

To look for those cases where someone recorded non-digit characters (which leaves out the final observation), use the following code:

```
> pumpkins$weight[grep(pattern = "\\D", pumpkins$weight)]
[1] "2.3"        "2.4kg"       "3.1 kg"       "2700 grams"
```

What if we want to look for cases where units were not recorded? We can look for a digit followed by an end of the string as shown in the following code:

```
> pumpkins$weight[grep(pattern = "\\d$", pumpkins$weight)]
[1] "2.3" "24"
```

The final thing we will introduce here are character classes, which really make regular expressions very powerful. As an example, instead of telling R to search a string for any of the following elements: a, b, c, d, e, and so on, we can use the regular expression [[:letters:]]. A table of character classes recognized in R is shown in the following table:

Character class	Meaning
[aeiou]	This character means a lowercase vowel.
[AEIOU]	This character means an uppercase vowel.
[0-9]	This character means a digit.
[a-z]	This character means a lowercase letter.
[A-Z]	This character means an uppercase letter.
[a-zA-Z0-9]	This character means a letter (either upper or lowercase) or a digit.
[^0-9]	This character means anything except a digit.
[[:alpha:]]	This character means an upper or lowercase letter.
[[:punct:]]	This character means a punctuation character.
[[:print:]]	This character means a printable character.
[[:digit:]]	This character means a digit character.

The last four character classes are examples of the POSIX character classes, which is a UNIX standard compatible with many other languages. There are other POSIX complaint expressions with significant overlap with other regular expressions in R.

We will use pattern matching to clean up the previous dataset. Now, in this example, we have only five observations, so we could clean it up by hand, but we will try to come up with some general rules that can be used to yield a data frame with one column of numbers using the same units and one column of strings using the same naming convention. As we will see, cleaning up datasets is often not a matter of statistical or mathematical decision making, but a series of decisions as to how data entry can go wrong and how to interpret this.

Firstly, there are a few ways where data entry can go wrong, such as:

- Record the units (rather than just the number), as illustrated in the pumpkin dataset earlier in this chapter.

- Record the data in the wrong units (we want kilograms not other units).

- Record the data in error in a manner we can't be sure about. An example of this is the fifth entry in the pumpkins dataset. Is this an accurate weight in the right units? Is it missing a decimal point? Is it just a complete error?

If data entry goes wrong in the first or second way, we can figure out exactly how to correct it easily, and we will write some R code to do this. If data entry goes wrong the third way, it is a bit of a problem, and we have to ask ourselves if we want to guess where things went wrong, or if we want to just call those observations missing. Any time that manual data entry is involved, the third type of problem is usually present. For example, if looking at human temperature in degrees Fahrenheit, a temperature of 999 is not right, but it may be 99 with a third digit accidentally typed or 99.9, which we are not sure about.

There are many ways to do this. Here, our general approach will be to first clean the text out of all weight entries. Then we will identify those entries recorded in grams instead of kilograms. We will then come up with a consistent naming paradigm for the locations. Once this is done, we will create a new cleaned data frame. Finally, we will get rid of elements of the data frame where the weights don't make sense.

Firstly, let's get rid of the text from the weights column. Here we just substitute alphabetical characters with nothing and coerce these to numbers. Let's have a look at the following example:

```
corrected.data <- as.numeric(gsub(pattern = "[[:alpha:]]", "",
pumpkins$weight))
```

We then identify those cells where the units are in grams based on the number of digits, assuming that a series of four digits represents something measured in grams rather than in kilograms, and we divide these measurements by 1000. If there were other units measured in pounds or ounces, we would need to figure this out ahead of time and add another statement. The number of digits is passed using the {4} argument. In general, this is the technique used to identify the number of consecutive instances of the character class that one is seeking. Let's have a look at the following example:

```
units.error.grams <- grep(pattern = "[[:digit:]]{4}", pumpkins$weight)
corrected.data[units.error.grams] <- corrected.data[units.error.grams]
/ 1000
```

We then fix the locations. Here we will use approximate pattern matching, because there are many ways to misspell "Europe", and we don't want to think of all of them. We will use the agrep function here, which looks for approximate matches. In order to look for an approximate match, agrep needs to know what the true match looks like, given by the pattern argument. Since we are doing approximate pattern matching, we also need to figure out what we consider as an approximate representation of the pattern versus something that is not a representation of the pattern at all. We will do this with the max.dist argument, which tells agrep how far off from the pattern a string of text can be and still be considered an approximate representation of the pattern. We tell agrep how many single character insertions, deletions, and substitutions are allowed. Let's have a look at the following example:

```
european <- agrep(pattern = "europe", pumpkins$location, ignore.case =
TRUE, max.dist = list(insertions = c(1), deletions = c(2)))
american <- agrep(pattern = "us", pumpkins$location, ignore.case =
TRUE, max.dist = list(insertions = 0, deletions = 2, substitutions =
0))
corrected.location <- pumpkins$location
corrected.data[european] <- "europe"
corrected.data[american] <- "US"
```

Finally, we create a new data frame with the consistent data as shown in the following code, and review what our new data looks like. Let's have a look at the following example:

```
> cleaned.pumpkins <- data.frame(corrected.data, corrected.location)
> names(cleaned.pumpkins) <- c('weight', 'location')
> cleaned.pumpkins
  weight location
1    2.3   europe
2    2.4   europe
```

```
3    3.1       US
4    2.7       US
5   24.0       US
> summary(cleaned.pumpkins)
     weight        location
 Min.    : 2.3   europe:2
 1st Qu.: 2.4    US    :3
 Median : 2.7
 Mean    : 6.9
 3rd Qu.: 3.1
 Max.    :24.0
```

Uh oh! The median weight is 2.7 kg with a mean of 6.9 kg, and a maximum of 24 kg. Clearly, there is an error here. Any pumpkin with a weight over 10 kg (two digits) is likely to be an error, so we get rid of these. (This is not a statistical question, but a judgment on the part of the researcher based on non-statistical knowledge of what is an implausible value.) We can either create a new data frame or fill it in as missing data.

Create a new dataset using the following code:

```
cleaned.pumpkins.2 <- cleaned.pumpkins[cleaned.pumpkins$weight <= 10,]
```

Fill in nonsensical values with missing values as follows:

```
cleaned.pumpkins[cleaned.pumpkins$weight >= 10,1] <- NA
```

Floating point operations and numerical data types

From the standpoint of mathematical operations, we usually think of numbers as just that. However, a computer takes a more broken down approach to numbers. Most of the time this doesn't matter, but when we have to deal with large datasets and are concerned about either memory or speed, it can make a big difference. R essentially has two numeric data types; integer and double precision (also called numeric). The integer data type handles exact values denoted as integers. As per the IEEE floating point standard, the double precision type handles values as rounded decimals. R has no single data type as is used in languages like C.

Here, we will create two vectors of integers, x and y, and divide one by the other. Mathematically (but not computationally), we get whole number results. Let's look at the following code:

```
> x <- as.integer(seq(1, 10, by = 1))
> y <- as.integer(seq(2, 20, by = 2))
> x
 [1]  1  2  3  4  5  6  7  8  9 10
> y
 [1]  2  4  6  8 10 12 14 16 18 20
> y/x
 [1] 2 2 2 2 2 2 2 2 2 2
```

The y/x vector has 10 members that look like integers (and all single digit integers). It should supposedly be the same size as x and y, but when we look at the size, it isn't. It's almost twice the size in memory. Let's have a look at the following code:

```
> object.size(x)
88 bytes
> object.size(y)
88 bytes
> object.size(y/x)
168 bytes
```

The reason is because the division operator has coerced the results of y/x to be a double precision data type, as we can see in the following code:

```
> typeof(x)
[1] "integer"
> typeof(y)
[1] "integer"
> typeof(y/x)
[1] "double"
>
```

Keeping values that are integers in integer form in memory can save a substantial amount of memory. As shown in the earlier code, the as.integer command is a generic command that can accomplish this.

 The command for creating a sequence, seq, by default returns the type integer. So the as.integer command was not strictly necessary in the previous code.

Memory management in R

One of R's classic weaknesses is its difficulty in handling very large datasets, which is because R, by default, handles data by loading the full datasets in memory.

Using data analysis tools designed for large datasets, such as CERN's Root (available online at `http://root.cern.ch`), is one obvious solution to this problem. Root is a completely different data analysis software, and it is not easy to switch to a new data analysis platform if one has already built tools for another environment.

Some third-party R builds, including Revolution R or Renjin, have been built with memory management in mind to get around this problem. Revolution has the disadvantage of costing money to commercial users (contact Revolution about academic use). Renjin runs on the Java virtual machine, but it has the disadvantage of not being fully compatible with all R packages. For users who routinely work with very large datasets (that is a few gigabytes) and want to do it in R, it is probably best to use an R implementation that can handle this and deal with the out-of-pocket costs or the occasional compatibility problems.

For users who simply want to be able to deal with occasional large datasets that come their way, there are a couple of things to keep in mind. The first is that R is actually much more capable than it used to be. While 32-bit versions of R could only handle up to 3 GB of memory, 64-bit versions of R can handle up to 8 TB of RAM. With RAM becoming relatively inexpensive nowadays, simply upgrading the amount of RAM in your computer and running a 64-bit version of R on a 64-bit operating system is probably an upgrade that any data analyst should be making, if data size is an issue.

Basic R memory commands

The amount of memory available to R can be obtained with the `memory.limit` command. This command can also be used to increase the memory available by telling R to use a certain amount of virtual memory. Here, we see about 6 GB of memory available (the amount of RAM in the computer) and tell R to use up to 8 GB, as follows:

```
> memory.limit()
[1] 5999
> memory.limit(8000)
[1] 8000
> memory.limit()
[1] 8000
```

If we close the R session and then reopen it, R will reset its memory limit to the default of the total available RAM, and will no longer have this virtual memory available to it.

Using virtual memory can significantly slow down R, so if memory use is a concern, it is best to do a couple of other things before resorting to this.

When performing large computations, the first thing to do is delete all unnecessary objects in memory with the `rm()` command. We can remove a particular element or all elements.

First, we create three reasonably large vectors and then tell R to delete one of them, as follows:

```
> A <- c(1:2E8)
> B <- c(1:2E8)
> C <- c(1:2E8)
> ls()
[1] "A" "B" "C"
> rm(A)
> ls()
[1] "B" "C"
```

If we want to clear all objects from memory, we can use the following code:

```
rm(list=ls())
```

Some people will point out that not all objects have really been deleted from memory, because garbage collection still has to happen. R will do this on its own, but if the user wants to force R's garbage collection to happen, this can be done with the `gc()` command.

If we want to look at the size of memory used already, we can call R's `memory.size` command. Here, we recreate the same two objects and examine the amount of size occupied. Let's have a look at the following code:

```
> A <- c(1:2E8)
> B <- c(1:2E8)
> memory.size()
[1] 2333.96
```

Handling R objects in memory

Regardless of dataset size, one easy mistake to make in R that will slow down the handling of even relatively small datasets is constantly recreating the object. This is in effect what is done with object resizing, and this is often what is responsible for slowing down R's notoriously slow loops so much.

For example, if we want to look at the NHANES data and don't want all five ordinal responses, but want to condense things to binary responses, we can do this in a relatively straightforward manner in R. We will go through three different looping functions that do this in the following sections. The first and third functions dynamically resize the vector of interest. The second function creates a vector of the appropriate size, and then it simply replaces it with the appropriate values.

Quite possibly one of the worst ways to create a vector in R is as shown in the following code:

```
physical.data <- read.csv('phys_func.txt')[-1]
condense.to.binary <- function(input.vector) {
  output.vector <- c()
  a <- 0

  for (i in 1:length(input.vector)) {
    if (input.vector[i] == 1) {a <- 0}
    if (input.vector[i] > 1){a <- 1}

    output.vector <- c(output.vector, a)
  }

  return(output.vector)
}
```

Here, we create the vector and fill it with some arbitrary values early on, then simply change a value of the vector with each iteration of the loop. No copying of the vector or resizing is needed, as shown in the following code:

```
condense.to.binary.2 <- function(input.vector) {
  output.vector <- rep(NA, length(input.vector))
  a <- 0
```

```
      for (i in 1:length(input.vector)) {
        if (input.vector[i] == 1) {a <- 0}
        if (input.vector[i] > 1){a <- 1}

        output.vector[i] <- a
      }

      return(output.vector)
    }
```

In the preceding example, we declare the vector early on and use R's index method to grow it implicitly. Since the vector is still growing with each iteration, this requires dynamic resizing and will still run slowly, as shown in the following code:

```
    condense.to.binary.3 <- function(input.vector) {
      output.vector <- c()
      a <- 0

      for (i in 1:length(input.vector)) {
        if (input.vector[i] == 1) {a <- 0}
        if (input.vector[i] > 1){a <- 1}

        output.vector[i] <- a
      }

      return(output.vector)
    }
```

We can use the system.time command to compare performances. As we can see, the second method runs much faster than the other two. Here, we use a vector that repeats the first variable of the data frame 20 times just to exaggerate the impact of the difference in coding styles, as shown in the following screenshot:

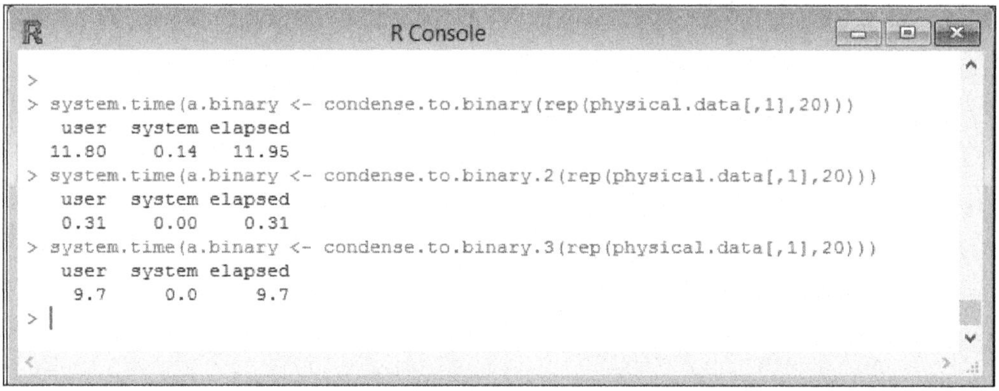

Dynamically resizing objects in R is a major bottleneck in code performance, because it requires memory reallocation of the entire vector in each iteration. Sometimes, it has to be done, but it should be done as rarely as possible.

Missing data

One of the biggest problems in real-world data is missing data. In carefully planned experiments on inanimate chemicals, small samples of rats, or highly mechanized factories, missing data may not be such a problem. However, whenever a dataset gets large enough, or starts to involve humans, missing data is almost a certainty. Let's begin by pointing out that if you have missing data, then you have a missing data problem, and you have to do something with that missing data; the question is, what? The answer lies in what kind of bias you are dealing with as a result of missing data.

Computational aspects of missing data in R

Before we delve into the statistical aspects of missing data, we need to review the computational ones. There are at least two different kinds of data missing in R, and they are NA and Null. NA is a missing value, but there are multiple types of NA, and R will automatically coerce missing values to be what it thinks is the appropriate type. For example, in the `cleaned.pumpkins` data frame, we would expect NA to be of numeric type, because the column was coerced to a numeric vector type when we created it. Let's have a look at the following code:

```
> cleaned.pumpkins
  weight location
1    2.3   europe
2    2.4   europe
3    3.1       US
4    2.7       US
5     NA       US
> cleaned.pumpkins[5,1]
[1] NA
> typeof(cleaned.pumpkins[5,1])
[1] "double"
```

We can see here that R keeps in mind that the NA values in the first column are still of double data type. Let's compare this with a nonexistent value. Let's select the first row and third column (notice that the cleaned pumpkins dataset has no third column), and let's assign it to a variable, as follows:

```
> b <- cleaned.pumpkins[1,3]
> b
NULL
> typeof(b)
[1] "NULL"
```

We can see here that b does not contain an NA but rather contains a NULL value, and this NULL value has no type other than NULL itself. Programs in R that are designed to handle missing data with imputation operate on the NA operator rather than the NULL operator.

Statistical considerations of missing data

We speak of a particular variable in a dataset being missing, and there can be three kinds of missingness in that variable, as follows:

- **Missing completely at random (MCAR)**: This missingness has nothing to do with any variable relevant to the entire dataset.

- **Missing at random (MAR)**: This does not mean what it sounds like. The missingness is not due to the particular variable, but may be due to other variables in the dataset.

- **Missing not at random (MNAR)**: The missingness is due to the variable itself.

Data that is MCAR has no bias. For example, let's say you are carrying a stack of papers that describe survey responses in your study and drop them, then the wind blows half of them away. Which half? It is completely random—we would expect the half that remains to resemble the half that blew away, so there is no bias introduced by the mechanism of missingness.

Data that is MAR will have bias. For example, let's say that we have a study of age and income. Let's say that younger people simply ignore the survey in the mail—then we have missing income data, and this is missing at random (a terrible name), because it is an income data that is missing based on age and not on income, once age is controlled for. As you can imagine, this may introduce bias.

In our age and income study, if those with higher incomes opted not to report incomes, then it would be data that is MNAR. In this case, the missing income data is an effect of the income value. This will surely introduce bias, because in general income, estimates will be lower because of the missing data.

We can try to deal with missing data in one of two ways, as mentioned below:

- Leave it out of our study and pretend it never existed (called deletion)
- Make up some values that we think would be present if the data were not missing (called imputation)

If our data is MCAR, then the first option is the better option because ignoring missing data only gives us a smaller sample with no bias. Unfortunately, data is rarely MCAR, and choosing the first option may introduce bias. Believe it or not, if the data is MAR or even MNAR, then it is better to make up some values than to simply ignore missing values. However, imputation itself can introduce its own biases, so sometimes deletion is the only viable fallback option.

Deletion methods

If we are going to rely on ignoring missing values, then there are a number of different approaches to deletion that we can use. These include listwise and pairwise deletion.

Listwise deletion or complete case analysis

The simplest approach to handling missing data in R is listwise deletion, and this is often the fallback method for handling missing data. Listwise deletion is simply leaving out all individuals who do not have all relevant data elements available. This is probably the simplest and most common method for dealing with missing data. As stated earlier, this can cause biased data, and may decrease one's sample size significantly if a large number of individuals have only a single data element missing.

Listwise deletion can be accomplished in R with the `complete.cases` command as follows:

```
> library(mice)
> data(nhanes2)
> complete.cases(nhanes2)
 [1] FALSE  TRUE FALSE FALSE  TRUE FALSE  TRUE  TRUE  TRUE FALSE FALSE
FALSE
[13]  TRUE  TRUE FALSE FALSE  TRUE  TRUE  TRUE FALSE FALSE  TRUE  TRUE
FALSE
[25]  TRUE
```

Pairwise deletion

Pairwise deletion ignores missing data like listwise deletion, but rather than outright excluding members who lack complete data on all variables, it makes use of the data that is observed for each member. For example, if in many statistical analyses, the computer creates a covariance matrix (for example, regression methods), each element in the covariance matrix comes from the covariance of two of the variables. Thus, with pairwise deletion, all available data for any of the two variables is used to compute their covariance. This helps to preserve sample sizes, but it has other problems. It may create bias as listwise deletion, and this means that the sample used to compute each element of a pairwise computation method can be slightly different, which can lead to problems like not being positive definite covariance matrices. Many R functions (or functions available in packages) offer a choice of listwise or pairwise deletion.

When is it appropriate to use deletion as a method of dealing with missing data?

While deletion is usually not the preferred method, in some cases it is. If less than five percent of your data is missing, this is probably an acceptable method (some might even say 10 percent). Likewise, if more than half of your data is missing, you may just want to acknowledge the bias created by ignoring missing values and do a complete case analysis so as to avoid analyzing a dataset that is mostly synthetic data.

Visualizing missing data

Let's start by loading the nhanes2 dataset from the mice package and summarizing the dataset.

This tells us that we certainly have missing values (denoted by NA), but what if we want to know a little more about the patterns of missingness? For example, what if we want to know what proportion of the sample has complete data, is missing data variables, and so on? The VIM package has convenient tools for this, such as an aggregation plot, as follows:

```
library(VIM)
aggr(nhanes2, numbers = TRUE, col = c('black', 'gray'))
```

The result is shown in the following plot:

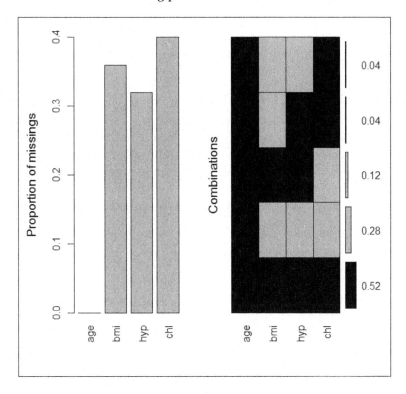

The preceding plot gives the proportion of missingness in each variable on the left, and then combinations of missing values on the right. In the previous example, black cells indicate complete data, and gray cells indicate missing data. The bottom row tells us that 52 percent of the sample has no missing data. The second to last row tells us that 28 percent of the population has a recorded age (as noted in black), but is missing the other three variables (as indicated in gray). The remaining eight percent of the sample has a missingness pattern given in the top two rows. Thus, if we were to do a complete case analysis, we would lose 28 percent of our (already small) sample.

> The mi package contains the mp.plot function for missing data visualization, which displays a graphic. The mice packages contain the md.pattern function, which returns a table with the same data as is contained in the right panel of VIM's aggr function.

An overview of multiple imputation

Multiple imputation is the method of creating new data to fill in missing values, which we alluded to as an alternative to case deletion earlier. Here we will give a big picture discussion of imputation before delving into how it can be done in R.

Imputation basic principles

The alternative to ignoring missing data is to fill in the missing data with some educated guesses. As indicated previously, this is quite frankly making up data, a fact important to keep in mind. The success of imputation relies on our ability to make up data that informs the data analyst, rather than leading them astray. The general approach to imputation is to assume that there is some other information available in the data that can tell us what a missing value would have been if it were not missing.

The simplest imputation method is to fill in each missing data value with a single replacement value, a method called **single imputation**. With the advent of fast personal computers and statistical advances over the past few decades, this has largely been replaced by multiple imputation, in which each missing value is replaced by multiple substitutes, effectively yielding multiple datasets. The problem with single imputation is that it replaces an unknown value with a single certain value. Of course, we don't actually know the value of the missing data element, so it is a bit unfair to pretend that we know it with certainty, and as such single imputation will tend to minimize the variability of the real data. Multiple imputation replaces the single unknown value with a distribution of known values, retaining the appropriate uncertainty or variance in the dataset. (At least this is how the theory goes.)

Approaches to imputation

Imputation is active area of statistical research for which new methods are constantly being developed, and older methods improved upon. There are not necessarily universal rules for imputation, and the type of imputation chosen may depend on the type of analysis one wishes to do.

Broadly speaking, the two main approaches to imputation that have been used are a multivariate normally distributed approach and an imputation by chained equations approach. We will first go over the `Amelia` package, which assumes multivariate normality, and then the `mice` package based on chained equations with an imputation method designed for non-normal data.

The Amelia package

Amelia is probably the newest multiple imputation package to be given to the R community. Amelia makes the assumption of multivariate normality, and in a moment we will see where this matters in terms of its use in R.

> **How important is the assumption of multivariate normality in imputation?**
>
> Many of the datasets we deal with in real life are not multivariate normally distributed, which might at first seem like a serious limitation to such an assumption. However, as the creators of Amelia point out, violations to this assumption usually don't make any practical difference. If this does bother an analyst, possible solutions include using the `mice` package that does not make this assumption or transforming the variables under study to be normally distributed.

We multiply impute data with the `amelia` command, which takes a number of arguments including the number of imputations to compute and descriptors for which variables are not continuous. By default, Amelia computes five imputations, but the optimal number is debatable. In general, the more missing data you are dealing with, the more imputations you will probably need to create. Traditionally, five imputations are considered adequate, but if there is a large amount of missing data, then 20 or even 50 imputations may be desirable. More imputations will create a significant computing burden later on, since analyses done on imputed datasets will have to be done separately on each imputed dataset.

In the following example, we impute data for the physical function dataset with missing values:

```
phys.imp <- amelia(phys.func.rm, ords = c(1:20))
summary(phys.imp$imputations)
```

We apply the `ords` = argument to tell Amelia which variables are ordinal in nature. Amelia will constrain imputations to take ordered integer values for imputations done for these variables, but it is questionable whether this is optimal. Leaving this command out will give continuous value estimates based on a multivariate normal assumption. While a value of 1.5 does not make sense as a person's response on a scale, which has only integer answers, it has a clear substantive interpretation and can be statistically analyzed.

As we discussed earlier, multiple imputation relies on making up data using some assumptions. So an important question is, "How can we test our imputed data?". A commonly used method is plotting observed versus imputed distributions of variables; if the missing at random assumption is true, then the two distributions should be similar.

Amelia provides the built-in `plot.amelia` command, which does just this. In the following code, we get such a plot for the second variable in the dataset:

```
plot(phys.imp, which.vars = 2)
```

The plot is shown in the following diagram:

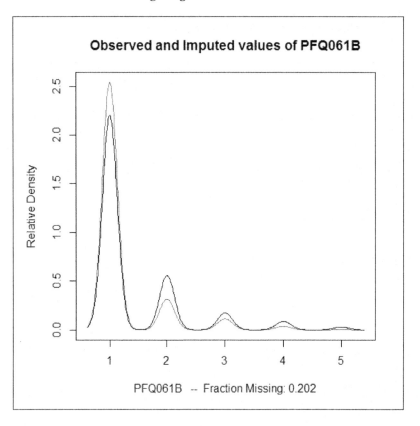

As shown in the preceding plot, the imputed values are in red, while the observed values are in black. The two distributions look sort of similar, so the imputation of this variable may be adequate. However, the imputed values seem to have a greater portion of responses of one, and a smaller proportion of the other responses.

Amelia also comes with a second imputation diagnostic approach, which was developed by its authors, called over-imputation. The idea of this method is to apply our imputation procedure to data that is not missing. If we impute non-missing data, then we can compare our imputed data to the observed values that these over-imputations are filling in for. If the two are drastically different, then there may be a problem with our imputation approach. This is done with the `overimpute` command. This command produces a multi-colored plot on its own, but we will store the data generated from this command and create our own plots. (As often happens with plots of large datasets, individual points with important information may be lost in a plot that tries to show too much.) Let's have a look at the following example:

```
B.ov.imp <- overimpute(phys.imp, var = 'PFQ061B')
summary(B.ov.imp)
```

The result is shown in the following screenshot:

```
> B.ov.imp <- overimpute(phys.imp, var = 'PFQ061B')
> summary(B.ov.imp)
      row                orig           mean.overimputed
 Min.   :   1    Min.   :1.000    Min.   :0.5973
 1st Qu.:1134    1st Qu.:1.000    1st Qu.:1.0737
 Median :2260    Median :1.000    Median :1.2195
 Mean   :2267    Mean   :1.422    Mean   :1.4204
 3rd Qu.:3399    3rd Qu.:2.000    3rd Qu.:1.6093
 Max.   :4528    Max.   :5.000    Max.   :4.8089
 lower.overimputed   upper.overimputed    prcntmiss
 Min.   :-0.69836    Min.   :1.615    Min.   :0.05
 1st Qu.: 0.01989    1st Qu.:2.063    1st Qu.:0.20
 Median : 0.18296    Median :2.248    Median :0.25
 Mean   : 0.35850    Mean   :2.419    Mean   :0.24
 3rd Qu.: 0.55965    3rd Qu.:2.624    3rd Qu.:0.30
 Max.   : 3.26388    Max.   :6.004    Max.   :0.60
>
```

In the preceding screenshot, we overimpute the data and then examine the matrix contained within the object returned by overimputing.

Let's just start by creating `boxplot` of the overimputed data (third column) verses the original data (first column) and adding a diagonal line, along which a perfect match between imputed and observed values would fall as follows:

```
boxplot(B.ov.imp[,3] ~ B.ov.imp[,2], xlab = 'Observed', ylab =
'Imputed', main = 'Overimputed vs Observed Values')
```

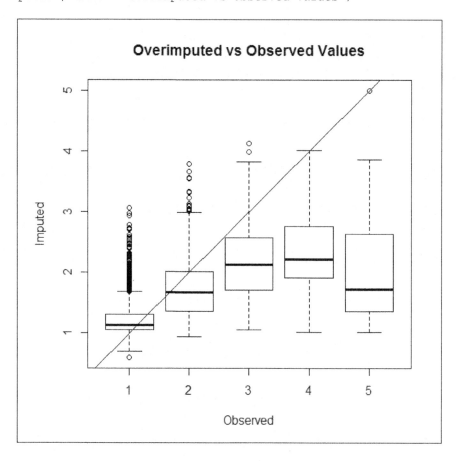

As we can see in the plot, overimputations for observed values of **3**, **4**, and **5** come nowhere near the diagonal line, indicating that the overimputations for these values systematically underestimate them. Why might this be? Let's examine the observed variables using a single sample t-test as follows:

```
> t.test(phys.func.rm$PFQ061B)

        One Sample t-test
```

```
data:   phys.func.rm$PFQ061B
t = 106.1534, df = 3612, p-value < 2.2e-16
alternative hypothesis: true mean is not equal to 0
95 percent confidence interval:
 1.395550 1.448071
sample estimates:
mean of x
  1.42181
```

We can see here that the mean of the observed data is 1.42, and the 95 percent confidence interval assuming a normal distribution is 1.39 to 1.45. This data is actually quite far from normally distributed, and high values are quite rare. As such, Amelia ends up imputing values much closer to the most commonly observed value, which is 1. Does this matter? When we look at the mean overimputed values and the mean observed values, there is practically no difference, so it may not matter.

Getting estimates from multiply imputed datasets

After going through the previous code, we have successfully completed a multiple imputation procedure, which we will accept as sufficient. However, instead of a single dataset, we have multiple datasets and still no new answers to any analytical questions. How do we actually get estimates out of the multiple new datasets? The answer is with Rubin's rules, which we will go through in the following sections. Here, the number of imputations is denoted by m, and the scalar quantity that we wish to estimate is Q. We will walk through Rubin's rules with the mean.

Extracting the mean

The mean of the multiply imputed data is simply the mean of the means of each of the m datasets (and Q is the mean), as shown in the following formula:

$$\bar{Q} = \frac{\sum_{i=1}^{m} Q_i}{m}$$

If we wish to find the mean value of each of the 20 items in the multiply imputed physical functioning dataset, we first need to find the mean of each imputation and then calculate the mean of these means, which we can do with the following code:

```
imputation.means <- sapply(phys.imp$imputations, colMeans)
rowMeans(imputation.means)
```

The result is shown in the following screenshot:

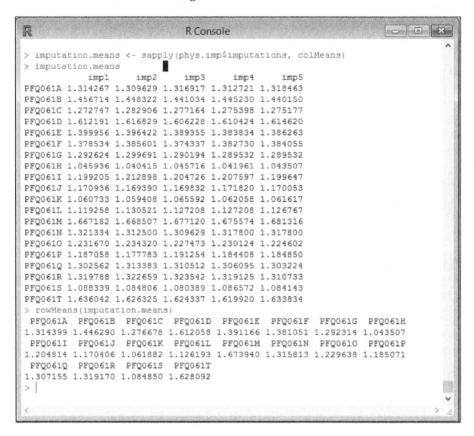

Lists are the most versatile data structures in R, but the most demanding to perform operations on, if we wish to apply a function to more than one element of a list. The `lapply` command conveniently applies a function to all elements of the list, but it returns yet another list. The `sapply` command returns a vector, matrix, or an array instead, which are usually easier data structures to work with than lists.

Extracting the standard error of the mean

To get the total variance of the multiply imputed datasets, we need to do a little more. Firstly, we find the average within imputation variance (the mean of the variance of each dataset), using the following formula:

$$\text{Variance}_{within} = \frac{\sum_{i=1}^{m} \text{Variance}_i}{m}$$

We then calculate the variance between each dataset using the following formula:

$$\text{Variance}_{\text{between}} = \frac{\sum_{i=1}^{m} (\text{Mean}_i - \text{Mean})^2}{m-1}$$

We can then compute the total variance using the following formula:

$$\text{Var}_t = \text{Var}_w + \left(1 + \frac{1}{m}\right)\text{Var}_b$$

The square root of the total variance approximates the standard error of the sample.

We can implement this in R easily. We start by creating a function that does for variance what the built-in `colMeans` function dose for means, after which the following code looks very similar to the code for imputed means in the previous code:

```
colVars <- function(input.frame) {
   return(diag(var(input.frame)))
}

imputation.vars.within <- sapply(phys.imp$imputations, colVars)
imputation.vars.within
avg.within.var <- rowMeans(imputation.vars.within)
```

We then calculate the between imputation variance, as follows:

```
between.var <- colVars(t(imputation.means))
```

Finally, we calculate total variance, and take the square root of this value to estimate the standard error, as follows:

```
total.var <- avg.within.var + (1+1/5)*between.var
```

This same approach will work for any other statistic we wish to estimate (for example, regression coefficients). Conveniently, the `mitools` package has implemented Rubin's rules so that we don't have to go through the tedium of writing fresh code for each function that we wish to write. Here we will use the `nhanes2` dataset from the `mice` package. We will start with our imputation (describing the appropriate columns as ordinal and nominal). We will then extract the actual imputed datasets and place them in an imputation list object, which will be used for further analysis. We will then apply regression to each dataset, using the `with.imputationList` command, the application of the `with` command to an object of `imputationList` type.

Finally, we will combine the results to get coefficient estimates from the multiple regression models on multiple imputations using the `MIcombine` command as follows:

```
library(mitools)
data(nhanes2)
nhanes2.imp <- amelia(nhanes2, ord = 1, noms = 3)
nhanes2.implist <- imputationList(nhanes2.imp[[1]])
lm.nhanes2 <- with(nhanes2.implist, lm(chl ~ age + bmi))
MIcombine(lm.nhanes2)
```

The preceding code gives the following output:

```
Multiple imputation results:
      with(nhanes2.implist, lm(chl ~ age + bmi))
      MIcombine.default(lm.nhanes2)
              results         se
(Intercept) -12.63903 79.719185
age40-59     49.77736 22.478038
age60-99     92.71007 49.483384
bmi           6.51795  2.494955
```

We will now go through multiple imputations using a different approach.

The mice package

The `mice` package provides an alternative approach to imputation, being based on a Bayesian procedure without assuming multivariate normality. The approach used by `mice` relies upon a procedure known as "chained equations". The basic operation goes as follows:

1. Some preliminary starting imputation values are filled in for all missing data.

2. The imputation starts for some particular variable, which we will call X. Starting imputation values are removed from X and missing data in X is, once again, treated as missing. Preliminary imputations are left in place of all other variables. Observed elements of X are regressed on, or somehow matched to the other variables (values of these other variables may be observed or imputed). Based on this regression or matching, the missing values of X are filled in.

3. Step 2 is then repeated for the next variable in line Y. Step 2 is then repeated for variable Z, and this goes on until the imputation has been done for all variables.

4. Steps 2 and 3 are then repeated over and over again. The imputed values at the end of step 2 are tracked with each imputation, and once they are no longer changing much, the imputation is thought to have converged.

 An important note here is that many different functions can be used in step 2 to perform the regression or matching, and the user must select which function he or she wishes to use.

Imputation functions in mice

The `mice` command in the `mice` package supports a large range of imputation methods, many of which do not assume normality. For categorical data, `mice` uses logistic regression or multinomial logistic regression. The default method for handling numeric data in `mice` is with predictive mean matching, which relies on filling in missing data with donated values from observed data. The donor values are selected based on the closest match from linear regression. The advantage of this approach over a simple regression-based approach is that it is less sensitive to violations of normality, and since it borrows observed values to fill in missing data, nonsensical imputed data is less of a concern.

The `mice` command also supports a range of other imputation functions, which the user can specify.

Before we go on, we will rename the variables with their respective letters for simplicity, as follows:

```
names(phys.func.rm) <- LETTERS[c(1:20)]
```

The `mice` command allows us to specify which variables will be used in the imputation of other variables as a matrix. Typically, we try to use all of the relevant variables to perform imputations. This consideration is especially important if the dataset has a large number of variables. This means, for instance, a variable like hair color would not be used to impute something like age. Here, we demonstrate the use of the predictor matrix in the physical functioning dataset, which has only 20 variables. In the prior section, we discussed the possibility that some of these variables relate to social engagement and cognition, some relate to leg function, and some relate to arm function. We will use this grouping for imputation prediction.

We create a square matrix. Each row represents the variable to be imputed (for example, the first row is A, the second row is B, and so on). Each column represents the variable being used as a predictor. Let's have a look at the following matrix:

```
predictor.matrix <- matrix(
  c(
  0,0,0,0,0,0,0,0,0,0,0,0,0,0,0,0,1,1,1,0,
  0,0,1,1,0,0,0,1,1,1,0,0,1,1,0,0,0,0,0,0,
  0,1,0,1,0,0,0,1,1,1,0,0,1,1,0,0,0,0,0,0,
  0,1,1,0,0,0,0,1,1,1,0,0,1,1,0,0,0,0,0,0,
  0,0,0,0,0,1,1,0,0,0,1,1,0,0,1,1,0,0,0,1,
  0,0,0,0,1,0,1,0,0,0,1,1,0,0,1,1,0,0,0,1,
  0,0,0,0,1,1,0,0,0,0,1,1,0,0,1,1,0,0,0,1,
  0,1,1,1,0,0,0,0,1,1,0,0,1,1,0,0,0,0,0,0,
  0,1,1,1,0,0,0,1,0,1,0,0,1,1,0,0,0,0,0,0,
  0,1,1,1,0,0,0,1,1,0,0,0,1,1,0,0,0,0,0,0,
  0,0,0,0,1,1,1,0,0,0,0,1,0,0,1,1,0,0,0,1,
  0,0,0,0,1,1,1,0,0,0,1,0,0,0,1,1,0,0,0,1,
  0,1,1,1,0,0,0,1,1,1,0,0,0,1,0,0,0,0,0,0,
  0,1,1,1,0,0,0,1,1,1,0,0,1,0,0,0,0,0,0,0,
  0,0,0,0,1,1,1,0,0,0,1,1,0,0,0,1,0,0,0,1,
  0,0,0,0,1,1,1,0,0,0,1,1,0,0,1,0,0,0,0,1,
  1,0,0,0,0,0,0,0,0,0,0,0,0,0,0,0,0,1,1,0,
  1,0,0,0,0,0,0,0,0,0,0,0,0,0,0,0,1,0,1,0,
  1,0,0,0,0,0,0,0,0,0,0,0,0,0,0,0,1,1,0,0,
  0,0,0,0,1,1,1,0,0,0,1,1,0,0,1,0,0,0,0,0
  ),
  nrow = 20,
  byrow = TRUE
)
```

We will then impute the missing values obtaining five imputations, and allowing up to six iterations to obtain the imputations, as follows:

```
imputed.phys.func <- mice(phys.func.rm, predictorMatrix = predictor.
matrix, m = 5, seed = 10, maxit = 6)
```

Once again, we now have five imputed datasets, but we have not found any new results. What if we want to ask whether the total leg function score is predicted by the total arm function score? We can use the `with` command to apply a regression model to each individual dataset as follows:

```
legs.v.arms.models <- with(imputed.phys.func, lm( I(B+C+D+H+I+J+M+N) ~
I(E+F+G+K+L+O+P+T) ))
```

We can then pool the results to get estimates as follows:

```
leg.v.arm.pool <- pool(legs.v.arms.models)
```

The summary function on a `mipo` object (returned by `pool`) will give additional interesting information, as follows:

```
summary(leg.v.arm.pool)
```

Let's have a look at the following screenshot:

```
R                              R Console                          ─  □  ✕
>
> legs.v.arms.models <- with(imputed.phys.func, lm( I(B+C+D+H+I+J+M+N) ~ I(E+F+G$
> leg.v.arm.pool <- pool(legs.v.arms.models)
> summary(leg.v.arm.pool)
                                      est          se         t        df
(Intercept)                     4.5689783 0.14504376  31.50069 145.12519
I(E + F + G + K + L + O + P + T) 0.5965278 0.01409243  42.32966  83.49253
                                    Pr(>|t|)      lo 95      hi 95 nmis       fmi
(Intercept)                            0 4.2823073 4.8556494   NA 0.1741114
I(E + F + G + K + L + O + P + T)       0 0.5685009 0.6245546   NA 0.2344096
                                      lambda
(Intercept)                        0.1628075
I(E + F + G + K + L + O + P + T)   0.2162875
> |
```

We get the estimation of the intercept and slope for the regression model in addition to the standard error and typical regression model statistics. However, we also get the fraction of information missing (column `fmi`) and the variance attributable to missing data (column `lambda`). As we can see here, a little over a fifth of variability is attributable to missing data.

Summary

This chapter has gone through techniques for data handling. Prior to data analysis, it is important to get the data into a consistently structured format, which string processing and pattern matching are helpful in doing. We have also gone through some basic memory management considerations. Finally, we discussed how to handle missing data using deletion, and two imputation approaches. The techniques of this chapter yield no new scientific insights or information about relationships in the data, yet they are often crucial preliminary steps prior to descriptive or inferential analyses. For large-scale projects, additional technologies designed just for data management, such as database platforms, will be important adjuncts to R by itself.

Index

covariance matrices 212
CRAN distributions page
    URL 63
CRAN page
    URL 301
CRAN R project Time Series Analysis
        website
    URL 94
Cronbach's alpha
    calculating 201, 202

D

data
    loading, in R 28-30, 57
data frames
    about 25-27
    saving 31-33
dataset
    about 178, 179, 212, 213, 252
    cleaning, in R 376
    Holzinger-Swineford 1939 dataset 252, 253
    physical functioning 213
    physical functioning dataset 252
    political democracy 252
    red wine 212
data structures, in R
    about 10
    atomic vectors 10-13
    attributes 19, 20
    data frames 25-27
    Factors 21
    heterogeneous 10
    homogeneous 10
    lists 15, 17
    multidimensional arrays 22
data variability
    about 61, 62
    confidence intervals (CI) 62
data visualization 313-315
data wrangling 375
DCT
    in R 206-209
debugging tools 52-54

deletion methods
    about 391
    complete case analysis 391
    listwise deletion 391
    pairwise deletion 392
density functions 324, 325
descriptive statistics
    about 59, 60
    data variability 61, 62
diagonal matrix 177
dimension reduction
    PCA for 220, 221
dim() function 19
distributions
    fitting, statistical tests used 73
dnorm() function 64

E

EFA
    about 233
    advanced EFA, with psych
        package 246-250
    centroid method 237-239
    communality 233
    covariance algebra 235
    direct factor extraction, by principal
        axis factoring 240
    estimation 236
    extraction methods 241
    factor rotation 242
    implied 233
    in matrix model 235
    latent trait or common factor 233
    multiple actors 239, 240
    oblique factor structure 234
    observed 233
    orthogonal factor structure 234
    path coefficient 233
    principal axis factoring, performing
        in R 240, 241
    uniqueness 233
effective degrees of freedom (edf) 118
eigenvalue decomposition 193-195

Thank you for buying
Mastering Scientific Computing with R

About Packt Publishing

Packt, pronounced 'packed', published its first book, *Mastering phpMyAdmin for Effective MySQL Management*, in April 2004, and subsequently continued to specialize in publishing highly focused books on specific technologies and solutions.

Our books and publications share the experiences of your fellow IT professionals in adapting and customizing today's systems, applications, and frameworks. Our solution-based books give you the knowledge and power to customize the software and technologies you're using to get the job done. Packt books are more specific and less general than the IT books you have seen in the past. Our unique business model allows us to bring you more focused information, giving you more of what you need to know, and less of what you don't.

Packt is a modern yet unique publishing company that focuses on producing quality, cutting-edge books for communities of developers, administrators, and newbies alike. For more information, please visit our website at www.packtpub.com.

About Packt Open Source

In 2010, Packt launched two new brands, Packt Open Source and Packt Enterprise, in order to continue its focus on specialization. This book is part of the Packt Open Source brand, home to books published on software built around open source licenses, and offering information to anybody from advanced developers to budding web designers. The Open Source brand also runs Packt's Open Source Royalty Scheme, by which Packt gives a royalty to each open source project about whose software a book is sold.

Writing for Packt

We welcome all inquiries from people who are interested in authoring. Book proposals should be sent to author@packtpub.com. If your book idea is still at an early stage and you would like to discuss it first before writing a formal book proposal, then please contact us; one of our commissioning editors will get in touch with you.

We're not just looking for published authors; if you have strong technical skills but no writing experience, our experienced editors can help you develop a writing career, or simply get some additional reward for your expertise.

R Object-oriented Programming

ISBN: 978-1-78398-668-2   Paperback: 190 pages

A practical guide to help you learn and understand the programming techniques necessary to exploit the full power of R

1. Learn and understand the programming techniques necessary to solve specific problems and speed up development processes for statistical models and applications.

2. Explore the fundamentals of building objects and how they program individual aspects of larger data designs.

3. A step-by-step guide to understand how OOP can be applied to applications and data models within R.

Instant R Starter

ISBN: 978-1-78216-350-3   Paperback: 54 pages

Jump into the R programming language and go beyond "Hello World!"

1. Learn something new in an Instant! A short, fast, focused guide delivering immediate results.

2. Basic concepts of the R language.

3. Discover tips and tricks for working with R.

4. Learn manipulation of R objects to easily customize your code.

Please check **www.PacktPub.com** for information on our titles

open source
community experience distilled

Instant Heat Maps in R How-to

ISBN: 978-1-78216-564-4   Paperback: 72 pages

Learn how to design heat maps in R to enhance your data analysis

1. Learn something new in an Instant! A short, fast, focused guide delivering immediate results.

2. Create heat maps in R using different file formats.

3. Learn how to make choropleth maps and contour plots.

4. Generate your own customized heat maps and add interactivity for displaying on the Web.

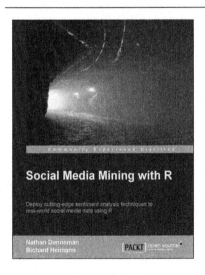

Social Media Mining with R

ISBN: 978-1-78328-177-0   Paperback: 122 pages

Deploy cutting-edge sentiment analysis techniques to real-world social media data using R

1. Learn how to face the challenges of analyzing social media data.

2. Get hands-on experience with the most common, up-to-date sentiment analysis tools and apply them to data collected from social media websites through a series of in-depth case studies, which includes how to mine Twitter data.

3. A focused guide to help you achieve practical results when interpreting social media data.

Please check **www.PacktPub.com** for information on our titles

CPSIA information can be obtained at www.ICGtesting.com
Printed in the USA
BVOW09s2355130415

395716BV00001B/1/P